Proven Paths

Proven Paths

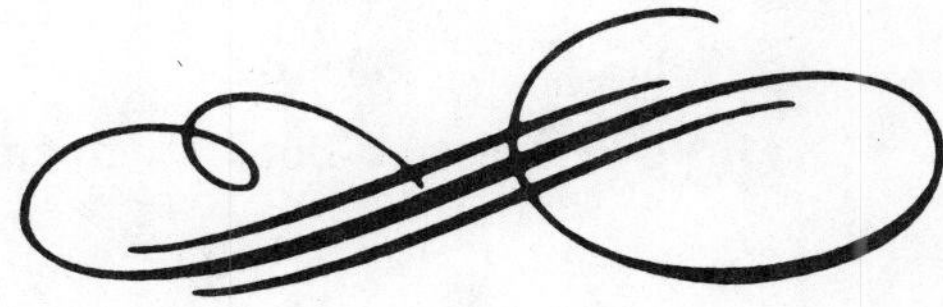

Robert L. Simpson

Published by Deseret Book Company
Salt Lake City, Utah
1974

Library of Congress Catalog Card No. 74-84540
ISBN 0-87747-537-7

Lithographed by

in the United States of America

CONTENTS

1

Using authoritative sources for guidance and information

PROVEN PATHS

Have you ever heard the beautiful song, "No Man Is an Island"? Seclusion is incompatible with the spirit of the gospel, particularly the priesthood. When you really analyze it, what can a man do for himself with the priesthood? Our young men administer the sacrament for others. They usher and do things around the chapel for the convenience and comfort of others. The priests bless the sacrament that others might partake.

Brethren of the Melchizedek Priesthood bless the sick. We do not bless ourselves with the priesthood. We call in others who have the priesthood to bless us. We are always thinking in terms of someone else when we use the priesthood. To willfully hide ourselves and live as hermits would be to allow our priesthood to wither and die. The Savior showed us the way; he set the pattern. His was a life of thinking and doing for others. This was the sum and substance of his entire existence in mortality.

Our great challenge here in mortality, then, is in the overcoming—the overcoming of things in mortality, these obstacles of the flesh; and in due course all appetites and habits must be brought under control that we may feel comfortable in the presence of the Lord. "To him that overcometh will I grant to sit with me in my throne, even as I also overcame, and am set down with my Father in his throne." (Revelation 3:21.)

Is there a Latter-day Saint who does not have as the foremost desire of his heart the great possibility of one day regaining the presence of his Heavenly Father? This is the sum and substance of it all. To aspire to this great blessing should supersede all else in the mind and heart of each member of the Church.

All of us need help in this important process of overcoming. The person doesn't live who is capable of doing it on his own. "No man is an island"; no being can stand alone.

One of the wisest things that we can do is to benefit from others who have passed this way. Our first loyal band of pioneers who entered the beautiful Salt Lake Valley in 1847 had scouts exploring many dead-end canyons and impossible mountain passes in order to select the best possible route for covered wagons. Subsequent companies found it much easier. The mistakes had already been made. Why make them again?

It would be foolish for us to waste time in remaking all of the mistakes of our predecessors. In the first place, we would not live long enough to make all the mistakes, so we must do the wise thing. We must take advantage of mistakes that have already been made. Perhaps the Lord had this in mind when he gave us the thought that "the glory of God is intelligence." Certainly that person is intelligent who would take advantage of a path that has already been clearly marked.

And so, the intelligence to benefit from those who know is really the key to our success. And now we ask, Who are those who know? Whom can we trust as we seek counsel on vital matters?

It is easy to be misled. It is so simple to seek our information from the improper source. I once heard a story about a jeweler who kept a fine-looking chronometer in his store window to attract attention and as a suggestion of accurate timekeeping. Early each morning he noticed a man stop by the window, look at the chronometer, and then carefully adjust his watch accordingly.

One day the jeweler was outside sweeping the walk in preparation for his day's business when the usual passer-by stopped for his usual watch-setting ceremony, and the jeweler asked the man why he always stopped to set his watch at the same time every morning.

"Well, you see," said the man proudly, "I happen to be the timekeeper at the plant. One of my jobs is to blow the whistle at precisely 8:00 A.M. and at 4:30 P.M. They all depend on my whistle to be accurate."

The jeweler smiled and said, "Well, do you know, for over a year now I have been setting my chronometer by your whistle?"

So you see, sometimes we are misled, uncertain as to where the real authoritative source might be. Sometimes we see a fine-looking chronometer, but it has to be working properly and it has to be set properly. Sometimes we see men who are esteemed men in the community, but they are not always the best source for the question that we have.

We have three main authoritative sources for our information. The first is our Heavenly Father, and just as surely as the Prophet Joseph received an answer to his humble question more than 150 years ago, so we may expect guidance from a loving Heavenly Father.

The second authoritative source of correct counsel and guidance is available from the one we affectionately refer to as "Dad." Dad, I hope the door is open for your son or daughter. I hope the door is open wide, that they may seek counsel when it is required. I hope they can come to you and talk about vital matters without being embarrassed. I hope we dads are living close enough to our family situations that we may sense the appropriate time and place for a few minutes of kindly talk—and lots of listening! I think this is the key to effective counseling with our young people. We have to do lots of listening. We need to have the full story before we can counsel properly.

The third authoritative source is our wonderful bishop, one who has been ordained and set apart to be the father of his ward, and especially a friend to the Aaronic Priesthood boys and to girls of corresponding age.

Bishop, are you too busy to counsel with your young people? If you are too busy, then the work load must be reorganized. How about assigning additional jobs to your counselors? How about letting them carry some of the other loads so you can free yourself for the all-important job of counseling with your young people at convenient and frequent intervals?

How do we interview, bishops? We interview with the spirit of love, and this should be the entire purpose of every interview—love. This should be the underlying factor. There should be no other source but love as we talk to our young people and seek to guide them in the proper direction. And like dad, the bishop should be a good listener too, with the wisdom of Solomon.

Communication — heart-to-heart communication! I wonder how much better off the world would be today if proper communication—not just words, but proper communication—were taking place where we feel the spirit of what is being said and receive the true interpretation? Then counseling could go on properly. Men's minds would come to a common understanding, and there would be peace.

We read in Proverbs: "Where no counsel is, the people fall: but in the multitude of counsellers there is safety." (Proverbs 11:14.) I am certain that the Lord meant exactly what we are talking about when he refers to the multitude of counselors—thousands of dads, hundreds of bishops.

Now, it takes determination to do the right thing at the right time. To illustrate, let me recount a story that comes from far-off New Zealand, one of the finest stories that I have heard in a long time. It concerns a world champion named Peter Snell, who holds several world records, including the mile run. Do you know how Peter Snell trains? Do you know what he goes through? When he goes out to train, he does all of his running uphill, and then when he meets his competition on a flat track it seems like running downhill. Then he will go out and run in the deep sand, and when he gets on a flat cinder track, he feels just as if his feet have wings on them. You will see Peter Snell out running on the wettest, most blustery, wintry day, and when you ask him why he is out running on such a day as this, his answer is, "The opposition is all home by the fire. Now I can get the edge on them." These are the thoughts of a champion.

Tomorrow's challenge *is* great. Why don't you exert the effort to do some running in the sand? Do a little plugging uphill, and work when it is not always convenient, when it might be a little stormy out; and I want to tell you that you will be headed in the direction of a champion in the family of your Heavenly Father.

2

How each person can bear true witness of Jesus Christ

GIFTS OF THE SPIRIT

Know ye not that ye are the temple of God, and that the Spirit of God dwelleth in you?" (1 Corinthians 3:16.) So it is with every son and daughter of our Heavenly Father. Some choose to magnify and amplify that great privilege by sponsoring the gifts of the Spirit within them; others ignore them and go blindly through life missing some of the great joys that can be theirs.

I have had the great privilege of hearing in person the certain, unwavering testimonies of those called and ordained as prophets, seers, and revelators in this day. My entire being seems to tingle as these special witnesses declare in clarion tones, "I know that God lives; I know that Jesus is the Christ and that his true church and kingdom has been restored in this final dispensation of time." Such knowledge is a gift from God through the power of the Holy Ghost.

Many of us have vivid recollections of a close friend or perhaps a family member who has been restored to health by the marvelous gift of healing, through the divine power of the Holy Ghost.

There are scores of returned missionaries who could bear witness that by the gift of the Holy Ghost, words of truth and life were spoken by their lips in a foreign tongue long before their own capabilities could justify it.

Yes, there are hundreds of thousands who have accepted counsel from the "still, small voice," and in that right decision they have avoided another snare, another pitfall. On those occasions theirs has been the gift of the Holy Ghost.

Such spiritual gifts have always been an important function of Christ's true church. The prophets of old were not without these gifts. Marvelous were the manifestations of the Spirit to the prophet Noah. His gift was the gift of revelation, and thus was the seed of Adam saved from destruction in the flood. Abraham enjoyed the gift of faith as he stood willing to sacrifice his beloved son if need be in the fulfillment of a commandment received from God. The prophet Moses was blessed with the gift of miracles as he parted the Red Sea and turned the walking stick into a serpent. The prophet Isaiah enjoyed the gift of prophecy as he so eloquently told of things to come, even down to our day.

The New Testament abounds with demonstrations of the Spirit, first by the Savior himself and then by those called and commissioned, but only as their faith and personal worthiness made them eligible for such experiences. We are all well aware of these faith-promoting stories from the Old and New Testaments, the Book of Mormon, and the beginning days of the Church in this dispensation. We have heard them since childhood—at the knees of our mothers, in Sunday School, in Primary, and so forth.

But how about today? Are we entitled to similar outpourings of the Spirit?

President Marion G. Romney has declared that without the spiritual gifts of the Holy Ghost, there could be no Church of Jesus Christ upon the face of the earth. How true that statement is! Without these gifts, there would be no prophecy, no revelation, no prophet, seer, and revelator, and no Council of the Twelve. So how could there be a church of our Heavenly Father on the face of the earth without these great manifestations that come through these great men?

". . . no man can say that Jesus is the Lord, but by the Holy Ghost," declared Paul to the Corinthians two thousand years ago. (1 Corinthians 12:3.) The Prophet Joseph corrected one word in that quotation. Instead of "no man can *say*," the Prophet Joseph declared that the wording should be, by proper interpretation, "no man can *know* that Jesus is the Lord, but by the Holy Ghost." I suppose that anybody could *say* it, even a counterfeit person, but only one who is convinced can really *know* it and *say* it with conviction.

Speaking of these various gifts of the Spirit, we must be cautious, because we are told in section 46 of the Doctrine and Covenants (verses 8 and 9) that there is danger of being deceived by apparent gifts of the Spirit that really do not qualify. We read: "Wherefore, beware lest ye are deceived; and that ye may not be deceived seek ye earnestly the best gifts, always remembering for what they are given; For verily I say unto you, they are given for the benefit of those who love me and keep all my commandments."

I suppose that we may say, "Well, what is the use? I have not been able to quite bring myself to keep *all* of Heavenly Father's commandments, so I suppose that rules me out!" Then in the next line we receive hope, for he says, ". . . and him that seeketh so to do." So I suppose we all qualify after all. We are seeking to keep all of Heavenly Father's commandments, and hopefully we will do a little bit better tomorrow than we are doing today.

As we seek to keep his commandments and do the very best within us, we are qualified for these gifts of the Spirit, ". . . that all may be benefited that seek or that ask of me, that ask and not for a sign that they may consume it upon their lusts."

Herein lies the problem with most of the world today—people who are seeking a sign, who want things to happen quickly and dramatically without being of service, without study, without all that we know is necessary to excel and be pleasing in the sight of our Heavenly Father.

Seldom, if ever, has testimony come in a miraculous burst. Manifestations are but confirmation to those who have lived worthily and have found their testimonies in the proper manner.

"For all have not every gift given unto them: for there are many gifts, and to every man is given a gift by the Spirit of God." (D&C 46:11.) Each of us has a gift from God. Is your gift being developed? Are you giving it room to grow? Are you making way for other gifts that could be added to you? This is the way we grow in the kingdom of our Heavenly Father, "line upon line, precept upon precept" (D&C 98:12), and gift upon gift, I might add.

If you do not recognize your gift, I think it is well that you seek it from your Heavenly Father and let him manifest through you what that gift is, so that you might amplify it. "To some is given one, and to some is given another, that all may be profited thereby." (D&C 46:12.)

I think that the key was probably given to us by President Joseph Fielding Smith when he pointed out that only the President of the Church is entitled to *all* of the gifts, but we may have *many* gifts—more than we ever dreamed possible—if we will but make our lives worthy and available for that purpose.

Now may we reiterate the most important and precious gift of all: "To some it is given by the Holy Ghost to know that Jesus Christ is the Son of God, and that he was crucified for the sins of the world." (D&C 46:13.)

This is the most precious gift of all gifts—to know that Jesus is the Christ. With that sure knowledge, our lives are tempered, always in the right direction, as we seek to gain the perfection that will one day bring us into his holy presence.

"To others it is given to believe on their words" (D&C 46:14)—on the words of those who can proclaim that they know that Jesus is the Christ. So as those who have been appointed and ordained as prophets, seers, and revelators say with conviction, "I know that God lives! I know that Jesus is the Christ!"—so you too, if you have not arrived at that point, can have the gift of being thrilled by their testimony and believing to a large degree yourselves, preparatory to having that sure knowledge which will come with time and proper effort.

I have been interested in a quotation from Heber C. Kimball. Speaking in terms of having a partial testimony, being able to stand and say, "I believe the Church is true, hoping that some day I might be able to stand and say, 'I know the Church is true,'" Brother Kimball said:

> The Church has before it many close places through which it will have to pass before the work of God is crowned with victory. To meet the difficulties that are coming, it will be necessary for you to have a knowledge of the truth of this work for yourselves. The difficulties will be of such a character that the man or woman who does not possess this personal knowledge or witness will fall. If you have not got the testimony, live right and call upon the Lord and cease not until you obtain it. If you do not, you will not stand. . . . The time will come when no man nor woman will be able to stand on borrowed light. Each will have to be guided by the light within himself. If you do not have it, how can you stand? (Orson F. Whitney, *Life of Heber C. Kimball*, Salt Lake City: Stevens & Wallis, Inc., 1945, pp. 449-50.)

How important it is that we learn to stand upon our own two feet, spiritually speaking. Many of us cling to the testimony of a good bishop, a quorum leader, a church leader, a church teacher, or our parents, without going through the motions that are necessary to one day bring *us* the light and knowledge we must have that we might be able to stand alone in the last days.

Let me tell you about a good man in California a few years ago. He would stand on fast and testimony Sunday and bear a fine testimony—he would tell us how he would willingly give his life for the Church when the persecutions come upon us again—someday. It sounded true, it sounded real. Then we would meet this good brother out in the foyer afterward and shake his hand and thank him for sharing his testimony with us. We would say something like, "Now, Brother So-and-So, how about home teaching next Tuesday night?" "Well," he would reply, "I am sorry, but my favorite TV program is on Tuesday nights, and I will not be able to make it. But someday I am going to give my life for this great church, someday I am going to make the great sacrifice, but I cannot be available next Tuesday night. I have some personal interests to take care of."

You know as well as I that when that someday comes, this good man will not be available to his Heavenly Father. He will not be standing in defense of what he believes, because he will perhaps have a personal interest that will take priority.

"And again, verily I say unto you, to some is given, by the Spirit of God, the word of wisdom. To another is given the word of knowledge, that all may be taught to be wise and to have knowledge." (D&C 46:17-18.) I hope you have found that knowledge is power. But more important than knowledge is in the preceding verse, which says: ". . . to some is given, by the Spirit of God, the word of wisdom." Now we are not talking about a law of health here, as recorded in section 89 of the Doctrine and Covenants. We are talking about the wise use of your knowledge. This is what the Lord means. With all of this getting of knowledge, we must use it wisely, for "the glory of God is intelligence." I want to tell you that there is no greater exemplification of the word *intelligence* than the proper and wise use of the knowledge that we gain. If we do something less than that, then we will be left wanting.

May we be diligent in hearing the word of God, attending our sacrament meetings, informing ourselves by finding some time in our busy day when we might be able to communicate with our Heavenly Father and when we might have a regular time every day to spend fifteen or twenty minutes with the scriptures. I do not know how it is in your busy lives, but in my life I have had to reach over and turn that alarm clock up twenty minutes or thirty minutes earlier. That is not an easy thing to do, but if you are looking for a quiet time, you try it at 4:30 or five o'clock in the morning. That would be an excellent time for you to get close to your Heavenly Father and spend those few minutes communicating with him, learning how he would have you live, and being available for some of these gifts of the Spirit. Those of you who might perhaps feel a little reluctant because of whatever your shortcomings might be, I tell you that the Lord will bless you if you will put forth your effort and do the very best you know how. The Lord will supplement and make you equal to these tasks. He will make you available for these spiritual blessings.

Let me conclude by telling you about a young man who was called into the mission field. He felt inadequate for the call—his grammar was poor, he did not know how to talk to people, and he felt that he could not carry out his mission. The reason he had this inferiority complex was because he had to quit school when he was fifteen years of age because his father passed away. This boy became the family breadwinner—he had to take over the ranch in Wyoming. The bishop assured him, however, that his place was in the mission field now that he was nineteen.

So into the mission field he traveled, halfway around the world, and there on his very first day he was told that Sister Johnson had invited the missionaries home to dinner. Sister Johnson's husband was not a member of the Church. He knew the scriptures very, very well—he knew everything that a Mormon missionary did *not* know on his first day in the mission field. After dinner he would get these missionaries in a corner and try to embarrass them, and he found great delight in doing so. More often than not the missionaries went home determined that that was not going to happen to them again, so they would set their alarm clocks up thirty minutes earlier in order that they might get some extra studying in.

Here comes our young cowboy from Wyoming, feeling inadequate in his calling. Mr. Johnson was in the corner with him after dinner, and the missionary was embarrassed and tears came to his eyes. The thought came into his heart, "I will go to my mission president in the morning and tell him that I must be released. I have come prematurely into the mission field." Just then something lifted him right out of his chair, and he stood up to his full six-foot-four-inches. He reached over and took Mr. Johnson by the shoulders and said, "Now, Mr. Johnson, I do not know how to argue these things with you. I do not know how to debate with you. I have not had a lot of schooling, but I know *why* I have come halfway around the world. If you will just stand here for four or five minutes, I am going to tell you about it."

Mr. Johnson had no choice. The young elder from Wyoming had a captive audience. Then, for the next five or six minutes, he told the man the Joseph Smith story—the story that rang true in his heart. He had been taught the story at the knees of his mother. He used to read the story as he rode the range. He loved it and he knew that it was true, and so he told it to Mr. Johnson with all of the sincerity of his heart. After five or six minutes had gone by, there were tears in their eyes.

To make a long story short, there was a baptism about four or five weeks later. Mr. Johnson had heard the Joseph Smith story from every missionary who had ever been in his home—some had been through college, some who had their gifts developed; but never had he heard it with the gift of the Spirit of God like he heard it from the unschooled lips of a cowboy from Wyoming on that wonderful day. He was listening to something beyond the words that were traveling from lip to ear. There was something from the heart of this young missionary into his heart, bearing witness to him. So he joined this great church.

President David O. McKay said: "The only thing which places man above the beasts of the field is his possession of spiritual gifts. Man's earthly existence is but a test as to whether he will concentrate his efforts, his mind, his soul, upon the things that will contribute to the comfort and gratification of his physical instincts and passions, or whether he will make as his life's aims and purposes the acquisition of spiritual qualities." May we live worthy of the spiritual gifts that God has for us, may we ever stand true to the faith and be willing to carry out the foreordination which is ours, is my humble prayer.

3

The covenants we make with the Lord

COMMITMENT

At a patriotic rally recently, a group of us earnestly vowed a pledge of allegiance to the flag of our country. Every citizen, whatever his nationality, makes strong commitments to uphold and honor his government. This is as it should be.

Few, if any, go through life without committing themselves to a sacred trust and promise of one type or another. In proper perspective and with lofty and worthy objectives, such covenants can and should be stimulating, motivating, and indeed a most stabilizing influence among men.

But any and all social or civil promises, commitments, and oaths entered into by man with man fade into relative insignificance when compared with those promises and covenants between man and God, the Eternal Father. Could any commitment be more important than a sacred covenant between mortal man and his Maker?

A long, long time ago—yes, even before the foundations of this earth were laid—the plan was clear; the process for the successful undertaking of building souls for eternal purposes was established. The covenant procedure was decided upon as an essential element to that end.

The Prophet Joseph has recorded this explicit observation from the Lord himself: "For all who will have a blessing at my hands shall abide the law which was appointed for that blessing, and the conditions thereof, as were instituted from before the foundation of the world." (D&C 132:5.)

Now, no one is suggesting that it is inappropriate for men to establish some mutual understandings and contracts from time to time, provided such agreements stimulate, motivate, and bind us more closely together in a good and worthwhile cause.

It is expedient, however, that we place first things first, and any agreement that we make with the Lord through his Holy Priesthood takes precedence over all else, regardless of its source or its apparent value. Speaking further through the Prophet Joseph, the Lord declared that "all covenants, contracts, bonds, obligations, oaths, vows, performances, connections, associations, or expectations, that are not made and entered into and sealed [by proper authority] . . . are of no efficacy, virtue, or force . . . ; for all contracts that are not made unto this end have an end when men are dead." (D&C 132:7.)

He then gives this reassuring promise: "Behold, mine house is a house of order, saith the Lord God, and not a house of confusion." (D&C 132:8.) Then, thinking in terms of eternity, he states: "For whatsoever things remain are by me; and whatsoever things are not by me shall be shaken and destroyed." (D&C 132:14.) The sacred agreements that we have entered into with our Heavenly Father must be kept first and foremost and above all else.

Most of us have taken upon ourselves the name of Jesus Christ through the waters of baptism. By virtue of this sacred ordinance, we have come forth in a spiritual birth, just as real and necessary as our birth into mortality. Woe be unto that child of God who would enter such a sacred covenant deceitfully or with ulterior motives. Little better is he who enters the waters of baptism without the intention of valiance or effort. Nothing is sadder in all this world than those who, after participating in this great blessing, regard it as of little or no consequence in their lives and then proceed to lose the possibility of life eternal by default. There can be no room for indifference in the wake of such an honor and blessing as that found in the sacred ordinance of baptism.

Indeed, it has been appropriately observed that where much is given, much is expected. All who have had the privilege of baptism in his appointed way and by his appointed authority are indeed richly endowed. Commitment of the highest order has been made. The obligation to bear his name worthily becomes paramount.

As man was being created, surely our Maker must have realized how short our memories and how weak the flesh in this temporal setting. Consequently, his great plan provided for a regular reminder to all who took upon them his name in the waters of baptism.

The sacrament was revealed by the Savior himself, first of all to his very closest associates in the ministry with the specific instruction that "it is expedient that the church meet together often to partake of bread and wine in the remembrance of the Lord Jesus." (D&C 20:75.) It is, therefore, most important for members of his church to recommit themselves every week.

Commitment No. 1: That they are willing to take upon them the name of his Son.

Commitment No. 2: And always remember him.

Commitment No. 3: To keep his commandments which he has given them.

These are not idle thoughts and words but rather sacred obligations and promises entered into with God, the Father, as each worthy member partakes with contrite spirit and deepest reflections concerning the atoning sacrifice of the Only Begotten of the Father.

Show me the man, woman, or child who truly and sincerely covenants to take upon himself the name of Jesus

Christ, and I will show you a person who is upright and honest in all of his dealings.

Show me the man, woman, or child who truly commits himself to always remember, and I will show you a child of God who is without guile, one who is understanding and quick to forgive.

Show me the man, woman, or child who makes it a matter of daily and hourly endeavor to keep God's commandments and lives that pledge in his every act, his every word, to the very best of his ability, and I will show you one who radiates the true Spirit of Christ and who, if unwavering to the end, will inherit eternal life, which is, according to the Lord, "the greatest of all the gifts of God." (D&C 14:7.)

Unfortunately, there are those who choose to commit themselves by covenant to the adversary. Conspiring men have formed secret combinations all through the ages to promote wickedness and evil. Immediately preceding the advent of the Savior on this continent 2,000 years ago, we are told of such a group who "did enter into a covenant one with another, yea, even into that covenant which was given by them of old, which covenant was given and administered by the devil, to combine against all righteousness. Therefore they did combine against the people of the Lord, and enter into a covenant to destroy them. . . ." (3 Nephi 6:28-29.)

Times have not changed. Some time ago an article appeared in our newspaper about a group of individuals who have established a so-called satanic church, with the sole purpose to participate only in the realms of evil and darkness. They are in open defiance of and diametrically opposed to all of His holy purposes. Without a goodly number of God-fearing men committed to the cause of truth, these advocates of evil could well take over our society.

The only effective tool against evil and darkness is truth and light, particularly truth and light held in the hands of those bearing God's Holy Priesthood: worthy, dedicated men. No man or boy who has accepted the commitment of priesthood can stand idly by, for if we do not abide in this covenant with the Lord, if we are less than anxiously engaged in doing something about it, he says: "ye are not worthy of me." (D&C 98:15.)

The oath and covenant of the priesthood stands singularly supreme among God's covenants with his children. The Spirit of the Lord is companion to the priesthood. ". . . all they who receive this priesthood receive me, saith the Lord; . . . And he that receiveth me receiveth my father." (D&C 84: 35, 37.) These reassuring promises from the Lord, as though there were not enough, are climaxed by what has to be the most generous reward ever accorded to mortal man. He confirms his part of the contract as repayment for complete faithfulness in these words: "And he that receiveth my Father receiveth my Father's kingdom; therefore all that my Father hath shall be given him. And this is according to the oath and covenant which belongeth to the priesthood." (D&C 84:38-39.)

Can't we see the folly of any course except it be that course which is priesthood-centered and points toward eternal life? The yoke is easy, the burden is light, the Savior tells us. (Matthew 11:30.) The only difficult way is the cobblestone byway of periodic indifference, broken covenants, and half-hearted effort.

If ours has been the commitment of baptism, then we must stand up tall and bear his name with honor and dignity, for the promise is that as we prove faithful over a few things, he shall make us rulers over many things. (See D&C 52:13.)

If our commitment is in the form of the sacrament, may we partake each time worthily, that we may always have his Spirit to be with us. (See D&C 20:77.) Such is the unqualified promise from our Heavenly Father.

If ours is the commitment to honor the priesthood, may we do so nobly, using it for the blessing of mankind, that our inheritance may indeed be "all that the Father has."

The commitment we make through our covenants with the Lord is serious business. All else is secondary. His rewards are certain, for he has declared for all to hear: "I, the Lord, am bound when ye do what I say; but when ye do not what I say, ye have no promise." (D&C 82:10.)

Let every father stand fearlessly at the head of his family and accept Joshua's challenge that has stood through the ages: ". . . choose you this day whom ye will serve; . . . but as for me and my house, we will serve the Lord." (Joshua 24:15.)

May we commit ourselves without reservation, and may ours be the whole armor of God, that our calling and election may be made sure.

4

The importance of setting and reaching for goals

ORGANIZING FOR ETERNITY

Heavenly Father has a goal and an objective, and, strange as it may seem, he has stated it in one simple sentence. That simple sentence is this: "For behold, this is my work and my glory—to bring to pass the immortality and eternal life of man." (Moses 1:39.)

I have spent a few years of my life in the South Pacific. The wonderful Maori people in New Zealand have a stated goal and an objective that is frequently expressed through one of their proverbs, which contains only four words, although it summarizes the entire objective of their mortal existence. These four words are, "*He wahine, he oneone.*" In this the Maori summarizes his main objectives—the things that he needs most to succeed in life. These two things are "a loyal companion and a plot of fertile soil," and with these two, the Maori considers all else secondary.

Fundamental truth has a habit of remaining unchanged through the ages. Perhaps we, too, could accept as fundamental in our lives these two Maori goals for this life: a loyal companion and an honorable occupation. Then, in terms of eternity, we will never go wrong following the objectives of our Heavenly Father. We do not have to worry about one of them, for immortality has been given to us as a gift by our Elder Brother, Jesus Christ. It has all been accomplished. All we have to do is die, and we surely do that; and then we will be resurrected following the pattern set by our Elder Brother, and immortality is ours as the greatest gift of all time. We also have the gift of the opportunity of eternal life, but eternal life depends on you and me. Something must be done about it. It depends upon individual performance, upon doing what needs to be done, upon scoring a few points every day.

For nearly twenty years I had the great privilege of being associated with one of the nation's largest and most successful corporations. I would like to share with you four of the main attributes that we looked for in the selection of future leaders for this company. We tried to find:

1. Those who had the ability to state a goal and to reach it.
2. Those who could do it through cooperation of other people.
3. Those who were able to satisfy those whose judgment must be respected (the bosses).
4. Those who could perform under conditions of stress.

Now, let us go to the first—the ability to state a goal and to reach that goal. The scriptures tell us that "where there is no vision, the people perish." (Proverbs 29:18.) Without a little vision in your life, without a few well-established goals each day, you will not make it. Even the stock boy the first day on the job should try to improve the order of the stock on the shelf, and after a few days, perhaps, he might even be bold enough to offer a written suggestion to the boss. It will probably be turned down, but he ought to write another one anyway. This is progress; this is vision.

We talk about long-range goals, those goals concerning eternal life or regaining the presence of our Heavenly Father. And we realize, I am certain, the complete necessity of a loyal companion and the importance of an honorable occupation or profession en route.

I think it would be a good idea if we would also consider some immediate goals. This could be the most important segment of all, for no sailor ever reached a given port without first charting a course—not only charting his course, but also checking those bearings every day and a few times every day to make certain he is located where he thinks he is. So, to the extent they as we are effective in charting our course, checking our bearings every day, will we be successful in going toward the goals that we might set for ourselves.

A missionary who felt the need for charting a course wrote down his major objectives for the next five years. He called it his "five-year plan." On this five-year plan, he had such entries as an honorable release from his mission (which was then just starting); graduating with a particular grade-point average; and being married in the house of the Lord. He had a notation about continuing worthily in the Church while he was achieving all of these things: worthy with regard to tithing, the Word of Wisdom, and attendance at sacrament meetings. He also planned to be available to his bishop and to serve as a home teacher or whatever else might need to be done that would be compatible with his busy schedule.

Having prepared his list, he made about five or six copies, with plenty of room at the bottom for additional signatures. Then he had witnesses to those objectives that he had set; he had his parents, his mission president and wife, his bishop back home, and his athletic coach all sign as witnesses to these commitments that he had made for himself. He was the kind of boy who would not want to disappoint those whom he loved. He would want to do these things so he would not have to say to all of us, "I failed."

This young man has now accomplished those goals. He is ready now to take his place in the world. He feels prepared to meet whatever comes next, and, most important of all, he has already prepared a brand-new set of goals that is going to carry him for the next five years, during the struggling days of beginning his business. And I know he will make it because he has established sound goals and has the self-discipline to pursue them effectively.

A very successful businessman, one of the heads of a large corporation and a self-made man, had not had much opportunity for formal education but he went right to the top. On one occasion when I had a few quiet moments with him, I said, "How do you do it? What is the secret to your success?"

He reached inside his shirt pocket and took out a three-by-five card. He said, "Do you see these entries on the card?" There were six or eight items. "I was up at five o'clock this morning deciding what things needed to be done today, and I jotted them down on this card. You notice that about three of the items have been crossed off. I still have the rest to do. If I reach the end of the day and there are one or two that have not been crossed off, they will be at the head of tomorrow's list, and I will do them before I turn to the others."

He concluded, "As far as I am concerned, this is one key to my success. Each day I decide what needs to be done most. I make a note of it; then I do not allow the little incidents of change to deter me from that objective."

One of the greatest stake presidents that I have known has a ruled pad. Every time he meets with his counselors, with the high council, with his bishops, or with his auxiliary heads, this pad is in front of him. He has already noted on the pad many things that he feels should be done for the success of that stake. As the meeting progresses, he adds things to the list. Then he proceeds to make his assignments. At the end of each line that has a given job on it, he writes the initials of a counselor, of a high councilor, of a bishop, or of an auxiliary head; and that remains on his list until the person has reported back and has given a satisfactory accounting of his assignment. No assignment ever dies for this stake president.

The second point in the management training course is to achieve goals through the cooperation of other people. The Savior said, "Come, follow me." When people followed him, it was not always a nice, easy trail. He involved them; he got them to do things to be involved in the work of the kingdom. And that is the way it is with every good bishop and every good stake president and every good employer. They involve people in doing things and achieving. Aren't you grateful to be a member of a church that involves about 200-plus people to operate every ward in the Church? This is the very essence of the success of the gospel of Jesus Christ—involvement, where people lose themselves in the service of others.

I remember hearing my great mission president, Matthew Cowley, say, "You don't have to worry about really being successful. All you have to do is serve the people, and the people will make you famous." Have you ever thought about that? Serve the people, and the people will make you great. They love you, and they put you upon their shoulders. That is how people really become exalted in this world, not by locking themselves in a closet and deciding how they are going to do it, in and of themselves, but through the forgetting of self and through service to others.

Remember the great prophet Moses, as he came with the Israelites out of bondage, standing on the threshold of the vast wilderness area. He apparently did not know exactly how to get things organized, because the Lord finally had to have Jethro, his father-in-law, come to the rescue. The Lord inspired Jethro to counsel with Moses. And Jethro said something like this: "Moses, you can't do it this way. The thing that thou doest is not good. Thou wilt surely wear away."

Then he continued with the advice that the Lord wanted Moses to have: "Get some able men around you, and organize them into groups of a thousand with someone at the head of each group. Then have groups within the thousand—groups of a hundred; groups of fifty; groups of ten; and each of these groups will have their file leaders. Then you will be successful." (See Exodus 18:17-25.) This is exactly what Moses did. Without some kind of organization, without getting other people to cooperate with him and help him, Moses could not have accomplished those things that the Lord gave him to do.

I believe with all my heart that the true value of a man is not in the man who can do the work of ten men, but rather in that man who can get ten men to work.

On an assembly line in an automotive plant in Detroit, a man was putting hub caps on new automobiles. He became the best man on the line. He had been putting hub caps on for ten years. One day the boss came by and said, "How are things going?"

"Well, I am glad you dropped by. I think I deserve a raise. I am the best man on this line. Do you realize I have ten years' experience putting hub caps on?"

The boss smiled and said, "No, George. You have one year's experience ten times. It doesn't take ten years to learn how to put on a hub cap."

Think about that for a moment. If you find yourself down in a rut putting on hub caps and you think you have got ten years' experience, get out of that rut and reach out into other areas. Learn how to do new things, and become useful in this world in which we live.

We have talked about stating a goal and reaching that goal through the cooperation of other people. Now, just a word about satisfying those whose judgment must be respected.

All the qualified leaders that I have ever observed have first been good followers. Heavenly Father has given us a commandment that we should honor our father and mother. He has given a promise associated with that commandment, and if we will do it, the Lord will bless us. Our parents love us. Let us listen to their counsel. Let us do those things they would have us do. God has said, "If ye love me, keep my commandments." (John 14:15.) The rules of life our parents would have us follow are exactly the same as Heavenly Father's commandments, because there is nothing that mothers and fathers would like more than to have us follow in the pathways of the truth and light of the gospel.

Next, we should listen to our bishop. Who loves us more than our bishop? Here is a man who has been ordained and set apart to help us specifically as a member of his ward. We should sustain our bishop and follow his suggestions, for he is counseling us and giving us the advice that we need. He is giving us opportunities for service for our growth and for our development and for those things which will equip us for the uncertainties that lie ahead.

I would mention also our public officials, our elected officials, and our law enforcement agencies. These are people whose judgment must be respected, and we must obey the law or we are not going to get very far.

The fourth condition is to do all of these things under conditions of stress. This could be the most important consideration of all, for almost anyone can succeed and excel on calm waters or while coasting down hill when everything is fine. But when we find the man or woman who can do it when all closes in around him, then we have a winner. Then we have a team that will not give up when every muscle in their bodies says, "I don't want to go any further."

James Freeman Clark said: "All the strength and force of man comes from his faith in things unseen. He who believes is strong. He who doubts is weak. Strong convictions precede great actions. Clear, deep, living convictions rule the world." And I bear you my testimony that they do.

So, as we face life, whether it be in a physical way, a mental way, or a spiritual way, these are our challenges. These are the things that we must do. We must learn how to do things under stress and learn our lessons well. That is the only difference, really, between someone who succeeds and someone who fails. He who is prepared is ready for any eventuality—prepared as the Savior was when he knelt in Gethsemane. That was an hour of great decision, but he met that hour—the greatest hour that any man has ever faced in the history of the world.

Think of George Washington at Valley Forge, his men without shoes, without food. But George Washington did not give up, and because he did not give up, his men kept going and there was victory. Abraham Lincoln could easily have said, "Who cares about all of this?" But he had determination, and he had a conviction in his heart; and when the nation was on the brink of disaster, this great leader carried the nation through. Think of the Prophet Joseph Smith as he stood on the threshold of martyrdom. All he had to do was deny his testimony. But that he was not going to do. Brigham Young could have turned back many times; but, no, the Lord told him what he wanted him to do, and he did it.

Let us do what needs to be done. Let us not think of our own personal convenience. Let us think of the Lord's convenience. Let us not always think of the easy way.

I like to think of the great basketball player, Bill Bradley. Do you know the three secrets of his success?

First, he practiced a basketball shot until he made the same shot twenty-five times consecutively before he moved from that position, and if he did not finish doing it one day, he came back the next. And if he got up to twenty-four and then missed, he started all over again. Until he made that shot twenty-five times, he had not perfected himself, and he went back and kept trying.

Rule number two in his life was that studies come first, and he studied, and he excelled. He was a Rhodes scholar.

Number three: the Sabbath day was the Lord's day, and he did not do any playing or anything else contrary to that holy day. He went to church and took care of his devotions and those things that were proper in his faith.

If we follow rules such as these, the Lord will bless us. He will magnify us. He will give us everything we need. Then when the going gets tough in this church, we will be ready to stand on our feet and make an accounting of ourself. We will be prepared mentally to rise above the crowd, and we will excel, and we will achieve. Then one day we will have the greatest privilege that ever comes to any man as we stand on the threshold of God himself and feel a kindly hand on our shoulder as he speaks the sweetest words that any man could ever hear: "Well done, thou good and faithful servant: . . . enter thou into the joy of the Lord." (Matthew 25:21.)

5

Developing the courage to resist and overcome evil

STAND UP AND BE COUNTED

True greatness has a habit of surviving the years. I am certain that every member of the Church has thrilled to the words of a stalwart young man of Aaronic Priesthood age who lived approximately twenty-six hundred years ago. When faced with a difficult situation, he said, "I will go and do the things which the Lord hath commanded, for I know that the Lord giveth no commandments unto the children of men, save he shall prepare a way for them that they may accomplish the thing which he commandeth them." (1 Nephi 3:7.)

This young man, destined to become a great prophet, had a most important quality. He had courage—courage to stand on his own two feet rather than follow the so-called easier way, the more popular way, the beckoning of the crowd, in this case his own brothers.

Let us quickly span twenty-six hundred years and review a story of Aaronic Priesthood courage in our day. My heart was touched as I had the privilege of reading an excerpt from a serviceman's letter to his parents. Apparently, his training instructor had made it a habit of starting each day's discussion with a few off-color stories.

One morning, quite by surprise, the instructor asked if anyone objected to a couple of "good" stories before starting the day's instruction. This young Mormon boy said that almost as though he had been ejected from his seat by an unseen power, he shot up and said, "Yes, sir, I object."

After a long, stony silence, the instructor said, "Are there any others?" You can imagine the feelings of this boy's heart as one by one another dozen or so young army recruits stood in defense of what they really believed. Those standing were invited to leave the class, and then halfway out, they were called back with a comment from the instructor, "I guess we can skip the stories this morning."

Wouldn't you like the privilege of shaking hands with that kind of Aaronic Priesthood courage? Isn't it gratifying to know that you don't have to turn the pages of history back twenty-six hundred years to find the courage of a Nephi or a Daniel in the lions' den or a David meeting Goliath? And isn't it also gratifying to know that for every courageous heart with the fortitude to stand up and be counted, there will be a host of others willing to rally to the cause of truth and right?

Now, courage is an easy word to say. To be effective, there must be action, positive action in the right direction, which can only happen when that courage is inspired through positive, proper motivation.

Now join with me through a thought sequence, which should prove helpful to serious-minded Church members as a basis for motivation in the right direction:

First, let us reconfirm in our minds that there is a Heavenly Father, that he is the Creator of heaven and earth and directs all that we survey.

Second, let us be assured that his house is a house of order, even to the extent that you and I have come to mortality now, in this day, by specific assignment for a real purpose. Have you ever asked yourself, "Why wasn't I born two hundred years ago, or a thousand years ago?"

There is only one reason: because the Lord wanted you born now, in this important day.

Third, can we know for certain that a young boy knelt in a grove of trees in the year 1820 and there received a personal visitation from God the Father and his Son Jesus Christ? Have you read the Joseph Smith story lately, with a real desire to know its truthfulness?

Fourth, why are you a member of this church and kingdom? Could this be by chance? By your selection only? The Savior has this to say: "Ye have not chosen me, but I have chosen you, and ordained you. . . ." (John 15:16.) I know that foreordination is a real part of the plan, and that we have a responsibility—a divine commission, if you please—conferred prior to mortal existence that can neither be disregarded nor taken lightly without far-reaching consequences.

Fifth, the Lord has given us a most precious gift that we call free agency. And after all is said and done, the final decision is ours with regard to our talents, our divine commission, our choice between left or right, right or wrong.

Youth of Zion, do you have the courage to do right? I sometimes wonder how we could have the courage to do anything but right if we really believe in the foregoing steps of logic. Let us just enumerate them again briefly:

1. God lives.
2. His house is a house of order.
3. The heavens have been opened and remain open today.
4. We are here by appointment, by foreordination.
5. And finally, the choice is ours as to what we do about it.

Now, not only do we need courage in choosing our way, but we also need help. The best source of help is from those who love us. I would like to reconfirm the truth that no one loves us like our parents, like our bishop, like our Heavenly Father. May we always seek our counsel and guidance from these three sources.

Youth is energetic; youth is aggressive. The mind of youth is inquisitive, sometimes beyond sound judgment, which often leads us into dangerous territory. The Prophet Joseph Smith had this to say to Martin Harris in kindly reprimand: "When a man designedly provokes a serpent to bite him, the principle is the same as when a man drinks deadly poison, knowing it to be such. In that case, no man has any claim on the promises of God to be healed." (*DHC*, 2:95-96.)

By the same token, can we expect the protection we need when we knowingly step beyond the limits of good judgment? Moroni's reiteration of Mormon's teachings gives us the key for keeping a solid footing:

> For behold, the Spirit of Christ is given to every man, that he may know good from evil; wherefore, I show unto you the way to judge; for every thing which inviteth to do good, and to persuade to believe in Christ, is sent forth by the power and gift of Christ; wherefore ye may know with a perfect knowledge it is of God.
>
> But whatsoever thing persuadeth men to do evil, and believe not in Christ, and deny him, and serve not God, then ye may know with a perfect knowledge it is of the devil; for after this manner doth the devil work, for he persuadeth no man to do good, no, not one; neither do his angels; neither do they who subject themselves unto him. (Moroni 7:16-17.)

Yes, youth of Zion, history is still being made, and whether you like it or not, you have a hand in it. You will need courage—and lots of it. You will need the help of those who love you and the support of loyal friends, real friends, friends who would encourage you in "every thing which inviteth to do good," as stated by Moroni.

Now in conclusion, may I suggest that this church is not idly named. We are The Church of Jesus Christ of Latter-day Saints. These are the latter days; this is the final dispensation of time, and the programs of the Church are all moving toward a sort of finalization or culmination. There is an urgency as never before about what needs to be done; and be sure of this, what needs to be done will be done on schedule, we hope by those initially foreordained to the task. But just as surely as night follows the day, if we choose not to accept our station, or if we grow weary along the way, placing less important things first, there will be substitutes raised to take our place, for the Lord's time plan and ultimate purposes will not be thwarted.

Youth of Zion, stand up and be counted, have the courage of your convictions, and whatever you do, don't allow someone else to be a substitute for you in the kingdom of your Heavenly Father.

6

The joy that comes to those who perform compassionate service

"GO, AND DO THOU LIKEWISE"

It has been truthfully said that the Savior is even more concerned for our success here in mortality than we ourselves are, the reason being, of course, that he has greater capacity for concern and love than do we mortals. He also has a superior knowledge of the gospel plan and man's potential in God's divine, eternal scheme. As stated by one prophet, God's work and glory is achieved through our attainment of immortality and eternal life. (See Moses 1:39.)

Someone once suggested that it would be relatively simple for Christ to do all of the religious teaching here on earth. How easy it would be for the Creator to deliver every sermon and to teach every Sunday School class by means of closed-circuit television. Each religious meeting place could be equipped with a large video screen, and the Master Teacher of all time could then present every gospel lesson and deliver every sermon in a way that would hold us spellbound and indeed convert even the most critical. I suppose it would also be within his power to take over all the compassionate service for mankind, but such is contrary to the development of God's children.

Before the foundations of this earth were laid, a glorious decision was made allowing you and me to be our brother's keeper. By faith and service we would be able to achieve a degree of glory in the hereafter suited to our Christlike efforts and our Christlike attainments.

Adversity, heartache, bitter disappointment, grievous transgression, and disability are but a few of the obstacles that beset the inhabitants of this world. Few, if any, escape. None would have to linger in despair for long, however, if man could just bring himself to heed that one great teaching recorded in the 25th chapter of Matthew.

On this occasion the Savior was describing the day of judgment, wherein those to be judged were divided, some on the right hand and some on the left. Finding themselves in a favored position, those on the right expressed surprise and wanted to know why the reward had come to them. The Savior replied:

"For I was an hungered, and ye gave me meat: I was thirsty, and ye gave me drink: I was a stranger, and ye took me in:

"Naked, and ye clothed me: I was sick, and ye visited me: I was in prison, and ye came unto me." (Matthew 25:35-36.)

Then the righteous answered, stating that not once had they found him hungry or thirsty or a stranger; and then the Savior's classic teaching: "Verily I say unto you, Inasmuch as ye have done it unto one of the least of these my brethren, ye have done it unto me." (Matthew 25:40.)

Other expressions of the Savior further confirm the same charges. He said, "Feed my sheep." (John 21:16.) ". . . all things whatsoever ye would that men should do to you, do ye even so to them." (Matthew 7:12.) Then, having set the perfect example of service during his ministry, he concluded by saying, "Go, and do thou likewise." (Luke 10:37.)

In recent years it has been my privilege to work closely with many emotionally disturbed people; others who have transgressed; some who have found themselves out of harmony with society; still others who have been lonely and afraid. It has not been a time of discouragement and despair, however, because the vast majority of these people have made an important decision; they have said, "I want to change my life. I am ready to take direction from someone who really cares." And in this church, we have bishops and stake presidents who really care.

How touching it was to hear a hardened prisoner say, "That is the first time anybody ever told me they loved me." This was after a six-year-old girl kissed him on the cheek during a Church-sponsored family home evening visit in the prison.

Consider with me an unwed mother who came to her bishop with some reluctance. Her heart was belligerent, and she also had a drug problem; but months later, following compassionate service by many, she was heard to say, "Life was over for me. I didn't want to live anymore, but things are different now, and I know the true meaning of God's love."

A confirmed alcoholic found a new lease on life because an assigned couple had won his confidence, and they were there when he needed them. His problem is now history. His own family is back together for the first time in years.

A sexual deviate discovered with help that his problem was not God-given, as so many had told him in the past, but rather self-acquired from an early age. He recently declared with confidence, "I have conquered Satan himself. Nothing can stop me now."

Every success story has been the result of special effort on the part of people who cared. They cared enough to give some time and to be sincere and compassionate; in other words, to follow the great example set by the Savior.

The only joy that is comparable with the joy of the one receiving the help is the glow that seems to emanate from the one who has given so unselfishly of his time and strength to quietly help someone in need.

The Savior did not seem to be so much involved in giving money. You will remember that his gifts were in the form of personal attention, in performing an administration, and in sharing the gifts of the Spirit. In fact, it was the Savior who said: "Peace I leave with you, my peace I give unto you: not as the world giveth, give I unto you. . . ." (John 14:27.) We could add to peace the gift of love, the gift of immortality, the gift of eternal life, the gift of understanding, the gift of compassion, the gift of eternal justice. All of these gifts are beyond monetary consideration and could well be our gift to someone sometime, if we weren't "too busy."

Members of this church understand clearly that baptism is essential for entrance into the celestial kingdom. We also know and understand that total fulfillment can only be found in that ultimate celestial state called eternal life or exaltation, which, of course, is to live eternally in the Savior's holy presence.

Only those who have been justified and sanctified through service to their fellowmen can hope to reach such a lofty goal. To be justified is to be found acceptable in our "good works" as well as by our superior faith. James used this excellent example:

"If a brother or sister be naked, and destitute of daily food,

"And one of you say unto them, Depart in peace, be ye warmed and filled; notwithstanding ye give them not those things which are needful to the body; what doth it profit?" (James 2:15-16.)

After citing other similar examples, he concludes with this thought: "Ye see then how that by works a man is justified, and not by faith only." (James 2:24.)

Moroni explained that we are sanctified "by the grace of God" as we become "perfect in Christ" and "deny not his power." (Moroni 10:33.)

No man can become "perfect in Christ" without a deep, abiding, and sincere concern for his fellow beings. The preceding example from James cites physical needs. However, there are also emotional problems about us in every direction. Loneliness and discouragement, for example, are two of Satan's most effective tools against us.

Is there someone you know who needs a friend, a friend who is willing to listen to him? The Church is reaching out to such people as never before. Resource volunteers are being organized throughout the Church to help carry out one of the Savior's most sacred challenges.

There are those who associate high calling in the Church with guaranteed rights to the blessings of heaven, but I wish to declare without reservation that the ultimate judgment for every man will be on the simplest terms, and most certainly on what each has done to bless other people in a quiet, unassuming way.

If this life's effort is to be justified, then there should be a major and continuing attempt to justify or, in other words, to conform our actions with the example of the Master. The central theme of his mortal span was purely and simply serving those about him. He fulfilled an eternal truth which should be a part of your life and my life. "And whosoever will be chief among you, let him be your servant." (Matthew 20:27.)

If our life's effort is to be sanctified or ratified by the standards of eternal truth, then our actions must be in harmony with the sanctifying principles of the gospel, which most certainly include sincere concern for others and a concerted effort to alleviate their problems.

I can think of no better guarantee for the future, your future and my future, than to follow the admonition of the Savior when he said at the beginning of his ministry: "Come and follow me" (Matthew 19:21); and then, after showing the way, he said very simply, "Go, and do thou likewise."

7

The purpose of the programs of the Church

THAT ALL MAY BE BLESSED

The Savior declared: "Inasmuch as ye have done it unto one of the least of these my brethren, ye have done it unto me." (Matthew 25:40.) This is the key to the gospel of Jesus Christ, doing for other people.

We have a great mechanism in the Church for getting this job done for Heavenly Father—of helping the Savior of the world to bring to pass the immortality and eternal life of man. We have our great priesthood programs, the auxiliary programs, and wonderful ordinances that we participate in. We partake of the sacrament and renew our covenant with our Heavenly Father. We recommit ourselves, that we are going to do what he has asked us to do.

And then we have the wonderful principles of the gospel—principles like repentance and forgiveness; principles like loving our brother as ourselves. These are the motivations that we have as Latter-day Saints to help us accomplish that which Heavenly Father has placed us here to do.

May I place my emphasis on the blessings that come to people through our efforts as we follow the programs of the Church. No one can deny the effort that goes forth with all of the programs in the Church and with all the implementation of the programs through stake conferences, regional conferences, meetings, meetings, and more meetings—but until we filter these programs down to an individual and lift that individual just a little bit, and until we can bless a family and make that family more united in the faith, then I say that these programs, these implementations, are all in vain. We must bless *people*, and unless we bless people, we are falling short of that objective given to us by our Heavenly Father.

Now, we have a rather substantial membership in the Church today, a little over three million people. Do you know that it took us 115 years to achieve a million members in this church? One hundred and fifteen years! But it took only fifteen to get our second million people, and our third million has come in much shorter time than that.

How thrilling it is to be living in this time in the world's history when great things are happening!

Along with this wonderful increase in membership, we have an increase in every dimension. I remember when I was just a lad—I guess I was a priest in the Aaronic Priesthood—and my ward bishop had us together one day, trying to catch us on fire and show us the vision of this great church. He said, "Now, young men, the average attendance at sacrament meeting throughout the Church today is about 19 percent." Then he said, "If you young men do what you are supposed to do and if you accept the reins of leadership and prepare for it now so that when you come back from your missions you can do what the Lord wants you to do, I can see the day when we might have as many as 33 percent of our people coming out to sacrament meeting." Well, we have exceeded that. Now it appears that more than 35 percent of the members are attending sacrament meeting regularly—not 19 percent, as it was just a few years back. Our challenge now is the challenge of doing the things that need to be done in this church so that even greater devotion will push us past the 50 percent mark.

Oh, how wonderful it is to see the great missionary force we have in the Church, ever increasing the membership, going out to every nation, kindred, tongue, and people, for the Lord has declared, "And this gospel of the kingdom shall be preached in all the world for a witness unto all nations. . . ." (Matthew 24:15.) And that is exactly what we are doing.

How grateful I have been to travel through some of these missions of the world. And do you know why I am thrilled most of all about our missionary service today? Because we have better techniques. We are doing a much better job. I blush sometimes when I compare the job I did in the mission field with the job that our young missionaries are doing today. My, how thrilling it is to hear them give their discussions with perfection and with the Spirit of the Lord, in simplicity and in humility and with sincerity.

How grateful I am for the great program that was introduced by President David O. McKay, "Every member a missionary." And while we don't all give the discussions, we can be finders. We can go out and find people who are prepared to listen to the discussions, and we can make arrangements for the missionaries to come into our homes to teach the gospel to these wonderful people.

And then I think, best of all, we have a fellowshiping program in the Church today that far exceeds and excels anything we have ever had in the past.

This church is going forward. It is wonderful. It is thrilling.

Some time ago Sister Simpson and I had the privilege of touring some of the stakes of the South Pacific, and in Australia particularly. On the flight down to Australia, a stewardess came down the aisle, pouring coffee and tea. "No, thank you. None for us," we said. "Do you have any milk?"

"You must be Mormons," she said.

Then she came back after she finished her job and she said, "You know, I can't wait to get back to my home in Sacramento."

I said, "Why is that?"

She said, "Well, I'm not a member of your church, but I'm taking the discussions, and when I get back, I will have discussion number three, and I'm going to be a member just as soon as I possibly can."

It wasn't more than a week later, still down in the South Pacific, that we were flying on another airline, and another stewardess came along serving dinner and pouring the drinks. "No, thank you. Do you have any milk?" we asked. "You must be Mormons." Right again.

And so she came back a little later and said, "You know, I'm not a member of your church, but I was over in France last year—I spent twelve months over there—and when I came home I found that my parents had been baptized into your church, and it's the greatest thing that has ever happened in our family."

And I said, "Well, how about you?"

She said, "That's coming. I have a few things to overcome, but I was in the roadshow last month just before I came on this trip, and I am going to be a member of your church just as soon as I can get things in proper order."

So that is the way the gospel is being spread around the world. No matter where we go, we hear wonderful things, and people are talking about this great Church of Jesus Christ of Latter-day Saints.

May I say just a word about some of the great priesthood programs? Let me begin with the home teaching program. Home teaching is the process whereby the bishop can multiply himself by dozens of times. Motivated by love unfeigned, the home teachers have as their only objective to strengthen the home, and this can only be done effectively as the family leaders—the parents—are strengthened. The home teacher draws on every resource in the ward, both priesthood and auxiliary, in order to lift the family. Home teaching is for no other purpose than to lift families and to bind them together.

A famous clergyman visited Salt Lake City a few years back. He studied the Church from all angles. He looked at all the priesthood programs and auxiliary programs, and after several days as he was about ready to leave, one of the Brethren said, "What has impressed you most about the Church organization?"

He said, "The greatest single thing you have, without a doubt, is the home teaching program."

And then the question was asked, "I suppose you are going back to start it in your church then?"

He said, "No, we're not able to do that because we don't have the lay leadership that you have in your church. It would be impossible for us to even attempt it."

And so you can see the great blessing that we have, and the great inspiration that comes from the Lord in carrying out these tremendous programs.

Let me take just a minute on the great welfare program, the priesthood arm of the Church that takes care of Heavenly Father's work in caring for the poor and the needy. You know the Bible talks about love unfeigned (2 Corinthians 6:6) and then it goes on to say we are to take care of the widows and the fatherless (James 1:27). This is love unfeigned—the great welfare program—where we abolish the dole; there is no such thing as a "something for nothing" program in Heavenly Father's church; the welfare program is only for those folks who are incapacitated, those who cannot do for themselves. Every time we do for someone who can do for himself, we weaken that man.

There are three basic concepts in the welfare program: (1) the individual is responsible for his own well-being; and (2) if the individual cannot do it, then the family must step in and take over and provide the needs of that individual; and (3) if the individual cannot do it, and the family cannot do it, then the Church will come to the rescue and do what needs to be done.

My, you would be thrilled to go into a Deseret Industries plant, where we employ hundreds of our handicapped people who without Deseret Industries in the Church would be at home probably watching television all day long. Wouldn't that be a terrible existence? But they can go to a Deseret Industries plant and produce something according to their abilities. Some produce a lot, some not very much; many of these people eventually qualify themselves for work in outside industry, which, of course, is the continuing objective of the program.

I shall never forget the great lesson I was taught in welfare as I visited the Deseret Industries plant in Logan, Utah. There was a little old sister working away—she must have been in her eighties. I stopped to chat with her and said, "My, isn't this work a little difficult for you?" And she looked up and said, "Why, I raised twelve children! This is the easiest job I've ever had." She was just thrilled to have an opportunity to work for her commodities; even though she could not support herself in the usual way, she was working in the Lord's way, and she felt good about it.

There are wonderful projects throughout the Church, projects to produce those things that people need. Did you know that 75 percent of all the commodities that we use in the welfare program are produced by the people of the Church? I would like to say further that the greatest storehouses we have in the Church are not the bishop's storehouses located throughout the Church; the greatest storehouses we have are in the pantries of the members of the Church, where members of the Church are advised to store up one year's supply for an emergency. Can you see what a great source of strength this would be in this nation in emergency, if every Latter-day Saint home were doing what a prophet of God has advised us to do?

Sometimes people criticize the Church; they say, "Well, that's all well and good, but why don't we take care of people outside of our church boundaries?" I would like you to know that every week dozens of people passing through Salt Lake City are given help and assistance at Welfare Square, given an opportunity to work, to receive money to buy gas for their cars that they might go on to their destinations, or that they might reestablish themselves, even though they are not members of our faith.

We have sent tons and tons of food, clothing, and bedding to far-away places to bless nonmembers of the Church in time of disaster. An earthquake in Iran, an earthquake in Chile, a flood in California, a terrible hurricane in Samoa—yes, tons of material have been sent all over the world to bless people in need, whether they be Latter-day Saints or not. This is a work of compassion indeed.

The world looks at us, and they like what they see. Yet we take so much for granted!

Did you know that nearly a million hours of compassionate service were given by the Relief Society last year? Did you know that last year some five million visits were made by the visiting teachers? Spiritual living, cultural refinement, social relations, homemaking—these are the exposures that our sisters have each month. It is not happening, as far as I know, to any comparable group of women in the world. These subjects are so vital to the rearing of future generations. Yes, children are being taught in truth and light and touched by the mothers of this church.

Let me tell you just quickly about the blessings of a little girl named Vicki, who was found on an Arizona desert living with her grandmother, abandoned by her real mother. Her cheeks were hardened by the desert sun, and her grandmother didn't know what to do with her. Here came the Relief Society—and now little Vicki is living with a family in Salt Lake City, Utah, an adopted child.

I met her just last week; she was radiant, she was alive, she had a new lease on life, all because of the Church's great adoption program. And many such adoptions take place every year.

We met another young man who was just fourteen years of age when he was discovered in a detention home. When the Church social workers were called to see if they could help him, they were able to place him in an LDS foster-care home where he had the influence of family prayer and the family home evening. This young man rallied to that kind of teaching; he wasn't a bad boy, he was just a boy who hadn't had a chance, who hadn't had proper parental care and direction. Well, foster care led him into the mission field. And then we met him with his new bride, married in the house of the Lord.

"What do you plan for the future, young man?" we asked.

"I'm enrolled at Brigham Young University. I am taking social work because I want to do for someone else what the Church has done for me," he replied.

This is the spirit of the gospel of Jesus Christ.

Aren't you grateful for the Primary Association? At the Primary Children's Medical Center is a display board showing photographs of some patients both before and after treatment. And here you see children who come into the hospital unable to walk, their arms and legs curled up, just able to scoot along on the floor; they leave the hospital a few months or years later, their bodies repaired. They go home to their countries of origin all over the world, and no one can judge the blessings that are coming through this service.

I am gratefully humble for all that has been going on in the Church. I hope you feel the same way. We have had great success, but we haven't had enough success; we will depend on you young people, the generation for tomorrow's leadership.

I want to promise our young people there will be no miracles, there will be no great signs in the heavens that will bring millions of people into this church. It will happen only as we bear an effective testimony, as we work through the auxiliaries and through the priesthood.

I testify that this is his work. It you want to please the Lord, just keep your ears attuned to that message he gave 2,000 years ago. Nothing has changed. If you were to talk to the Savior today he would give you the same word. He would say, "Love thy neighbor as thyself," "Come, follow me," "Feed my sheep," and indeed he would say, "Inasmuch as ye have done it unto the least of these my brethren, ye have done it unto me."

Let us rejoice in this day of salvation, but may we do so in humility and with a determination to do even better in the future than in the past because the Lord has given us the tools to do it with.

8

The peace that comes from living God's commandments

NOT AS THE WORLD GIVETH

May I share a great experience that I had at the age of eight years. This was an experience of learning and taught me a lesson that I shall never forget.

I remember the thrill of being taught simple division. Three goes into fifteen five times. It seemed almost like a miracle as the teacher further taught us that all we had to do was multiply the answer by the divisor, and we would have the number that we started with. She said that by following this simple plan and procedure we could check any division problem and make certain that the answer was right.

A few days later we had our first test in simple division. I shall never forget turning to my school chum and announcing, "I got an 'A.'" He said, "How do you know? We haven't even graded the papers."

"I know I have an 'A' because I checked every answer. I multiplied the answer by the divisor, and I was certain that it was exactly the same number we started with. I know I got an 'A.'"

And sure enough, it was an "A" because I was standing on solid rock. There was no doubt in my mind. I was dealing with an exact science, and for the first time in my life I felt really secure in something that I had been taught in school. This was an exact science, and I was able to prove my answer beyond question.

Now in the world today, I think if there were one common wish among all mankind, that wish would be for peace—peace in the world; peace in each nation; peace in the community; even a feeling of peace in each home; and perhaps most important of all, peace of mind.

Our day will probably go down in history as the day of psychiatry, psychology, and tranquilizers. Now, I don't mean to suggest that there is no place for the professionally trained to treat the mentally disturbed or for the prescribing of proper medicine for the overwrought, but I do believe with all my heart and soul that most of these anxieties found in the hearts and minds of men today can be eliminated by a return to faith in God and the resultant desire to obey his commandments.

To me, and I am sure to you, God's plan is like a superhighway. This superhighway is built on solid rock; it is built well above the fog-shrouded valleys; and it is built well above the swamps of infidelity, selfishness, and immorality. The Lord himself has said, "I am the light of the world: he that followeth me shall not walk in darkness, but shall have the light of life." (John 8:12.)

Heavenly Father has also said that there are laws irrevocably decreed in the heavens upon which all blessings are predicated. (See D&C 130:20-21.) If we keep the law, we reap happiness. If we violate the law or ignore the law, we have problems, and we have unhappiness. It is just as simple as that.

And so, as we think back to my third grade experience, how much the same are God's laws. His laws are also undeviating, certain, proven, and all we need do is keep his laws, and we will be happy, we will be successful, and we will regain his presence.

With you, I invite all men, all women, all children, all people everywhere to join in God's plan. Let's consider his law of health, for example. Why have all the upset that we have in the world through lack of health, when all we need do is follow God's plan as revealed in this day, and then we will most likely have the peace of mind of a strong, healthy body.

With you, I would share with the world the great truth that all we have to do is give back to Heavenly Father one-tenth of our increase, and again we have peace of mind, as we help build his kingdom unselfishly.

With you, I would give to the world the great truth that we must have love and unity in our homes, and here again we can achieve a peace of mind unattainable in any other way.

The same thing can be said of the Sabbath day, of keeping it holy, and of the peace that comes to all who keep that great commandment.

The same thing can be said about the principle of prayer. As we communicate with our Heavenly Father, we let him know that we love him and that we intend to keep his commandments to the very best of our ability.

Yes, there are eternal truths. Two parts hydrogen and one part oxygen is water. It was so when Heavenly Father was creating the earth. It is so today, and it will be so forever. This is an eternal truth of chemistry. PiR^2 has always been and always will be the formula to find the area of a circle. One hundred and eighty-six thousand miles per second always has been and always will be the speed of light Einstein has given us in our day that E is equal to MC^2, the theory of relativity.

As we quote these basic truths, they are simple. They are not complicated. All basic truth seems to be simple. It is only when we go beyond the realm of truth that we become complicated, that we become mixed up in our minds and our emotions.

Can we simplify our lives, simplify our living, take time to do the things that need to be done? If there is not time in our lives for the family home evening, there is something wrong, and we are getting away from the way Heavenly Father would have us live. If there is not time in our lives for personal prayer, then we must take stock of ourselves. If there is not enough faith or money to give back to Heavenly Father his one-tenth, then we are mismanaging our affairs, and we are getting away from those things that would bring us pure and simple happiness.

So the gospel is peace of mind, and only as rapidly as we get back to the standard works and give heed to his basic principles will we have the peace of mind that Christ himself spoke of when he proclaimed to the world: "Peace I leave with you, my peace I give unto you: not as the world giveth, give I unto you. Let not your heart be troubled, neither let it be afraid." (John 14:27.)

The world giveth differently from the way Christ giveth, and when we partake of the world as the world giveth, we start reaching for our tranquilizers. But as we reach for the standard works of the Church and the truths revealed therein, then I say we are going to have joy in our lives, and we can promise to all men there will be happiness in their lives. We can further say that theirs will be a peace of mind that will bring a surety to their souls and give them the happiness to which all Heavenly Father's children are entitled.

9

The faith of our Maori brothers and sisters

THE LORD IS MINDFUL OF HIS OWN

The book of Alma in the Book of Mormon has a very significant statement concerning a man called Hagoth, who set sail from the Americas many centuries ago.

> And it came to pass that Hagoth, he being an exceedingly curious man, therefore he went forth and built him an exceedingly large ship, on the borders of the land Bountiful, by the land Desolation, and launched it forth into the west sea, by the narrow neck which led into the land northward.

Now where would the west sea be? The west sea would be the Pacific Ocean, and the narrow neck of land leading into the land northward must mean the Panama Canal area.

> And behold, there were many of the Nephites who did enter therein and did sail forth with much provisions, and also many women and children; and they took their course northward. And thus ended the thirty and seventh year.
>
> And in the thirty and eighth year, this man built other ships. And the first ship did also return, and many more people did enter into it; and they also took much provisions, and set out again to the land northward.
>
> And it came to pass that they were never heard of more. And we suppose that they were drowned in the depths of the sea. . . . (Alma 63:5-8.)

In a great gathering of Polynesians held in Salt Lake City just prior to 1915, a prophet of the Lord, President Joseph F. Smith, addressing a group of Polynesians who had come to Salt Lake City to participate in their temple endowment work, made the statement that without a doubt this man Hagoth and his company were the progenitors of the Polynesian races, and that this migration was the beginning of the Polynesian population in the South Pacific.

Now up until very recently men of science have said no, the Polynesians have come from the Malay states, they have come from the Asian side of Africa, and they have migrated from a westerly direction to the Polynesian islands—not from the Americas. This was popular thinking until about 1940, when a very bold scholar by the name of Thor Heyerdahl made the observation that indeed these people must be from the Americas. He set out to prove this by building some balsa rafts on which he set himself adrift off the shores of South and Central America. He and his companions drifted for about one hundred days; and depending only on the prevailing tides and winds of that area, they found themselves cast upon the shores of these South Pacific islands, not far from Tahiti. It seems rather significant that all of a sudden scientific opinion began to change, and Thor Heyerdahl, since that day, has presented additional evidences that have further made it a very important consideration—that the Polynesians did originate from the Americas.

Now the Maories themselves have something to say about this theory. They all have the same answer to the question: "Where did your people come from? Where did you originate?" The answer is always the same:

"*I haere mai matou i tawhiti nui, i tawhiti roa, i tawhiti pamamau i te hono i te wai e rua.*" ("We came from a great distance, from a still greater distance, from a very, very great distance, from the joining place of two great waters.")

Perhaps they came by way of the narrow neck of land that separated the two great waters, the narrow neck of land that led into the land northward. This is Maori tradition, and those who have joined the Church believe without reservation that these things I have told you are part and parcel of Mormon doctrine.

There is another part to this story. You know that down through the ages the Polynesian people have clung tenaciously to their genealogical records. Here is a people strewn through the South Pacific islands without a written language, only a spoken language, and it has been the obligation of each male member to memorize and to know his genealogy without fail. Why?

"We do not know why," answers the Maori; "only that our father told us and his father told him and his father told him, as far back as we know, that we must preserve our genealogical record." So the Maori had what was called the *whare wananga*, or house of learning, before the coming of the white man. In the *whare wananga*, the Maori boy at the age of eight or nine was taught his genealogy, hundreds and hundreds of names. These names had to be memorized to stay with him until it was time for him to pass them on to his children.

I remember, on my mission to New Zealand, going up to the Bay of Islands to Brother Otene's house. Brother Otene wanted me to take down some genealogical records for him. I was a rather new missionary, but I was delighted with the opportunity. He would bury his head in his hands and close his eyes, and he would repeat from memory, "*Kua marena a mea, a ka puta mai a mea, nana i marena a mea,*" etc. ("So and so was married to so and so, and the children were thus and thus and thus.")

I was writing just as quickly as I could, and soon there were eight or nine pages, name after name. I said to myself, "Now I wonder if all this memorization could really be correct. I wonder if this record is *really* right." It was not more than a few weeks later that I had occasion to be transferred to another part of New Zealand a couple of hundred miles away. There I was also invited to take down some genealogical records from another old brother, and as far as I know, these two had not compared notes. I thought I recognized about halfway down through the first page that these names were sounding very familiar. I could not wait to get back to headquarters after taking down that second record, and I found that page after page, these names were identical. They were authentic records.

Why were they keeping their genealogical records? Because the Lord knew that one day the gospel was going to be restored, and that when it was restored, it would need to come to this branch of Israel scattered in these islands of the South Pacific. These people would have to have these names in order to do justice to their ancestors who had gone before. We have two lovely temples now in the Pacific Isles. The Lord does watch over his people. These Polynesian people have been choice in the eyes of our Heavenly Father, and their genealogical records have been preserved as a result.

May I tell you also of an experience in a humble Maori home. There a mother and father and twelve children were living the gospel as well as anyone I have ever seen in all my life. As they would gather around each evening to have their family devotional, scripture readings, and participation by the children, there was a time in the evening when the father would put a few pennies in a glass jar sitting on the mantle. The house was lighted by candles and kerosene lamps. In this humble home this little jar was always there, just a few pennies each day—this was their family temple fund. (Imagine a family of fourteen trying to save a few pennies a day, knowing that they would have to travel thousands of miles, at least to Hawaii, in order to get to the house of the Lord to do what they wanted to do.) Then they would kneel down in prayer, and from the smallest child they would take their turns and ask Heavenly Father that they might enjoy the rich blessing of having their family sealed together in order that they might have the fulness of the gospel come into their home.

I used to sit there and wonder how these wonderful people would ever realize this blessing. A few pennies a day—they just could not possibly get a family of fourteen to the temple on a few pennies a day. But they prayed in great faith, and they prayed with devotion, and they meant what they said.

If someone had told me at the time that within my lifetime there would be a temple built within sixty miles of this very home, I would have said, "I don't believe it," because I did not have the same faith these people had. I am not sure that they visualized the building of a temple in New Zealand either, but they knew that their family was going to be sealed and receive the rich blessings of the gospel. I want to tell you that the Lord is mindful of these people. He was mindful of their plea, and he poured his blessings out upon this family—and this family was multiplied by many hundreds throughout the length and breadth of New Zealand. It is a wonderful thing to contemplate the great blessings of the Lord to these Polynesian people as he listens to their prayers of faith. The Lord does move in mysterious ways, his wonders to perform. He protects his people and he watches out for them. He is mindful of his own.

As I was being set apart for my mission, President Rulon S. Wells of the First Council of the Seventy laid his hands upon my head and said, "I bless you, Brother Simpson, with a knowledge of the language of the people amongst whom you will labor," and I was grateful for this blessing. So I went to New Zealand feeling elated that I was going to learn a foreign language and that this blessing had been given to me, and no one could take it away from me.

But as I got to New Zealand I did not do very much about learning the language. I was with a companion who was on the verge of going home and he had other things to think about, so we did not spend much time studying the Maori language.

After about three or four weeks had gone by with not much activity on the Maori language, I had a dream. To me it was very real. It is one of the significant events of my life. In this dream I had returned home from my mission. I was getting off the boat in Los Angeles harbor, and there were my bishop, my stake president, my mother and dad, all of my friends. As I came down the gangplank of the boat they all started talking to me in Maori, every one of them—my mother, my father, my bishop—all talking in Maori, and I could not understand a word they were saying. I was so embarrassed. I was humiliated. I thought to myself, This is terrible. How am I going to get out of it? And I started making excuses.

Right then I woke up and sat straight up in bed, and two thoughts came forcefully to my mind. Thought number one: You will *have* to do something about learning this language. The Lord has given you a blessing, but you are going to have to do something about it yourself. Then thought number two: You are going to need this language when you get through with your mission. These thoughts kept ringing through my ears all through that day, so arrangements were made and we allotted time each day to study the Maori language. The Lord blessed me and I was able to bear testimony in the language after a short time. (To make a long story short, when the mission was finished and I came home and into Los Angeles harbor, they were all there to meet me, but they all spoke English. Not one of them spoke Maori to me.)

Then World War II broke out, and all of the missionaries were called home. I thought, Now if I am called into the Army, I am just sure that I will be sent right back down to New Zealand where I can also help President Matthew Cowley. Maybe the Lord will send me down there to help him with the mission activity between military assignments.

I went into the Air Force, and sure enough, when it came time for overseas processing after a few months, I was sent to San Francisco. All the Pacific processing was done here. I thought, Here I go right back to New Zealand. However, about two days before the ship was to sail with our group of several hundred men, about five of us were taken out. This is all—just five—and we were sent all the way back to the Atlantic seacoast for shipment across the Atlantic. I thought, Well, I guess I can always preach to the Maori spirits in prison after I'm shot and get to the other side!

We joined a convoy and went across the Atlantic Ocean. I saw the Rock of Gibraltar go by, and finally the ship stopped in Egypt. We got off the ship in Egypt and were taken to our American air base, where there was a very small Air Force group. You cannot get further from New Zealand than Cairo, Egypt. I thought, I don't know what the Lord has in mind, but I'll just do the best I can, and I am sure that everything will work out all right.

Well, not more than forty-eight hours had gone by when I found that right there within the very shadows of this American air base was the entire Maori battalion! This was *their* overseas base for processing, for all of their fighting in North Africa and Italy. For nearly two years I had the privilege of being there and meeting each Sunday with these Maori boys, bearing testimony with them in their own tongue, organizing them into small groups as they went up into the front lines in order that they might have their sacrament meetings and do the things that they needed to do. They needed me. I needed them. I want to tell you that the Lord had a hand in writing military orders, because of all the places in this world that Air Force men were being sent, very few were sent to Cairo, Egypt. Why one of them should be selected who knew a few words of Maori and who had an abiding love for the Maori people, only the Lord can answer.

Yes, the Lord is mindful of his own. The Lord was mindful of Hagoth. The Lord guided Hagoth. The Lord was mindful of these Maori people and their genealogical records. He preserved their records for them through their minds and he inspired them to do so. The Lord was mindful of a humble prayer in a Maori home as those family members put a few pennies in a jar each day, and he caused that a great temple should be built almost in the shadows of their home. I also want to tell you that military orders can be written by our Heavenly Father as he takes care of his people.

So as we bear testimony to our Heavenly Father, let us remember that this is his work and that he governs in the affairs of men. May we live up to this foreordination and be prepared not only to be the leavening influence of this great nation, but indeed, to be saviors of the world during very perilous times.

10

The solid rock of God's true church

BUILDING A FOUNDATION OF PERSONAL REVELATION

During World War II, I walked near the Mediterranean Sea by a city known anciently as Caesarea Philippi. I was all alone. I had come there with the hope of recapturing some of the surrounding influence that gave background to one of the significant discussions of all time. I refer to that occasion when the Savior had asked his disciples: "Whom do men say that I the Son of Man am?

"And they said, Some say that thou art John the Baptist: some, Elias; and others, Jeremias, or one of the prophets."

Then Christ became more direct: "But whom say ye that I am?

"And Simon Peter answered and said, Thou art the Christ, the Son of the living God." (Matthew 16:13-16.)

As never before, the strength, the power, the conviction of that testimony declared so many centuries before had become mine to cherish and harbor as an integral part of my own personal testimony.

What happened to me that beautiful morning on the coasts of Caesarea Philippi was not unique nor was it physical in any way. As Christ explained to Peter: ". . . flesh and blood hath not revealed it unto thee, but my Father which is in heaven." (Matthew 16:17.) Peter was the recipient of personal revelation! And in like manner this same sweet confirmation of testimony can permeate the hearts of all truth-seeking, conscientious Latter-day Saints the world over. This great gift of personal revelation is unmistakable; it is direct. It is a more sure communication than the audible spoken word; for that which we hear through mortal ears is sometimes distorted, so often misunderstood. This precious gift of spirit speaking to spirit is infallible and direct and, in the case just cited, came from a loving Heavenly Father to his faithful disciple Peter.

During this same conversation, Peter's revelation was referred to as a rock—a rock firm and immovable. ". . . and upon this rock," the Savior declared, "I will build my church." (Matthew 16:18.) He selected rock as the perfect symbol of uncompromising truth, the only possible foundation upon which to build his true church—the rock of revelation.

This same rock of revelation is broad enough for all mankind to build upon. It beckons to all individuals who are willing to put on his yoke, for it is easy and the burden is light. The author of all truth has declared it so.

As a child of God, man is never forsaken by him. War and contention among men, whether it is an international conflict or a form of family disunity, is not God's will. Man's unhappiness is of his own making, a direct result of nonconformity to the plan of life as contained in Heavenly Father's blueprint for happiness. Men never fail because of God's revealed word, but rather, in spite of it.

So how can we know as Peter knew? How can a person achieve this reassuring, motivating certainty that God lives? Surely, if there were no doubts, our course would be undeviating. Can it be that only a few are chosen to receive this most precious gift of personal assurance?

The purpose of all creation is, hopefully, that all men may qualify to return to His presence. Now, there are those who spend most of a lifetime debating with themselves. They ask: Is it worth it? or, How can I truly know that this or that is God's will?

As the Savior taught in the temple on one occasion, the Jews marveled at his wisdom and knowledge. "How knoweth this man letters, having never learned?" they asked.

"Jesus answered them, and said, My doctrine is not mine, but his that sent me.

"If any man will do his will, he shall know of the doctrine, whether it be of God, or whether I speak of myself." (John 7:14-17.)

The key phrase, of course, is, "If any man will do his will." The doing is of prime importance. Only in the doing can we be assured of a confirmation by the Spirit; yes, by good works we do become eligible for personal revelation.

May we now turn to another important key to this vital and sought-after knowledge of Deity. Two thousand years ago the great high priest Alma was traveling from city to city. He knew something about personal revelation and seemed most anxious to share it with those he attempted to teach as he declared: "Behold, I testify unto you that I do know that these things whereof I have spoken are true. And how do ye suppose that I know of their surety?

"Behold, I say unto you they are made known unto me by the Holy Spirit of God. Behold, I have fasted and prayed many days that I might know these things of myself. And now I do know of myself that they are true; for the Lord God hath made them manifest unto me by his Holy Spirit; and this is the spirit of revelation which is in me." (Alma 5:45-46.)

Now, Alma points out here that he did something more than just carry on the work. He hastened his process of sure knowledge through fasting and prayer. "I have fasted and prayed many days that I might know these things of myself." These same principles will work for each of us today. Fasting has been practiced by men seeking spiritual strength from the very beginning of time.

If prayer was important for Alma, it is important for us, too. It is folly to think in terms of having this highly spiritual information made known to us by the Holy Spirit without first parting the veil through prayer. It was this important step that led to this greatest of all dispensations, the dispensation of the fulness of times. The young lad Joseph Smith was touched by the invitation of Holy Writ, the promise given for all men alike: "If any of you lack wisdom, let him ask of God, that giveth to all men liberally, and upbraideth not; and it shall be given him." (James 1:15.)

When we want bus travel information, we go to the bus terminal; when we want financial assistance, we seek out a banker; so why not go directly to God for a confirming testimony of him and his work?

> Ask, and it shall be given you; seek and ye shall find; knock, and it shall be opened unto you;
>
> For every one that asketh receiveth; and he that seeketh findeth; and to him that knocketh it shall be opened.
>
> For what man is there of you, whom if his son ask for bread, will he give him a stone?
>
> Or if he ask a fish, will he give him a serpent?
>
> If ye then . . . know how to give good gifts unto your children, how much more shall your Father which is in heaven give good things to them that ask him? (Matthew 7:7-11.)

There is no sweeter work than his work. There is no joy to compare with the blessed assurance of obedience to his laws and ordinances. But we only do his work and obey his law when we are convinced that it is important. This is why we must remove with all haste those barriers that would prevent such assurance from a loving Heavenly Father who is so anxious that we receive. May we guard against the condition that Laman and Lemuel found themselves in. They refused to cooperate in God's work even after receiving unmistaken direction from an angel and the still small voice. Nephi records that they were "past feeling," that they "could not feel his words." (1 Nephi 17:45.) It is interesting to note that it was they, not God, who broke the bond. This seems to be the pattern, and our day is no exception.

I feel sorry for the man or woman who has become so negative that he is "past feeling" so far as the things of God are concerned. But we all rejoice as we see those who stand out in the crowd as a beacon on a hill, declaring with Alma that "the knowledge which I have is of God" (Alma 36:26); those who reconfirm the testimony of Job, "For I know that my redeemer liveth, . . ." (Job 19:25); those who stand firm with Joseph Smith and Sidney Rigdon in their famous declaration, "And now, after the many testimonies which have been given of him, this is the testimony, last of all, which we give of him: that he lives!" (D&C 76:22); and then those who can feel with Peter, "Thou art the Christ, the Son of the living God" (Matthew 16:16).

The world needs assurance. The world needs some solid rock to replace shifting sand. The world needs men with conviction about things most important. The world needs the added strength of several thousand more clarion voices that teach only truth because they live by the truth.

To my mind, the main strength of the world we live in is the strength of his true church. And where is the main strength of his true church? Not in our buildings, nor is it found in any group of men who might be designated as leaders for a short season. In my opinion, the Church has its foundation in the heart, in the home, and in the testimony of every worthy member. The widow cannot pay her mite, nor is it possible for an unselfish scoutmaster or quorum leader or dedicated bishop to take time to help a boy, except the kingdom of God on earth is strengthened and the world is made a little more secure on its foundations.

Indeed, the Savior of the world has declared that if a foundation is built on the solid rock of revelation, be it an individual, a group, a nation, or the world, "the gates of hell shall not prevail against it." (Matthew 16:18.) Peter heard it on the shores of Caesarea two thousand years ago. I found it still there undiminished a few years ago, and you can find it in your quiet place today, tomorrow, and forever. May we ever be available for that most precious gift of the Spirit—personal revelation—is my prayer.

11

A free gift from God to those who are willing

HOW TO GAIN AND HOLD ONTO YOUR TESTIMONY

Joseph Smith was a visionary and subject to hallucinations. There is no truth to his story." Such was the announcement made to me by one of my best friends while attending junior high school.

His comment was in reaction to our previous conversation on religion at which time I had relayed to him the story of the first vision in detail. My friend documented his opinion with a library reference book supplied him by his parents. There it was in black and white, and from the public library no less. Certainly there could be no more authentic source in the mind of thirteen-year-old boy than the public library.

For the first time in my young life, all that I had been taught by those I loved and trusted seemed to be in jeopardy. Just two years before, in Primary, it had all been so simple. My parents had been good, my acceptance of their teachings complete. Now suddenly all that had been so secure and neatly packaged for me was under attack.

Sooner or later such a moment comes to every Latter-day Saint. The day of childhood faith and unquestioned reliance on the word of others fades and eventually must be replaced by personal conviction if one's faith in the restored gospel of Jesus Christ is to survive.

Heber C. Kimball, counselor to President Brigham Young, foresaw the day when the Church would be under attack on prime social issues and even fundamental doctrine. Addressing himself to the individual members of the Church, he said:

> To meet the difficulties that are coming, it will be necessary for you to have a knowledge of the truth of this work for yourself. The difficulties will be of such a character that the man or woman who does not possess his personal knowledge or witness will fall. . . . The time will come when no man nor woman will be able to stand on borrowed light. Each will have to be guided by the light within himself. If you do not have it, how can you stand? (Orson F. Whitney, *Life of Heber C. Kimball*, Bookcraft, 1967, p. 450.)

There seems to be a worldwide return to thought about God, which is a reversal of the "God is dead" fad that was so prevalent a few years ago. Traditionally in the Church, teenage and young adult baptisms have been more numerous than those of other age groups. Lately this trend has been even more pronounced. In some cases new converts know more about the Church and develop stronger testimonies than many young members who have been in the Church all of their lives and who seem to take for granted that which should be a most urgent factor in their lives.

A firm and abiding testimony of this great latter-day work is not reserved for your bishopric and a select circle of high priests in the ward. A testimony of the truth is a free gift from God to everyone who is willing to go through the process of building a testimony. A young lad of fourteen was chosen to open this dispensation for many good and sufficient reasons: His mind was not set. He was teachable. He was young and believing. He was not too far removed from the faith of his childhood, a faith that is too often left behind for a life of skepticism and doubt. In my opinion a young mind and heart can be a most fertile field for seeds of testimony to take root and grow.

A person's search for testimony can start in earnest only if it becomes a matter of vital concern with him whether or not the Joseph Smith story is true, whether or not the Book of Mormon is an inspired document, whether or not this a prophet-led Church. Only then can a person really be ready for the noble quest of light and truth. But the acquisition and maintenance of a testimony require effort. Without strong desire, without study, and without the necessary self-discipline to live worthily, answers to questions will not likely come.

My teenage years were very much like those of many youth I talk to from day to day. They frequently say: "If the Lord would only let me know for sure, then I would certainly be willing to dedicate my entire life to the work." Testimonies built on miracles alone are at best shallow and can only be perpetuated by other miracles. Such is not the eternal process considered best for the acquisition of a testimony that can withstand the troubles spoken of by Heber C. Kimball.

Even President David O. McKay went through this mental process as a teenage boy. He has told us about kneeling by a serviceberry bush as a boy in Huntsville to find out once and for all about the truth of the work. May I quote President McKay as he tells of that occasion:

> I knelt down and with all the fervor of my heart poured out my soul to God and asked him for a testimony of this gospel. I had in mind that there would be some manifestation; that I should receive some transformation that would leave me absolutely without doubt.
>
> I got up, mounted my horse, and as he started over the trail, I remember rather introspectively searching myself and involuntarily shaking my head, saying to myself, "No, sir, there is no change; I am just the same boy I was before I knelt down." The anticipated manifestation had not come. . . .
>
> However, it did come, but not in the way I had anticipated. Even the manifestations of God's power and the presence of his angels came; but when it did come, it was simply a confirmation,

it was not a testimony. (*Treasures of Life*, Deseret Book, 1962, pp. 229-30.)

There are no shortcuts to eternal life with our Father. Knowledge and testimony must come "line upon line, precept upon precept." (D&C 98:12.) The Savior said, "Search the scriptures"; then he refers to eternal life about which the scriptures teach, and concludes, ". . . they are they which testify of me." (John 5:39.)

A wonderful brother whom I admire very much, especially for his knowledge of the scriptures, was discussing the Book of Mormon one day. Someone asked him how one could ever begin to gain such facility with the scriptures as he possesses.

His answer was classic. "Why, it is very simple," he explained. "You begin on page one, and then turn to page two, and so on." Few of us are willing to start on page one. May I reemphasize, there are no shortcuts to life eternal. To learn gospel principles, we start on page one, then go to page two, and hopefully unto a perfect knowledge.

Concerning the principles we learn about, we need to remember that the gospel of Jesus Christ is undeviating. As you know, man is continually seeking to rationalize the scriptures, fitting them to a here-and-now expediency or perhaps fitting them to meet a temporary convenience, but the Lord says in latter-day revelation: "Search these commandments, for they are true. . . . What I the Lord have spoken, I have spoken, and I excuse not myself." He concludes with an observation that should be taken as a guide for every young Latter-day Saint: ". . . whether by mine own voice or by the voice of my servants, it is the same." (D&C 1:37-38.) Isn't it reassuring that we have access to day-to-day direction from living prophets?

"Jesus answered them, and said, My doctrine is not mine, but his that sent me. If any man will do his will, he shall know of the doctrine, whether it be of God, or whether I speak of myself." (John 7:16-17.)

As a missionary arrives in the mission field, he can find joy and success only as he decides to jump in and get wet all over. Youth all over the world are being "turned on" in one way or another. Recently I saw a group of high school seniors in California "turn on" as they worked on a special project side by side with some handicapped employees at a Deseret Industries plant. One young man said, "I'll never be the same again."

While on their summer vacation a quorum of deacons in Australia decided to go all out as volunteer laborers on the construction of their new meetinghouse. They still refer to it as *our* building. A class of Laurels in Salt Lake City selected a nearby hospital for volunteer service during the summer. They donated over 600 hours for others. In a testimony meeting at the end of the summer, one girl said, "It was like heaven on earth."

Then there was the bishop's youth committee in Logan, Utah, that decided to fix up a widow's home. One young man commented, "When I saw her cry, I decided then and there that I had finally found the key to real happiness." A girl commented, "I never knew till now what my teachers meant when they taught us about 'pure religion and undefiled before God.'" (James 1:27.)

There are hundreds of such examples all over the Church as young people in every part of the world gain a sweet confirmation of testimony by the gift of the Spirit as they do his will. Just learning about it is not enough. You've got to get in on the action yourself.

"And when ye shall receive these things, I would exhort you that ye would ask God, the Eternal Father, in the name of Christ, if these things are not true; and if ye shall ask with a sincere heart, with real intent, having faith in Christ, he will manifest the truth of it unto you, by the power of the Holy Ghost.

"And by the power of the Holy Ghost ye may know the truth of all things." (Moroni 10:4-5.)

This scripture alone has led more people to a testimony of the Book of Mormon than any other prompting or encouragement. Fasting and prayer are the means used by all of the prophets who have ever lived to gain spiritual strength and to communicate better with our Father. All of them have encouraged us to do likewise.

Every Latter-day Saint must gain a firm testimony for himself—a personal knowledge that Jesus is the Christ and the Son of the living God, that Joseph Smith is the prophet through whom the gospel has been restored, and that The Church of Jesus Christ of Latter-day Saints is "the only true and living church upon the face of the whole earth. . . ." (D&C 1:30.)

Anyone can acquire this testimony by following the established procedure by which the Lord gives a testimony. There are no shortcuts. A desire to know is imperative. To learn the doctrine is essential. To do his will will sanctify that teaching in our hearts. To pray often will open the way and make all things possible through him, for he has said, ". . . without me ye can do nothing." (John 15:5.)

May each of us be capable of standing on our own testimony, for borrowed light may not be sufficient as we face the future.

12

Gaining a strong testimony of the calling of a prophet

"THE PROPHETS ARE REAL—BE TRUE TO THEM"

While visiting New Zealand in April 1958 for the purpose of attending the dedicatory services of the New Zealand Temple, I had a spiritual experience that has had special meaning for me.

All my life I had been raising my right arm to the square in sustaining the presidencies of the Church as prophets, seers, and revelators. The term "prophet" had definite meaning, as did the term "revelator," but the term "seer" was just a little illusive in my mind, as I had not taken the time to anchor its true significance firmly to my understanding.

It was the third day of dedication. All of the meetings had been extremely spiritual, and all who had participated in this special tour were so grateful to be a part of this historic occasion. On the third day of dedication, I was walking by myself down the hallway of this lovely temple when a friend intercepted me as I walked past one of the sealing rooms. He invited me to step inside, and I was completely overwhelmed to notice that the only other people in the room were President and Sister David O. McKay.

My friend said, "President McKay, this is one of our returned New Zealand missionaries, Brother Simpson."

President McKay extended his firm right hand and, placing his left hand on my shoulder, looked into my eyes and, more than that, into every fiber of my being. My feeling at that time was one of complete peace; my entire being seemed accelerated. After a few seconds, he gave my hand a friendly pump, my shoulder a squeeze, and said, "Brother Simpson, I am pleased to *know* you." Not, "I am pleased to meet you," but "I am pleased to *know* you." Every detail of this special meeting in this very special place registered indelibly on my mind, although it was quite by chance and completely unarranged.

During the ensuing days and weeks, the memory of this introduction kept recurring. It was a vivid, clear, and comforting, to say the least. Approximately three months later, while I was sitting in my office in Los Angeles, my telephone rang, and after a brief confirmation by the long distance operator, the voice on the other end of the line said, "This is David O. McKay speaking." There could be no mistaking this kindly voice. I was asked if I were prepared to return with my family to my former mission field, New Zealand, to preside over the people I loved so much. President McKay went on to remind me that we had had a personal interview in the New Zealand Temple at the time of the dedication (as though I needed reminding—this choice opportunity I could never forget). He said that based on our interview, he felt impressed to issue this call.

Following the brief conversation and after regaining my composure, I thought to myself how unlike the business world. Had I been considered by my company to take charge of an overseas operation, surely there would have been many questionnaires to be filled out and hours of personal interviewing by department heads and personnel people.

In the work of the Lord, a modern-day prophet can look into the eyes of a fellow Church member and search his very soul without so much as a question being asked, but even though there were no verbal questions on this occasion in April of 1958, there must have been many answers, perceived only in the heart and mind of one ordained a prophet, *seer*, and revelator.

One more story to illustrate this marvelous testimony concerning prophets: A pioneer grandmother lay on her deathbed in Salt Lake Valley a few years ago. She was a great pioneer grandmother who had lived a good life and had reared a good Latter-day Saint family. She was in her ninety-third year, and as she lay there on the last day of her life, with her life waning and her strength ebbing away, she took her daughter by the hand and said, "I have just had a great experience. I would like to tell you about it before I go. The Lord has given me the privilege of seeing beyond the veil, and now I have the great opportunity of being here to tell you about it."

Then, looking into her daughter's eyes, she said, "I have seen the prophets. They are real. Be true to them." Yes, the prophets are real! May we always be true to them.

13

Keeping a firm eye on our basic goals, based on eternal truth

HE KNOCKS—WE OPEN THE DOOR

Living in this jet age of accelerated pace and challenge causes serious reflection on some fundamental issues. We might ask ourselves a few basic questions; for example, How can precious time and energy be spent most profitably? What comes first? To what shall we turn our hand next? Does a loving Father really dwell in the heavens?

These all-important questions have been asked by practically every person who has ever lived. Sometimes we avoid dedicating ourselves to the direction that common reason tells us is right until a circumstance forces the issue. I shall never forget a thought-provoking experience that came to me at the outbreak of World War II, which I would like to share with you briefly.

The British Empire had just declared war on the Axis powers. At the time I was a missionary in far-off New Zealand, and that country was busily engaged in adjusting itself to wartime footing. Various projects were launched by the government in an attempt to make the people sense the seriousness of their situation. One beautiful morning as I was walking with my companion down the main street in New Zealand's largest city, our attention was captured by a group of low-level bombers approaching rapidly over the city. Their markings were indistinct, and we thought to ourselves, Might this be the enemy? Just at that moment the bomb bays began to open. It was a very ominous sight. Then what appeared to be bombs were released from the bomb bays and everyone stood transfixed and amazed—and very much relieved to see that these would-be bombs disintegrated into thousands of leaflets, fluttering down over the city.

Being tall, I was one of the first to reach a falling pamphlet, and bringing it quickly into focus, my companion and I read this brief but startling message: "If this were a bomb, where would you be?" Now, you can be certain that our thoughts were very serious on that occasion, and I want to tell you that the gospel of Jesus Christ and its importance to mankind seemed foremost, above all else.

The gospel, as set down by the Savior of the world, was never intended to be the least bit confusing, for he is the author of truth and light. Our Heavenly Father has but one desire, and that is to have as many of his children as possible regain his presence.

You know, I had a business acquaintance who once complained that to him, religion had become a mass of confusion. He said that the road immediately ahead was covered with thick fog—that the bright goals which seemed so clear and discernible in his childhood now seemed obscure and questionable. He was losing his faith! He was standing alone!

We ofttimes lose sight of basic goals as we struggle against the adversary in this mortal realm of existence. Nothing would please him more than to have us distracted in our attempts to regain the presence of our Heavenly Father, and such was the plight of my friend.

Often we hear folks say, "I can't see the forest for the trees." How important it is for us to ascend a vantage point from time to time, above the fog that my friend referred to, to check direction and relative position, decide on things of most importance, and reevaluate our goals.

The Lord gave the key to all men nearly two thousand years ago when he said:

"Behold, I stand at the door, and knock: if any man hear my voice, and open the door, I will come in to him, and will sup with him, and he with me.

"To him that overcometh will I grant to sit with me in my throne, even as I also overcame, and am set down with my Father in his throne." (Revelation 3:20-21.)

How grateful we should be to have this key to live by! How grateful we should be that as we face the tremendous task of overcoming the imperfections of mortality, he assures us of his presence and sustaining help; but not without one very important stipulation—that the incentive must come from us. Remember, he said, "Behold, I stand at the door, and knock." In other words, he is always there, ready to enter, ready to be with us, but too often we fail to recognize the knock.

How can any man look into the heavens and witness the order of God's creations without hearing that knock? How can any witness the wonders of this electronic and nuclear age without hearing the knock? How can we participate in the revealed wonders of medicine without indeed knowing that his mercy and love extend toward all men?

He goes on to say, ". . . if any man hear my voice"—not just some special, select group of men, but "any man," any or all of more than three billion who live on the face of the earth and who may accept of this invitation freely.

". . . if any man hear my voice, and open the door, I will come in to him." What must we do? It is up to us to open the door! He knocks; we recognize his voice; and then we open the door.

It is not the Lord's plan to force his will upon anyone. Holman Hunt, the artist, felt inspired to capture this stirring scripture on canvas. One day he was showing his picture of "Christ Knocking at the Door" to a friend. Suddenly the friend exclaimed, "There is one thing wrong about your picture!" "What is it?" asked the artist. "The door on which Jesus knocks has no handle." "Ah," replied Mr. Hunt, "this is not a mistake. The handle is inside. It is from within that the door must be opened. Man must take the initiative."

Yes, we are weak; we do need help; we need help in overcoming. Where should we turn for spiritual and moral strength? Should we desire to become a doctor, we do not hesitate to seek qualified doctors to train us. If our interest is in the field of law, we turn to those who are graduates in law in order to become experts ourselves.

Almost all men have the goal of our Heavenly Father's presence, so why do they not recognize the knock? Why do they not seek his counsel and listen to the voice? Let's open the door and let him in. Let's partake abundantly of this one great source of truth and light, for his promise rings ever true:

". . . I will give unto him that is athirst of the fountain of the water of life freely.

"He that overcometh shall inherit all things; and I will be his God, and he shall be my son." (Revelation 21:6-7.)

After we open the door, graciously accepting the help that is so necessary to our success, the Lord gives us another great promise, and how appropriate that it follows his promise of help, for it is unlikely that man could ever achieve this promise on his own. He promises, "To him that overcometh will I grant to sit with me in my throne, even as I also overcame, and am set down with my Father in his throne."

Now, as the Lord draws close to us in fulfillment of his promise, his advice and counsel will be direct and clear and undeviating from that original theme which has been the very core of his message from the beginning of time. He will tell us that our overcoming can best be accomplished in terms of others.

What can we do for ourselves with the priesthood? We only do for *others* with the priesthood. We bless others, we perform ordinances for others, we perform service for others. Such is the admonition given by the Savior to all mankind. Matthew has recorded the Savior's words as follows: "Verily I say unto you, Inasmuch as ye have done it unto one of the least of these my brethren, ye have done it unto me." (Matthew 25:40.)

Another great prophet, speaking from this hemisphere, expressed it in this way: ". . . when ye are in the service of your fellow beings ye are only in the service of your God." (Mosiah 2:17.)

Selfishness and ingratitude are tools of destruction. The civilized world rocks and reels today because of selfish attitudes. I like the expression given in the following poem:

Lord, help me to live from day to day
In such a self-forgetful way
That even when I kneel to pray
My prayer will be of others.

Others, Lord, yes, others.
Let this my motto be.
Help me to live for others
That I may live for Thee.

May we constantly strive to be worthy of the blessings of our Heavenly Father. None can do it alone. We must open the door wide. We must extend the arm of fellowship to those about us, forgetting self, thinking of others, always others—not waiting until tomorrow, but today, for who can tell: "If this were a bomb, where would you be?" God grant us the vision to see the way clearly ahead.

14

Only as we forgive may we be forgiven

FORGIVENESS

Biblical history tells us that no mortal man has ever been subjected to the humility, the pain, the suffering that were experienced by the Savior of the world during his final hours of mortality. Following a number of false charges, he was betrayed by one considered to be among his closest circle of friends. He was then subjected to a so-called trial, which produced a sentence that was dictated by political convenience and public sentiment rather than justice.

Then in rapid agonizing succession: there was the long struggle to Calvary as he bore the heavy cross; he was jeered at and spat upon by the multitude all along the way; there was the offering of vinegar, climaxed by the cruel spikes; and finally, there he hung, his body broken and bleeding, still taunted by his enemies; and it was in the midst of all this that Jesus pleaded perhaps quietly, with deep reverence, "Father, forgive them; for they know not what they do." (Luke 23:34.)

With this plea of forgiveness in behalf of his oppressors, Jesus indeed practiced what he taught, for it was during his remarkable Sermon on the Mount that he said: "Love your enemies, bless them that curse you, do good to them that hate you, and pray for them which despitefully use you, and persecute you." (Matthew 5:44.)

It is most enlightening to observe the overwhelming importance of this oft-neglected principle as a necessary prerequisite to individual salvation and exaltation. First of all, it must be recognized that the great principle of repentance is largely dependent upon forgiveness. He who has transgressed and then decides to repent is expected to seek out those he has offended, to solicit their forgiveness. I know of one man who carried his grudge to the grave after forty long, bitter years of refusing to forgive. What a tragedy! His light was never able to shine forth as intended. As recorded in 1 John, "But he that hateth his brother is in darkness, and walketh in darkness, and knoweth not wither he goeth, because that darkness hath blinded his eyes." (1 John 2:11.) Paul wrote to the Saints at Corinth about the importance of forgiving readily, "Lest Satan should get an advantage of us: for we are not ignorant of his devices." (2 Corinthians 2:11.)

Only as we forgive do we earn the right to be forgiven. This is an eternal principle, so taught by the Savior when he said: "For if ye forgive men their trespasses, your heavenly Father will also forgive you." (Matthew 6:14.)

Paul certainly understood this great truth, for he taught: "And be ye kind one to another, tenderhearted, forgiving one another, even as God for Christ's sake hath forgiven you." (Ephesians 4:32.)

Not only need we forgive to be forgiven, but we must also repent to earn this great blessing. A prophet of our day has recorded that the repentant "shall be forgiven, according to the covenants and commandments of the church." (D&C 68:24.) Then this sweet assurance followed: ". . . and I, the Lord, remember them no more." (D&C 58:42.)

This is the hope of mankind, to have our mistakes wiped clean. There is no other way; there are no shortcuts in the kingdom of God. We repent, we forgive, we progress; and may we remind ourselves once more, it all starts with our own willingness to forgive one another. Yes, after all is said and done, the Golden Rule still stands supreme: "Do unto others as you would have others do unto you." (See Matthew 7:12.) First forgive and then stand eligible in the sight of God to be forgiven. The simplicity of the process testifies of its divinity.

Now, in case someone has forgotten the extent of our obligation in forgiving that wayward neighbor, just remember that 70 times 7 is 490. But we will never make it to 490, because if we follow the Lord's formula with sincerity, something very special always comes into our lives and into the lives of our neighbors long before we achieve 70 times 7.

Another interesting observation is made by the Lord for the benefit of all who come close to him with their lips but whose hearts are far from him. Too frequently we come to worship and to leave our offerings without attempting to prepare our inner selves to the same degree of perfection that we achieve in our outward dress and grooming.

It was Matthew who advised such folks to "leave there thy gifts before the altar, and go thy way; first be reconciled with thy brother, and then come and offer thy gift." (Matthew 5:24.) So it appears that a generous offering of time, talent, or means to the building of the kingdom is not fully acceptable if we bear such gifts without first truly forgiving our offenders. In so doing, we guarantee forgiveness for our own weaknesses.

Lillian Watson has recorded an interesting episode from the ministry of Phillips Brooks, a great American clergyman, as he addressed his affluent, well-dressed congregation on a Sunday morning in Boston nearly 100 years ago:

He looked into the faces of men and women he long had known, men and women who had come to him with their problems, who had asked for his help and guidance. How well he knew what seethed behind the pleasant, smiling masks of their Sunday-best respectability! How well he knew the petty spites that embittered their hearts, the animosities that set neighbor against neighbor, the silly quarrels that were kept alive, the jealousies and misunderstandings, the stubborn pride!

Today his message was for those bitter, unbending ones who refused to forgive and forget. He must make them realize that life is too short to nurse grievances, to harbor grudges and resentments. He would plead for tolerance and understanding, for sympathy and kindness. He would plead for brotherly love.

"Oh, my dear friends!" he said, . . . and it was as though he spoke to each separately and alone:

"You who are letting miserable misunderstandings run on from year to year, meaning to clear them up some day;

"You who are keeping wretched quarrels alive because you cannot quite make up your mind that now is the day to sacrifice your pride;

"You who are passing men sullenly upon the street, not speaking to them out of some silly spite, and yet knowing that it would fill you with shame and remorse if you heard that one of those men were dead tomorrow morning;

"You who are letting your friend's heart ache for a word of appreciation or sympathy, which you mean to give him someday;

"If you only could know and see and feel, all of a sudden, that the time is short, how it would break the spell! How you would go instantly and do the thing which you might never have another chance to do."

As the congregation poured out of the church that Sunday morning, people who hadn't spoken in years suddenly smiled and greeted each other . . . and discovered it was what they had wanted to do all along. Neighbors who had disliked and avoided each other walked home together . . . and were astonished to find how very much they enjoyed doing it. Many who had been grudging and unkind firmly resolved to be more generous in the future, more considerate of others . . . and all at once felt happier and more content, felt at peace with themselves and the world.

"Forgive," Phillips Brooks urged his audience. "Forget. Bear with the faults of others as you would have them bear with yours. Be patient and understanding. Life is too short to be vengeful or malicious. Life is too short to be petty or unkind. . . ."

So spoke Phillips Brooks one hundred years ago, that great humanitarian who, incidentally, composed the words to that favorite Christmas hymn, "O Little Town of Bethlehem."

We need not reach back one hundred years for an example of bitter hearts. Such feelings are common in these very last of latter days. Unwillingness to forgive on a person-to-person basis is indeed a major and chronic illness of today's world.

"Love the Lord thy God!" This is the number one foundation of all Christianity, and the second is like unto it, "Love thy neighbour as thyself." How can you love God and hate your neighbor? You cannot! So forgive right now, today. That is the beginning of love, for forgiveness is indeed that prime ingredient of love. It is the function of love.

Not one of us is incapable of calling to mind, this very instant, a person who has offended in some way; and if my understanding of the scriptures is correct, we had better make it a matter of urgent business to forgive that person, whether he asks it or not. Woe unto that man who stands stubbornly in the way of another's plea for repentance by failure to forgive, "for he that forgiveth not his brother's trespasses standeth condemned before the Lord; for there remaineth in him the greater sin. I, the Lord, will forgive whom I will forgive, but of you it is required to forgive all men." (D&C 64:9-10.)

Yes, forgiveness enlarges the soul, for "he that loveth his brother abideth in the light. . . ." (1 John 2:10.) To abide in the light is to abide in the pathway that leads to the very presence of our Heavenly Father. In forgiveness there is a divine satisfaction that is also sublime. The fruit is sweet, the way is easy, and the time is so short. Slow forgiveness is almost no forgiveness.

Yes, as long as man lives in his mortal state, we will be confronted with imperfection, with our main chore to overcome that imperfection. As we forgive, we achieve the right to be forgiven. As we forgive, we increase our capacity for light and understanding. As we forgive, we live beyond the power of the adversary. As we forgive, our capacity for love expands toward heaven. And as we forgive, we approach the ability to stand one day in the midst of oppressors who do their ugly deeds out of ignorance and misdirection with the capacity to say, "Father, forgive them; for they know not what they do." (Luke 23:34.)

15

The blessings of paying an honest tithe

"WHAT WOULD THOU HAVE ME DO?"

In the tradition of the Easter season, all Christendom pauses with bowed head and contrite heart to contemplate the terrible agony, the pain, the suffering, and the indignities of the Lord and Savior of the world as he gave himself to be crucified for the sins of all mankind.

But with the rising of the sun of another Easter morning, there also wells up within each of us a glorious assurance of hope, a brilliant ray of peace, for he lives! Death is overcome! And life will be eternal.

Let us suppose that by some miraculous arrangement the privilege would be granted for each to spend one precious minute in private audience with the resurrected Christ on Easter day. What would you do? What would you say? Surely there would be great emotion because of your love for him. Then I am certain that many would ask the simple question: "What would thou have me do?" And he might conceivably answer: "If ye love me, keep my commandments." (John 14:15.) "Feed my sheep." (John 21:16.) "Love thy neighbour as thyself." (Matthew 19:19.)

There is no reason to believe that his counsel and advice today would be any different than it was 2,000 years ago. For his house is a house of order. His gospel is the same yesterday, today, and forever.

And because he would be most anxious for us to overcome selfishness and lack of faith, which I believe are the two major sources of man's problems today, don't you think he might have some advice to give with respect to the mastery over worldly possessions? For surely "where your treasure is, there will your heart be also." (Matthew 6:21.) Yes, this great principle of faith and the willingness to share our temporal increase go hand in hand. In fact, someone has properly observed that it doesn't take money to pay tithing—it takes faith.

In this respect, I shall always remember the faith of an old Maori brother in New Zealand. As the missionaries came to his humble little fishing shack located well off the beaten track, he hastened to find an envelope that contained a letter addressed to him and in which he had also stuffed a sizeable sum of hard-earned money. He promptly handed the envelope containing the money and the letter to the missionaries. This fine brother didn't have the ability to read the letter when it arrived, for it was written in English and his native tongue was Maori, but he could read the financial figures contained in it, and he recognized the letterhead as being from the mission office. He thought the mission needed the cash amount mentioned for some special purpose, and he had it all ready for the missionaries. After the letter had been translated for him, it was now clear that it merely confirmed his annual tithing settlement and stated the total amount paid for the previous year. His faith was such that he stood ready to pay the same amount all over again if the Lord's servants needed it for the work.

Let me tell you about a beautiful little chapel located in Maromaku Valley in New Zealand. When Brother Matthew Cowley was presiding over the New Zealand Mission, he wrote to President Heber J. Grant and his counselors, telling them of this faithful branch of English members. He expressed a recommendation that because of their devotion and tithing record over many years, a modest chapel be built for them without local participation, entirely from the general tithing funds of the Church. Soon the answer came back that the recommendation was approved. Immediately a special meeting was called in the community schoolhouse, and for the first time these wonderful people heard what had transpired in their behalf.

At first they just sat. No one seemed elated by the news, and then, one by one, each family head stood to explain how he would be disappointed if he were not allowed to accept financial responsibility for a certain phase of the proposed chapel. Within twenty minutes, the entire amount had been subscribed to. These faithful people were in the habit of going the extra mile in helping to finance the needs of the kingdom, and this is the way they wanted it. You see, people overcome selfish desires as they practice the Lord's law of giving.

Recently a man said, "Today's cost of living makes it impossible for me to consider ten percent of my income for tithing." By every standard of today's economic and financial teaching as figured by the mind of man, his reasoning seems justified. But the spiritual law is different. Do you remember how perplexed the multitude was when the Savior said this: "He that findeth his life shall lose it: and he that loseth his life for my sake shall find it"? (Matthew 10:39.) How much like this law is the law of tithing, wherein we receive by giving away. It just doesn't add up by worldly standards, and most men consider such teachings impractical and even abstract.

But it works! And hundreds of thousands can bear that witness today because their faith has been such that they were willing to accept God's invitation when he said, "Bring ye all the tithes into the storehouse, that there may be meat in mine house, and prove me now herewith, saith the Lord of hosts, if I will not open you the windows of heaven, and pour you out a blessing, that there shall not be room enough to receive it." (Malachi 3:10.) No business proposition in all this wide world can begin to match this offer. Here is the only real answer to today's cost of living.

We can't make the family budget stretch far enough on our own, so we had better form a partnership with the Lord by giving ten percent to him. "I, the Lord, am bound when ye do what I say, but when ye do not what I say, ye have no promise." (D&C 82:10.) Now, it is just that simple. And when we decide to accept his terms, we'll be amazed to learn that we can do far better on nine dollars with the help of the Lord than we can do with ten dollars on our own.

Many of us remember the tremendous enthusiasm of President Stephen L Richards of the First Presidency on the subject of tithing. He had this to say concerning partnership with God: "I like to think of the Lord as a partner because the essence of a partnership is a sharing of profits. It is, however, indispensable in a partnership that there shall also be a sharing of the burdens of the enterprise. The honor and the satisfaction that come to one in realization that he lives his life in partnership with God is to me a lofty and exalting thought. One cannot hope to realize the profits from that venture without bearing his portion of the expense—the giving which is requisite."

President Richards went on to say that our part of that partnership could only be confirmed through the payment of an honest tithe. He also made this observation with regard to the spiritual power that comes to one who is willing to give of his substance to the Lord: "Observance of tithing brings spiritual power, and after all that to me is the main thing. . . . It makes for the growth of the soul; it cultivates all of the virtues. So one who is serious about religion will be willing to give it the things which are vital to himself." (*Where Is Wisdom?* Deseret Book, 1955, p. 292.)

Let me share with you the testimony of a wonderful brother who had been impressed by one of the Church leaders as he explained the law of tithing. Meeting the leader on the street about three months later, he took some money from his pocket and said, "Do you see this? It is all mine. It does not belong to the butcher, the baker, or the loan agency. For the first time in my life I am free of debt. I can walk down either side of the street with my head held high. I no longer have to cross from side to side, avoiding the shopkeepers holding my delinquent accounts."

Then he went on to tell how all this came about because he took time to sit down with his family and they decided how they were going to meet their obligation to the Lord.

This man has peace of mind today. He is now a leader in a branch of the Church and a blessing to scores of other people. While wearing the chains of indebtedness, he was literally in bondage and unavailable to the Lord for service. Tithing had been the answer, and he found financial freedom.

The personnel manager of a large Los Angeles plant, who is not a member of the Church, relates this story: "I asked one of your returned missionaries seeking employment with our firm if he paid his tithing, and when he said yes, I hired him on the spot. I knew that he would be a man of integrity, I knew that he loved the Lord, and I knew that he would be true to his wife."

So you see, the payment of tithing means many things to many people.

We often hear the comment, "I believe all you say about tithing, but I am so hopelessly in debt right now that I will have to wait until next year to start." The only trouble with that is that next year never comes. Meet with your bishop right away and receive his kindly counsel. Then call a special meeting of all the family. Invite them to participate in the possible solutions to the problem. Maybe your son Johnny ends up with a paper route—that's great! And teenager Susan finds work on Saturdays—wonderful! I think all of our teenagers should learn well this wonderful principle of work. Not only that, but the entire family might agree to rough it for a few years by settling on a five-year-old car that uses regular gas and has roll-up windows. This important family meeting on finances could be the turning point toward eternal exaltation and salvation.

Few topics have received as much time and attention as has the subject of tithing. There is good reason for such emphasis. Compliance to the great law of tithing develops and trains men in the vital attribute of obedience, without which there could be little hope for anyone, and also in the vital attribute of unselfishness, man's most immediate need for solving the world's dilemmas in this day of hate, greed, and distrust.

Speaking through the Psalmist, the Lord said, ". . . the world is mine, and the fulness thereof." (Psalm 50:12.) He doesn't really need our ten percent—it is all his in the first place; but we need the experience of giving. Just as the Sabbath was created for man rather than man for the Sabbath, so it is with tithing: the value of the human soul is most important.

The God and Creator of heaven and earth could surely lay all the riches of the world at the feet of his leaders here in mortality if this were the important factor. But most important is that we demonstrate our love for God by making our means available to him according to his perfect plan and supreme wisdom.

Each dollar of tithing is for the blessing of people, the edification of the soul, the perfection of man; and in this, all who participate can find added comfort to the Savior's observation that "inasmuch as ye have done it unto one of the least of these my brethren, ye have done it unto me." (Matthew 25:40.) We make wonderful things possible for many wonderful people when we return the Lord's tenth to him.

I bear solemn witness to all that the law of tithing is God-given and that the purpose for which these sacred funds are used is sanctified by divine direction.

Old Testament prophets taught the law of tithing, for they said: "Honour the Lord with thy substance, and the first-fruits of all thine increase: So shall thy barns be filled with plenty, and thy presses shall burst out with new wine." (Proverbs 3:9-10.) This admonition has never been rescinded.

On one occasion just prior to that first Easter morning two thousand years ago, the Savior admonished his disciples: "Lay not up for yourselves treasures upon earth, where moth and rust doth corrupt, and where thieves break through and steal: But lay up for yourselves treasures in heaven, where neither moth nor rust doth corrupt, and where thieves do not break through nor steal: For where your treasure is, there will your heart be also." (Matthew 6:19-21.)

To justify the purpose of the Savior's suffering and to fulfill the opportunity that he has afforded us of life eternal, man must break the restricting chains of selfishness. There is no better way than to do it in the Lord's way. He gave his life that we might truly live, not just exist. He established the pattern, declaring: "I am the way, the truth, and the life. . . ." (John 14:6.) He beckons all to "come . . . follow me." (Matthew 19:21.) He pleads with seemingly indifferent children: "If ye love me, keep my commandments." (John 14:15.) He says that if we are to preserve life, we must be prepared to give it away—our time to the blessings and comfort and edification of others, our means to the building of the kingdom and the blessings of mankind here and now.

Yes, in my opinion, God issued the challenge of the ages when he said, ". . . prove me herewith," and quickly followed it with a resulting promise that he would "open you the windows of heaven, and pour you out a blessing, that there shall not be room enough to receive it."

There has never been a more definite promise than this. Let us not forget that the "windows of heaven" can only be operated by the remote control switch in our hand. We must make the first move. This is the very foundation of the eternal principle of faith. Once that faith has been demonstrated, God stands ready and anxious to fulfill his part of the agreement.

16

Spiritual blessings for the faithful Saints

THE LAW OF THE FAST

One of the most neglected and yet most needed laws for this troubled generation in a modern world of acceleration and distraction is the law of the fast. Fasting and praying have been referred to almost as a singular function from the earliest times. Adam's generation fasted and prayed, as did Moses on Sinai. (Deuteronomy 9:9-11.)

The Prophet Elijah traveled to Mt. Horeb under the influence of fasting and prayer. There he received the word of the Lord. His preparation had not been in vain. (1 Kings 19:8.)

Mordecai's advice from Esther as he faced an emergency at Shushan pointed out that he and his people should "neither eat nor drink three days, night or day. . . ." (Esther 4:16.) This was the true fast, abstinence from both food and drink. This is still the manner of the true fast in our day.

There were significant changes made at the time of Christ's mission in mortality. The law of sacrifice, for example, was replaced by a higher law. We are told that following the Master's visit to this, the western hemisphere, the people were told to continue in "fasting and prayer, and in meeting together oft both to pray and to hear the

the word of the Lord." So complete and sincere were the people in obeying his commandments "that there was no contention among all the people, in all the land; but there were mighty miracles wronght among the disciples of Jesus." (4 Nephi 12-13.) Wouldn't it be thrilling to enjoy such a condition today!

His law has been reconfirmed in our day, for through a modern prophet in the year 1832, he said: ". . . I give unto you a commandment that ye shall continue in prayer and fasting from this time forth." Then in the very next verse he mentions gospel teaching almost as a prime product of the prayer and fasting process. In the words of the Lord: "And I give unto you a commandment that you shall teach one another the doctrine of the kingdom.

"Teach ye diligently and my grace shall attend you, that you may be instructed more perfectly in theory, in principle, in doctrine, in the law of the gospel, in all things that pertain unto the kingdom of God, that are expedient for you to understand." (D&C 88:76-78.)

No man or woman can hope to teach of things spiritual unless he is directed by the Spirit, for "the Spirit shall be given unto you by the prayer of faith; and if ye receive not the Spirit ye shall not teach.

"And all this ye shall observe to do as I have commanded concerning your teaching, until the fulness of my scriptures is given.

"And as ye shall lift up your voices by the Comforter, ye shall speak and prophesy as seemeth me good;

"For, behold, the Comforter knoweth all things, and beareth record of the Father and of the Son." (D&C 42:14-17.)

Oh, that every teacher might catch the spirit of this promise and claim this offered partnership, available to all who are engaged in the teaching of truth.

There are no better examples of teaching by the Spirit than the sons of Mosiah. The Book of Mormon tells us how they became "strong in the knowledge of the truth; for they were men of a sound understanding and they had searched the scriptures diligently, that they might know the word of God.

"But this is not all; they had given themselves to much prayer, and fasting; therefore they had the spirit of prophecy, and the spirit of revelation, and when they taught, they taught with power and authority of God." (Alma 17:2-3.)

Is there a priesthood or auxiliary leader any place in this church who wouldn't give all to possess such power, such assurance? Remember this above all else, that according to Alma, they gave themselves to much fasting and prayer. You see, there are certain blessings that can only be fulfilled as we conform to a particular law. The Lord made this very clear through the Prophet Joseph Smith when he declared: "For all who will have a blessing at my hands shall abide the law which was appointed for that blessing, and the conditions thereof, as were instituted before the foundation of the world." (D&C 132:5.)

Now, the Lord could not have stated the position more clearly, and, in my opinion, too many Latter-day Saint parents today are depriving themselves and their children of one of the sweetest spiritual experiences that the Father has made available to them.

In addition to the occasional fasting experience for a special purpose, each member of the Church is expected to miss two meals on the fast and testimony Sunday. To skip two consecutive meals and partake of the third normally constitutes approximately a 24-hour period. Such is the counsel.

Competent medical authorities tell us that our bodies benefit by an occasional fasting period. That is blessing number one and perhaps the least important. Second, we contribute the money saved from missing the meals as a fast offering to the bishop for the poor and the needy.

And third, we reap a particular spiritual benefit that can come to us in no other way. It is a sanctification of the soul for us today just as it was for some choice people who lived 2,000 years ago. I quote briefly from the Book of Mormon: "Nevertheless they did fast and pray oft, and did wax stronger and stronger in their humility, and firmer and firmer in the faith of Christ, unto the filling their souls with joy and consolation, yea, even to the purifying and the sanctification of their hearts, which sanctification cometh because of their yielding their hearts unto God." (Helaman 3:35.) Wouldn't you like this to happen to you? It can, you know!

Did you notice the scripture says that those who do this have their souls filled with "joy and consolation"? The world in general thinks that fasting is a time for "sackcloth and ashes," a time to carry a look of sorrow, as one to be pitied. On the contrary, the Lord admonishes: "Moreover when ye fast, be not, as the hypocrites, of a sad countenance: for they disfigure their faces, that they may appear unto me to fast. Verily I say unto you, They have their reward.

"But thou, when thou fastest, anoint thine head, and wash thy face;

"That thou appear not unto men to fast, but unto thy Father which is in secret: and thy Father, which seeth in secret, shall reward thee openly." (Matthew 6:16-18.)

Now, may we turn to the most important part of this great law. So far we have only discussed those areas that bless us. The real joy comes with the blessing of the poor and the needy. For it is in the fulfillment of this wonderful Christlike act that we practice "pure religion and undefiled" spoken of by James. Can you think of a better or more perfect Christian function than "pure religion and undefiled"? I can't.

The Lord speaking through Moses observed: "If there be among you a poor man of one of thy brethren within any of thy gates in thy land which the Lord thy God giveth thee, thou shalt not harden thine heart, nor shut thine hand from thy poor brother: But thou shalt open thine hand wide unto him. . . ." Then he goes on to promise him who gives: ". . . the Lord thy God shall bless thee in all thy works, and in all that thou puttest thine hand unto." He concludes: ". . . therefore I command thee, saying, Thou shalt open wide thine hand unto thy brother, to thy poor, and to thy needy, in thy land." (Deuteronomy 15:7-8, 10-11.)

Amulek had something to say on this subject. After instructing the people for some time on various vital matters, he turned his thoughts to the poor and the needy, advising the congregation that even if they are diligent in all of these other things, and "turn away the needy, and the naked, and visit not the sick and afflicted, and impart of your substance . . . to those who stand in need—I say unto you, if ye do not any of these things, behold, your prayer is vain, and availeth you nothing, and ye are as hypocrites who do deny the faith." (Alma 34:28.)

Yes, the law of the fast is a perfect law, and we cannot begin to approach perfection until we decide to make it a part of our lives. When you start and stop the fast is up to you, but wouldn't it be nice to culminate it and be at your spiritual peak for the fast and testimony meeting?

How much you give the bishop as a donation is also up to you, but isn't it thrilling to know that your accounting with the Lord has been paid willingly and with accuracy?

Why you fast is also up to you. But suppose the main reason was simply that you wanted to help someone in need and to be a part of "pure religion undefiled." Wouldn't your faith be lifted and sanctified? Of course it would. And incidentally, have you ever noticed how satisfying it is way down deep inside each time you are obedient to Heavenly Father's desires? There can be no equal to the peace of mind that always comes as the reward for obedience to truth.

The world needs self-discipline. You can find it in fasting and prayer. Our generation is sick for lack of self-control. Fasting and prayer help to instill this virtue.

The world's future depends upon an urgent return to family unity. Fasting and prayer will help to guarantee it. Each person has greater need for divine guidance. There is no better way. We all have need to overcome the powers of the adversary. His influence is incompatible with fasting and prayer.

There can be no greater joy than in helping others, for "inasmuch as ye have done it unto one of the least of these my brethren, ye have done it unto me." (Matthew 25:40.)

And now, my dear brothers and sisters, although not as worthy perhaps, but equally enthusiastic in the cause we represent, I join my testimony with Alma of old when he declared: ". . . Behold, I testify unto you that I do know that these things whereof I have spoken are true. And how do ye suppose that I know of their surety?

"Behold, I say unto you they are made known unto me by the Holy Spirit of God. Behold, I have fasted and prayed many days that I might know these things of myself. And now I do know of myself that they are true; for the Lord God hath made them manifest unto me by his Holy Spirit. . . ." (Alma 5:45-46.)

17

The Word of Wisdom: a commandment with a promise

GOD'S LAW OF HEALTH

A great prophet who lived 2,500 years ago stated that "men are, that they might have joy." (2 Nephi 2:25.) The Church of Jesus Christ in this day holds fast to this inspired scripture as an eternal truth.

The quest for joy and happiness is common to all regardless of race, color, or creed. While the objective is common, the understanding on how to achieve it is often another story.

The existence of man in this mortal sphere finds him involved in a grand system of physical force and physical law, all held together and seemingly pre-set into a magnificent system of amazing order and synchronization. We marvel at the seasons, the celestial bodies. All about us is evidence of natural law and an overwhelming suggestion of divine assemblage. The laws of gravity, heat, and motion all follow precise patterns under given conditions. If we enter the fiery furnace, we die. If we attempt to defy the laws of gravity, we are killed. If our car sweeps along the highway uncontrolled, we crash; and we must all agree that the human body in similar manner is subject to the law and order of the universe, for it is physical.

Obedience to the law, whether it be physical, intellectual, or spiritual, brings harmony, peace, joy, and happiness. This thinking was confirmed by the Master, who said through the Prophet Joseph Smith: "There is a law, irrevocably decreed in heaven before the foundations of this world, upon which all blessings are predicated—And when we obtain any blessing from God, it is by obedience to that law upon which it is predicated." (D&C 130:20-21.) We are blessed by obedience to law. Transgression of the law always brings unhappiness. Carried to the extreme it could mean death.

I believe with all my heart that natural law is the handiwork of a loving Father in heaven, and I further bear record that this same loving Father has not left us without specific instruction concerning the care of our physical bodies, for he created us, and he knows that true happiness and total growth, moral, spiritual, and intellectual, are largely dependent upon our physical well-being.

Through this same great latter-day prophet, Joseph Smith, the Lord has revealed an entire volume of scripture known as the Doctrine and Covenants.

In the 89th section of this inspired work, the Lord gives to all men who would listen what he calls "A Word of Wisdom." Let us note a part of this inspired revelation, starting with the fourth verse:

> Behold, verily, thus saith the Lord unto you: In consequence of evils and designs which do and will exist in the hearts of conspiring men in the last days, I have warned you, and forewarn you, by giving unto you this word of wisdom by revelation—
>
> That inasmuch as any man drinketh wine or strong drink among you, behold it is not good, neither meet in the sight of your Father. . . .
>
> . . . strong drinks are not for the belly, but for the washing of your bodies.
>
> And again, tobacco is not for the body, neither for the belly, and is not good for man, but is an herb for bruises and all sick cattle, to be used with judgment and skill. (D&C 89:4-5, 7-8.)

We are further instructed that the "evil designs of conspiring men" has reference to those who would ply us with a never-ending tidal wave of propaganda in an attempt to convince us that it is not only popular but safe and smart to violate this God-given law of health.

Now to clarify a few terms—this also by revelation. Strong drink signifies all alcoholic beverages. Tobacco is explicit and needs no clarification; this reference includes all forms of tobacco. The term "hot drinks" has reference to coffee and tea. To summarize quickly: alcohol and tobacco, tea and coffee are all contrary to the Lord's law of health, and all who violate the law for a borrowed moment of so-called pleasure must be prepared to sacrifice some real and lasting joy and happiness that should rightfully be theirs.

Thomas A. Edison has said, "To put alcohol in the human brain is like putting sand in a machine." He further commented: "I employ no one who smokes cigarettes."

I wonder whether we are all aware of the scientifically proven facts about alcohol. Alcohol is not a stimulant but a depressant of the brain and nervous system. It is a habit-forming drug and has poisonous effects on the body. It has no value as a food. In the United States there are nearly a million alcoholics with nearly two and a quarter million well on the way. This is a national disgrace. Mental accuracy is impaired by alcohol, and in chronic cases, the brain cells degenerate. Approximately 12,000 alcoholic patients are given psychiatric treatment in a single New York hospital each year.

Gladstone has observed that "the ravages of drink are greater than those of pestilence and famine combined." Now we must surely agree with this great man, for alcohol has contributed to the loss of more homes, led to more bankruptcies, more crime, more accidents, more broken marriages, more cases of blindness, more derelicts of society, more immorality, more suicides, than any other single influence known to man today.

Yes, it is certain that out of compassion for his children, a loving Heavenly Father has given a modern-day revelation that strong drinks are not for our benefit.

A similar wake of destruction follows the careless rampage of tobacco among men, women, and children. Would you believe that tobacco costs the American people well over three and a half billion dollars a year? Do you know that the purchase of cigarettes in one recent year in the United States increased about four percent? This means that the vast majority of smokers are ignoring the overwhelming evidence of competent medical authority now available concerning the lethal effect of tobacco on the human anatomy.

The American Cancer Society reports that lung cancer is ninety-five percent fatal, and then the report goes on to say that evidence proves that three-fourths of all lung cancer cases can be traced to the use of tobacco.

The American Public Health Association estimates that one million American children now in school will die of lung cancer before they reach their God-granted life expectancy. Now, in a sense, this is a form of national suicide, and we do not have the right to shorten human life. And perhaps the saddest of all commentary is that a staff of experts studying the tobacco problem has concluded that the upward trend in the use of tobacco among children can be traced directly to a more permissive attitude on the part of parents. Perhaps we shouldn't talk so much about what the schools aren't doing as we should talk about what parents should be doing, and this is as it should be. Our children should be taught in the home. I would like to make an appeal to every parent who loves his children: why not start today and set the proper example for those we love?

The Lord has also recognized coffee and tea as habit-forming stimulants contrary to the freedom he wants so much for all of his children.

Now, if you really knew that your child was in danger, if you were told that conspiring men were meeting your children on their way home from school, going all out to attract their attention and condition their minds toward the acceptance of a bad habit, wouldn't you feel compelled to do something about it? Why, of course you would—you would do something that very day. But why let the conspiring men stand on a cold corner? We are allowing them to accomplish the same evil practice in the comfort and convenience of our homes every day. Here's a challenge for us; let's do something about it.

Let me read a letter from a confused youngster. I think this has some real merit. This young man was a typical sports fan. He is writing to his favorite baseball player: "You are my favorite baseball player. I saw an advertisement where you say you smoke cigarettes and that you like them. I guess they help you. My mother says cigarettes are bad and good players don't use them. I want to be a good player. Can you tell me? Are they good for you? Would you please tell me?" Signed "Hector. P.S. I am ten years old."

Well, the answer was slow in coming, but after a few weeks: "Dear Hector: Yes, I was in a cigarette commercial on television. I would not recommend for anyone to ever start smoking. It does not help one in athletics. I hope you will take your parents' advice not to smoke."

As these young minds are being conditioned by conspiring men, we see history repeating itself. This is the same technique that took eleven years back in the late '20s and '30s to make it appear smart, modern, and acceptable for a woman to be seen in public with a cigarette. This all started back in 1927 when the first billboard ad appeared that showed a man and woman relaxing on a beautiful hilltop. He was smoking, and her comment was simply this: "Please blow some my way." Rather harmless—"Please blow some my way." From this subtle beginning, the well-planned campaign took eleven years before the billboard dared to show a woman with a cigarette in her hand or mouth. Had the latter billboard been shown at first, we would have been up in arms, and something would have been done about it in a hurry. And now, unfortunately, in this campaign for the approval of our children's minds, there is hardly a tobacco advertisement that does not include a child admiring a bribed athlete who is making a statement that he probably doesn't believe in. Or perhaps we see a family situation, an apparently wholesome family situation, Dad rollicking with the children but with a cigarette in his hand. It's the same type of campaign all over again, this time aimed at children.

Now, all of this talk is not designed to show how foolish we are. We're just being victimized. The Lord understood all of this well in advance, and he told us that the very elect would be deceived by the "evils and designs . . . of conspiring men." I am sure he had this in mind. So we condemn no one at this point, but forewarned is forearmed.

May we not stand idly by and allow the cream of the nation, our hope for tomorrow, the finest youth in all history to be quietly and softly led away to habits of bondage and unhappiness. Their only hope is a parent who cares enough.

Incidentally, would you like to be a better citizen? Would you like to contribute the maximum effort to your nation and community? Only those who are physically fit can expect to make the maximum contribution and fulfill their obligation to society as they should. Much is being said about national fitness in all countries. Let us join with other clear-thinking citizens who are not adverse to happiness and joy. Let's prove that it's smart to do what is right. There is no doubt at this point what the instructions from the Lord are.

One country in a recent national survey found that nine percent of its national income was being spent for liquor and tobacco. Assuming that many of this nation were abstainers, certainly more than ten percent of the income of those indulging was being spent to satisfy their poor habits.

It is interesting to note that the Lord has promised to open the "windows of heaven" to those willing to impart ten percent of their income to the upbuilding of his kingdom. (Malachi 3:10.) This is perhaps the most gracious, the most promising, the most generous of all contracts offered by the Lord to those he loves; and yet, there are millions who are spending more than ten percent for an enslaving habit, and instead of opening the "windows of heaven," they are slamming the door on a promise of happiness and joy that no man, in my opinion, has the right to deny himself.

And so I conclude this plea by returning to the 89th section of the Doctrine and Covenants, and here is the promise the Lord concludes with, the most stimulating promise of all holy writ concerning the day-to-day welfare of his children:

> And all . . . who remember to keep and do these sayings, walking in obedience to the commandments, shall receive health in their navel and marrow to their bones;
>
> And shall find wisdom and great treasures of knowledge, even hidden treasures;
>
> And shall run and not be weary, and shall walk and not faint.
>
> And I, the Lord, give unto them a promise, that the destroying angel shall pass by them; as the children of Israel, and not slay them. (D&C 89:18-21.)

And so, when we obtain any blessing from God it is by obedience to that law upon which it is predicated.

Let's heed Elijah's challenge: "How long halt ye between two opinions? if the Lord be God, follow him: but if Baal, then follow him. . . ." (1 Kings 18:21.)

"I, the Lord, am bound when ye do what I say; but when ye do not what I say, ye have no promise." (D&C 82:10.) May we be obedient to law that we may have true joy, eternal happiness, and peace of mind.

18

Reaping rich dividends and satisfaction in everyday life

THE WONDERFUL WORLD OF WORK

One recurring theme among the teachings of the Church is "Faith without works is dead." One of the very first commandments given to man was that he should "eat bread" by the "sweat of [his] face." (Genesis 3:19.) In our time the welfare plan has been reemphasized in loud, clear terms. The fundamental message of God's welfare plan is that man must reenthrone work as the ruling principle in his life. All of this, of course, is in sharp contrast to governmental welfare plans that invariably seem to foster the character-weakening dole systems of rendering aid.

Not long ago the periodical *Christian Economics* made this thought-provoking statement:

> There are certain truths which are true no matter how much the world may question or deny them. In the economic realm, for instance, you cannot legislate the poor into freedom by legislating the wealthy out of it. You cannot multiply wealth by dividing it. Governments cannot give to the people what they do not first take away from the people. And that which one man receives without working for, another man must work for without receiving it. Nothing can kill the initiative of the people quicker than for half of them to get the idea that they need not work because the other half will feed them, and for the other half to get the idea that it does no good to work since someone else receives the rewards of their labors.

There will always be a place in the world for voluntary giving and true charity—without it we would surely degenerate into a society ruled completely by selfishness and greed; but voluntary giving and true charity must never be confused with dole systems, wherein those without in the community are encouraged to live on the goods produced by certain others without any arrangement to work for them or to pay back later. Such plans unfortunately are too often made binding, legal, and "honorable" by established laws. These laws not only make "honorable" the practice of "something for nothing," but they also help to guarantee perpetuation and even expansion of this character-damaging process.

You see, when a successful, hard-working man is continually deprived of a considerable share of what he produces, his incentive for all-out production soon diminishes. The one who receives quickly catches the idea that he has a good thing going and, consequently, his incentive for production is also diminished.

With total production lagging, history has shown that the heads of state next step in with threats and even dictatorial punishments in order to maintain required production levels to insure the national economy. History has proven time and time again that man never works his best under threats and force. You see, in these cases, free agency is no more; and under the hand of tyranny, even the "something for nothing" culprits become the victims of the very scheme that they helped to contrive. Such plans will always fail in the end, for their foundation is sand, and, most significant of all, they are diametrically opposed to God's law that man should eat bread by the sweat of his brow.

While the world at large thinks first in terms of "better qualified to earn more money," may I make this plea that we think first of all in terms of "better qualified to serve mankind." This kind of thinking will result in greater temporal dividends because of a healthy attitude that will produce important by-products of happiness and peace of mind. The world spends millions every day in pursuit of these important but elusive qualities.

I am reminded of the story about three laborers who stood beside a building under construction. A man passing by asked, "What are you doing?" The first looked up with a blank expression and said, "Cuttin' stone." The second shrugged his shoulders and replied, "Puttin' in time—until a better job comes along." The third seemed almost radiant as he answered, "I'm building a cathedral!"

After some years in the business world, I am satisfied that the vast majority of employees are not motivated to their best efforts because of the pay involved nearly so much as by the cause in which they are engaged and the degree of favorable human relationships in their business.

Vivid in my memory is the episode that transpired during the building of the New Zealand Temple. The prime minister of that country had made a special trip to the project just to see what the Mormons were doing. As Elder Rosenvall, the construction superintendent, stood with him watching several Maori boys pouring foundation, he said, "My, you Americans are fortunate to have the money to be able to pay high wages. I've never seen Maoris work like this on the wages we give them." This great leader was dumbfounded to learn that these men were building missionaries who were working with a purpose—they received no wages as such for their efforts. They were happy in their work and demonstrated it by extra effort.

I feel sorry for people who respect tools only for their labor-saving convenience. In my humble opinion, each tool should be evaluated only in terms of its contribution to greater efficiency—getting more accomplished in a twenty-four-hour period. To seek only more leisure time is dangerous thinking and contrary to God's law of work for man.

Now, lest I be misunderstood, may I quickly suggest that a time to play is indeed necessary, and any person who rules recreation out of his life is headed for trouble. The important consideration is that when we work, we should *really* work; when we play, we should play with all that is in us; and when we worship, we should worship with an eye single to God. At least one of the prophets made this important discovery, for he told his people, "Whatsoever thy hand findeth to do, do it with thy might." (Ecclesiastes 9:10.)

Balance in life is so important! But to think work during recreation time is to destroy the value of that hour of respite from duty. Equally damaging to the balance of life is in allowing frivolous distractions of the mind to rob our working hours of the planned objectives.

Happiness has always been an important by-product of a job well done. As David Grayson puts it:

> Happiness loves to see men at work. She loves sweat, weariness, self-sacrifice. She will be found not in palaces but lurking in cornfields and factories and hovering over littered desks; she drowns the unconscious head of the busy child. If you look up suddenly from hard work you will see her, but if you look too long she fades sorrowfully away.

Emerson was inspired when he wrote: "The reward of a thing well done is to have done it." And Bailey observed that "the fire-fly only shines when on the wing. So it is with man; when once we rest we darken."

To do less than we are capable of is a crying waste in today's world. In fact, one shrewd observer went so far as to say: "That man is idle when he does less than he can." (Anonymous.)

May our efforts be significant whether our contributions be recognized or not, for someone has said: "He that would move the world must first move himself." Just remember the stirring advice of Charles Kingsley when he said: "Thank God every morning when you get up that you have something to do which must be done, whether you like it or not. Being forced to work, and forced to do your best, will breed in you temperance, self-control, diligence, strength of will, content, and a hundred other virtues which the idle never know."

Yes, it's a wonderful world—that wonderful world of work. At least, it can be, but that is a decision that each person must make for himself. The dividends are rich when we learn to work for the sheer joy of accomplishment. Work is indeed the second most important subject in the world, but only when accomplished through and by virtue of the most important thing in the world, which is love!

19

An important question for every Latter-day Saint youth

DO YOUR STANDARDS SHOW?

A story was told in the Brigham Young University *Daily Universe* about a young lady who is a student there from out of state. Evidently her roommates had been giving her a bad time. She didn't have a wardrobe that was exactly in accordance with Church standards. The young members who were her roommates, not having a husband to "provoke to good works," were sort of practicing on their poor roommate, whom I will refer to as Sylvia. Their kindly but persistent needling had prompted Sylvia into four main areas of thought:

1. Am I really being inconsistent, or are they being narrow-minded?
2. What is wrong with a strapless formal and some fad dancing as long as there is no evil in my mind?
3. Why do I have to live by BYU standards while I am off campus?
4. Isn't someone making a "mountain out of a molehill"?

This sort of rings in my ears, too, because it hasn't been many years since I was thinking some of these same thoughts about the activities I was engaged in and some of the restrictions that I felt were placed upon me as I attended junior college in Southern California and tried to be a good Latter-day Saint at the same time.

Let us talk about the first point. Sylvia's number one question was, "Am I really being inconsistent, or are my roommates just being narrow-minded?"

In order to properly evaluate any problem, I usually go to the standard works to see if it squares with the gospel of Jesus Christ. I would like to establish this one cardinal principle at the very outset: there is no inconsistency in the gospel plan that Heavenly Father has given us. Indeed, Heavenly Father's house is a house of order. We are told that it is the same yesterday, today, and forever.

The instability and frustrations of the world today are largely due to too many people who are straddling too many fences. To live one's life on a foundation of inconsistency is to live on shifting sands. As the Savior said:

> Therefore whosoever heareth these sayings of mine, and doeth them, I will liken him unto a wise man, which built his house upon a rock:
>
> And the rain descended, and floods came, and the winds blew, and beat upon that house; and it fell not: for it was founded upon a rock.
>
> And every one that heareth these sayings of mine, and doeth them not, shall be likened unto a foolish man, which built his house upon the sand:
>
> And the rain descended, and the floods came, and the winds blew, and beat upon that house; and it fell: and great was the fall of it. (Matthew 7:24-27.)

We must never confuse the solid rock of truth and revelation with narrow-mindedness. Any and all information or advice that comes from proper priesthood authority is for our benefit, for our happiness, and for our ultimate exaltation. Yes, Sylvia, you will be smart to rule inconsistency out of your life, for it is not only frustrating and character weakening, but it also puts out a big welcome mat for trouble—trouble that is not apparent at the outset, real trouble that you did not bargain for. Inconsistency has been a favorite tool of the adversary from the very beginning of time.

If rationalization and selfish interests are suggesting to your mind that sound Church policies be classified as narrow-mindedness, perhaps a serious reevaluation would be important for you, and might I suggest that it be soon.

Question number two: "What is wrong with a strapless formal and some fad dancing as long as there is no evil in my mind?"

If unsavory thoughts have not entered your mind as your partially exposed body is allowed to contort in a most unladylike manner, you are most likely just beginning in your fad dancing recreation. But I can promise you that there are others on the same dance floor, those with whom you have chosen to affiliate, who are not as naive as you are. One or more of the opposite sex is very likely watching you rather closely. He is likely making plans for you in his future. But I promise you, young lady, his future plans so far as you are concerned don't even extend beyond tomorrow's dawn. They are all included in tonight. It is a rather remote possibility that a worthy priesthood holder who thinks only in terms of eternity would be anything but repulsed but such an exhibition.

I suppose it boils down to the same old question: a few fleeting moments of temporary excitement versus holding out for true and eternal happiness, which can only come by observing the rules that a loving Heavenly Father has set down for those seeking to reenter his presence.

Question number three: "Why do I have to live BYU standards while I am off campus?" Well, Sylvia, I suppose free agency is just about the most basic element of Heavenly Father's plan of salvation. We all have our freedom, and nothing helps to guarantee that freedom as effectively as obedience to the gospel of Jesus Christ.

But sometimes we make a major decision that automatically dictates a host of smaller ones that are all inseparably connected to it. Putting it quite simply, if I should decide to ride the train to San Francisco, I have decided automatically that I am going to go by whatever route the track carries that train. I have no choice after I have made my first decision. Not only have I decided to go along with the routing, but I have also made a decision to spend a night on the train, because it takes that long to get to San Francisco. There are, of course, many other conditions that I automatically must accept as I decide to go by train.

To my mind, that is what we have done at the waters of baptism, and we reconfirm that decision each time we partake of the sacrament as we witness unto our Heavenly Father that we are still willing to take upon ourselves the name of his Son, and always—not sometimes, but *always*—remember him, and keep his commandments which he has given us, that we may always have his Spirit to be with us. (See Moroni 4:3; D&C 20:77.)

To make a commitment of this nature and then to fail in living by that commitment is to be, as James put it, a double-minded person. He tells us that "a double minded man is unstable in all his ways," (James 1:8.) He further reminds us that God does not tempt his children, but that as our selfish lusts and desires conceive, then sin moves in rapidly. (See James 1:13-14.) But we must open the door; we must give the initial invitation by our selfishness and by our desires that are in this direction. He goes on to state that the results are usually death, and I am certain that he was referring to spiritual death, which is the sure fate of all who do not live by those things they know to be true. (See James 1:15.)

When Paul was writing to the Ephesians, he warned against this divided allegiance when he admonished: "Wherefore take unto you the whole armour of God, that ye may be able to withstand in the evil day, and having done all, to stand. Stand therefore, having your loins girt about the truth, and having on the breastplate of righteousness." (Ephesians 6:13-14.)

The Savior said: "Let your light so shine before men, that they may see your good works, and glorify your Father which is in heaven." (Mathew 5:16.)

To my mind Brigham Young University stands as a showcase for Mormonism. I do not know of a more effective showcase in all the world than this university provides as its representatives travel to South America, to the Far East, to Europe, and almost every country, performing with excellence, but, more importantly, exhibiting the standards they have been taught as a result of the gospel of Jesus Christ.

Let me read what a businessman in far-off Ceylon had to say: "The sincerity and healthy youthful exuberance displayed by the BYU group is indicative. There is something of intangible significance connected with a faith that creates such innate comradeship as I was fortunate in being witness to during the group's limited stay in Ceylon."

A Navajo tribal chief made this inquiry, after seeing BYU students in action: "Who is the man I should see so that my grandchildren can have this influence? They need school. I want them to study with your people."

The American Consul General at Madras, India, concluded his flowery appreciation by stressing the importance of international communication. He observed that the BYU group "did it without once making a speech, or getting involved in controversy, just by joyfully being themselves." Yes, ofttimes actions speak louder than words.

I was fortunate to survive World War II, because while I was in Turkey, the children were sent out to throw rocks at us as we drove by in our jeeps. Listen to their feelings today about BYU: "Because of the efforts of this group, Brigham Young University is certainly one of the best-known (if not the best-known) American universities in western Turkey, and the name of your institution has become a household phrase in Izmir. It was especially satisfying to read enthusiastic press reviews in Greek Cypriot newspapers which have ceaselessly attacked the United States for many months, and you may be interested in knowing that attempted boycotts by hostile groups in Limassol and Larnaca failed completely. Your students made an excellent impression on the many Cypriots, students and adults, they met during their brief stay here."

I was thrilled to read the expression of the late Adlai Stevenson, United States ambassador to the United Nations and former governor of Illinois, as he stood before his colleagues of the United Nations following their exposure to BYU youth: "I am completely captured! These glorious young people have represented superbly the ideals of my country. I only wish to congratulate them with all my heart. . . . These glorious young people should be sent on a nationwide tour to show Americans what Americans can produce. How can so much talent be found in one university?" And then he added: "We never should have let the Mormons out of Illinois."

King Hussein of Jordan was delighted. From Iraq comes this: "You are still the talk of Baghdad, and those who attended your performance will never forget you."

Yes, our students at Brigham Young University are, indeed, the showcase to the world.

I love what the Prophet Joseph Smith had to say, as we think of our young people minding themselves properly as they tour around the world. He said, "We teach our people correct principles, and they govern themselves."

I think this is the way it should be for Sylvia. We teach correct principles, and then everything else falls in line.

We stand as a beacon to the world, whether we like it or not. This is one of our commissions. Thus, we have a grave obligation to make certain that Heavenly Father's work is represented in a true and proper fashion.

Some talk about Brigham Young University standards. There is no such thing as a Brigham Young University standard. There are only Church standards. As soon as the Brigham Young University chooses not to observe Church standards, it will not be a Church university; it is just as simple as that. We are talking about those standards set down by prophets, seers, and revelators—men who know what the pitfalls are, men who would be upset and distressed if we were going in the wrong direction, or if we were headed for a rocky abyss.

To illustrate, let me attempt to create a picture in your mind's eye.

Suppose you were standing on a beautiful green hill. It is springtime. The grass is green; the trees are beautiful. The day is perfect. The temperature is just right. There is a gentle breeze blowing. You feel as if the world is at your command. You are all alone on this hill. You see this beautiful, peaceful river as it winds around the hill. My, what a beautiful sight it is!

But as you turn around and look on the back side of the hill, you notice that the beautiful, peaceful river drops over an abrupt waterfall and crashes onto some rocks at the bottom. Then all of a sudden you hear music. You hear voices. It sounds familiar. You look back, and right down there on the same river is a boat with about eight or ten of your friends. One is playing a guitar; all are singing together. They are truly enjoying life as they allow the current to take them downstream. You say, "My, isn't that delightful! How I would love to be with them!" There they are, just drifting, not knowing where the river is going to take them.

Then all of a sudden it dawns on you—the waterfall! The jagged rocks at the bottom! What are you going to do? Will you just fold your arms and say, "Now, this should be interesting. Let's see what happens here"? You are not going to do that, are you? You are going to jump up and down; you are going to shout; you are going to get excited about it.

That is exactly what we do. We do a little jumping up and down, and we get excited, because we know where the jagged rocks and pitfalls are. Our prophets have told and continue to tell us the things that we should do as well as the areas to avoid in order that we might get back into the presence of our Heavenly Father.

So as we who love you get excited, as we raise our voices, as we wave our arms, would you forgive us, please; and would you just know it is because we love you so much. We don't want you to get into any situation that would not be a blessing to you. We want to be with you when the greatest day of your life or our lives comes; when we feel that friendly arm on our shoulders and the kindly voice of someone who is over all, as he says, "Well done, thou good and faithful servant: . . . enter thou into the joy of thy lord." (Matthew 25:21.)

Yes, we have guideposts to follow, and only by following these things that have been set down can we hope to gain the rewards that are there for us.

20

Breaking down barriers to understanding

IF YOU WOULD COMMUNICATE WELL

The world seems forever plagued with a lack of understanding between nations. Traditionally we humans have been without the ability to communicate well across international borders. Our very own nation within recent years has been torn by vicious riots, partly because large and important factions of our citizenry are failing in their ability to communicate with one another. Oh, true enough, the transmissions have been loud and clear—but sometimes I wonder what has happened to the receivers. We only seem to listen to and to hear that which we want to hear.

Perhaps saddest of all is the fact that family units, the basic and most important of all units in our social order, seem to be breaking up by the thousands each week—all because husbands and wives, parents and children, or next-door neighbors find it difficult to establish a simple and clear line of communication between them.

The greatest need in the world today is for the gospel of Jesus Christ. The greatest challenge you and I have as the custodians of this truth is the ability to communicate better in a world that needs what we have.

Now for the sake of interest and to start some thought processes in motion, come with me for a minute as we roll back the calendar about a hundred years. By contrast, we can better contemplate the miracle of communication in our time. Too often we take for granted the convenience and ease of today's methods of communication. From the hills around our valleys, Indian smoke signals could be seen less than a hundred years ago as messages were sent across the miles to signal the success or failure of a hunting party or perhaps the approach of a covered wagon train. Yes, after thousands of years there had been few advances in the field of communication. Jungle drums, tom toms, smoke signals—and, oh yes, we mustn't forget the revolutionary new Pony Express of that day—but all this seemed to be about the best the mind of man was capable of after all that time.

An interesting sidelight of United States history suggests the ingenuity and the inventive genius of 1825 as the top brains of that day were employed to devise a sure and quick way of notifying the population of New York City about the departure of the first barge from Albany as it headed down the newly completed Erie Canal. The canal was a historic feat. It provided a new avenue of commerce and trade from the Great Lakes to New York City. All the citizenry of New York, some 430 miles downstream, were eager to start a giant celebration as the new waterway was officially declared in operation with the departure of this first barge.

Now this urgent need for a better way of communication was solved as follows: forty-three cannons from the War of 1812 were stationed ten miles apart along the length of the Erie Canal and the Hudson River. As the barge entered the canal, cannon number one fired; nearly a minute later, the attendant of cannon number two heard the sound, and he lit the fuse and cannon number two was fired; and so the sound was relayed until all forty-three cannons had been fired in rotation. At last the people in New York City heard the report of the last cannon, and at that instant the celebration was underway. Total elapsed time for the message—approximately one hour. It had to go 430 miles.

You see, sound travels slowly—only about 740 miles per hour. As a matter of fact, if we had a hollow tube telephone system in this country with some means of sending our voices through the tube instead of allowing our voice patterns to ride piggyback on electromagnetic waves, a person in Utah calling someone in California would shout "Hello" into the mouthpiece, and that hello would take about one hour to travel to the coast. Then the person in California would shout back "Hello," and two hours would have gone by and all you have said is "Hello." The only thing worse than the service would be the bill, especially if it were at today's rates!

Let me give you one more interesting contrast in comparing the speed of sound with electromagnetic waves. The next time you watch a World Series baseball game on TV and see the batter hit a long fly ball to center field, just remember that the sound of the bat hitting the ball hops into a microphone not far from the home plate and then speeds on electromagnetic waves directly into your living room. That speed is 186,000 miles per second —about 7½ times around this earth in one short second. The center fielder in the ball park has had to wait for those lumbering slow sound waves to reach him some 300 feet away; and although he will probably catch the ball, TV viewers perhaps 3,000 miles away heard the crack of the bat before he did. All of this is made possible through the miracle of our modern-day electrical communication.

Yes, we are living in a great day; and we read and hear about coaxial cables; we hear about microwave radio relay systems; we hear about earth-orbiting satellites, moon robots talking back to earth, and even "hot lines" between heads of nations, providing us with an absolute miracle of communication from a pure technological and mechanical standpoint. But as a world filled with more than three billion people, we are failing miserably in our ability to really get the message through. I think we can conclude that the source of our failure is human. It stems from the uncompromising, the selfish—yes, even at times the deceitful—heart and mind of man. No one, in my opinion, can be a good transmitter unless he has first learned to be a good receiver.

One of the great communication problems of our day is the communication of empty words—just words, no real message, no stimulus for thought. As children of our Heavenly Father, he would have us say something as we give utterance.

Any person who reads and understands the scriptures is better prepared to speak with wisdom. How glorious that we have a divine, uncontaminated source of light and knowledge. Speaking through the Prophet Joseph Smith, the Lord declared unto Oliver Cowdery and David Whitmer as follows:

> These words are not of men nor of man, but of me; wherefore, you shall testify they are of me and not of man;
>
> For it is my voice which speaketh them unto you; for they are given by my Spirit unto you, and by my power you can read them one to another; and save it were by my power you could not have them;
>
> Wherefore, you can testify that you have heard my voice, and know my words. (D&C 18:34-36.)

In Isaiah, we are taught: "Incline your ear, and come unto me: hear, and your soul shall live. . . ." (Isaiah 55:3.)

As King Mosiah attempted to stimulate the listening ability of the people of his day, he made this plea: ". . . open your ears that ye may hear, and your hearts that ye may understand, and your minds that the mysteries of God may be unfolded to your view." (Mosiah 2:9.)

Now, nearly every day someone calls at 47 East South Temple. Their plea is simple: "Won't you please help me!" Many of these visitors come in pairs—husband and wife finding themselves on the verge of real trouble in their marital situation. And in too many cases, each is equipped with a powerful transmitter and one-tube receiver with dead batteries—no interest in listening; all they want to do is transmit.

Let me tell you about a young man. I've known him all his life, and he's a fine young man. One day he called in to tell me about his pending temple marriage. He had standing at his side a beautiful young lady who seemed to be as thrilled with life and the spirit of the Church as he was. They were obviously very much in love. I wished them well, but just a few months after their marriage they came back. They were calling for help. They were in difficulty. I was looking at two unhappy people. They were both anxious to tell me their side of the story; they were anxious to be transmitters, but they had no desire to be receivers, and this is the way it had been for many weeks.

She claimed that in spite of a heavy course at the university, he chose to go bowling with his buddies three nights a week, because this is the way it had been before they were married, and he didn't want to break up a pleasant relationship. It was his choice to go to the library and study on the other evenings instead of coming home for dinner because he felt that there were the reference books he needed to do his studying.

He was claiming that although his wife was kind and generous in trying to support him through school with a full-time job, he saw no reason why she had to work overtime on Sunday just to pick up that extra money. Why wouldn't she go to church with him? He was also complaining that the house didn't look as tidy as he thought it should—and she, of course, was complaining of being a slave and not being able to keep up. As he complained about things being strewn around, she was quick to remind him that their meager little home had just one cupboard, and she couldn't get it all in. And so it went—on and on and on.

Well now, the solution turned out well. I think it was a great day when he decided to sever relations with his former bowling buddies—I don't think he severed the friendships, but he decided not to go bowling with them. He decided that he would keep up his bowling interests by taking his wife together with a neighbor and his wife and going out and bowling some mixed doubles. It was very well arranged.

She decided not to work on Sundays—she decided she should be with her husband in church—and they decided between them that there were many economies that could be effected in their little home, that they wouldn't have to have that extra money after all.

So every night they had dinner together—no bowling with his friends, no studying at the library (he seemed to find some way of getting the reference books he needed); and then, in addition to all this, he was able to help with some of the housework, and they worked together side by side. They found when it was all over that not only were they able to pay the bills better than ever before, but they were able to pay their tithing, something that had been neglected. They carved an hour out of each week for family home evening, just the two of them, and they found great comfort there. They had traded in their one-tube receiver with a broken-down battery for a good five-tube receiver and some new batteries, and they were listening, and they were able to communicate with one another. As far as I know this young couple is very happy today.

Another couple had been married for twenty years and had five children. Her complaint was that she had a robot husband who sat in front of a TV all night and who was unsympathetic to her needs. She hadn't been on a date for more than five years—not even out to dinner once. His complaint was that he had a nagging wife. This complaint was not original with this man. We have heard it before. She was irritable and so on and on. The list became longer.

Do you know what happened? I give you the scene just two years later. This good wife had a very important operation. She had been suffering with something that he was not anxious to be sympathetic about or admit. But after the operation, she was a new woman. She took on a new glow, and he fell in love with her all over again. He attended his priesthood meetings and soon he was ordained to the Melchizedek Priesthood. They were sealed in the temple, and he is now the elders quorum president. They had a boy whose mind was furthest from a mission call. Now he was not only called on a mission, but he was a mission leader. These people had been overmodulating their transmitters with bitterness, and after twenty years they are now communicating well, and they are happy.

Yes, communication is the key—not only transmitting but receiving as well, and as we transmit, transmitting something worthwhile.

One other couple had been married for ten years and had three children. For three hours they poured out their complaints—no major transgression on either part, just nagging little complaints that seemed to go on and on. After analyzing everything that had been said, we determined that the answer was just as simple as a few evenings of financial counseling from a member of the high council who had qualifications in this direction. Ninety percent of all their grievances had been distorted and amplified due to their financial mismanagement. But after seeing the way and after being willing to communicate on the subject not only with one another but with someone else who knew what he was talking about, they found those problems had blown away into the thin air, and happiness now prevails in this home.

If you would communicate well, be a good listener. Keep that reservoir filled to capacity so that as your opportunity comes you will be able to transmit something worthwhile. The Lord can help us to recall. The Lord can help us to remember. The Lord brings out the best that is in us, but there is an eternal principle, an eternal law: you can't get something out of nothing, and that pertains to your mind and my mind, to your heart and soul and to my heart and soul. As we contemplate all that needs to be done in learning, I like the attitude of a wonderful old-timer down in Arizona whom I met not too long ago. I thought his remark was classic. He said, "I can't learn nothin' while I'm a-talkin'." There is a lot of truth in that. Sometimes when we are always transmitting, we find that all of our power is being used in that direction while we should be diverting some of that power to our receiver.

If you would communicate well, become better informed. Have you read a good book lately? Have you had a stimulating conversation yet today? If TV viewing is regular with you, do you select your programs carefully; and probably more important than that, do you have the will power to switch it off at the appropriate time?

It was Victor Hugo who observed, "When the disposition of time is left to the incident of chance, chaos will reign." Has there been a little chaos in your life lately? Maybe a reevaluation and reorganization of your time might help to solve this problem. We have been told time and time again that knowledge is power. I would add that only when knowledge is intelligently used does it become a part of the glory of God.

No radio transmitter has ever been any better than its programming, its music, the spoken word; and so it is with you: if you wish to communicate well, become better informed so that your programming will be superior.

If you would communicate well, learn the importance of simplicity. Simplicity can be a wonderful thing. Have you listened to a child pray lately? I think we can take great lessons from the prayer of a child. The Savior himself has said, "Except ye become as little children. . . ." (Matthew 18:3.) As we think in terms of little children, we think in terms of simplicity.

Simplicity and sincerity seem to go together, and perhaps this is what Paul had in mind as he made that very famous statement: "For if the trumpet give an uncertain sound, who shall prepare himself to the battle?" (1 Corinthians 14:8.)

Remember the simplicity of our Heavenly Father as he gave utterance in various passages handed down through the prophets. Remember his message on the Mount of Transfiguration, when he said to Peter, James, and John: "This is my beloved Son, in whom I am well pleased; hear ye him." (Matthew 17:5.) No extra words—simplicity and clarity.

To the Nephites on this continent, he said, "Behold my Beloved Son, in whom I am well pleased, in whom I have glorified my name—hear ye him." (3 Nephi 11:7.)

Then a third time, in the Sacred Grove, as the young lad, Joseph, knelt to pray, in the year 1820: *"This is My Beloved Son. Hear Him!"* (Joseph Smith 2:17.)

The Savior himself said with such admonition and clear simplicity, "Follow me." (Matthew 9:9.) "Feed my sheep." (John 21:17.) "Father forgive them; for they know not what they do." (Luke 23:34.) "Go, and sin no more." (John 8:9.)

These are direct, uncomplicated, meaningful, simple. Yes, if you would communicate well, learn the importance of simplicity.

If you would communicate well, communicate with enthusiasm. It is not so much what you say as how you say it. The world loves enthusiasm. The world loves people with spirit.

I remember an athletic team. They were headed for almost certain defeat, until one man's enthusiasm caught the whole team on fire. That team won a great victory that day.

I remember three candidates for a very important job. Each one was almost equally prepared academically. One was less handsome than the other two, but his enthusiasm was contagious. He got the job.

I remember a man in New Zealand. He had been approached by scores of missionaries, and his wife seemed to pray in vain for his conversion to the Church. Then that same plan of salvation that he had heard many dozens of times was explained with the spark of enthusiasm—well-placed enthusiasm—and he was caught on fire with a desire to be baptized. Today that man is a priesthood leader in New Zealand, and he is praising the name of an enthusiastic young missionary who made him want to sit up and listen.

Speaking of enthusiasm, I remember going to Yellowstone National Park. As we went by snowmobile into this winter wonderland in the middle of winter with snow about eight or ten feet deep, the park rangers had to guide us and show us where to go. We were awe-struck with the beauty of it all. Then finally we went right into the geyser basin. We didn't know what time Old Faithful would erupt. The park was empty, and there was no one there to tell us when the last eruption took place. We knew it was due about every hour. While we waited, we watched a mudpot—blupe, blupe, blupe. Then all of a sudden there it went—beautiful Old Faithful geyser spouting up against an azure blue sky in the middle of winter. I had never seen a more magnificent sight. At that moment someone nudged me and said, "You know, the only difference between that old mudpot and Old Faithful is enthusiasm."

So, that is about the way it is. Don't you be an old mudpot; be enthusiastic like Old Faithful. I promise you it will pay you handsome dividends throughout your entire lifetime.

Now the last point I would make, if you would communicate well—consider the virtue of love. Love is true empathy for the other person. Love is compassion. Love means the golden rule. Love means charity. I think Paul hit it squarely when he said: "Though I speak with the tongues of men and of angels, and have not charity, I am become as sounding brass, or a tinkling cymbal." (1 Corinthians 13:1.)

May we think of the other person as we learn to communicate with love. Section 121 of the Doctrine and Covenants is one of my very favorites. It talks about the power and influence of the priesthood being maintained through persuasion, through long-suffering, gentleness, meekness, and love unfeigned. Isn't that a beautiful term—love unfeigned!

I am reminded of the young father who was anxiously getting his children ready for Sunday School on a tight time schedule. He had involved the older children to help him, and they were taking delight in their new authority and responsibility and were rushing the younger ones here and there, washing faces, combing hair, and all the rest. Finally this one son had his little brother out on the driveway, his hair combed, his face washed, and he wanted to get him into his jacket and into the car. The younger fellow had one arm in his jacket, and he pulled it out, looked up at his big brother, and said, "I don't have to put on my jacket if I don't want to. I don't have to get in the car, I don't have to go to Sunday School, because just the other night in our family home evening Daddy told me I have my *free agency*."

He was standing there and then on his free agency. At that very moment Dad came out the back door and heard the rebellion. The little fellow came to his father crying and obviously seeking sympathy. This father could have been like most of us and said, "Yes, you have your free agency all right, but you get in that car and do it now!" and boom, in he goes.

But he didn't do that. He went down on one knee, put a loving arm around the little fellow, and said, "Young man, free agency is the most important thing you have in this life, and don't you ever forget it." Then giving him just a little squeeze of confidence, he said, " Now hurry and put on your jacket, or we are going to be late." The little one put on his jacket, looked up at his big brother, and said, "See, I told you so."

What a great victory for this little fellow! But the real victory was with Dad—love unfeigned!—giving this young son the courage and confidence that he needed; letting him know that he was needed with the family at Sunday School, and that is where he wanted to be all the time, I am sure.

Now, returning to this same verse of scripture, it justifies our "reproving betimes with sharpness, when moved upon by the Holy Ghost. . . ." Not lashing out in anger; not unguarded, but when moved upon by the Holy Ghost, reproving betimes with sharpness. There is a place for it, but in the proper way. My, how wonderful! Then, of course, after reproving with sharpness, "showing forth afterwards an increase of love. . . ." (D&C 121:43.)

What are the rewards for this kind of consideration toward our fellow beings? As we gain love unfeigned, as we are able to conform ourselves in this way, the Lord promises: "The Holy Ghost shall be thy companion, and thy scepter an unchanging scepter of righteousness and truth; and thy dominion shall be an everlasting dominion, and without compulsory means it shall flow unto thee forever and ever." (D&C 121:46)

Yes, if you would communicate well, consider well the virtue of love.

We have a message—a vital message about man's eternal destiny; a vital message about the importance of free air to breathe. These are messages that the world needs, and it can't wait. Do you believe in these things? Do you believe that you can do the job? I know you can, and I pray that the Lord will bless you that you will do something about it, that you will get excited about this great experience of living and of communicating with people and of letting the world know what you know and sharing it with them in an effective manner.

21

Timely counsel on keeping our thoughts and minds clean

POLLUTION OF THE MIND

Before drawing the breath of life on this earth, we were all spiritual beings living in the realm of God, the Eternal Father. Scripture reveals that even before our spiritual birth, each of us had individual identification as an intelligence. Before all else could take place, there had to be that beginning spark of light, that spark of intelligence or, if you please, the marvelous mechanism that controls our every thought, that controls our every act. We might think of this spark of intelligence as perhaps the nucleus of a human mind.

No wonder it has been said: "As a man thinketh, so is he." The master control center within each individual must be regarded as the key. Signals flashing out to the various parts of the body bring instant reaction; in sum and substance, this center dictates the character, the conscience, the strength, and yes, even the weaknesses of every man.

From the beginning of time, there has been a never-ending struggle to influence and control the human mind. Too often, the false promises and enticements of conspiring men have been successful. How much more effective to capture the control center than a mere outpost.

The mind of man must first depend upon quality input before it can be counted upon to render good decisions. Like the most sophisticated computer, only with its properly designed control panel in proper place and in working order can the system be depended upon to produce the desired results.

It was Paul who made the observation that the whole must be fitly framed before the properly functioning church can be recognized and identified. It must naturally follow then that the pollution of a single church member's mind will indeed affect the whole. If pollution touches even a segment of the church, then the entire church is weakened. The church can be no stronger than its members. By the same token, the degradation of a family member weakens the entire family unit. Applied to a nation, when a segment of its citizenry becomes contaminated by frequenting the cesspools of its society, that nation indeed is weakened.

Thousands have said: "Printed filth will never become an obsession with me. I am a mature adult, and I have the right to see what is going on in the world without becoming trapped." But hardly a day passes that we don't listen to alcoholics and drug abusers who are now looking back with regret on their beginning days of social drinking and mild drug experimentation just to satisfy a so-called curiosity.

Evidence is conclusive that mind-polluting pornography is just as addicting and just as devastating as Satan's other tools of destruction and degradation. As expressed in the last line of Alexander Pope's poem: "We first endure, then pity, then embrace."

The gradual infiltration of this mind-polluting material has quietly engulfed us on a wide front. Today's so-called acceptable motion picture would have been banned from public viewing just a few short years ago. Many of the recommended reading lists of our public schools would have been classified as unacceptable less than a generation ago. All of us, by the flip of a switch, allow much highly questionable and some downright objectionable filth to occupy the center stage of our family circle. Public attitude against smut has very gradually been lulled into a state of mild resistance—so mild, in fact, that the adversary has already won a major victory whether we are ready to admit it or not.

Now the question follows: Is there really anything that can be done? Why, of course there is, and if every God-fearing citizen would band together on a few fundamental steps, this entire trend could be turned around.

How about taking a few minutes, for example, to voice objection to the local supermarket manager about easy availability and prominent display of unacceptable material on his periodical display rack.

How about taking just five minutes each week to review the TV log and then establishing a few rules that all the family agrees to concerning viewing time and on which channel.

Why not make some effort to find out something about the next movie that will engage your family's undivided attention for two and a half or three hours and will probably cost you far more than you contributed to the poor and needy that month. It goes without saying that all X- and R-rated movies are automatically eliminated.

Perhaps we should all become a lot more interested in what the school is recommending and making available to our children. How many school meetings or visits did you make during the past year?

Do the persons you vote for feel as you do on these vital matters? Is there some legislation that needs to be encouraged, some petitions that need to be circulated, some telephone calls that need to be made? God gave us a democratic process for a good reason. Do we use this process to help his cause? Not enough! The opposition is certainly misusing it, all in the name of free speech. You and I must keep the record straight on what God intended by freedom of speech and some of the obligations connected with it.

Satan is the master of deceit. He diverts man's God-given attributes from their noble and divine purpose onto a downward track. All seem to agree that one of man's most demanding and ever-present drives is centered in his desire for companionship and sexual fulfillment. To have this highly sensitive and divine human mechanism falsely aroused by unnatural processes creates a serious conflict in that vital control center, the mind. Rationalization quickly rallies to the side of the victim of off-color literature, because rationalization helps him to live with his conscience. He tells himself that his drives are God-given and, therefore, not that bad. He also tells himself, "Nearly everybody does it. I am not so different," and while he may not be so very different, he is just exactly 100 percent wrong in the eyes of God.

Now a mind that has been deceived into receiving trashy input cannot but send false signals to the feet, the hands, and the tongue. Future decisions will all be colored by the impurity allowed to enter that control center of his entire being.

As you invite unclean thoughts to become a part of your total being, be assured some of your faculties will become considerably sharpened. Your temper will be sharpened. Your tongue will be sharpened. Your desire for more trash will be sharpened. Your ability to shade the truth will be sharpened. Yes, just about every negative part of your character will be enhanced.

There will also be a noticeable diminishing effect in your life. Your personality will be diminished. Your family relationships will be impaired. Your ability to pray will be lessened. Your spirit will be affected adversely, and your testimony of the truth will start to slip away, probably so gradually at first that you won't even realize it is happening until it is too late. The Lord has said: "Be ye clean that bear the vessels of the Lord." (D&C 38:42.)

Every prophet from the beginning of this earth has had foreknowledge of our day with its pitfalls and hazards. The scriptures alone give us the formula for avoiding disaster. I like what the Lord says in the 121st section of of the Doctrine and Covenants: ". . . let virtue garnish thy thoughts unceasingly; then shall thy confidence wax strong in the presence of God; and the doctrine of the priesthood shall distil upon thy soul as the dews from heaven." (Verse 45.)

We have been admonished to read good books and to avoid idleness, and as President David O. McKay used to say so eloquently: "The true measure of a man is how he spends his time when he doesn't have to do anything." This, of course, brings us around to self-discipline, which is the major key in the total avoidance of illicit literature.

Are there any books or literature in your possession that would have no place in the personal library of the President of the Church? Someone has said: "Which way to go, the leader will know." Don't you think we should follow his example? Do you allow material to enter your mind that would be incompatible with entrance into the celestial kingdom of God?

Church membership contemplates only one thing—to qualify for his holy presence. Why jeopardize that possibility? The oft-quoted wisdom of President Heber J. Grant bears repetition here: "That which we persist in doing becomes easier for us to do; not that the nature of the thing itself has changed, but the power to do is increased." (Ralph Waldo Emerson.)

It works in both directions: the power to accept pornography, as our senses become numbed, or the power to reject as we declare with Joshua of old: ". . . choose you this day whom ye will serve; . . . as for me and my house, we will serve the Lord." (Joshua 24:15.)

To whom shall we turn for our direction in these vital matters? A prophet of God has spoken, and here are the exact words of the First Presidency on this vital subject:

> Pornographic filth continues to flood this country as well as other nations of the world.
>
> There is abundant evidence of the damaging effect of obscenity on the solidarity of the family, on the moral fiber of the individual.
>
> We, with many leaders outside the Church, are deeply concerned about this growing obscenity in print, on record and tape, on television, and in motion pictures.
>
> We therefore urge Latter-day Saint parents to teach their children to avoid smut in any of its many insidious forms. "Let virtue garnish thy thoughts unceasingly." (D&C 121:45.)
>
> The Lord has also said: "Set in order your houses; keep slothfulness and uncleanness far from you." (D&C 90:18.)
>
> We also encourage Latter-day Saints as citizens to exert every effort to fight the inroads of pornography in their communities. History is replete with examples of nations which have fallen in a large measure through licentiousness.

May we accept this timely counsel. Your personal welfare and the eternal future of your entire family unit may depend upon it.

22

Our most important challenge:
to teach our children

"FOR OF SUCH IS THE KINGDOM OF HEAVEN"

I'm certain that the Lord recognized the value of children in the kingdom. The Savior saw the value in teaching and blessing those who would lead the kingdom in another generation. I feel certain that he had this in mind as he admonished those about him to allow the little children to come near that he might teach and bless them. He was thinking of the church in the kingdom twenty or thirty years from that time. The Savior has set the pattern in all things, so be assured that children are precious in his sight, and to the extent that we prepare them well, I am convinced that we honor our Lord and Savior in the highest degree.

Have you ever paused to think about the strength of the Church after another generation? Now we don't have to wait to see how strong the Church is going to be twenty years from now—the strength or weakness of this latter-day work and in other generations to follow is going to be just as strong as the Primary and Sunday School classes that are being held today and the teaching being given these children in every Latter-day Saint home. For each effective lesson, we provide another guarantee for tomorrow's world. The Church today is the product of yesterday's teaching, and so it will be in another generation.

Neither you nor I can take much of the credit for the strength of the Church today. We are pleased with the growth and progress, but don't you think that most of the honor goes to our teachers and to our parents, for the examples of righteousness planted in our hearts as their children?

The opening verse of the Book of Mormon is rather significant: "I, Nephi, having been born of goodly parents, therefore I was taught somewhat in all the learning of my father. . . ." (1 Nephi 1:1.) We are all familiar with Abraham Lincoln's tribute: "All that I am or ever hope to be, I owe to my angel mother."

Yes, we were taught well, and those who taught us should take the bows for the encouraging progress we see in the Church today.

Tomorrow we step aside, for those we teach now will fill our shoes. I pray that we may look back and be satisfied that we taught well. Could anything be more rewarding than that assurance? The Old Testament says: "Cast thy bread upon the waters: for thou shalt find it after many days." (Ecclesiastes 11:1.)

Man's greatest joy comes in building. Could there be anything more noble and rewarding than in building human souls? This is the obligation we have toward our children.

What kind of legacy might we be preparing? Will the work progress or retrogress by virtue of our efforts?

It's my feeling that these future Church leaders of ours can't possibly qualify for their great challenge by virtue of one solitary hour in Primary or Sunday School each week. Hours are much too short, and there are too few weeks in a year. But an hour is long enough to plant a fertile seed, long enough to spark the germ of an idea, long enough to suggest to the mind another interesting new avenue of eternal truth.

After the seed is planted, the idea sparked, the truth defined, we need help from someone who loves them just as much as we do, from someone who has access to their minds not for just an hour but for many hours each week, someone who cares enough to water the seed, to cultivate the ground, and to keep up our beliefs.

Who cares enough for all of this? The answer is simple. It's mother and dad. There is really no one else who has the time, the tools, and the God-given love required.

President Stephen L Richards once gave the best definition of home and its noble purpose that I have ever heard. He said that home should be "a divinely appointed institution in which a servant and handmaiden of the Lord prepare themselves in righteousness to receive chosen spirits coming from our Eternal Father in heaven and give them bodies in the flesh for mortal probation, and then undertake with all the power at our command to lead these spirit children entrusted to their care back into the presence of God whence they came." Isn't that the sum and substance of it all?

Some parents will say, "I can't find the time." Of course we can't find the time. Time doesn't just make itself automatically available. We must *make* the time. We must plan the time. The Lord's house is a house of order. We always seem to find time for the things we want most. Let's put first things first in the organization of our time and our talents.

It was Victor Hugo who said, "When the disposal of time is surrendered to the chance of incidents, chaos will reign." This is contrary to the admonition that the Lord's house is a house of order, and if we are going to have the Spirit of the Lord in our homes, it must be a house of order.

There are no shortcuts in the Lord's plan. Our children must be taught properly, for just as surely as Heavenly Father lives, only those who are able to overcome selfish interests can ever hope to feel comfortable in his presence. No Latter-day Saint parent who understands the first thing about his religion would ever think in lesser terms than regaining the presence of our Heavenly Father as a complete family unit.

One great religious thinker observed, "Anyone who thinks long in terms of Christ, who acts long enough in terms of Christ and lives long enough in terms of Christ, will surely become like Christ." This seems to be the formula, but it doesn't happen without effort, not without help—preferably at an early age and preferably in the home.

Leaders and teachers, are you planting fertile seeds? Are you conditioning the soil before planting through reverence and other classroom arrangements conducive to good gospel planning and teaching? Are you really and truly available to the Spirit of the Lord for that single vital hour you have? Has the preparation been complete? Are gospel standards being maintained in your own home? You are the leader, and they look to you for direction and motivation! Is your direction and motivation carried out through the gift and power of the Spirit? Every Latter-day Saint leader should have as his motto that left by the Savior when he said: "Come, follow me!" Is your life such that you can say that? You must set the standard, and if the Lord did not know that you could do it, you would not have been called into service.

May we allow the Lord to bless and magnify us as leaders, that we may measure up to the charge given us in the Doctrine and Covenants wherein the Lord affirms that "no one can assist in this work except he shall be humble and full of love, having faith, hope, and charity, being temperate in all things, whatsoever shall be entrusted to his care." (D&C 12:8.) And may we not forget that most important challenge—one that is beautifully simple and simply beautiful: "Suffer little children . . . to come unto me: for of such is the kingdom of heaven." (Matthew 19:14.)

May we let nothing stand in our way as we accomplish this charge, for God lives—this is his church. Our callings have come through proper authority. May we never betray that sacred trust.

23

Our basic relationships in the family of God

"WHAT IS MAN, THAT THOU ART MINDFUL OF HIM?"

Not too long ago a schoolteacher, anxious to extract some participation from her class of third graders on the subject of modern-day progress, asked her little ones a simple question: "Can anyone here name one important thing in this world that was not here ten years ago?"

After a few moments of thinking, an eager and confident eight-year-old boy near the back raised his hand. His answer: "Yes—me."

As humorous as this incident might sound on the surface, I am certain that Heavenly Father smiled approvingly at the boy's response, a response that was made in all seriousness.

This lad, in my mind, is a modern-day David, for it was he who declared centuries ago:

> When I consider thy heavens, the work of thy fingers, the moon and the stars, which thou hast ordained;
>
> What is man, that thou art mindful of him, and the son of man, that thou visitest him?
>
> For thou hast made him a little lower than the angels, and hast crowned him with glory and honour.
>
> Thou madest him to have dominion over the works of thy hands; thou hast put all things under his feet. (Psalm 8:3-6.)

If the world could but learn and have feelings about this one basic concept of God to man, of father-to-son relationship, many of our mortal frustrations and contentions could be greatly diminished. Our Primary children sing a song in which we are reminded: "I am a child of God, and he has sent me here." This is a basic doctrine, and all mankind needs to believe it.

We seem so inclined to forget that there are certain basic and fundamental relationships within the human family that do not alter as the scene changes from one side of the veil to the other. One of those concepts, in my opinion, is the right that every child has to communicate with and obtain assistance from his father, mortal and heavenly. Each of us has two fathers—a spiritual father and an earthly father. Not only that, but I have also been taught that every parent has the right and the capacity to know and be concerned about the welfare of his children. It is an eternal commission and right shared by the father of your physical body and the Father of your spirit.

Why must we continually limit God, our Eternal Father, and his abilities by our own mortal incapabilities, immaturities, and our earthbound, physical restrictions? Should he who has the ability to create worlds and father billions of children be denied the right to know his offspring? Of course not. Every father has that privilege. To think otherwise is inconsistent with all that we hold as basic and fundamental in life—life here, life before, and life hereafter.

May I be bold enough to suggest that our Heavenly Father knows us personally and can call us by name—yes, us plus three billion other children who share this world with us. And we can add to that family circle the billions upon billions who have lived and died since Father Adam. This thought itself is admittedly almost beyond the comprehension of mortal understanding, but please, let us not limit the Creator of heaven and earth in any way, for his powers are limitless, and the basic concept must hold that a father knows his children.

As a child of God kneels to pray, that individual must believe implicitly that his prayer is being heard by him to whom the prayer is addressed. The thought that our Heavenly Father is too busy or that our message is being recorded by celestial computers for possible future consideration is unthinkable and inconsistent with all we have been taught by his holy prophets.

It was thrilling to listen to a father relate this story about his three-year-old youngster, as they knelt by the crib in the usual manner for the little fellow to say his simple prayer. Eyes closed, head bowed—seconds passed, and there were no words spoken by the child. Just about the time Dad was going to open his eyes to check the lengthy delay, little Tommy was on his feet and climbing into bed. "How about your prayers?" asked Dad. "I said my prayers," came the reply. "But son, Daddy didn't hear you." Then followed the child's classic statement: "But Daddy, I wasn't talking to you."

Even three-year-olds have personal, private matters to discuss with Heavenly Father from time to time. But most important of all is the implicit faith that the communication is not in vain. Each word is finding its way to a Father who is not too busy, a Father who has the ability to hear, to judge, and to act for our benefit. This must be the personal faith of us all regardless of our age, regardless of our station in life, regardless of how long it has been, regardless of how grievous the confidence might be.

". . . this is my work and my glory—to bring to pass the immortality and eternal life of man." (Moses 1:39.) His total purpose and plan is involved in our success. It's natural for a father to want success for his offspring. A son or daughter should want to please his parents and to help guarantee an eternal relationship with them.

"What is man, that thou art mindful of him?" A loving Father in heaven, concerned for the welfare of his child, might well answer: "Why, you are my son, you are my daughter. I love you very much. I listen carefully each day, hoping to hear from you. I want so to have you back one day where you belong. Please share with me your innermost thoughts, your hopes, yes, and particularly your problems. I know I can help, but listen carefully, child—don't close the door when I give you the answer. I need you very much, just as you need me." And I suppose that a fitting climax to such comments that a loving Heavenly Father might conceivably utter to any one of his children could well be couched in the same language that the Savior used as he spoke tenderly through John: "I am the vine, ye are the branches: He that abideth in me, and I in him, the same bringeth forth much fruit: for without me ye can do nothing. . . . If ye abide in me, and my words abide in you, ye shall ask what ye will, and it shall be done unto you." (John 15:5, 7.) What a promise!

We are the children of God. He is our Father in very deed. May we revere that relationship. Without this lofty concept as the foundation of our lives, our chances for temporal happiness and true success are extremely limited; our possibilities for eternal joy and exaltation are nonexistent. But with it in sharp focus and meaningful on a daily basis, we will best be able to comprehend and realize the great statement that "men are, that they might have joy." (2 Nephi 2:25.)

24

Lessons we can learn from the faith of a child

"EXCEPT YE BECOME AS LITTLE CHILDREN"

The faith of children has always helped me to realize how close our Heavenly Father really is to us. Children's prayers have also taught me that our Heavenly Father doesn't expect each prayer to be long or for us to use big words. My granddaughter Lisa doesn't pray very long, and she doesn't use big words. But I know that her prayers are heard and answered because she loves her Heavenly Father and he loves her.

When I was six years old, my mother took me to the groundbreaking service for our new chapel in Santa Monica, California. As we arrived, Mother noticed that I had brought the small sand shovel that I usually took on our family outings to the beach. I had hoped that I could help by digging some ground at the chapel site. They let me use my shovel that first day, and my faith was increased because I helped to build a church for our Heavenly Father. My, how good I felt! The seeds of service and faith were planted in my heart. It is my wish to keep that same feeling of faith and desire to serve that I had as a six-year-old child.

Years later when my childhood dreams of a mission were realized, I was called far away to New Zealand. There I first met the Maori people, who have brought so much into my life by their simplicity, sincerity, and great faith.

One of my first assignments was to a Maori village called Judea, where the missionaries were helping in the construction of a small chapel. At that time I was trying to learn the Maori language. Each day I prayed to our Heavenly Father for help. And then one day I was surprised to be surrounded by Primary children. My prayer for help with the new language had been heard, and our Heavenly Father had inspired the branch president to send these children to help me. They followed me everywhere I went for weeks, talking to me in Maori. Their first lesson I shall remember forever:

Hei tito tito te ngeru me te whiro
Te kau peke runga te marama
Ka kata te kuri ki tana mahi pai
Ka oma te rihi me to punu.

The words sounded beautiful, but they were meaningless to a new missionary. I thought I was learning an old Maori war chant. What a surprise to me when I found out the children were teaching me "Hey, diddle diddle, the cat and the fiddle, the cow jumped over the moon. . . ."

How grateful I shall always be to those children of New Zealand for the wonderful blessing they brought to their new missionary!

Our family will not forget our little friend Becky, who invited us to hold our family home evening in her home. Even though her daddy was not a member of the Church, she wanted him to participate in a family home evening. Most of all, she wanted him to become a member of the Church.

Becky's daddy said he would be glad to have us go to their home for family home evening. We had a beautiful time together. The spiritual lesson was followed by refreshments, some games, and family prayer. As we were saying goodnight, Becky looked up at me and asked, "Bishop Simpson, will you do me a favor?"

"Of course," I answered, "anything you say."

"Will you please baptize my daddy for me?"

That request, filled with the hope and faith of a child, sank deeply into the heart of her daddy, and it was just a few weeks later that his baptism was performed.

No wonder Jesus said, "Except ye . . . become as little children, ye shall not enter into the kingdom of heaven." (Matthew 18:3.)

25

Teaching gospel principles in the home

OUR RESPONSIBILITY TO OUR CHILDREN

Recently I was invited to visit the detention home of a large city. In accepting the opportunity of interviewing some of the youngsters, as on previous occasions, I was not surprised to be confronted with some rather typical American youths who seemed to be anything but juvenile delinquents or so-called criminals in embryo. Too frequently, the story that came from their lips was about parents who were either completely indifferent or whose heavy hand in extracting obedience had seemingly forgotten the great example of love as taught and demonstrated by the Master some two thousand years ago. The innermost feelings of these youngsters in trouble seemed to be expressed in the two most frequently requested hymns at their regular devotional hour. They were: "Do What Is Right" and "Love at Home."

Many persons today are successful beyond question. By all of the usual standards of measurement for success, they have "got it made," as we say.

But we mustn't feel too relaxed on this "all's well" philosophy until we consider some facts that are even more important than social acceptance, professional and technical skill, or financial security. A report issued by the FBI reveals that a six-year population increase of 8 percent in this nation was accompanied by an appalling 40 percent increase in crime. In simple fact, lawlessness is moving ahead of us and five times as fast! This same report reveals the equally disturbing fact that 70 percent of our auto thefts and more than 50 percent of all robberies, burglaries, and larceny are committed by youngsters nineteen years of age and under.

These misguided youth cannot be dismissed from our minds lightly as that "unruly bunch from the other side of town." They are ordinary, everyday teenagers from all types of homes from both sides of town. They are our sons and daughters with the same deep-down desires for social acceptance, success in business, and a happy family life that you and I were dreaming about not too many years ago; and no matter how well we seem to be, generally speaking, we have never "got it made" until our children are raised and successfully launched into a happy and well-adjusted maturity of their own.

Yes, home is the very core of human society, and love must be the basis of human endeavor and happiness. President David O. McKay said: "No other success can compensate for failure in the home." Too often we look to the Sunday School teachers, the public schools, or someone else to make up the difference, but there is nothing in all this world that can take the place of home and the fundamental instruction of unity, love, and moral teaching that each parent owes his children.

No sooner had Moses passed the Ten Commandments to his people than the admonition came to Israel as recorded in the sixth chapter of Deuteronomy: "And these words, which I command thee this day, shall be in thine heart; And thou shalt teach them diligently unto thy children, and thou shalt talk of them when thou sittest in thine house, and when thou walkest by the way, and when thou liest down, and when thou risest up." (Deuteronomy 6:6-7.)

Since the beginning of time, God has never revoked this admonition to parents. We have a continuing obligation to teach God's laws diligently to our children and we should do it inside the home or, in the Lord's words, "when thou sittest in thine house." If the Lord were speaking today about this obligation, he would probably add a warning about addiction to the TV screen. This teaching of children must be a full-time job, from morning till night, "when thou liest down, and when thou risest up."

The most profitable time parents could spend today would be a prearranged family home evening, by appointment, with all other matters set aside; a precious hour or two when parents and children would communicate with one another and perhaps learn together about some meaningful scriptures and resolve a family problem or two without bickering and selfishness. It could be a time to discuss and appreciate more fully the blessings of living in this day of the world's history and in this great land of liberty. This family home evening could include some planned social activity and, to the added delight of all the youngsters, some refreshments.

Such a planned evening once each week could do so much to better guarantee family unity, which after all is the source of practically all real happiness and in very fact the foundation of America's strength. A kind and loving Heavenly Father has instructed us how to teach our children. As Paul wrote to the Ephesians: "And, ye fathers, provoke not your children to wrath; but bring them up in the nurture and admonition of the Lord." (Ephesians 6:4.)

How often we unthinkingly drive our children from us through selfish, impatient directions when all we need do is follow the Lord's way with "love unfeigned, reproving betimes with sharpness, when moved upon by the Holy Ghost; and then showing forth afterwards an increase of love toward him whom thou hast reproved, lest he esteem thee to be his enemy." (D&C 121:43.)

An unknown poet has indeed captured the importance of the parents' role during a child's formative years when he said:

I took a piece of plastic clay
And idly fashioned it one day,
And as my fingers pressed it, still
It moved and yielded to my will.

I came again when days were past:
That bit of clay was hard at last.
The form I gave it still it bore,
And I could fashion it no more!

I took a piece of living clay,
And gently pressed it day by day,
And moulded with my power and art
A young child's soft and yielding heart,

I came again when years had gone:
It was a man I looked upon.
He still that early impress bore,
And I could fashion it no more!

Are we too busy, parents? Isn't there enough time to carry out our sacred trust and partnership with God? He sends us spirit children to occupy for a short season the temporal bodies that we provide. Then we must teach them the pathway they must travel for day-to-day happiness and, most important of all, for the privilege of eventually regaining his presence after a fruitful and profitable mortal existence. If we are too busy for this, we are just too busy, and we must make some changes in order to fulfill our first and foremost obligation to God, the proper training and teaching of our children.

26

Finding the key to the hearts of young people

OUR YOUTH: THE HOPE OF THE WORLD

It was once my privilege to listen to an outstanding talk given by John M. Claerhout, director of the Explorer Division, Boy Scouts of America. He discussed the dilemma of youth and in the process delineated some very interesting findings about today's young people. His conclusions were based on some authentic national surveys, some personal interviews involving the reactions of thousands of young people, and some in-depth studies. The conclusions were clear and, to me, extremely significant. I would like to share some of them with you.

1. Today's youth are better trained intellectually than ever before in the history of the world.
2. Today's young people, on the other hand, are more lonely. (Their friendships are shorter in duration and more shallow in nature.)
3. They have more trouble with authority (home authority, school authority, and civil authority).
4. Today's youth are prone to silence and withdrawal. (In my opinion, this is the greatest danger sign of all.)
5. Most young people today are less willing or able to postpone gratifications.

6. Our youth of today seem less able to tolerate probabilities and compromise. They demand results. It must be black or white. Anything less than absolute is considered hypocrisy in their eyes.

7. Youth are found to be more afraid of risk or error.

As a church, we have a tendency to shrug our shoulders and say, "Well, that's the other segment of society. It doesn't apply to us." I've got news for those who draw such hasty conclusions. It does apply to some of our youngsters, and enough of them that we all need to be deeply concerned.

There are those of us who do a great job of providing spiritually rewarding experiences for the young people who are active and cooperative but would rather not be bothered with those young people who might rock the boat a little or be inconvenient to reach.

We need to re-read the Savior's admonition about the lost sheep. We need to tell ourselves each day: "If this is Christ's church restored, best we be about his business in his appointed way." We boast to the world that the gospel has been restored in all of its fulness. It has been! Our obligation is to all.

Indeed, we live in a time of grave concern. We live in an age of protest, but even this is not without its lighter side. For example, this article from the Ames (Iowa) *Daily Tribune*: "As was probably inevitable, the form of protest against something or other that started out with the burning of draft cards is spreading. Somebody in St. Joseph, Missouri, burned his library card to protest an increase in the overdue book fine. A student at the University of New Mexico burned his Social Security card to protest policies which required one to work for a living.

"This isn't the ultimate," the article goes on to say. "We're waiting for somebody to burn his birth certificate for having been brought into this 'vale of tears' without his consent and then being required to perform the involuntary act of breathing in and out all day long."

An anonymous questionnaire was once given to almost a thousand sophomores in college. Two of the questions were: "Do you love your parents? Do you respect your parents?" Ninety-three percent answered the first question affirmatively. But only 51 percent checked "yes" for the second answer. Love parents? Why, of course. Respect parents? Well, we're not quite sure.

Every eighth student was called in and asked, "Can you help us understand the difference between the 93 percent and the 51 percent?" One girl's response covers most of the answers. She said: "Sure, I love my parents. They mean well. But respect? Well, let me put it this way. I came home one day and told my mother that our high school club was going to have an overnight party at our house. My mother turned pale. I told her that chaperones were no longer in, and she turned even paler. You see, I hoped that she would say, 'No, you aren't,' and get me out of it, because I didn't have the courage to say 'no' to the others. But instead, my mother called the parents of the other girls and asked them what she should do. Listening, I could hear that the other mothers wanted us girls to be popular. They didn't want us to seem like 'kooks' to the others, and so they decided: 'Let's say yes this time.' In short, my mother discovered her values and mine by taking a telephone poll!"

Now anyone with even the most casual contact with the principles of the Church would never need to rely on a telephone poll of neighbors to give a straight answer. Above all people, we have the key to the hearts of youth. That key is found in our programs for our youth where they become involved with others, put into motion by worthy, conscientious leaders, and interpreted at the local level to meet the needs of youth in the ward or branch.

You would be thrilled to see a group of young people down in the Mesa, Arizona, area who developed a "Grow a Friend" program as a missionary effort. It was their idea. They drew up the rules; they implemented it; and each of these young people went out to "grow a friend"—not just over the weekend. They took weeks and weeks to grow a friend, and you would be amazed at the number of convert baptism that came into the Church through these ideas of our young people and their program.

In Logan, Utah, another group of young people gathered around their bishop, who had vision and foresight. This bishop decided that digging post holes or thinning beets wasn't exactly the young people's idea of meaningful participation in the welfare program of the Church, and so he asked them to decide what they would like to do. Do you know what these young people decided? They decided that on Friday evenings they would like to go to the homes of shut-ins and there perhaps prepare dinner; then have a little program afterwards, and, where the occasion was appropriate, and with the bishop's approval, conduct a sacrament meeting service, that they might be able to bring to these shut-ins a blessing that they were not otherwise receiving.

And so young people have great ideas. They want to be involved; they want to do things; but sometimes we don't give them all the room they need to make these decisions and carry out their plans.

One of the important aims of our Aaronic Priesthood youth programs is to provide for maximum youth involvement, to give the youth an opportunity to assist in the planning of those activities found in the regular priesthood and auxiliary programs of the Church.

Another important objective is to provide maximum opportunity for youth leadership training. President David O. McKay made a statement that is very significant for all of us. He said: "The spirituality of a ward will be commensurate with the activity of the youth in that ward."

Simply stated, our aim is to involve the youth and thus raise the level of spirituality in the wards, stakes, and missions—yes, throughout the entire Church. Now, spirituality depends upon activity. I believe in youth. As we involve them in meaningful responsibilities, they rise to the challenge. You've seen it, and I've seen it. Youth will usually set their own standards of performance even higher than we set them.

Let me take you to another group of young people. The bishop thought it might be a good idea for them to perhaps be the sacrament meeting speakers on the fifth Sunday night in those months where there was a fifth Sunday. And so he asked the class officers of the young people to decide how they might want to handle the first meeting. He gave them some guidelines, but he was holding his breath. He had no idea what they might come up with. But as he came back into their meeting, which had been left under the direction of the priests group leader, a fine young man and a good leader, they were bubbling over. They said: "Bishop, we're excited about this, and we want to talk about reverence. We're not happy with the reverence in our ward." Why, this bishop couldn't have been more pleased. Here were the young people who wanted to do something about reverence; and many ward members have testified that it was their finest sacrament meeting in a long, long time.

There is a teenage bundle of energy and enthusiasm living at our house. He has just become eligible for driver training, and all of a sudden even food takes second place. It's absolutely fantastic. He has only one thing in mind. He wants to get behind that wheel all by himself. He wants to solo. He wants to decide whether the car goes right or left. He wants to start and stop the car when he wants to start and stop. He wants to be in the driver's seat! There are nearly half a million teenagers in the

Church who want to do more than we are letting them do. They want to be part of the action. They no longer feel content in the back seat, and while we get upset about it, I supppose Heavenly Father just smiles and would probably call it a part of eternal progression. And I think that is just about what it is. Each human being is endowed with a God-given desire to achieve, to peek over the next horizon, to develop and mature on schedule. It's just as natural as the night following the day.

As new maturity comes to our wonderful young people, there is an automatic device inside that turns a bright green light on and says GO! It says DO!—try out those new muscles; use that newly acquired concept, that new bit of knowledge that is now yours. And "go" they will, and "do" they will. The only thing that is uncertain is "when" will they go and "what" will they do? That's where you and I come in. This church has a divine program conceived through the hearts and minds of men whom we sustain as prophets, seers, and revelators.

The official activities of this Church are wholesome. They are fulfilling. They are activities that lead to exaltation and provide the key to happiness every inch along the way. But something has to happen—something needs to happen inside of you and me—something has to happen to us as leaders before the ultimate can be achieved. And this can only happen provided priesthood leaders learn their duty and live worthy to lead with inspiration; provided our priesthood and auxiliary programs are used as intended by our wonderful leaders; provided officers and teachers live worthy of emulation; provided also that officers and teachers live worthy of the personal inspiration that will temper the program appropriately to meet the local needs of our youth; and provided parents are willing to encourage their young people in the ways of truth and right.

These are our challenges. And in conclusion, may I give you this final challenge: listen to the pleas of youth. Listen carefully. They are talking to us every day. It may not always be in a word; sometimes it's in an act, but listen to the youth. They are sincere; they are trying to tell us something.

Recognize the strength of youth. They are no longer little babes; they are no longer little children. They are young adults. They want to get out of the back seat. They want to sit at our side, and once in a while they want to take hold of the wheel, and I think they should have that opportunity as appropriate.

Each of us must live in such a way that the Lord can use us in order that we might train our youth, for they are the hope of the world. There is no hope greater than this, for this is his church, and this is his work. May God bless us to realize it and do something about it.

27

The special privileges and potentialities of LDS women

A FRANK TALK WITH YOUNG WOMEN

One evening a faithful and wonderful Laurel adviser stood to present a carefully prepared lesson when suddenly she was prompted to forgo the regular lesson and discuss the tragedy of immorality. About halfway through the lesson, impatient horn honking was heard from the church parking lot. Finally, it stopped, and the car with its youthful male occupant sped away. Following the inspirational discussion in the classroom, one tearful young lady lingered after the others had departed to confide in her leader that the honking had been for her. Then she said: "I had decided that tonight was going to be the biggest night of my life, and that horn toot was the signal that all of the arrangements were complete, and he was waiting. What you said and how you said it has saved me from the most serious mistake of my life, and I shall never forget it."

A few years ago, I listened intently as President David O. McKay issued a most vital challenge to a new Presiding Bishop of the Church. Among other things, Bishop John H. Vandenberg was told about his prime responsibility for thousands of young men throughout the world. Then came a most explicit direction from the lips of a living prophet: "Bishop," he said, "your concern must be just as great for the girls of corresponding ages."

In the spirit of this firm but kindly direction, I choose to talk frankly with the girls—those young women with stars in their eyes, great hope in their hearts, but, in far too many cases, uncertain minds in a fast-moving, impatient, and ever-changing society. I approach this subject with a fervent prayer in my heart, a prayer that you girls will consider my intrusion into your private world of hopes, dreams, and aspirations in a kindly way, that you will welcome me as a friend, deeply concerned for your happiness, anxious for your well-being. Yes, also concern for that eternal but elusive hope of fulfillment that floods the heart of every normal young woman as her thoughts turn to things tender, things loving, and things spiritual. Yes, tender thoughts about possible motherhood, loving thoughts about loyal and eternal companionship, spiritual thoughts about a sacred commission given only to the daughters of a kind and loving Heavenly Father. You received this commission personally from Heavenly Father upon leaving his presence not too many years ago.

Once I heard a girl say, "What's the use? What am I good for?" Well, one mighty important point would be that you are here by assignment from your Heavenly Father to prove yourself worthy of his ultimate blessing. In his own words: ". . . we will prove them herewith, to see if they will do all things whatsoever the Lord their God shall command them." In this passage of scripture, Heavenly Father talks about passing a test in order to come to this earth. This you have done. You have already demonstrated your ability to excel. Then in referring to our performance in this life, he makes the wonderful promise that "all who prove obedient shall have glory added upon their heads for ever and ever." (Abraham 3:25-26.)

God's house is a house of order, and you exist by personal and direct commission as part of that order and plan. It is important to you that you are created in his image.

". . . God created man in his own image, in the image of God created he him; male and female created he them." (Genesis 1:27.) How fortunate you are to know and understand this simple truth. Relatively few in the world accept it. Your every thought and action should be on a higher plane just in the knowledge that you are a part of him, that you know that God personally fathered your spirit, that in you is a spark of divinity, and that with it comes the power to reason and to think to achieve dominion and eternal glory, but it can only happen on his terms, on his terms of righteousness.

"What's the use?" "What am I good for?" Why, young lady, without you and others like you, life would stop, and the very foundation of God's master plan would be frustrated.

Can any young woman remain unmoved in the thought that within her is the potential of creation, of providing earthly bodies for spirits previously created by him? No mortal has honor greater than this. Yours is a possible partnership with Heavenly Father in perpetuating the process of life. The very thought is overwhelming. The decision to participate with him demands the best that is in you. It must be premeditated, planned, never by impulse. This sacred process requires worthiness.

Just the other day our family purchased a new radio. We were all anxious to try it out when a member of the family called attention to the bold print on the attached booklet which read: "Before playing your radio, read this instruction book carefully." The first thing we found out was that if it had been plugged into an improper source, costly damages would have resulted. Several other facts were revealed that proved important to the successful operation, preservation, and enjoyment of the instrument.

Vital instructions pertaining to your life have been given through a long line of prophets. These instructions must be understood and carried out if you are to enjoy happiness and success. Is human life less important than a forty-dollar radio? You must know the rules if you are going to play the game. If you want a particular blessing, you must be willing to abide by the law upon which that blessing is predicated. (See D&C 130:20-21.)

It was never intended that we spend our time groping in the dark. The prophets have provided us with the greatest handbook of instructions ever published. In the scriptures we find the guidelines, the rules of life, the answer to every problem. It is recorded that "where there is no vision, the people perish. . . ." (Proverbs 29:18.)

How is your vision, girls? Is vision possible without knowledge? Can you really expect to do well in any game without knowing the rules of that game and then following those rules to the best of your ability? May I invite you to know God's will concerning you.

If you are to be faced with the sacred obligation of someday providing bodies for God's spirit children, it seems to me that your personal health habits should be just as perfect as you can make them. Liquor and tobacco have been forbidden by the Lord. We are all expected to eat proper food, to rest adequately, to work vigorously. Partaking of those barriers to good health and a sound mind just for the sake of social acceptance while turning your back on an obligation to be physically prepared for a divine partnership is, to my way of thinking, inexcusable.

Allow me to share with you just one brief example of how important it is. Did you know, young ladies, that a recent survey revealed that the incidence of stillborn children among premature births is 400 percent higher among smoking mothers? No wonder God has declared: "Know ye not that ye are the temple of God, and that the Spirit of God dwelleth in you? If any man defile the temple of God, him shall God destroy; for the temple of God is holy, which temple ye are." (1 Corinthians 3:16-17.) In reality, it is we who destroy ourselves by ignoring his counsel.

"Nevertheless neither is the man without the woman, neither the woman without the man, in the Lord." (1 Corinthians 11:11.) This is God's equation for exaltation. It is just as true as 2+2=4. It is an eternal truth. It is unchangeable.

Everyone talks about the "new morality." Any departure from God's moral code is unapproved in his sight. He is the same yesterday, today, and forever. His plan for our happiness is no different. It, too, is unchangeable. On this premise, there may be a new immorality advocated by deceitful men, but there can never be a new morality. Only the adversary has a vacillating, ever-changing program always geared to trap the uninformed, the misled, those who choose to run the risk of questionable company.

Oh, youth of the noble birthright, don't give yourselves to the father of all lies—that deceitful one who would consider your downfall as a major victory. Don't be impatient.

Speaking of impatience, a faithful young lady in Southern California had this perplexing problem. Jim, who was in the service, was leaving for overseas duty immediately. He was pushing for marriage before his departure but had to overcome a particular problem before he could offer her the kind of marriage she had always dreamed of. She did love him. She did want to marry him, but her wonderful parents were insistent that the three-month courtship had scarcely been long enough to really know. Finally, the decision was made to wait. Their correspondence during the ensuing twelve months while he was away was on a very high plane. Their love grew. Each discovered an ability to discuss things in letters that had found no place in their lighter conversation during a date. Then he returned. I am happy to report their love for one another has been sealed in the house of the Lord; their first little one is a reality, and another wonderful family unit is well on its way to exaltation and eternal life.

Young ladies, the highway of disillusionment is teeming with girls who said, "Just this once" or "Everybody else does it." Do these phrases sound familiar? Another favorite trap sounds like this: "You would if you really loved me." Just imagine the irony of giving up all that is good, all that is truth, all that is sacred, including the trust and faith of loved ones, Church leaders, plus your own good name and personal dignity just on the basis of a smooth talker who feigns love with his lips but wants only to use you for a few minutes of selfish lust and animal gratification. Girls, you stay sweet. If you've made a mistake, correct it. It will be about the best decision that you will ever make. The Lord stands ready to help, for we have his word: "Behold, I stand at the door, and knock; if any . . . hear my voice, and open the door, I will come in to him, and will sup with him, and he with me." (Revelation 3:20.)

But please remember, you must make the first move. It is you who must open the door. He will be there and very likely in the form of a faithful teacher who feels prompted to change her prepared lesson. It could be you who will say in return, "Thanks. What you said and how you said it saved me from the most serious mistake of my life, and I shall never forget it."

God loves you wonderful girls. Don't you let him down. You have a special function to perform with him as your partner. Be worthy of that privilege. And this final thought, girls: the priesthood cannot achieve its ultimate destiny without a faithful female companion. No girl will ever achieve her ultimate destiny without a worthy priesthood companion at the head of her home. May this be your undeviating goal.

28

Why priesthood leaders are specially chosen servants

MANY ARE CALLED, BUT FEW ARE CHOSEN

Those who hold the priesthood in The Church of Jesus Christ of Latter-day Saints are specially chosen servants of the Lord in this day. Why are they special? Let me give you five important things to think about:

1. God the Father and his Son Jesus Christ have appeared in this time of the world's history.
2. All of the keys and powers of the eternal priesthood of God, with all of its attendant authority and blessings for mankind, have been restored to the earth, nevermore to be removed.
3. No less than nine heavenly beings have appeared by assignment in our time of the world's history to assist in this restoration: God the Father, his Son Jesus Christ, the apostle Peter, accompanied by James and John, John the Baptist, Moroni, Elijah, and Elias.
4. Three additional books of scripture, totalling 835 pages, have been revealed for the further guidance of mankind and to lend additional direction in these perilous times.
5. Last but not least, a living prophet stands at our head and presides over us and gives us the will of the Lord, up-to-the-minute evidence of continuous revelation.

Now, any one of the foregoing facts should rate banner headlines in every newspaper in the world, but about the only response we get from more than three billion people who are supposedly thirsting for truth is, in effect, "Don't rock the boat," or "Who do you think you are to make such fantastic claims as visits from on high, the only true priesthood, additional scriptures, and a living prophet?"

I do not know all there is to know, but there are a few things I do know by personal revelation, and I think the Spirit of the Lord is anxious to confirm these same truths within each member of the Church if he has not done so already.

The scriptures declare that many are called, but few are chosen. Do you think that there might be a possibility that you have not only been called but may be chosen as well? Why not!

"Behold, there are many called, but few are chosen. And why the they not chosen?" The Lord tells us why they are not chosen, and here are his reasons:

"Because their hearts are set so much upon the things of this world, and aspire to the honors of men, that they do not learn this one lesson—

"That the rights of the priesthood are inseparably connected with the powers of heaven, and that the powers of heaven cannot be controlled nor handled only upon the principles of righteousness." (D&C 121:34-36.)

You are special! And furthermore, the Lord has something in mind for you to do about it starting right now. The Church has need of every member. A recurring theme during the life of the Savior as he taught the people was that each man is his brother's keeper. No priesthood obligation is more important. The scriptures say something very similar but in another way that I like very much: ". . . when thou art converted, strengthen thy brethren." (Luke 22:32.)

No one takes upon himself the covenant of baptism nor the honor of the priesthood except he also receives the obligations associated with Church membership and priesthood affiliation.

The world today tells you to leave your friend alone. He has the right to come and go as he pleases. The world tells you that persuasion to attend church or priesthood meeting or to discard a bad habit might lead to frustration and undue pressures; but again I repeat the word of the Lord: You are your brother's keeper, and when you are converted, you have an obligation to strengthen your brother.

"But," you say, "I wouldn't know what to say or how to go about it. I am just a deacons quorum president." And to this the Lord answers that he gives no assignment to the children of men except he prepares a way for them to accomplish that which he has given them to do. He also says: "Therefore, verily I say unto you, lift up your voices unto this people; speak the thoughts that I shall put into your hearts, and you shall not be confounded before men; for it shall be given you in the very hour, yea, in the very moment, what ye shall say."

Now at this point the Lord gives a commandment that we must speak in his name with solemnity of heart and in the spirit of meekness, and then he concludes with this promise: ". . . inasmuch as ye do this the Holy Ghost shall be shed forth in bearing record unto all things whatsoever ye shall say." (D&C 100:5-8.)

Following this divine formula will take your contact with a friend out of the usual lip-to-ear communication category. With the help of the Holy Ghost, there will be a penetration into the heart of your friend. He will be persuaded through a wonderful spiritual process that is reserved for worthy members of the Church. It is the same process by which converts are brought into the

Church and will be an important spiritual gift for each of you to develop and improve on a continuing basis.

Yes, the Church has need of every member, and the list of indifferent members is much too long; it concerns the First Presidency; it concerns the Lord.

There will not be a sign or miracle in the heavens to wake people up. It was decided aeons ago that people would be helped by people so far as the Lord's work is concerned. This is an eternal principle and process: ". . . when thou art converted, strengthen thy brethren." The task is largely up to those of us who are active in our priesthood quorums, and the responsibility is upon the newest deacon as well as the high priest of longest standing.

May I conclude with a word of caution as the Lord gave it to the Prophet Joseph Smith. He said this: "What I say unto one I say unto all; pray always lest that wicked one have power in you, and remove you out of your place." (D&C 93:49.)

"Many are called, but few are chosen." What a tragedy to be foreordained or to be chosen or to be called and ordained only to have the adversary "remove you out of your place." Don't allow it to happen. Live beyond his grasp, for I can promise you that there are limits beyond which Satan cannot reach. He will not have claim on the righteous. The challenge for each of us is to stand worthy that we might better assist our brother back into the circle of activity, and may our efforts to do so be centered in that glorious revelation which is pure poetry in a scriptural setting:

". . . let virtue garnish thy thoughts unceasingly; then shall thy confidence wax strong in the presence of God; and the doctrine of the priesthood shall distil upon thy soul as the dews from heaven.

"The Holy Ghost shall be thy constant companion, and thy scepter an unchanging scepter of righteousness and truth; and thy dominion shall be an everlasting dominion, and without compulsory means it shall flow unto thee forever and ever." (D&C 121:45-46.)

What a promise! What a challenge! Are you special? Why, of course, you are! Are you your brother's keeper? Most certainly! If not you, who? Who else would do it if you didn't do it as a priesthood holder?

Are you converted? You most certainly are, whether you recognize it or not, and "when thou art converted, strengthen thy brethren"—for the Church has need of every member.

29

Helping heads of families magnify their priesthood

THE ROAD BACK

As we visit stake conferences each week, few experiences are more satisfying than that little nudge on the arm from the stake president as he points out some good brother just taking his place on the third row, and then he whispers a few choice comments about some recent changes in that man's life. Sometimes it is about response to a faithful and patient home teacher; frequently, about the faith and prayers of a patient wife being answered in a glorious way. Too often the change has come about following adversity. Some are adversities that might have been avoided, but most important of all, he is back. He is on course again. He is feeling the joy of service to others, perhaps to some other wonderful men who need the same kind of helping hand that was extended toward him at that right moment. There are far too many who trod the futile path that leads to nowhere.

An air traffic control tower recently established radio contact with a plane that was streaking across the radarscope, obviously not on proper course. The pilot was asked to report his situation. The controller's voice seemed urgent. The pilot responded to the tower with this classic observation: "We are making wonderful time, but we are hopelessly lost."

I wonder how many persons there might be in the world who are making wonderful time but without direction. Of what value is speed if the direction is without purpose? Someone has written: "A destination is a fine thing to have. If a man does not know to what port he is steering, no wind is favorable to him; and if he doesn't know where he is now, he cannot very well set a course. How hard he rows, or how good his engine is—these do not count in his favor unless he has a good definition of his objective. Hard work is often robbed of its reward by poor planning."

I was touched by the story of one highly successful business executive who responded graciously and humbly to a call to serve in his elders quorum presidency. Upon being asked the direct question: "What brought you back?" he responded, "Well, I have never told anyone before, but this is what happened:

"One morning while shaving, I overheard my six-year-old son singing from the next room. He was singing a little song I had heard him sing dozens of times before, 'I Am a Child of God'; but somehow that morning when he came to the part that says, 'Lead me, guide me, walk beside me, help me find the way,' I had the feeling that he was singing directly to me. I just stood there and listened. Within seconds, my whole life seemed to pass in review; and it really came home with full force that some changes had to be made, especially when he came to the part, 'Teach me all that I must do, To live with him some day.' "

This good man confesses today that these simple words from the lips of his own child reached his heart as a personal plea. The plea was from a child of God who has been placed in his custody to be delivered back some day into Heavenly Father's presence. He concluded his answer to this question by stating that he decided then and there that he had something important to do, something more important than anything else in the world for a little fellow who still loved his daddy in spite of many personal failings.

Let me tell you about a man who was attending a patio party one Sunday afternoon at the home of a business associate who happened to live next door to a Latter-day Saint meetinghouse. As the sacrament meeting got underway, the strains of the organ could be clearly heard over the back fence and seemed to be somewhat incongruous to the tinkle of ice being placed in the cocktail glasses. There were some uncomplimentary jokes and the usual snide remarks about religious fanatics, when all of a sudden the strains of the opening song broke the warm summer afternoon air. It was "Come, Come, Ye Saints." The party tempo was warming up, and by now the church music was all but unnoticed—unnoticed by all but one, a man whose grandmother had walked across the plains pulling a handcart. His mind withdrew from the party. For the first time in many years, he spent some minutes in sincere reflection concerning his birthright.

About ten minutes later, the sacrament song came drifting across the back fence. Unknowingly, a chorister—inspired in her calling, I am sure—had selected, "I Know That My Redeemer Lives." And way down deep, he knew it too, but it had been a long, long time. From that moment on, he was attending a patio party in body, but mentally and spiritually he was far above and beyond his environment of the moment.

It was almost an hour later, just about the time that he had lapsed back into the party mood, when the closing song, "We Thank Thee, O God, for a Prophet," reached his ear and mellowed his heart to the point of submission. Isn't it odd that a man should start his way back while attending a cocktail party? The Lord moves in a mysterious way, his wonders to perform.

The road back has been described by some as long and tedious and hard, but this is only as you stand at the starting end of that road. Those who have made the journey find that after the first difficult step, the road is sweet and pleasant to travel; the end rewards are beyond description.

God bless the home teacher who goes the extra mile, who conforms his love for the families he teaches with genuine interest and follow up. May I tell you about a pair of home teachers who felt impressed to discuss some recently published findings on lung cancer with a brother who had been plagued with the cigarette habit all of his adult life. As the home teachers said goodnight, the brother expressed appreciation for their message and concluded with, "I will try again, starting right now. I hope I can make it this time."

These home teachers could have been like most of us and waited until next month's visit to see if he succeeded, but they did not. They came by the very next morning at 6:45 A.M., unannounced and unexpected. They expressed keen interest in their visit of the night before and especially in his expressed desire to stop smoking. They went on to tell this brother that they had decided to fast and pray for him that day. "We will be thinking about you all day today, and not only that, we will also meet you here at your bus stop at 5:30 tonight to see how you made out." This man could not help but succeed. "These two wonderful home teachers are going to be fasting and praying for me. They are going to be thinking about me all day. Tonight they are going to meet me at the bus stop." He wanted to have a right answer for them. He did! With help, he succeeded. He came back.

A seventy-three-year-old man took that glorious road back after fifty long years of indifference. There were many tears on that occasion, tears of joy, yes—his and especially those of a loving companion who had waited those fifty long years for this most glorious moment. The tenderness of that occasion was mute evidence to the sanctification of that moment by a kind and loving Heavenly Father who stands always prepared to say, "Welcome back, my son."

Oh, that thousands might put aside their stubborn pride! Oh, that thousands might find the courage for that first giant step back! Oh, that thousands of fine upstanding men with great potential might place themselves in the hands of the Lord, for he has said: ". . . my yoke is easy, my burden is light." Oh, that thousands might give way to their real, deep-down inner feelings, for as President J. Reuben Clark, Jr., said: ". . . God has placed in every man's heart a divine spark, which never wholly goes out; it may grow dim, it may become hidden, almost smothered by the ashes of transgression; but the spark still lives and glows and can be fanned into flame by faith, if the heart is touched."

Those of you who sit reluctantly in the wings, find your patriarchal blessing, dust it off and read it again; contemplate deeply the Lord's personal message given to you alone. There is yet time. It's never too late to pick up the pieces. I feel confident that one of the Lord's favorite greetings is, "Welcome back, my son." May we find the way back where we belong.

30

The purposes and function of priesthood courts

COURTS OF LOVE

The hour was very late; the room was quiet except for the audible sobs of a young man who had just received the verdict of a Church court. Justice has taken its true course. There was apparently no alternative. The unanimous decision, following serious deliberation, fasting, and prayer, was excommunication.

After several minutes a weary face looked up, and the young man's voice broke the silence as he said, "I have just lost the most precious thing in my life, and nothing will stand in my way until I have regained it."

The process leading up to the court was not an easy one. Certainly, courage is a most important factor for every person who has seriously slipped but wants to get back on the Lord's side.

After the meeting was finished, the communications that followed the young man's dramatic statement of hope for the future were so reassuring. From some there were firm promises of help during the ensuing months of continuing repentance; from others a pat on the back and a handshake, with an eye-to-eye assurance that conveyed a feeling of confidence and the hand of fellowship. There was complete knowledge among all present at that meeting that all could be regained in the life of this young man if it were done in the Lord's way.

This young man had just taken his first giant step back. As an excommunicated member of the Church and with his heart determined to make things right, he was far better off than just a few days before with his membership record intact but carrying deceit in his heart that seemed to shout the word *hypocrite* with every move he made toward doing something in the Church.

This episode took place a few years ago. The young man's pledge has been fulfilled, and, in my opinion, no member of the Church stands on ground more firm than the man who has had the courage to unburden himself to his priesthood authority and to set things in order with his Master. What a relief to have once again the peace of mind that "passeth all understanding."

Priesthood courts of the Church are not courts of retribution. They are courts of love. Oh, that members of the Church could understand this fact!

The adversary places a fear in the heart of the transgressor that makes it so difficult for him to do what needs to be done; and in the words of James E. Talmage, "As the time of repentance is procrastinated, the ability to repent grows weaker; neglect of opportunity in holy things develops inability." (*Articles of Faith,* p. 114.) This simply means that doing what needs to be done will never be easier than right now. As in all other paths and guideposts that have been provided for us to achieve our eternal destiny of exaltation, there are no shortcuts.

Heavenly Father is not anti-progress: he is the author of eternal progression. In his own words, "For behold, this is my work and my glory—to bring to pass the immortality and eternal life of man." (Moses 1:39.)

Our achievement of eternal life adds glory to his name and is the only ultimate objective acceptable to a true Latter-day Saint.

Reduced to its simplest terms, our mission here in mortality is to overcome weakness of the flesh and all irregularities in our lives, to the point that our control of personal desires is sufficient to bring about a daily living and thinking pattern that will be compatible with his holy presence.

Be not disillusioned by doctrine of the adversary that there will likely be a magic point in eternity when all of a sudden selfish and improper actions are automatically eliminated from our being. Holy writ has confirmed time and time again that such is not the case, and prophets through the ages have assured us that now is the time to repent, right here in this mortal sphere. It will never be easier than now; and he who procrastinates the day or hopes for an alternate method that might require less courage waits in vain, and in the meantime, the possibilities grow dimmer. He is playing the game as Satan would have him play it, and exaltation in the presence of God grows more remote with each passing day.

To our bishops, may I say: Be available to your people. Let them know about the kindness and compassion that dominates your soul. Don't become so caught up in the business affairs of your ward administration that you fail to convey to your people all of these wonderful attributes referred to in the 121st section of the Doctrine and Covenants. I am talking about the attributes of kindly persuasion, long-suffering, gentleness, meekness, and love unfeigned.

Bishops, learn the great principle of delegation so that your heart and your mind can be free to counsel with the Saints. You are their common judge. There is no one else in the entire ward so designated by the Lord. It is to you that they must turn. You must be available to listen, and, equally important, you must live in such a way that the voice of heaven will find utterance through you for the blessing and edification of your people.

I am certain that a basic cornerstone of true justice is compassion. Perhaps even more important than the transgression itself is the sensitivity of a person's soul and his desire to repent and to follow the Master.

It would be so much easier for the sinner to talk about serious transgression to someone he had never seen before and would likely never see again; or better still, to talk in total seclusion to an unseen ear and receive forgiveness then and there from unseen lips. But in such a process, who would then be at his side in the struggling months ahead, as he attempts with great effort to make his repentance complete, as he strives to prevent a tragic recurrence?

Few, if any, men have the strength to walk that hill alone, and please be assured, it is uphill all the way. There needs to be help—someone who really loves you, someone who has been divinely commissioned to assist you confidentially, quietly, assuredly—and may I reemphasize the *confidentially,* for here again, Satan has spread the false rumor that confidences are rarely kept.

May I assure you that bishops and stake presidents are not in the habit of betraying these sacred confidences. Before being ordained and set apart, their very lives have been reviewed in that upper room in the temple by those divinely called as prophets, seers, and revelators. Without question, they are among the noble and great ones of this world and should be regarded as such by the Saints.

What a glorious plan this is! How reassuring to know that we all have hope for a total blessing, in spite of all the mistakes we have made; that there might be complete fulfillment; that we might enter his holy presence with our family units!

Even excommunication from this church is not the end of the world; and if this process is necessary in carrying out true justice, I bear you my personal and solemn witness that even this extreme penalty of excommunication can be the first giant step back, provided there follows a sincere submission to the Spirit and faith in the authenticity of God's plan.

These processes can only be carried out in this church through properly designated priesthood authority, for God's house is a house of order. All of this is made very clear in the Doctrine and Covenants:

> And again, verily I say unto you, that which governed by law is also preserved by law and perfected and sanctified by the same.
>
> That which breaketh a law, and abideth not by law, but seeketh to become a law unto itself, and willeth to abide in sin, and altogether abideth in sin, cannot be sanctified by law, neither by mercy, justice, nor judgment. Therefore, they must remain filthy still.
>
> All kingdoms have a law given;
>
> And there are many kingdoms; for there is no space in the which there is no kingdom; and there is no kingdom in which there is no space, either a greater or a lesser kingdom.
>
> And unto every kingdom is given a law; and unto every law there are certain bounds also and conditions.
>
> All beings who abide not in those conditions are not justified. (D&C 88:34-39.)

In other words, all beings who abide not in those conditions, all who fail to correct infractions of the eternal law by proper priesthood procedures that have been established for such corrections, are not acceptable to the Lord and will likely never be eligible for his presence. God bless us to accept eternal law and understand that there can be no other way.

31

The living water that comes from compliance with commandments

CONFORMING TO PRIESTHOOD PRINCIPLES

Throughout history men have always been looking for the easy way. There have been those who have devoted their lives to finding "the fountain of youth," a miracle water which would bring everlasting life. Today men are still seeking for similar treasures, some magic "fountain" that would bring forth success, fulfillment, and happiness. But most of this searching is in vain, because they are looking for shortcuts. Unless they turn to him who offered the Samaritan woman at Jacob's well a drink of living water, then their searching will indeed be in vain, for he told her: ". . . whosoever drinketh of the water that I shall give him shall never thirst; but the water that I shall give him shall be in him a well of water springing up into everlasting life." (John 4:14.) It is only this living water, the gospel of Jesus Christ, that can and will bring a happy, a successful, and an everlasting life to the children of men.

The living water that the Son of God offers is a set of divine principles. These principles are proven principles—they are priesthood principles which, when applied, can result in the blessings of eternity. How well you and I learn and practice these priesthood principles is not just important; it is *everything*. Everything worthwhile in your life, everything you hope and dream for, is embraced in priesthood principles.

The scriptures tell of some who have tragically disregarded priesthood principles. In the very beginning we can see Cain, a man whose birth gave his mother a great deal of joy, for she said, "I have gotten a man from the Lord. . . ." (Moses 5:16.) However, Cain departed from the principles taught to him by his parents and began to love Satan more than God.

"And Cain went into the field, and Cain talked with Abel, his brother. And it came to pass that while they were in the field, Cain rose up against Abel, his brother, and slew him.

"And Cain glorified in that which he had done, saying: I am free. . . ." (Moses 5:32-33.)

Cain's observation of a newfound freedom was false doctrine straight from the adversary. In reality he enslaved himself to a life of deceit and a life "shut out from the presence of the Lord." (Moses 5:41.) Cain brought this tragedy to his own life by disregarding priesthood principles. He refused to be his brother's keeper, and in so doing he sold his soul to the father of lies and murder.

We can also look at Saul, the promising young ruler of Israel who had every requirement of a great leader. Yet Saul disobeyed priesthood principles. He was given specific instructions by a prophet of God to lead the armies of Israel against the city of Amalek. But Saul rationalized and compromised those instructions. He acted on his own volition. He did that which he reasoned should be done rather than that which the prophet Samuel had instructed him to do.

On subsequent occasions Saul further violated priesthood principles, but just as with Cain, these misdeeds brought only tragedy and sorrow. Finally, Saul took his life by falling upon his own sword during a battle with the Philistines.

While the disregarding of priesthood principles has and does bring anguish and sorrow into people's lives, obedience to the principles of righteousness is that living water which brings a life of everlasting joy and fulfillment. The scriptures tell of many who have drunk of this living water and received everlasting joy.

One of the prime examples of a man who knew the value of adhering to priesthood principles and had the courage to live accordingly is Noah. In the face of ridicule and even at the peril of his life, Noah remained steadfast to the principles of the priesthood. The scriptures describe Noah's devotion in these simple, straightforward terms: "Thus did Noah, according to all that God commanded him, so did he." (Genesis 6:22.)

"And thus Noah found grace in the eyes of the Lord; for Noah was a just man, and perfect in his generation; and he walked with God. . . ." (Moses 8:27.) Noah tasted of the joy of life because he adhered firmly to the principles of righteousness.

In our time the distinction is just as clear; the living water on the one hand, sorrow and tragedy on the other. As the Lamanite prophet Samuel declared, ". . . for behold, ye are free; ye are permitted to act for yourselves; for behold, God hath given unto you a knowledge and he hath made you free.

"He hath given unto you that ye might know good from evil, and he hath given unto you that ye might choose life or death; and ye can do good and be restored unto that which is good, or have that which is good restored unto you; or ye can do evil, and have that which is evil restored unto you." (Helaman 14:30-31.)

The choice seems clear and obvious, but the sure test of truth must be applied by each of us. We must apply the principles of the priesthood in our own lives. To be taught truth is not enough. We must participate to be sure of the doctrine, to be certain of its truth. Only practice can bring peace of mind and that personal testimony which enables some to stand and declare, "I know that God lives." There stands not one man who speaks this kind of assuring testimony who did not have to first earn that right by compliance to priesthood principles.

No greater security can ever come into your life than the strength and power that comes through personal testimony. Your parents cannot give it to you without your cooperation. Neither can the Lord force it upon you, for that would be a violation of an eternal law called free agency.

Yes, that is the name of the game, free agency, and you are the team captain. You must direct the action in your life; and to do it intelligently, you must decide where the goal line is. You must decide which plays will work best to achieve that goal. Each day should mean another point or two scored in your favor. Which direction is the goal you seek? Why don't you think of a few major goals this very moment—can you think of one or two? Now ask yourself this question: "What are the rules in this vital game of life?" There is only one worthwhile direction. There is only one set of rules, and they are centered in priesthood principles.

What do you who hold the priesthood of God really want out of life? What do you see that is really worthwhile on that goal line that you are striving to cross? Would I be right in assuming that you would like a good portion of happiness in your life? Why, of course you would. Of what value is freedom to you, or perhaps peace of mind? I am certain that Heavenly Father would also like to see happiness be your lot, for he has said: ". . . men are, that they might have joy." (2 Nephi 2:25.)

Did you know that the gospel could guarantee freedom, for "the truth shall make you free"? (John 8:32.) The Savior of the world, I am sure, was talking about peace of mind when he said: "Peace I leave with you, my peace I give unto you; not as the world giveth, give I unto you. Let not your heart be troubled, neither let it be afraid." (John 14:27.)

Would you be interested in a guarantee of good health and physical strength to carry you along life's highway? There are some dramatic promises contained in the eighty-ninth section of the Doctrine and Covenants. Those who will observe God's rules of health may have all of those promises fulfilled.

Is knowledge one of your goals? The gospel teaches that man is saved no faster than he gains knowledge, and I am sure the Lord would have you use that knowledge intelligently, for "the glory of God is intelligence. . . ." (D&C 93:36.)

Are you interested in a financially sound future? You can be, if you stay out of debt and spend wisely. This has been the counsel of the Church leaders from the beginning.

Most holders of the priesthood would rather be industrious and progressive than lazy. The welfare plan of this great church tells us to reenthrone work as a ruling principle in our lives and to abolish the dole, which is a something-for-nothing program. There is no place for it in the gospel of Jesus Christ.

Then, of course, you would have as a goal the practicing of pure religion, undefiled, caring for the widows and the fatherless. Heavenly Father has given us the law of the fast, that the unfortunate might be provided for, and also a declaration that inasmuch as we do it unto one of the least of these, we have done it unto him; pure religion, undefiled, all a part of the gospel of Jesus Christ and implemented in the law of the fast.

We are all just human enough to ask the questions: What is in it for me? Is it worth the effort? What will the end result be? If the word of the Lord means anything to us at all, then the reasons for compliance are overwhelming, for in the seventy-sixth section of the Doctrine and Covenants, the Lord tells us explicitly about those who conform to priesthood principles in this life. May I quickly review some of the conditions and rewards that will most certainly be yours as you decide to conform and then do something about it. The seventy-sixth section of the Doctrine and Covenants says your friends and associates hereafter will be just like you:

Those who receive the testimony through compliance.

Those who were baptized in the right way by the proper authority.

Those who kept the commandments and received the Holy Spirit as a constant companion.

Those also who, with you, have prepared themselves for entrance into the house of the Lord, there to be "sealed by the Holy Spirit of promise" for all eternity to those who are nearest and dearest, the family unit.

Yes, it is they to whom the Father has promised all things.

It is they who will be anointed priests and kings of the Most High.

It is they who will receive of his fulness and of his glory.

This remarkable revelation further continues that "they are gods, even the sons of God." Does that mean anything to you? Is that worth striving for?

It states that all things are theirs, and "they are Christ's." As though that were not enough, it further states that they "shall dwell in the presence of God and his Christ forever and ever." Indeed, "These are they who are just men made perfect, whose bodies are celestial, whose glory is that of the sun, even the glory of God." (See D&C 76.)

I challenge all priesthood bearers to commit yourselves here and now to such a reward hereafter. How can anything be more important than this? The very next time you are faced with the decision of going along with the crowd in something that seems questionable or standing firm in what you know to be right, just remember that you are a priesthood bearer. Your commitment is to God; you must never defect to the enemy—you must remain above such things.

By so doing, you will find new strength. You will be given new power. You will discover the deep-down joy that comes with compliance to priesthood principles.

I testify to you that there is no success, no joy, no true fulfillment for us in this life or in the eternities unless our lives are in compliance with priesthood principles. This is the living water which can and should be a "well of water springing up into everlasting life."

I testify of the divinity of Him who offers the "living water" through compliance with the principles of the priesthood.

32

Eternal responsibilities for every Latter-day Saint man

OUR FUNDAMENTAL OBLIGATION: THE PRIESTHOOD

Our message to the world is that God lives, that the heavens have been opened, that priesthood authority has been restored, and that a living prophet stands at our head.

We regard as scripture that chapter of the Pearl of Great Price which records the precious thoughts and words of the Prophet Joseph Smith as he recounts the astounding events that occurred in the spring of 1820. He said he did it to "put all inquirers after truth in possession of the facts, as they have transpired. . . ." (Joseph Smith 2:1.) He further stated: ". . . I shall present the various events . . . in truth and righteousness. . . ." (Joseph Smith 2:2.)

You will remember that, after recounting some family history and commenting about religious unrest in the community, the Prophet told of being impressed by the scripture found in James chapter 1, verse 5, which reads: "If any of you lack wisdom, let him ask of God, that giveth to all men liberally, and upbraideth not; and it shall be given him." Then the Prophet said:

> Never did any passage of scripture come with more power to the heart of man than this did at this time to mine. It seemed to enter with great force into every feeling of my heart. . . .

. . . I at length came to the determination to 'ask of God,' concluding that if he gave wisdom to them that lacked wisdom, and would give liberally, and not upbraid, I might venture.

So, in accordance with this, my determination to ask of God, I retired to the woods to make the attempt. It was on the morning of a beautiful clear day, early in the spring of eighteen hundred and twenty. It was the first time in my life that I had made such an attempt, for amidst all my anxieties I had never as yet made the attempt to pray vocally. (Joseph Smith 2:12-14.)

Does this sound like a 14½-year-old boy? Then he said:

After I had retired to the place where I had previously designed to go, having looked around me, and finding myself alone, I kneeled down and began to offer up the desire of my heart to God. I had scarcely done so, when immediately I was seized upon by some power which entirely overcame me, and had such an astonishing influence over me as to bind my tongue so that I could not speak. Thick darkness gathered around me, and it seemed to me for a time as if I were doomed to sudden destruction.

But, exerting all my powers to call upon God to deliver me out of the power of this enemy which had seized upon me, and at the very moment when I was ready to sink into despair and abandon myself to destruction—not to an imaginary ruin, but to the power of some actual being from the unseen world, who had such marvelous power as I had never before felt in any being—just at this moment of great alarm, I saw a pillar of light exactly over my head, above the brightness of the sun, which descended gradually until it fell upon me.

It no sooner appeared than I found myself delivered from the enemy which held me bound. When the light rested upon me I saw two Personages, whose brightness and glory defy all description, standing above me in the air. One of them spake unto me, calling me by name and said, pointing to the other—*This is My Beloved Son. Hear Him!* (Joseph Smith 2:15-17.)

This is the most significant singular event in the world since the resurrection of the Lord and Savior Jesus Christ. The First Vision is the very foundation of this church, and it is my conviction that each member of this church performs his duty in direct ratio to his personal testimony and faith in the First Vision. How well do you believe this story?

No man having heard the Joseph Smith testimony can, in good conscience, remain on neutral ground.

Joseph Smith was an ordinary boy with a rather ordinary name, but he was now to become an extraordinary prophet. For nine long years following the First Vision Joseph prepared for the privilege of the priesthood. As you remember, it was John the Baptist who appeared on the banks of the Susquehanna in answer to a fervent prayer offered by Joseph Smith and Oliver Cowdery. How simple the words for such a historic occasion:

> *Upon you my fellow servants, in the name of Messiah, I confer the Priesthood of Aaron, which holds the keys of the ministering of angels, and of the gospel of repentance, and of baptism by immersion for the remission of sins; and this shall never be taken again from the earth until the sons of Levi do offer again an offering unto the Lord in righteousness.*
>
> He said this Aaronic Priesthood had not the power of laying on hands for the gift of the Holy Ghost, but that this should be conferred on us hereafter; and he commanded us to go and be baptized, and gave us directions that I should baptize Oliver Cowdery, and that afterwards he should baptize me.
>
> Accordingly, we went and were baptized. I baptized him first, and afterwards he baptized me—after which I laid my hands upon his head and ordained him to the Aaronic Priesthood, and afterwards he laid his hands on me and ordained me to the same Priesthood—for so we were commanded. (Joseph Smith 2:69-71.)

It was just a few weeks later that Peter, James, and John appeared to confer the Melchizedek Priesthood and the apostleship upon these same two men. That priesthood authority remains today in an unbroken chain. How reassuring to know that God's house is a house of order and that the same great leaders of 2,000 years ago were privileged to reestablish true priesthood authority on the earth. The logical sequence of events and the personages involved help to confirm the divine nature of all that transpired on that historic occasion.

It was in the following year, 1830, that the Church was organized. At last truth was established and continuing revelation was assured.

Then nearly six years later at the Kirtland Temple on a Sabbath afternoon, the Lord himself appeared in glorious vision to Joseph and Oliver. That same day Moses, Elias, and Elijah also appeared, each ancient prophet restoring an important function of the gospel. Listen again to the glorious description of the Savior's appearance as recounted by the Prophet Joseph Smith:

> The veil was taken from our minds, and the eyes of our understanding were opened.
>
> We saw the Lord standing upon the breastwork of the pulpit, before us; and under his feet was a paved work of pure gold, in color like amber.
>
> His eyes were as a flame of fire; the hair of his head was white like the pure snow; his countenance shone above the brightness of the sun; and his voice was as the sound of the rushing of great waters, even the voice of Jehovah. . . . (D&C 110:1-3.)

The Savior then delivered a message that we should all read on occasion. It is recorded in the 110th section of the Doctrine and Covenants.

Those of us who have accepted the obligation of priesthood have made a deep commitment, and there is really no excuse for failure, because "the Lord giveth no commandments [or commission] unto the children of men, save he shall prepare a way for them that they may accomplish the thing which he commandeth them." (1 Nephi 3:7.) With a promise like that, there is really no excuse for us to fail.

Now, after reviewing these divine appearances—God the Father; Jesus Christ, his Son; John the Baptist; Peter, James, and John; and other ancient prophets—doesn't this make you excited about this great work!

Knowing that these events transpired, if I were a young deacon all over again, I would pass the sacrament as if it were one of the most important things I had to do all week. My every act and my appearance would be in strict harmony with the dignity and honor of the position entrusted to me by the Savior.

The gathering of fast offerings would take on a rich, new meaning, and I would remind myself as I approached each home that I was the bishop's personal representative, that poor and needy people would be blessed more abundantly as a result of my efforts to participate in what James described as "pure religion and undefiled." (See James 1:27.)

If I were a young teacher or priest again, I would strive to really be an asset to my home teaching companion. I would try harder to cement friendships with the members we visit. I would attempt to lift people as the Savior did. My responsibility toward the sacrament would be regarded as a rich, spiritual experience, never to be taken lightly. To participate in a sacred ordinance with anything but our highest respect and best effort is a disservice to the people of the ward and a betrayal of the true Spirit of Christ.

If I were a young adult over 25 and still unmarried, I would start looking for someone who has the potential for perfection instead of someone who has already achieved it. Just off the record, and quite confidentially, it is my understanding that there is only one perfect girl produced in each century, and I have already found her; she is all mine.

If I were a young father just starting out, I would practice kindness, patience, and love unfeigned. I would check my priority system constantly just to make certain that my course was true and that eternal life was my destiny.

If I were a prospective elder, I would give myself to some kind of Church service and at the same time set out to improve my gospel scholarship on a daily basis so that my family could be sealed to me for all eternity.

If I were an active Melchizedek Priesthood holder, high councilor, member of the stake presidency, member of a bishopric, and especially if I had children at home, knowing all that I know about eternity, I would remember above all else the wise counsel of the past: that if you spend all your days and save the whole world but lose your own family, you will be counted as an unprofitable servant.

I would beseech all who hold the priesthood to ponder four great statements:

First, the words of God the Eternal Father, *"This is My Beloved Son. Hear Him!"* Not 2,000 years ago, but in our time.

Next, the memorable words of John the Baptist, who declared with authority: "Upon you my fellow servants, in the name of Messiah, I confer the Priesthood of Aaron. . . ." (D&C 13.) This also is in our day.

Third, the Savior's statement about "Peter, and James, and John, whom I have sent unto you, by whom I have ordained you and confirmed you. . . ." (D&C 27:12.) This is for us, in our time of the world's history.

And fourth, from Kirtland, as recorded by the Prophet Joseph: "We saw the Lord standing upon the breastwork of the pulpit, before us; and under his feet was a paved work of pure gold, in color like amber." (D&C 110:2.)

Indeed, fellow priesthood holders, these statements are not the idle words of men. We live in a remarkable time. The Lord has spoken in our day. You and I have received the message. Our fundamental obligation is to the priesthood of God, which cannot be regarded casually, as though it were a man-made club or a mere fraternal organization.

I testify with all the sobriety of my heart and soul that we are committed, that we are depended upon. All things are possible in the Lord. As we unite in our faith and determination, his work will be accomplished. May this obligation burn within us. May it never be dimmed. May we be excited about the opportunity that is ours as we move forward deliberately, in humility, and with constant preparation, and do what we have to do.

33

The grave obligations of those who hold the Aaronic Priesthood

A SEASON OF PREPARATION

One day in May I stood reverently with a large group of young Aaronic Priesthood bearers and their fathers on the banks of the beautiful Susquehanna River in Pennsylvania. We had assembled in quiet contemplation to commemorate one of the most significant events of history. The morning was fresh, the majestic river moved quietly and effortlessly southward, just as it has for ages. Only the songbird interrupted the silence. All was peaceful, perhaps very much like that eventful morning in 1829, for it was at this very location on May 15, 1829, that John the Baptist appeared—that same John whose privilege it was to immerse the Savior in the waters of baptism nearly 2,000 years ago. He had now been commissioned by heavenly priesthood authority to enact the important role of restoring the Aaronic Priesthood, thus confirming with priesthood authority the official opening of this final dispensation of time.

As we reflected on the magnitude of what had transpired at this place, each was lifted in his faith. The Holy Ghost reconfirmed in my heart then and there the truth of Joseph and Oliver's unusual experience at the hand of John the Baptist, and the continuity of authority from the ordination of Aaron by Moses, to this very time.

There are many who suppose that the Church was organized immediately following Joseph Smith's first vision. There was much to be learned, however, by this young lad. Many significant events needed to transpire, such as the translation of the Book of Mormon and the restoration of the priesthood before Christ's true church could be organized. It was nine years, for example, following Joseph's humble prayer before the conditions were right for this important step of priesthood restoration to be consummated on Susquehanna's banks, and still another year before the Church was organized.

President Joseph Fielding Smith made a most interesting observation concerning the events of that day of priesthood restoration:

> After the priesthood had been given to Joseph and Oliver and at the command of the heavenly messenger, they were baptized; then by the same messenger they were instructed to lay hands upon each other and *re-confer* the authority the angel had given them, thus placing the ordination and baptism in the proper relationship. These details, which would have been overlooked by imposters, tell us a significant tale and bear an appealing testimony of the truthfulness of these two men. (*Doctrines of Salvation,* Bookcraft, 1956, vol. 3, p. 91.)

Modern-day scriptures are explicit in designating the Aaronic Priesthood as preparatory: "And the lesser priesthood continued, which priesthood holdeth the key of the ministering of angels and the preparatory gospel." (D&C 84:26.)

Indeed the Lord's house is a house of order. It would have been out of sequence for the Melchizedek Priesthood to have been restored before the Aaronic. Consequently, it was several weeks before Peter, James, and John, those same stalwart apostles who held these keys during the meridian of time, appeared to Joseph Smith and Oliver Cowdery to make the restoration of the priesthood complete in this final dispensation.

Aaronic Priesthood is not only preparatory in the general sense, but certainly in a personal sense as well. Preparation for the higher priesthood should fill the expectant heart of every candidate for the Aaronic Priesthood, whatever his age or station in life. Before the babe is given solids, there must be milk. Before we run, we walk. Before we go to high school, we prepare through the elementary grades. So it is with priesthood. There needs to be a season of preparation for the active, growing Aaronic Priesthood holder before the greater obligations of Melchizedek Priesthood are received. That preliminary schooling for male members of the Church is, and always has been, Aaronic Priesthood.

Not only are individuals and dispensations prepared through the lesser priesthood, but great nations of people as well. So it was with ancient Israel. Due to immaturity and repeated failure in things of the "higher" law, Israel was given the carnal law through Moses as a preparatory process—a preparation that was to take centuries, down to the advent of the Savior.

From the beginning, Adam and those worthy leaders of recorded biblical history down to the days of Moses held the patriarchal order of the Melchizedek Priesthood. It was while receiving instructions face to face from God at Mount Sinai that Moses was commanded to ordain Aaron and his four sons to become priests in the Aaronic Priesthood: "And take thou unto thee Aaron thy brother, and his sons with him, from among the children of Israel, that he may minister unto me in the priest's office, even Aaron, Nadab and Abihu, Eleazar and Ithamar, Aaron's sons." (Exodus 28:1.)

Of course, this was a lesser order of the priesthood than that which permitted Moses to talk with God face to face. Aaron being the first to receive it, he has been honored to have this sacred authority identified with his name. This is the same practice we follow in referring to Melchizedek Priesthood. Rather than repeat the sacred name of Deity unnecessarily, it is wisdom in the Lord that we use instead the name of the great high priest Melchizedek, who according to history collected tithes from Father Abraham.

Our Heavenly Father's true priesthood was originally called "the Holy Priesthood, after the Order of the Son of God." (D&C 107:3.) The terms *Aaronic* and *Melchizedek* should always be used by Church members when referring to priesthood authority.

Because Book of Mormon history prior to the advent of the Savior makes reference to "priests and teachers," many persons are misled to suppose that Aaronic Priesthood authority was among them. The Nephites did not officiate under the authority of the Aaronic Priesthood. They were not descendants of Aaron, nor were there Levites among them. There is no evidence in the Book of Mormon that they held the Aaronic Priesthood until after Christ's ministry among them. On the other hand, the Book of Mormon tells us definitely that the priesthood they held and under which they officiated was the higher priesthood. The higher priesthood can, of course, officiate in every ordinance of the gospel. Jacob and Joseph were consecrated priests and teachers after this higher order. (See 2 Nephi 5:26; Alma 13:2; 43:2.)

To even suggest that Christ would establish a different gospel plan or priesthood organization on the western hemisphere is unthinkable. He personally spoke of "one fold" and "one shepherd" in referring to his contemplated visit to the American continent. (See John 10:16.)

During the Savior's ministry, the ancient role of the Aaronic Priesthood was changed to conform to the "new gospel" as introduced personally by the Son of God. As Paul said: "There is made of necessity a change also of the law." (Hebrews 7:12.)

The word *change* when applied to priesthood can be misleading. The power of the priesthood is unchangeable. Sometimes, due to misdeeds, man diminishes in his ability to handle priesthood authority. The word *change* above should be interpreted more accurately as "an alteration of implementation."

John the Baptist has been referred to as "the end and the beginning." It was he who terminated the ancient order of father-to-son succession of authority. It was he who witnessed an end to the carnal law of Moses through the atonement of Christ. It was also he who helped to usher in a new dispensation, as he baptized the Savior of mankind. His "changed" ministry continued with the full blessing and knowledge of the Christ until his imprisonment.

The following important alterations occurred in the Aaronic Priesthood during the ministry of Christ: (1) The office of bishop was added. (2) The office of teacher was added. (3) The office of deacon was added. (4) Formal dress for the priest was discontinued with fulfillment of the carnal law. (5) The passing of authority from father to son was no longer mandatory.

This new order of the Aaronic Priesthood as we have it today is a higher order than the carnal law given through Moses. We should feel honored to live in this final dispensation of time. All who hold the Aaronic Priesthood today have a grave obligation to live worthy of its promised blessings and preparatory purposes. Today each Aaronic Priesthood member carries a sacred obligation to prepare vigorously for the Melchizedek Priesthood and ultimate exaltation in God's kingdom.

34

The simplicity of the gospel's foundation principles

BEAUTIFULLY SIMPLE AND SIMPLY BEAUTIFUL

It was my rare privilege to serve as a missionary many years ago under a great mission president named Matthew Cowley, later to become an apostle of the Lord. One of his oft-repeated phrases was: "The teachings of the Savior are beautifully simple and simply beautiful." It was somehow easier and quite appropriate for President Cowley to make such an observation, for we were then involved in sharing the "beautifully simple" message of the Savior with a "simply beautiful" people—the Polynesian people of the South Pacific.

The genius and charm of Polynesia is simplicity—almost as a nation grown to adulthood without sacrificing the pure love, the complete faith, and the undeviating sincerity of childhood. They have often been referred to as a nation of children; and I assure you that this comparison is not meant to be disrespectful in any way, but rather most complimentary.

It was the Savior himself who said: ". . . of such is the kingdom of God." (Mark 10:14.) I feel certain he had in mind their sincerity, their simplicity. He also went on to say that "whosoever shall not receive the kingdom of God as a little child, he shall not enter therein." (Mark 10:15.) So it seems that we all have an obligation toward sincerity and simplicity—the simplicity of a child—in our faith, in our understanding.

May we turn our thoughts momentarily to the importance of simplifying our lives in this age of seeming turmoil and strife, this age of complication and harassment.

The end result of learning is most frequently simplicity itself. Einstein spent the better part of his life delving into the mysteries of the universe, and finally his great mind evolved what he called his theory of relativity. He expressed it in the simplest of terms: $E = MC^2$. This has never failed to amaze me that such a complicated theory could be expressed in this simple equation. How thrilling it must have been for the mathematicians of many centuries ago as they made the startling and simple discovery that πr^2 would always produce the area of a circle—simplicity. It seems that almost always when we arrive at the very base and core of a real truth, there is one thing most evident—simplicity. Even the chemist observes that water, the very lifeblood of this world, can be expressed in the chemical formula H_2O.

"A living symphony of simplicity" is one man's description of the Savior of the world. He was the perfect faith, the perfect knowledge, and in his perfection he reflected only the most elementary teachings in all that he did and all that he said. He did not come to confuse the world, but rather he came to bring light and truth and to bless the world, just as a beacon on a hill, that all might see and understand. No matter what level of education, even the simplest can understand that to love your neighbor is one of the greatest achievements of this mortal existence. The only ones who have not been able to understand these teachings of the Savior of the world are the proud, the haughty, those who refuse to accept the truth in its simple, uncomplicated reality.

As we go through life we sometimes fail to recognize our true station—just exactly where we are, how we fit in with the rest of all that we observe. One great philosopher has made the observation, "Man is but a reed." Can you visualize yourself down by the river bank, taking hold of a reed, so fragile, so brittle—and just with your fingertips you could snap that reed? So it is with man. Picture walking through a jungle and suddenly one of the mighty beasts of the tropical forest decides to attack, and with one mighty swipe of the paw he could break your body, because our bodies are fragile. So, man is but a reed.

When we look through the microscope and observe the smaller forms of life we feel mighty; we feel strong; indeed, we feel that we have all at our disposal. But at the same time, when we consider the smallest of all that Heavenly Father has created—the atom—and realize that when that very small atom is split it unleashes energy that is almost beyond man's comprehension, it makes us reconsider our so-called power.

How small is an atom? In just one drop of water there are more atoms than all the people living on the face of the earth could count in 10,000 years. How small is an atom? Certainly beyond our comprehension.

We are massive. We are giants. And yet, contemplate the wonder of the heavens. As we look at Heavenly Father's creation, we are informed that light takes thousands of light years to travel from one of those stars to our eyes. In other words, a star could have gone out of existence thousands of years ago and we wouldn't know about it until tonight because the light that left there thousands of years ago would just be arriving here and we would see it terminate. So, light traveling 186,000 miles (which equals seven and one-half times around our earth) in one second gives us some concept of the immensity of space. Truly we do feel insignificant by comparison.

Yes, man is but a reed. Then the philsopher added, "but he is a *thinking* reed." And this is the point. We are different from all other creations that Heavenly Father has placed upon the earth because we have the ability to reason. We have the ability to learn beyond all other creations. We are indeed created in his image. We are his children. We have the potential to become as he is.

May we guard, as a foundation in our simplicity, the fact that God lives. This is basic, it is fundamental, and without that knowledge and without that reality, there would be no tomorrow, for the sun would not rise and we would be doomed to mortal destruction. May we be reassured of this fact and may this become a controlling influence in all that we do and say. May it become the temperament of all that we learn. May it become our complete motivation and our first consideration in all decision making.

"So God created man in his own image, in the image of God created he him; male and female created he them." (Genesis 1:27.) This is found on the very first page of the Old Testament; and yet the world is drawing away from this simple truth because it is too simple. It is so simple that men fail to recognize its truth and its veracity.

May we never lose sight of the fact that we are his children, created in his image. May we never lose sight of the fact that he is the Son of God, the Savior of the world, the Christ-child born unto the virgin Mary—that this miracle birth literally happened, that it is not a fable, that it happened in all reality for a real purpose.

Then may we believe simply and implicitly that following his merciless crucifixion he was risen on the third day. The holy writ confirms to the believer that resurrection is a reality, and all shall live beyond the grave. We shall not only live beyond the grave, but if we live up to that very sacred covenant we took in the waters of baptism and do the very best we know how, we will also live back in the very presence of our Heavenly Father. No greater glory can come to any man. There can be no greater objective in all the world. And yet, it is a simple objective, clearly defined to those who would make the effort to be spiritually discerning and receptive to those things which come by the promptings of the Spirit from time to time.

Another foundation principle is that we have a simple, God-given health code in order to provide a firm physical body as a tabernacle for that spiritual faith which can be ours. I don't suppose there is any other subject in all the Church that is talked about more than the Word of Wisdom. You know, as well as I, all the things that Heavenly Father has said concerning care for our temporal bodies and making our mortal tabernacles of flesh a proper dwelling place for his Spirit that he might be able to guide us and direct us and give us comfort.

A very great man of medicine, a man who has performed hundreds of operations on people with lung cancer, made this theoretical observation:

> One hundred people with lung cancer have been brought together, and because of their common ailment they decide to have an annual reunion. So, they organize this little society—this club. You will be interested to know that at the end of the first year there will only be 60 people at the reunion, because 40 will have died during that first year.
>
> And without going into a lot of detail, let me skip to the fifth year reunion. There are only 5 there; 95 are dead because lung cancer is treacherous, because it takes its toll almost without exception, and it moves rapidly.

My point is that no man living under Heavenly Father's blue sky has the right to shorten his life even two minutes. God has given life, and he will decide when we have run our course, when we have made our contribution, when we have gained the facility we need. Only he should make that decision. And we don't have the right to shorten our life by even ten minutes, let alone ten years. Every man who desecrates his body with liquor and tobacco and all the other things that we talk about from time to time is running the jeopardy of shortening his life span contrary to the plan and will of our Heavenly Father.

Man has an obligation to keep probing. There are those who would say, "Let's be careful about probing too far into space." In some people's own private opinion man shouldn't be going to the moon or man shouldn't be trying to go someplace else.

Heavenly Father has given man an inquiring mind and will. He has given us an unquenchable thirst for exploration, for finding out what is over the next horizon. Now, there might be a boundary; there might be a limit; there might be some place out there beyond which our Heavenly Father doesn't want us to pass for our own good. In fact, I know that Heavenly Father has a fence built out there wherever it is—a fence that you and I can't see. And I thank God that we can't see it. He knows our ability, our capacity—and we won't quite be able to get over that fence, wherever it is. I think it would be a terrible thing if we knew where the fence was or even if we knew what our limitations were, so far as exploration and seeking and learning are concerned. So, I say, let us seek in all directions so long as we can keep our feet firmly planted in these basic truths of simplicity and faith that God lives.

Our last foundation principle of simplicity is that foundation stone of freedom and democracy, that we might exercise our God-given free agency. My, what a glorious thing it is! To the thinking person, freedom has much in common with simplicity. Our lives can be truly free only as we put forth the effort to keep them that way.

The shackling complication of tyranny, for example, cannot abide the peace of mind found in free agency. They are just not compatible. Some people are misled to thinking that all they have to do is vote for someone who is going to take complete control of everything, and then their lives will be simplified, and they can then sit back and fold their arms. In reality this is the beginning of complication in their lives. These people have been deluded.

The terrifying complication of fear cannot abide a true belief in God. That is why our number one platform is to form a partnership with our Heavenly Father. My, how grateful I am that Sister Simpson and I decided a long time ago—in fact, right in the very room in which we were sealed in for all time and eternity on that first day of our marriage—that there was no problem that three of us couldn't take care of, provided one of them was the Lord. We have always tried to keep him in our partnership, and he hasn't let us down once.

All who choose to participate within the limits of revealed truth must simultaneously choose to live in the light of noonday. The complicating factors of fear, hate, death, and ignorance can be found only as we turn our face from the direction of God, which is light, which is truth, which is everything worth having.

Some time ago I read a statement concerning our freedom that has made a tremendous impact on me:

> Great nations rise and fall—the people go from bondage to spiritual faith, from spiritual faith to great courage, from courage to liberty, from liberty to abundance, from abundance to selfishness, from selfishness to complacency, from complacency to apathy, from apathy to dependency, from dependency back into bondage. (Robert Muntzel, *Management Magazine,* January 1961.)

As we think about the course of this great nation, isn't that true? Our Pilgrim forebears come across the Atlantic

Ocean, purged from their homes of bondage and seeking spiritual faith. Yes, it was spiritual faith that brought them to the shores of America.

Then spiritual faith took them on to great courage as they moved westward, subdued the elements, built up their communities. Great courage carried them to liberty as they fought the Revolutionary War and founded the Constitution, which to my mind is the greatest single banner of liberty and freedom that any modern country has ever known.

From liberty came abundance, as free enterprise prospered in the only kind of climate it knows—freedom.

Then we went from abundance to a degree of selfishness. Do you remember how Patrick Henry said, "Give me liberty or give me death"? Today we abbreviate everything and it is just "Give me!" We have forgotten about the rest of it.

Apathy is the first cousin to complacency. We go from apathy to dependency as we vote those into power who are going to do everything for us, and all we have to do is to sit back, fold our arms, and be deluded into thinking that we are going to have a free ride. But it isn't so.

Then, of course, the last step from dependency is back again into bondage, because we know they are one and the same thing.

What are we going to do about it? I say that Heavenly Father has placed an obligation on us not to be apathetic, not to be complacent. We have freedom and we love freedom. If there should ever be a people in all this world who love freedom, it should be the Latter-day Saints, whose church could only be founded upon the soil of freedom. Heavenly Father waited until that freedom was assured before he restored the gospel of Jesus Christ in the fertile soil of this great land which we love so much.

May we reinforce the firm foundations upon which we have been established, and may we echo and re-echo the same declaration that was made by Joseph Smith and Sidney Rigdon when they said: "And now, after the many testimonies which have been given of him, this is the testimony, last of all, which we give of him: That he lives! For we saw him, even on the right hand of God; and we heard the voice bearing record that he is the Only Begotten of the Father." (D&C 76:22-23.)

May our faith be beautifully simple and simply beautiful, as we build our foundation of faith, as we provide a physical tabernacle worthy of that spiritual faith, and without which it cannot grow to full maturity. May we not neglect to keep probing and searching and reaching for the light and truth that Heavenly Father would have his children gain.

And may we do it all with an eye on that great pillar of freedom and democracy which is our heritage, which can never be taken for granted, and without which our great church will not be able to exist in today's society.

APPENDIX

The chapters in this book were adapted from the following speeches and articles:

1. Follow Proven Paths. Address at the 132nd Annual General Conference, April 1962.
2. Gifts of the Spirit. Address to BYU student body, October 18, 1966.
3. Commitment. Address at the 137th Annual General Conference of The Church of Jesus Christ of Latter-day Saints, April 1967.
4. Organizing for Eternity. Address to the BYU student body, April 20, 1965.
5. Stand Up and Be Counted. Address at the 133rd Semiannual General Conference, October 1963.
6. "Go, and Do Thou Likewise." Address at the 143rd Annual General Conference, April 1973.
7. That All May Be Blessed. Address to the BYU student body, October 29, 1968.
8. Not As the World Giveth. Address at the 135th Annual General Conference, April 1965.
9. The Lord Is Mindful of His Own. Address to the BYU student body, April 4, 1962.
10. Building a Foundation of Personal Revelation. Address to the 135th Semiannual General Conference, October 1965.
11. How to Gain and Hold Onto Your Testimony. Article in the *New Era,* March 1972.
12. "The Prophets Are Real—Be True to Them." Article in the *Improvement Era,* September 1963, and address at special meeting for bishops of the Church, April 5, 1963.
13. He Knocks—We Open the Door. Address at the 132nd Semiannual General Conference, October 1962.
14. Forgiveness. Address at the 136th Semiannual General Conference, October 1966.

15. "What Would Thou Have Me Do?" Address at the 136th Annual General Conference, April 1966.

16. The Law of the Fast. Address at the 137th Semiannual General Conference, October 1967.

17. God's Law of Health. Address at the 133rd Annual General Conference, April 1963.

18. The Wonderful World of Work. Address at the first convocation exercises of the College of Industrial and Technical Education, Brigham Young University, May 27, 1966.

19. Do Your Standards Show? Address to the Brigham Young University student body, October 19, 1965.

20. If You Would Communicate Well. Address to the Brigham Young University student body, February 6, 1968.

21. Pollution of the Mind. Address at the 142nd Semiannual General Conference, October 1972.

22. "For of Such Is the Kingdom of Heaven." Address at the Primary General Conference, April 1963.

23. "What Is Man, That Thou Art Mindful of Him?" Address at the 140th Annual General Conference, April 1970.

24. "Except Ye Become As Little Children." Article in the *Friend*, February 1972.

25. Our Responsibility to Our Children. Radio address produced by Marmon Productions, Inc., May 10, 1965.

26. Our Youth: The Hope of the World. Address at the Mutual Improvement Association June Conference, June 1967.

27. A Frank Talk with Young Women. Address at the 138th Annual General Conference, April 1968.

28. Many Are Called, But Few Are Chosen. Address at the 141st Semiannual General Conference, October 1971.

29. The Road Back. Address at the 139th Semiannual General Conference, October 1969.

30. Courts of Love. Address at the 142nd Annual General Conference, April 1972.

31. Conforming to Priesthood Principles. Address at the 138th Semiannual General Conference, October 1968.

32. Our Fundamental Obligation: The Priesthood. Address at the 143rd Semiannual General Conference, October 1973.

33. A Season of Preparation. Article in the *Instructor*, November 1967.

34. Beautifully Simple and Simply Beautiful. Address to Brigham Young University student body, August 2, 1966.

INDEX

JOHN GREENWOOD

Murder, Mr Mosley

WALKER AND COMPANY
NEW YORK

All the characters and events portrayed in this story are fictitious.

First published in the United States of America in 1983 by the Walker Publishing Company, Inc.

ISBN: 0-8027-5574-7

Library of Congress Catalog Card Number: 83-42881

Printed in the United States of America

10 9 8 7 6 5 4 3 2 1

One

'You are not contemplating,' the Assistant Chief Constable said, 'committing this to Mosley?'

Detective-Superintendent Grimshaw looked his master in the eye with a firmness meant to conceal the fact that he would rather have been looking almost anywhere else in the world. 'Chief Inspector Marsters is tied up with managerial crime – the Hartley Mason business. We've leave and sickness problems. Woolliams is looking after two divisions. Stout's going off on a course. And it *is* Mosley's patch.'

'But damn it, he couldn't even get to the scene of the crime.'

'He'd been up all night, sir: an epidemic of poultry-rustling over at Kettlerake.'

'Grimshaw – it will take Mosley until the middle of next year.'

'Oh, I don't know. He's good at talking to people – especially hill-folk. He *knows* everybody. They all like him – even when he's clapping his horny old hand on their shoulders. And we've got one here that has its roots well and truly in Mosley soil.'

'But have we ever let him loose within thirty miles of a murder before? Does he *know* that people sometimes kill each other? I'll grant you that when it comes to sheepdog-nobbling, cock-fighting and breaking into village halls –'

'Oh, yes, sir. In his thirty-four years in the force, Mosley has twice handled homicide – and in both cases he pulled it off. Once was back in 1954, when a man stabbed his wife in a Saturday-night domestic, and rang through to tell us he'd done it. I admit that he also complained about how long it took Mosley to get there.'

'And the second time?'

'A junkie on a camping-site, over on Back Moorside. He was leaning over the corpse with a dripping sheath-knife still in his hand, and a gang of Youth Hostellers cordoned him off and held him there as if they were photographing a still. Mosley spent two days satisfying himself that the chap wasn't being framed. That's what I like about Mosley: he's careful. And I'll keep a close eye on him, sir.'

'It strikes me you'd better gouge out an optic and attach it somewhere about his person. And Grimshaw – give him an up-to-date sergeant: someone who's heard about fingerprints and things.'

'Beamish, sir – on temporary transfer from Q Division.'

'Beamish! What's the betting they'll both have resigned from the force before the case breaks?'

So a cheerful-looking gentleman, who cultivated a shabby appearance and tried to seem older than his fifty-five years, arrived on a red service bus in the frontier village of Parson's Fold early one dusty afternoon in late October, after the scene-of-crime team had done all their work and departed. Parson's Fold ranks as a frontier village because it lies in that no man's land between Lancashire and Yorkshire where the county boundaries were changed early in the 1960s, and men had suddenly found themselves belonging to a neighbouring race which they had been brought up to hate from the cradle onwards. One local philosopher, interviewed on radio and asked how he felt about the change, said he did not know how he would be able to stand the climate.

Mosley travelled by bus because there had been a complex misunderstanding about the transport with which

Sergeant Beamish, fuming, was still waiting for him at Bradburn police station. Beamish did not know Mosley, except by improbable reputation, and was not yet in a position to suspect that the misunderstanding could have been an adroit piece of management on the old man's part.

Mosley went slowly straight into the public bar of an inn called The Crumpled Horn. It was against Section 178 of the Licensing Act of 1964 for him to consume intoxicating liquor on duty and equally illegal for the landlord to serve him. But the duration that he could spin out half a pint of beer made it a mild offence. He took off his black homburg, set it on a stool and leaned on the counter with his trench-coat flapping open. Any buttons it had were concealed, and he never seemed to fasten these up, even in wet weather. And he looked round the faces of the lunchtime drinkers as if he were glad to see them all. What is more, they seemed equally glad to see him. Perhaps there was general local relief that the murder in their midst had been left in the hands of a man so unlikely to create anything unpleasant out of it as Jack Mosley. He leaned sideways on the bar, his blue eyes twinkling at Parson's Fold in general, his long strands of sparse hair swept untidily across his bald head and – as predicted – he talked to people.

An hour later, leaving a quarter of a pint of beer to be poured back into the ullage, he came out and sat in the weak October sunshine on the wooden bench round the oak tree on Parson's Fold's parlous patch of green, and wrote at very great length in his notebook, in the tiny handwriting that looked so peevishly pinched.

The trouble had started (as Mosley patiently reconstructed it in his notes) a month ago, early one dusty afternoon in mid-September, when there was sudden activity in the main thoroughfare of Parson's Fold, a street unreasonably named The Pightle. As far as Parson's Fold was concerned, activity meant (the movements of hikers, cyclists, botanists and fell-walkers excepted) any perceptible variation from the daily pattern.

On this particular day, the daily pattern had been moving inoffensively along its accustomed course. At two minutes past two, Bill Clitheroe's mobile stores had moved ten yards downhill, from outside Emily Cotterill's on the east side of The Pightle to Carrie Bowland's on the west. At three minutes past, a rook had flown out of one of the elms behind the Old Rectory, and at three and a quarter minutes past, it had flown back again. At ten minutes past old Arthur Blamire, widower, left The Crumpled Horn and crossed The Pightle to his cottage; at twelve minutes past he returned. Arthur Blamire was always nipping back from the pub to his empty home for a minute. He invariably had an explanation for his conduct – today it was that he wanted to put the kettle on for eventual tea. Such rationalizations, however, were never believed, and theories in the Horn were facetious, disrespectful and sometimes imaginatively obscene.

But now there came major aberrations from custom – one at sixteen minutes past the hour, and another nine minutes later, both involving motor transport, and both inspiring women to report to each other in their kitchens. Nor were curiosity and a sense of involvement exclusively feminine traits. The active cells in the brain centre of The Crumpled Horn all made postural adjustments enabling them to see out of the window.

The first arrival was a Mercedes-Benz, a car that evidently did not know its way about Parson's Fold. It performed a clumsy reversing manoeuvre round the oak against which Mosley was later to sit, and then parked askew and obstructively in the forecourt of the pub. Its driver came into the public bar, a brisk and blustering man in his forties, who scorned refreshment of any kind and merely wanted to know the whereabouts of Jackman's Cottage. There was a long silence, perhaps a quarter of a minute, whilst the herd mind decided whether to answer him; and then they all told him at once.

The second immigrant was a green MG two-seater, pre-war to judge from its number-plates, yet clearly not an aficionado's car, though it could easily have been one. There was some buckling of the radiator grille, which an enthusiast would obviously not have left unattended, and the paintwork was scratched in several places under its patina of road-film. This was a vehicle that clearly did know where it was going, for it thrust its bonnet without hesitation up the alley that led to Jackman's Cottage, where its lady-driver got out, slammed its door and made a single unladylike comment upon the manner in which the Merc was blocking further progress up the lane.

She was an attractive woman in her mid-forties, with city-styled auburn hair, colourfully dressed in a green sweater that matched, perhaps, the original livery of her car, and corduroy slacks of a warm terracotta hue that went well with the knotted silk bandana that she wore round her neck.

'Inconsiderate sods!' she said, in a voice that carried down into The Pightle. She then entered the cottage, producing a key and opening the front door as if it belonged to her, and a minute or two later voices were raised, though not loud enough to be discernible to the forward reconnaissance elements that Parson's Fold had now discreetly deployed. They had not long to wait however for her to come out again, saying very angrily, and this time with a clarity that carried into The Pightle and beyond, 'And I tell you the house is not for sale.'

To establish which point she uprooted the estate agent's signboard and threw it petulantly into the long grasses of what had once been a lawn. It was seventeen years since anyone in Parson's Fold had set eyes on this young woman, but everyone knew who she was. Brenda Thwaites – as she was still thought of – was still rated an addled egg in Parson's Fold. And Mosley's memory went as far back as that. The year in which Brenda Thwaites had left home had also marked his promotion to detective-sergeant.

The brisk and blustering male followed her out of the cottage, attended by a woman in light tan suede who was evidently his wife. There was further conversation, which had to remain a mystery to the onlookers, but in which the man was evidently disbelieving what Brenda was saying. She seemed to have her way in the end, though, for presently the man began to upbraid her for placing her car where it was, preventing his exit from the alley. At first she seemed minded to leave it there, letting him stamp up and down until she had finished whatever business she had in the cottage. But then she thought better of this, got into the MG and reversed into The Pightle with a burst of querulous acceleration that had her wheels spinning in the September dust. Then, when the Mercedes had departed, she drove back to the cottage gate.

She was in there, silent and frustratingly beyond observation, for a full half hour. When she came out, she made sure the front door was locked, went and threw the estate agent's board even further out of sight in an overgrown herbaceous border. And then she walked down to the Old Rectory, where there was not a single native of Parson's Fold sufficiently courageous to follow her.

Inspector Mosley finished writing, looked at his watch – some of his superiors would have had their theories confounded by the fact that he had one – and made his own way up to Jackman's Cottage, a distance of some forty yards, which took him ten minutes, so many leisurely civilities did he have to exchange on the way.

Two

Jackman's Cottage was in fact a conversion, completed just before the outbreak of the Second World War, and achieved by throwing together four previous dwellings. It was built in the grey local stone and its original leaded windows had never been enlarged or modernized, so that the first impression was of austerity and hard living: the sort of home in which to face out the siege of a Pennine winter.

The garden had not been tended for a number of years. A profusion of sere Russell lupins and a population explosion of golden rod indicated where flower-beds had been. A roofed bird-table was broken and its plywood laminations had sprung apart. Near to it a gnome lay on his back, his nose broken and his colour bleached away, beside an ornamental stone trough whose water looked black under its green slime.

Mosley opened the front door with the key that Superintendent Grimshaw had handed him together with a large envelope of front-line documentation. He picked up the single letter that was lying on the mat – a credit card statement addressed to Mrs B. Cryer – and put it away in an inside pocket. It must have come by a very late morning delivery.

The interior of the cottage was as the scene-of-crime team had left it this morning: contents of drawers examined, likely objects dusted for fingerprints, possessions disturbed and put away again with a certain rough tidiness, even with respect, perhaps, but without tenderness. The outline where the body had lain was marked by a chalk-line. Mosley stood for a few seconds and contemplated it, ignoring it thereafter, unworried whether his feet obliterated it or not.

The furnishing of the home was such as a couple might have assembled who had married on a modest income in the early thirties – the beginning of the country cottage era in domestic interiors. A reproduction rural dresser, now losing strips of its veneer, dated back to that time. There had been one or two major replacements – a three-piece drawing-room suite from the utility years; that must have been bought when the couple had moved here from Bradburn, in a better though still vigilant state of affluence. And that had been, Mosley was well aware, in the mid 1950s. It was sometimes said of him that he knew everything and everyone in the twelve miles by twelve of moors, cloughs and valleys that were his territory – except, cynics added, the criminals. The rider was unfair, and the general proposition exaggerated: but he might certainly have been expected to know Arthur Thwaites, solicitor's scrivener in Bradburn since his boyhood before the First War, and managing clerk since the middle of the Second. Thwaites had been a colourless, industrious, unimaginative, meticulous man, well respected in Bradburn, and probably even more so in the almost absolute unsophistication of Parson's Fold. But not long after coming to this pasture, Arthur Thwaites had begun to suffer ill-health, had later died of a stroke, brought on, it was commonly believed, by the behaviour of that daughter who had come home in her MG a month ago.

The drawing-room furniture was not deployed as such. Sofa and armchairs had been pushed to one side, without regard for comfort or appearance and the main space was occupied by a three-quarter bed, still flanked by an invalid's side-table: a few bottles and pill-boxes – bismuth tablets, aspirin, a nasal dropper, a half-finished phial of oil of cloves – but among them no major prescriptions or regular doses. Mosley paid interested attention to the bed itself, turning back the coverlet, examining the pillows and holding a corner of sheet against his cheek.

He had known Nora Thwaites, too, Brenda's mother, who had married her husband at a time when there had seemed no likelihood of his ever advancing beyond the rank of a very humble pen-pusher indeed. Greenhill, her unmarried name had been, and she had come from a hill-farm some fifteen miles from here – a subsistence holding of the sort that is known as an intake: rough sheep pastures retrieved from the savage moor in a spirit of primeval and largely misplaced optimism. The Greenhills had been legendarily poor and her marriage to a man of letters – even the letters involved in merely engrossing conveyances for Fothergill, Fothergill, Foster, Sons and Fothergill – had been a rise out of class for her. She, too, had been ill for a long time. She had spent the last two years in a private nursing home. Then Brenda, the profligate absentee, had returned without notice after seventeen years and brought her mother back home.

All this Mosley knew, in a passive manner, which he had re-activated by laborious cerebration and quick reference before he left home to reams of his pinched-up writing in notebooks now decades old. His records of gossip were as rich as his talent for producing it.

Now he saw landmarks of his knowledge of the Thwaiteses' biographies in each room that he visited: a studio portrait of Nora Greenhill at the time when Arthur Thwaites had been courting her: in the late 1920s, it must have been, before Mosley had had any personal knowledge of the family. She was wearing fashions that dated from a few years before the photograph was taken: a characterless cloche hat and a shapeless frock from the age when women were disinclined to parade their femininity. It was a forced and unnatural Nora Greenhill, disciplining herself to face a camera in front of which she felt ill at ease, the end frustrated by the means. For Nora Greenhill had had the reputation of a certain wild beauty: the tangled, unconscious beauty of an impoverished girl brought up on a failed intake. She had rapidly lost it after marriage to a solicitor's clerk. There was one family group that occupied Mosley for a minute or two, dated about 1950. Arthur Thwaites was then in his early fifties, and at the apex of his career at law, the man who kept Fothergills, Foster and Company on the rails of office efficiency. Brenda was then a girl of about five – her parents had had her late in life – in floral patterned dungarees, her hair in a pony-tail. Her brother, twelve years older than she, was by now one of the promising fruitlings of Bradburn Grammar School. But Mosley knew relatively little about the boy, who had moved away into the world of redbrick university, a science degree and the mystique of industrial chemistry. He now lived in the Old Rectory, with a wife of whom Mosley knew nothing at all. There were no children.

Of Brenda he knew very little either – except what people said of her. It was true she had left home at seventeen for a marriage of which her parents disapproved, which they had declined to attend, but which their distaste for publicity had prevented them from legally opposing. It had surely been one of the shortest marriages on record, for Brenda – now Bryce – had got off the honeymoon train at an intermediate station, and was believed not to have been in touch with her husband again. An impetuous girl, people said, whose volatility led her into extremes. She had never returned home again until a month ago; and some said that this was because her parents had banned her. Her mother was believed to have been especially embittered, the more so because the girl had not even tried to make contact at the time of her father's funeral. She would probably have been rejected if she had – but this was not a logical sequence.

Certainly the characteristics of intransigence were latent in Nora Thwaites's face in the photograph that Mosley was now looking at: in her early forties, her figure gone and apparently not missed, her mouth turned down at the corners and her eyes resenting even the photographer.

What had happened to the girl after that rapidly stalled marriage? There were rumours. She had been spotted, so various claims went, in more than one Yorkshire or Lancashire town: Preston, Huddersfield, Heckmondwike, Bolton – always too far away, and lost in too impersonal a populace for there to be any great danger of a direct Parson's Fold connection. There had been rumours of more men – of course. In her sixth-form days, even in school uniform, there had been a patent sexiness that had people forecasting ill for her. She knew what she had, and what it was for, and maybe was just a little impatient to be exercising it. But there had been more to her than just that, Mosley seemed to remember: standards, if that wasn't too sentimental a label. It must have been something that ran significantly counter to those standards that she had learned about her husband on that honeymoon train.

The most comfortable room in the house had been turned into a sickroom, and there was no sign that Brenda had made her private headquarters in the kitchen: she would not be the sort of woman who wanted her leisure dominated by reminders of domesticity. Mosley therefore spent a long time in her bedroom, which bore some witness to her previously acquired skill in bed-sitter home-making: the ability, for one thing, to keep unaesthetic essentials out of sight. Brenda Thwaites – Bryce – Cryer – had been no slut. Her underwear, mostly St Michael, was well kept and put away with fastidious tidiness. There was only one thing in her wastepaper basket – an empty cigarette packet of an expensive King Size brand. There were no stubs in her bedside ashtray, but the stains in it suggested a medium-heavy smoker.

The pictures that had been on the wall when she came back had been taken down and stored flat on top of the wardrobe: parental treasures – Cader Idris in monochrome and an engraving of a sentimental group in a Victorian smithy. She had replaced these by framed watercolours, originals, but with signatures which told Mosley nothing. They represented industrial scenes, but with extravagant, abstract use of colour. Her musical tastes were catholic, to judge from the sleeves piled by her record player, and ranged from Lindisfarne and Fairport Convention to Mozart and Stravinsky. Her current reading was a paperback Beryl Bainbridge and she also had Edna O'Brien, Susan Hill and Nina Bawden.

In a drawer Mosley found contraceptives in a sponge bag: a Dutch cap backed up by a tube of jelly of which about a third had been used. He unscrewed its cap and found the nozzle dried but not crusty. It might or might not have been opened within the last month.

He moved into the front bedroom, the one that must once have been parental territory, and examined the bed with the same lingering curiosity that he had given to the one downstairs. It was made up with freshly laundered sheets that had not been slept in. There was no sign that he could find of recent occupancy of the room. There had been a putting away of things, probably ages ago, a more recent skirmish against the dust – in general a banishment of life that amounted to positive coldness. Mosley sat down on a chair, motionless, as if punishing his memory, bludgeoning it to make it give him something. Then at last he took out his notebook and added one further line:

1972 to present? Eight years unaccounted for – not even rumours.

He put his notebook away, stood up and looked out of the window: nothing, really – only stone walls, slate roofs and a passacaglia of chimney-stacks and cowls. Suddenly a car came to rest outside and seconds later there was a hammering on the door. Mosley went down patiently and opened it, looking amiably into the eyes of a very angry young man: Sergeant Beamish.

Beamish was the sort of detective who believed in saliva tests and computers. He did not quite think that the colour of a man's socks could be deduced from a seminal stain, but he did believe that the ultimate assembly of silicon chips would leave the human brain ranking as candidly second-rate, its inferences amateur, its recall inefficient, its retrieval taxonomy haphazard. Intuition, of course, was a joke that no one any longer made, a synonym for guess-work and cheerful muddling through. He and Mosley had heard of each other, but they did not normally move in the same internal circle.

In addition, Beamish was an advanced democrat, who believed in the inferiority of age, experience and rank.

'Is this the way you treat all your sergeants?' he asked without inhibition. 'Leaving them conflicting messages?'

'Did I? I'm sorry: no harm done, at any rate.'

'Only time wasted. What have you found here? Anything that scene-of-crimes missed?'

'I don't know, really. Eight years of a young woman's life that need looking for.'

'Was there anything in the on-the-spot photographs? I believe there was some polaroid stuff for instant assessment. Anything preliminary from pathology or forensic?'

'I don't know. I haven't looked yet.'

Mosley nodded vaguely at the buff envelope which he had put down, still unopened, on a corner of the bed.

'I like to leave all that till I've made my own impressions.'

'Mind if I take a quick glance?' Beamish asked.

'In principle, do by all means. But there was rather an urgent job that I'd hoped you would do for me, if you don't mind.'

Beamish's lower jaw had already dropped, ready to parry the irony. But there was something in old Mosley's tone that made Beamish wonder whether it was intended as irony at all. He closed his mouth again, giving Mosley the benefit of the doubt – and incidentally, degrading the inspector a point or two in his assessment. Good manners at this stage of case-work could be a sign of muddled priorities.

'You'll find an estate agent's sign in the garden,' Mosley said. 'Go down and take note of their address. It's in Harrogate. Go over and pay them a visit. Find out who was given an order to view on September 16th. Go and see those people, whoever they are, and discover whether there is any personal connection between them and Mrs Cryer. I think we'd better call her that for the time being, to avoid confusion.'

'Yes, Inspector.'

'Oh, and Sergeant – if it's in some other force's territory, get all the necessary clearances and go and see them yourself. One always misses points when one tries to do things secondhand.'

'Yes, Inspector.'

'Even if it's at the other end of the kingdom,' Mosley said.

He let them out of Jackman's Cottage, locked it and tested the latch, then walked over to the Old Rectory with the gait of a Senior Citizen, clutching the buff envelope in his hand.

Three

The Old Rectory was one of those residences that must have tested the fidelity, not to say hardiness, of any Old Rector not blessed with a private income. Who could have afforded to maintain winter warmth in those rooms thirty feet square and fourteen feet high? Who could have attempted to populate those eleven bedrooms? Mosley walked up a drive beside a lawn that would have competed with an Oxford quadrangle for spirit-level immaculacy and freedom from weeds.

He could not think that he remembered anything about the woman that Donald Thwaites had married, except that she came from somewhere up in the Trough – Sedbergh or Settle – or was it from somewhere down in Ribblesdale: Balderstone or Roach Bridge? And young Thwaites had met her while doing his two years' national service, back in the fifties.

She opened the door to him, a woman well past the forty mark, of non-fat-making metabolism, a type for which the Greeks had had a word which Mosley had forgotten, as gaunt in temperament as in physical frame. She was very grave, though naturally unsurprised in the circumstances to receive a visit from a criminal investigator. The flat intonation and glottal stops of her native speech were variegated by a sincere but calamitous attempt at south country vowels. Although he did not go quite so far as this, Mosley was also on his most gentlemanly behaviour, and conducted himself as if he expected Beryl Thwaites to feel some measure of grief at the loss of her sister-in-law.

She led him through a wainscotted entrance hall decorated with patent brass-ware of the type that keeps its shine without polishing: pans, kettles, ladles, skimmers and warming-pans, none of which had ever been used – or designed for use. The Rectory drawing-room had been given an even greater sense of vastness by the addition of an immense picture window that looked out across the motionless autumnal valley to the dark hulk of Pendle Hill. The prospect combined magnificence with a strong innuendo of the elemental, greatly enhanced by the manner in which the garden of the house had been landscaped as a proscenium to the main set, clipped hedges and converging parallels of chrysanthemum beds leading the eye to the backcloth behind the elms. The room itself was contemporarily furnished, with shelving and wall-lamps by Habitat. Dangling fern-like house-plants interrupted the tiers of Book Society spines, and there were exhibits suitably illustrative of Donald Thwaites's profession: an early twentieth-century laboratory balance in its square-cut glass case, and a microscope with triple objective, likewise protected from dust and dusters.

Beryl Thwaites quickly gave the lie to the notion that she might be mourning for Brenda Cryer. She made a progressive statement, obviously rehearsed, and Mosley did not deny her the comfort of her preamble.

'I know, Mr Mosley, that it is wrong to speak anything but well of the deceased, and I know that whatever she may have done with her life, no one has the right to do what was done to Brenda. And I know that perhaps all along she was more to be pitied than blamed – '

'I am sure that this has been a very great shock to you,' Mosley said.

'To tell you the truth, Mr Mosley, it has been a long series of shocks from the very first moment that she arrived without notice and insisted on bringing her mother back home.'

Mosley nodded sympathetically, sitting uncomfortably in his chair, as if admitting that the quality of the furniture out-classed him. He had left his trench-coat and homburg in the hall and was now displaying a herringbone suit of the shabbiest grey with a silver watch-chain across his waistcoat and a blue and beige tie which seemed to bring out the worst in the ensemble.

'I mean,' Mrs Thwaites said, 'she could have written. She could have rung up. She could have come and talked to us. We had not heard a word from her for seventeen years, not us, not her mother, none of her old friends, not a soul. Donald and I can only think that she saw in some paper or other that the house was for sale and that she was worried about not getting her share.'

'But she did not apparently want the house sold,' Mosley said.

'No – and what a way of doing it! It did not occur to her to come down here and discuss it with us. She just tore down the sign, under the nose of an interested enquirer, and set herself up in there. And the next thing we knew, she had brought my mother-in-law out of the nursing home, had made a sickroom out of the drawing-room and was making the most disgusting exhibition of herself in the village.'

'How long since you had the old lady taken into the home?' Mosley asked.

'Two years, and I know what you are thinking, but you are wrong. We had discussed it, coolly and without passion, the three of us. My mother-in-law understood that there were times when her mind became confused, when she forgot things. She appreciated that it is beyond my resources to run two homes – I have this one to keep up for Donald; I have to entertain his associates. Also, she refused point-blank to come here and live with us – and I would be telling less than the truth if I pretended that I heard that with anything but relief. She did not see eye to eye with us about so many things. She agreed that it would be better for her to be where she could be looked after, with the companionship of people of her own age.'

'And she had enough funds to pay for this?'

'She had savings in the Co-op, something put by in the Post Office, a few thousands that Donald's father had left her, the proceeds of a life policy that she had held on him.'

'And all this was beginning to run out?'

'You must understand, Mr Mosley, that Donald and I never counted on being left anything by his mother.'

'Of course not. I assume that your husband is reasonably well off. He is a works chemist, I believe.'

'Chief works chemist. But that does not mean that he could afford the fees that the nursing home are now charging. Mrs Thwaites's capital was, as you say, diminishing – but the value of Jackman's Cottage has also risen absurdly. We believe it would make something like £35,000 on the open market, and, as I say, Donald and I have never reckoned in terms of a legacy.'

'Did you often go and see her in the home?'

'Weekly without fail.'

'Both of you?'

'Sometimes Donald went alone.'

'I see. And had Mrs Thwaites's condition deteriorated?'

'Very considerably. Sometimes she did not even recognize us. But in heart and limb she was remarkably sound for her age.'

'Yes, many of our old people are like that,' Mosley said. 'How well do you think that Brenda was able to cope with her?'

'Remarkably well. I was surprised. That, of course, was before the novelty of it wore off.'

'There must have been some sort of reconciliation between them. Was the old lady mentally up to that, do you think?'

Mrs Thwaites Junior allowed herself an apology for a smile. 'I would think that her clouded mental condition was the only thing that made reconciliation possible. She had never forgiven her daughter.'

'Did you see much of your sister-in-law over the last month?'

'We had her to dinner, of course. And we went over to tea at Jackman's Cottage on the second Sunday. Then I have to admit that things became rather strained between us.'

But Mosley seemed barely interested in this aspect, and offered no help towards continuing her line of thought. He waited.

'Brenda was difficult. She always has been – from the stories Donald has told me of when she was a child. And when she got into the upper forms of the High School – '

Mosley still waited. Perhaps Beryl herself had not qualified for High School.

'Well, as I say, Donald and I did our best to be sociable. But it took only a week or so for Brenda to be up to her usual games.'

Mosley disobligingly did not ask what they were. Beryl Thwaites paused for the drama of her next revelation to build itself up.

'Quite apart from extremely regular visits to The Crumpled Horn for bottles of gin, there were men,' she said at last.

Mosley continued to torture her with patient silence.

'I hate to have to tell you this, Mr Mosley – but in her own home village, returning ostensibly to look after her sick mother, she was receiving men at Jackman's Cottage before she had been here much longer than a week.'

Quite unexpectedly Mosley asked a question.

'And who were these men?'

Mrs Thwaites allowed her shoulders to twitch at precisely the right moment. 'Would you expect me to know? At first we thought it was only village talk – of which, I might say, there has been no dearth. But then Donald and I heard the cars come and go. Late at night. On one occasion someone stayed all night, not driving away until almost seven.'

Mosley did not seem shocked.

'Of course, I told Donald he must go and remonstrate. In a house that you cannot by any charitable stretch of imagination say belonged to her, and with her mother lying ill on a downstairs bed! We have our own position to consider, you know, with Donald expecting a seat on the board at the next AGM, and him a sidesman, and in the running for next vicar's warden. We are not exactly lords of the manor here, but people do look up to us. And I do think that we owe something to this house. After all, it was a Rectory. It has always had an aura as a centre of moral astringency.'

'And did he approach his sister?'

'He did.'

'What was her reaction?'

'She was outrageously and indecently rude to him. Wild horses would not drag from me the things she said to him about his relationship with me. Then, of course, we heard the rumours that my mother-in-law was no longer at the cottage – that she had been sent away again somewhere. And we were the last to hear, even about that. That was what hurt.'

Mosley appeared to have dried up again as a source of guidepost questions.

'I can't describe to you what it was like, Mr Mosley, in a village like this, going into the post office or the grocer, knowing that all conversation will stop, and won't start again until after you've gone. It was the milk roundsman, young Smethurst, who first circulated the story. He was in the habit of knocking at Jackman's, because Brenda was always forgetting to put out her order. And he usually put his head into the hall and shouted something friendly to the old lady. Then one morning, a week ago, he saw that the bed was empty – actually stripped of its linen. Being inquisitive, like all these country folk, he asked me, next time he saw me, where she had gone. And then the villagers started getting up to their typical ways and made excuses to go there, to find out what they could. Mrs Cotterill, the know-all of The Pightle, even went touting for laundry and mending – and came back telling people that she was sure that my mother-in-law was no longer there.'

Mosley continued to listen.

'Well, Donald asked me to go over, to save him from another intolerable scene with his sister. And Brenda was most insolent; obscene again. She showed me the bed, made up certainly, with the covers turned back at one side, but nobody in it.

' "She's in the lavatory, if you must know."

'And she went up and hammered on the toilet door, and she shouted, "Oh, Mother, how many times have I told you not to lock yourself in? I'll have that bolt taken off." Then she looked at me and said, "I don't suppose you've ever wiped her posterior." That, of course, wasn't the word she used.'

'How very distressing for you,' Mosley said; and raised none of the obvious supplementary points. Had she really fallen for a trick as shallow as that? Had she or her husband attempted no follow-up in the week that ensued? Hadn't her husband wanted to see his mother again in that time? Or his sister? Or were relationships between the two houses now beyond succour?

Mrs Thwaites allowed a tear to strain through into the corner of her eye. 'I did my best, I am sure, in an extraordinarily difficult situation. Of course, it is horrifying that anyone should have wanted to *kill* her.'

'*Did* kill her. I think it's possible she may have been in with rather a rum set of people,' Mosley said mildly.

'But it's the old lady I am worried about. I do hope, Mr Mosley, that you are leaving no stone unturned – '

'Oh, we have all the stops out,' Mosley said.

'Of course, I dare say she simply got tired of nursing her, after the first flush of madness. I've no doubt she's found some other home for her. But at least she might have told us. Mrs Thwaites *is* Donald's mother, and I could not bear to think of her being looked after somewhere second-rate. Still, I suppose until we hear something different, we must look on the bright side.'

'Invariably,' Mosley said.

The bright side? Brenda Cryer had been shot through the back of the neck, at an inch or two's range, with a bijou automatic of the kind that is known as a lady's handbag model in circles where ladies carry such models in their handbags. But the stops had indeed been pulled out – largely as county office routine – on behalf of Mrs Thwaites. Grimshaw had set that in motion and a little cell of troglodytes, at a battery of telephones, were thumbing their systematic way through the Yellow Pages of an ever-increasing radius. But so far nothing had come in from a box-search of hospitals, private nurses and invalid homes.

Mosley went off again towards the nerve centre of The Pightle. He could honestly claim to know everybody who mattered – from his point of view – in Parson's Fold, and there was one man he was very anxious indeed to talk to. But that man was not at home; so, for the second time in one afternoon, he looked at his watch. It was evidently a keen sense of urgency that was impelling him. He knew from whom, in Parson's Fold, he could borrow a bicycle, and from that friend he now borrowed one. It was an emergency that he might even have been anticipating, for he drew a pair of clips from the pocket of his raincoat and fitted them round his ankles. With his coat flapping open and his homburg set squarely on the top of his head, he freewheeled down the hill out of the village.

Four

Mosley arrived at Murray-Paulson's in time to wheel his machine into the staff bicycle shed as the staff were wheeling theirs out; in time, too, to note that a large blue Vauxhall estate car still stood in the rectangle in the executive car park marked *Chief Chemist.* Otherwise, except for a small red mini in the space labelled *Company Secretary,* there was no indication of upper echelon life about the premises.

In a small way, Murray-Paulson's made paint: of very high quality and in custom-mixed shades. They were permitted to continue to do so in competition with the commercial giants, perhaps because their plant was so antiquated, their premises so dilapidated and their infrastructure so minimal that none of the giants was impressed by the viability of a merger. Donald Thwaites led Mosley through a laboratory reminiscent of a Dickensian blacking factory and settled them down in his office, a sort of minstrels' gallery overlooking his range of sinks, retorts, condensers and crucibles. Mosley, still wearing his bicycle clips, as if equipped for sudden flight if need be, maintained such dignity as was afforded by an adjustable armchair whose cushions appeared to have passed between the stones of a well serviced flour-mill. Thwaites's desk was a litter of paper-clips, promotional leaflets and routine analysts' reports on roneoed forms. His ashtray was that of a heavy smoker, and in it two filter-tipped stubs bore thick smears of lipstick.

Donald Thwaites was looking tired: it was not merely the

events of today that had been nearly too much for him to handle. He had the nerviness of a man whose equilibrium had for some time depended on his ability to manage a peripheral picket of unmanageable women. Mosley, somehow omitting to mention that he had called at the Old Rectory, led him without passion through the events of the morning.

It had been the milkman, peeping through the letter-box, who had seen Brenda's body, at about a quarter to eight, when Thwaites had been within ten minutes of leaving for work.

'I ought to have stayed home all day, I suppose. But we'd a significant new contract at a critical stage, EEC stuff, and a working party was coming over from Duisburg to discuss consumer parameters.'

The scene-of-crime team had arrived at about a quarter to nine. At nine fifteen, Superintendent Grimshaw had come in from County HQ, looking with imperishable confidence for Mosley, and taking charge on the spot in his absence. He had organized a slow-moving queue for preliminary questioning. By a quarter to eleven, Thwaites was told he could go.

'I don't even remember your face among the officers who were milling about this morning.'

'No. I came late on the scene. Been up all night, you know. Serious wave of naughtiness going on, over at Kettlerake. You can't expect people to respect law and order if their hens aren't safe in their own back yards.'

Donald Thwaites nodded vaguely. He did not appear to see anything amiss in Mosley's juxtaposition of priorities. He was too far gone in general discouragement.

'Still,' Mosley said. 'What's in an hour or two? It seems to me it's taken the best part of twenty years to build up the situation in which your sister was killed. There's no point in wearing ourselves into wafers for the sake of five minutes.'

'I suppose not.'

'Your sister, now: one could hardly describe relations

between you as cordial.'

'She was – shall I say? – difficult. Always had been. Even as a small child. We all spoiled her, her arrival being, well, late and unexpected. It seems improper talking about her like this, doesn't it? She was – well – difficult. Let's leave it at that.'

'Difficult in what way?' Mosley asked, relatively tenacious.

'She never seemed to know what she really wanted, and yet she wanted it badly. That doesn't make any sense at all, does it?'

Mosley expressed no opinion.

'I mean, at my wedding, for example, she was a bridesmaid. Very pretty. She was eleven. I was twenty-three. But she suddenly threw such a tantrum that she almost ruined the day for all of us. I know that she certainly did for Beryl. It was all about a spray of sweet peas that she didn't want to carry. They were deep maroon, and for some reason she'd pictured herself carrying light blue and lavender. She had preconceptions of what she wanted to look like, and she would not tolerate any variation.'

'Did she suddenly find, then, on a train, that this man Bryce didn't live up to her preconceptions?'

'Oh, Bryce! Bryce was a shyster. But he simply arose out of a situation. If it hadn't been Bryce, it would have been somebody else. My father even engaged a private detective, someone he knew through his office, to try to get a report on Bryce that might prove to her what he was. But it wouldn't have made any difference. If she hadn't found Bryce, she'd have found another – and it wouldn't have been anyone savoury. That wouldn't have suited her book at all.'

He looked Mosley in the eye. His own irises were tired and unhealthy, bloodshot, and occluded with yellow deposits of cholesterol in the corner veins. He lit a cigarette and drew in the smoke as if he depended on it for sustenance.

'I am trying to remind myself, Mr Mosley, that I shouldn't be talking like this – but it's true. The trouble was compounded, I suppose, when she went into the sixth form at the High School. That was back in the early sixties: Beatlemania years. And I don't mean the music, though she was pretty far gone on that too: Freddie and the Dreamers, Manfred Mann, the Rolling Stones. She used to play it so loud in her bedroom that even the table the radiogram stood on was dancing. My mother and father nearly went scatty. But it wasn't only Merseybeat. It was rebellion: adolescent rebellion. There was nothing new in that, but somehow there was a nationwide cachet about it, a sort of universal cohesion – even a uniform. My mother and father were the last people on earth to understand it. They hadn't a clue what was going on in Brenda. I, in my time, had been orthodox, compliant. Even my work had been different: concrete and tangible, dependent on weighing and measuring. Brenda went on the Arts side, did History, French and Art at A level. She was reading Baudelaire when she was seventeen – and contemporary authors who left nothing unsaid. She went wild over painters like Warhol. She didn't hide her contempt for Parson's Fold and the values at home. She treated her father like an ignoramus and her mother like a mental defective. There was a teacher at her school in her last year, a girl just out of college, who fanned the flames of all this, fed her with every idea that was different and rotten. She was a terrible influence. Everything she said, every view she held seemed to be accepted without question. No: more than accepted – raved about. She had to go, a year or two later – the teacher, I mean – after a major row with the headmistress.'

Thwaites stubbed out a good inch of cigarette and immediately lit a fresh one.

'It was a domestic calamity when Brenda set foot in the house after school, or came in from an evening out. To make it worse, she had set her eyes on university, but my father could not see his way to finance her. He was a sick man. He had suffered from hypertension for years. He did old-fashioned copperplate handwriting, and you might say he had a copperplate mind. He knew he wasn't going to make old bones and he wanted to see her settled in something respectable, gainful and local before he died: secretarial, accountancy, local government or such. So there lay another bone of contention, and there was a flaming row every time either side of the question was broached. My mother, of course, backed my father's view all the way. She hadn't the remotest idea of anything that was going on in Brenda's mind, whether it was poetry, painting, politics or progressive pop. And by now, Mother had got the idea pretty firmly fixed that it was education itself that lay at the root of the trouble. Believe me, it was little short of civil war. I suppose in the normal run of things, Brenda would have got her university place and gone on independently; not that that would have done my father any good. It was commonplace security he wanted to see. But then Bryce came along.'

'And who was Bryce?'

'Someone she'd met at a pop concert – though they tried to make out that that was a coincidence: he was in some way different from the run-of-the-mill people you got at those places. In all fairness, I think there was a trace of truth in that. He was in his late twenties, at least ten years older than her: an artist, he said – sometimes. Sometimes he called himself a technical consultant. Sometimes he admitted that he was in advertising. In fact he was drawing hack technical diagrams for promotional material, over at Sinkers', at Goosnargh. And not very good at it, either, my spies informed me; holding precariously on to the job from one month to the next. But he had a red mini, and that was very dashing, twenty minutes after the school bus had gone, the village empty, except for faces behind curtains, and Brenda waiting alone by the oak for him to come revving down The Pightle. He was a collector: that's what I told her. "He's a collector," I said. "And you're the next specimen he wants in mint condition in his album." And she laughed – she could be insufferable – "I'm already in his album," she said. "And I'm a collector, too. Only I keep mine in slide-out trays in a glass cabinet." '

'Collector or not,' Mosley said. 'He was prepared to marry her.'

'Well, he might have done worse for himself, mightn't he? She was attractive, she was witty, she had ideas of her own. She could have made him an interesting home. Outside the family circle, I dare say she could even be agreeable for hours at a stretch.'

'So why did she abandon him on a train?'

'Your guess, too. They were flying from Manchester to Tenerife. She said that was bourgeois, but not as bad as Torremolinos. She got out twenty miles from here. Maybe he had said something that made her see the light suddenly. She was no fool: only blindfolded – by herself and that silly chit of a teacher.'

'And didn't he ever come back here? Didn't he try to trace her through the family?'

'Never. I don't think Sinkers' tolerance had much longer to run. And maybe he pictured us Thwaiteses coming down from the hills fanning our hammers.'

He was capable of humour, then; but this was an isolated example of it.

'And Brenda?'

'We heard in a roundabout way that she was sharing a flat and had taken a factory job – assembly line stuff – somewhere in North Yorkshire: Rangate.'

'You didn't go to see her?'

'To be laughed and abused off the premises?'

'There was never anything between you that one could have called friendship?'

'Inspector, unilateral friendship is an uphill furrow. Brenda was only seven when I was doing my National Service. She was eleven when I came down from university.

We never got to know each other. And if we are going to be here much longer, Mr Mosley, I would like to phone my wife.'

'By all means.'

Mosley watched his face closely as he did so: the uneasiness, the frown – the shock when he realized that his wife had already been questioned.

'You didn't tell me that you'd already talked to Beryl.'

'Didn't I? I apologize. I assumed she'd have rung you. Now: do you mind if we change the angle a little, Mr Thwaites?'

'Does it matter whether I say yes to that or not?'

A midge-bite, rather than a wasp-sting: which Mosley did not even bother to slap.

'When did you last see your mother?' he asked, suddenly – and apparently unconscious that he had just uttered an inane and tasteless epigram.

'I suppose it would be about ten days ago. But I gather you have already had all the relevant information from Beryl.'

'I would like to hear your account.'

Thwaites did not actually wriggle, but he looked as if he would have liked to.

'I admit it must seem curious to you – but you must understand, Mr Mosley, that the circumstances are not normal – they have been abnormal with us Thwaiteses for years. It isn't a question of love, Mr Mosley – it's a basic absence of communication. Three quarters of the time my mother doesn't recognize me. When she does, the chances are that she will mistake something I say – or impute to me something I haven't said. Then she'll become insulting, obstreperous. She lives in a twilight world, and even when she acknowledges reality, it is a reality that moves without reason from present into past, from ancient history into sick fantasy. They call it senile dementia. I tried to handle it on a charitable family basis – and if I had gone on, it would have broken my home. My wife has tried very hard – but she lacks that common ground that remains from my boyhood years. Even after Brenda brought Mother home, we tried again – had the pair of them to dinner. I need hardly tell you that it was catastrophic.'

'And that is the state your mother was in when you put her into the nursing home?'

'That is how she was beginning to be. What would you have had me do, Mr Mosley?'

'I am not accusing you, Mr Thwaites.'

'No. I am accusing myself – I suppose. Beryl is always taking me to task for it. She says I am too soft-shelled.'

'Your sister must have been surprised by your mother's condition.'

'I know Brenda too well. At first she would refuse to accept it, refuse to believe it. She would see only what she wanted to see: just as she saw only what she wanted to see in Charles Bryce – until suddenly the truth caught her like a wet towel across the face. I tell you, I know the way her mind works. That's why I'm not as worried as you might think I ought to be about where Mother is.'

Mosley looked at him with hopeful enquiry.

'Brenda isn't unloving, unkind. She is obstinate, self-deceptive. She is an intellectual and aesthetic snob. She identifies with wrong-headed minorities to the point of perversion – '

All in the present tense – though by his own account, all his evidence for this was nearly twenty years old.

'She rides rough-shod over people's opinions; only her own beliefs count. But she's not totally irresponsible – not in the material, the humane sense. She wouldn't do physical harm, and she wouldn't see physical distress in a situation where she could relieve it. I am sure that she has sent Mother somewhere to be looked after – perhaps only on a temporary basis, to give herself a rest. Perhaps she even only wanted to clear the house as a rendezvous for one of those men who keep coming.'

'Somewhere private,' Mosley suggested. 'We, of course,

are covering all the public institutions – all those that are advertised or registered.'

'She wouldn't send her back to The Towers,' Thwaites said. 'That's one thing I'm certain about. I know Brenda too well. She'd never repeat history: that would be the abnegation of progress. That would be admitting us right and herself wrong. I know she'd try something new.'

'Could she afford to, do you think?'

Thwaites shook his head, disclaiming knowledge.

'She did her best to get it over to me that she's not done badly for herself. She was contemptuous of what I earn – and though I say it myself, I am doing quite comfortably.'

He looked down into his sub-standard laboratory, with its ancient brown woodwork, its stained benches and its sense of improvisation and archaic methodology.

'I know this doesn't look much, but the firm is flourishing, and the board knows it all starts in here. It would have to be a big offer to tempt me away. But Brenda looked down her nose at me. She may have been exaggerating, but she gave the impression that she'd been moving in circles that didn't think small over money matters.'

'But she gave you no idea of the nature of those circles?'

'None whatever.'

'Or of whether she had come away from them permanently?'

'She gave no hint. There was an aura of something, a suggestion that it would have been tampering with unstable dynamite to have asked. But surely, though – '

Thwaites paused, indecisive. Mosley got him to continue by simply raising one eyebrow.

'Surely that's what it's all been about – all these cars in the night – the bullet in the back of the neck. Doesn't it show that she was still as thick with unsavoury circles as ever she had been?'

'She may only have thought she'd escaped,' Mosley said, barely audibly. 'Well, Mr Thwaites, I know you are wanting to get home. I am sorry to have detained you so long. There's just one little thing –'

Thwaites had shown immediate relief at the suggestion that the interview was over. The anxiety returned to his eyes at the hint that some venomous question had been held in reserve.

'Did your mother suffer much from toothache?' Mosley asked.

'That's strange. Of course, she couldn't. She'd none of her teeth left to ache. But she did complain sometimes. I wondered if it was like the patient who has a pain in a leg that's been amputated. Or perhaps there was something amiss in her gums. But whenever we vaguely suggested getting her to a dentist, there always seemed to be a miraculous improvement.'

Mosley nodded. His face seemed to suggest that this slotted in neatly with views he had formed. He did not say what they were and gave the impression, not rare among strangers who had to deal with him, of being unable to clear his mind of irrelevant trivialities.

Thwaites saw him through the laboratory, across the factory floor and out by a side-door that opened directly on to the car park. As they passed the administrative suite, Mosley was aware of a door slightly open, where he would have expected it to be closed: *Company Secretary*.

And from the staff bicycle shed, as he tested the state of his tyres with his thumb, he saw a woman watching him from one of the ground-floor windows: a middle-aged woman, not saved from dowdiness by artificially blonde hair quite out of keeping with either her age or her heavy, plum-coloured costume.

Five

It was well advanced twilight by the time he was leaning his machine against the rose-trellissed porch of the modest country villa. Some of the residents had already been put to bed. Others were sitting round the walls of a day-room either watching or dozing through a moderately moronic television panel game: old ladies with their hair sticking out at the sides in ludicrous tufts; old ladies clutching the handles of their knitting-bags as if they suspected every other inmate of being a potential snatcher; old ladies staring unresponsively at the screen; others staring at nothing.

It was a good nursing home as such places went, which is to say that it did not waste money on extravagances, even on some of those extravagances that patients' relatives believed they were paying for. But an honest effort was in reserve for emergencies, and physical discomfort was alleviated where it could be. Mosley fortuitously knew – it was odds on that he would – the retired SRN who came in to help with the bedtime rounds. She was a woman to whom he would have committed the care of himself, if he had needed it.

Nellie Palmer put him in a corner of the small cubicle used as a nurses' common room, furnished him with a cup of gut-tanning tea and left him to catch up with his note-writing until she had delivered the evening pills. Tags and ends of patients' quarrels drifted in to him: 'You go back to your own place, Kathleen Darwent. This isn't your corner.'

And now and then Nellie's voice was raised in final judgement. 'Lizzie Armitt, you're old enough to know better.' Lizzie was eighty-eight.

Nellie Palmer came into the ante-room at last, carrying a cup of tea for herself. She was a woman of Mosley's own age-group, with kind eyes, brisk movements that made short work of work, and a lack of hesitation, even in snap decisions. She was a woman who had been involved on the edges of a great deal of suffering and stupidity – and had once or twice been plunged into the maelstrom on her own account.

'Nora Thwaites?' Mosley asked.

'We were shattered when that daughter came for her. And shattered when we heard what had happened to *her*. I suppose they've got you on it now.'

Mosley blinked.

'I'll give that girl her due. I know all that's been said of her, but she was shocked when she saw the state that her mother was in – shocked and angry.'

Mosley looked at her expectantly.

'It's that glazed look,' Nurse Palmer said. 'They all get it. I've seen them come in here, and for the first day or two they wander round talking to those who can't get out of bed, trying to show friendly. But within a week they give up. Then you see them sitting, looking at a wall – or out of the window at the roses and squirrels – and not seeing them.'

'Is that how she spent the last two years, then – with the glazed look?'

'Nora Thwaites was a mutterer. She muttered.'

'Muttered?'

'To people who weren't there: her son and her daughter and her daughter-in-law mostly. Always spiteful, always complaining, blaming them for putting her into situations that were unfair and inhuman.'

'How did she behave when they came to visit her?'

'They? There was only the son – he came alone after the

first two weeks. I respect that man, Mr Mosley. He scarcely ever missed a Saturday afternoon and sat loyally through his hour, no matter what mood she was in. She sometimes begged and screamed and demanded for him to take her home again. But most often of all she just ignored him, wouldn't look his way when he sat beside her, wouldn't even eat cake for him at tea-time. There were times, of course, when she didn't even know him – or mistook him for somebody else.'

'Who, for example?'

'Mostly for one of her own brothers, as a matter of fact – and he was a man that she didn't care too much for, either.'

Out in the ward someone moaned loudly. Nellie Palmer cocked her head on one side, but decided that it was not a case for intervention.

'I remember once,' she said, 'that he had another woman with him. I don't know who she was. Can't have been too close a friend of the family, because she wouldn't come in. Just stayed out in the car, reading a magazine, while he sat out his hour.'

'What sort of woman? Can you describe her?'

'Nondescript. About his age. Shapeless. Unattractive.'

'Relative of his wife's, I wouldn't wonder,' Mosley said. 'What I'm really wanting to know is about old Mrs Thwaites. What was the true state of her mind?'

'It's hard to tell. She had better days than others. They all do: me too. You ask my opinion: I'll give it you. I think Nora Thwaites knew more of what was going on than she ever let be seen. Some days, of course, she was not with us at all. On others, I'm pretty sure she knew where she was, why she was here – and just how hopeless it all was.'

A fresh cadenza of moaning broke out and Nellie Palmer got up and went out to the sufferer, treating her woes as if they were an offence by a naughty child.

'Be quiet, Gladys Bretherton, and let the others get some sleep.'

She came back to Mosley.

'Of course, you know, these people in here are all crafty, far gone though some of them are. In places like this little things are apt to loom large – like if there's half a slice of bread and butter over. And Kitty Spencer has got my jam, Nurse, the little jar Mrs Gilman sent in for me. They jockey for pathetic little advantages. They think themselves into situations where people are being unjust to them – and then use all the guile they can muster to get the tables turned. Sometimes we pretend to give way to them, let them win a round – as a bargaining point, I might say. Some of them have an irrational confidence in some drug or other – maybe nothing more startling than aspirin. Others take against a medicine they've been prescribed and will go to great lengths to get out of taking it.'

'And that's a general picture of Nora Thwaites, all the time she was here?'

'Not entirely. As I say, there were days when she knew who we were. You would see her eyes come unglazed, and she'd sit looking round at people, weighing them up – and hating them.'

'So what was the reaction when Brenda came for her? Did she know her own daughter?'

'We wondered what was going to happen. I might say, there were two or three of us at action stations in the wings in case of major upset. But it all went off quietly. Yet it had not been one of Nora's good days. And she didn't actually say anything, not a word, when she was taken into the office and confronted with Brenda. We'd brought her in in a wheelchair and she sat, oh for minutes, not looking at any of us, especially not at her daughter. Then she did glance at her, didn't smile, didn't speak, but somehow we got the message that she'd grasped the situation and wasn't going to create a scene. Of course, I didn't hear what Mrs Lumley said to her in the office after Brenda had gone. But still she didn't show any feelings, any joy, any bitterness – not even curiosity – when we eventually helped her into that bashed-up green sports car and the wheels crunched up the drive. More tea?'

Mosley said no, he would have to be going, and began tucking his notebook into his already bulkily overloaded inside pocket.

'There was one other thing, Nellie.'

'Oh, yes?'

'Can you tell me whether Mrs Thwaites ever suffered from toothache?'

Nellie Palmer gave a throaty little laugh.

'She did, yes – oh, I suppose about every six weeks or so. She had complete plates, upper and lower, and I looked two or three times to see if there was an abrasion, but there was nothing that I could make out. We'd give her an aspirin and she seemed to forget it. But there was one time when she nagged about it for two or three hours, and we told her we'd arrange for a dentist to come in and give her gums the once-over. The very thought of it seemed to cure her.'

'And the whole thing was forgotten about?'

'She didn't complain any more. We get very used to imaginary symptoms in here, Mr Mosley.'

He unleaned his bicycle from the porch and tested his lamps. The front one gave the sorriest flicker and the tail-lamp no sign of life at all. He pushed the thing philosophically out into the darkness.

Six

'Why,' the Assistant Chief Constable asked, 'has Mosley sent Beamish to Edinburgh?'

'Largely to get him from under his feet, I would imagine,' Detective-Superintendent Grimshaw said.

'I always hate asking for a clearance when it's already a *fait accompli.* I take it we can put up a reasonable case on paper?'

'On paper. In point of fact, I'd probably have done the same thing myself. The house-hunters that Brenda Cryer disturbed happen to be living in Scotland at the moment. Mosley wants to know how fortuitous the connection is.'

'Ten to one entirely fortuitous,' said the ACC. 'And what is Mosley himself doing, if anything, at the moment, do you think?'

'Going through several thousand pages of journal – I hope.'

'Journal?'

'Mosley keeps a daily diary – has done since he joined the force in 1946. He puts down everything that comes his way – everything he hears, everything anybody believes, any rumour that's current or public reaction that's seething. It runs to several hundred school exercise books, all carefully numbered. He does the index on Sunday mornings and his rest days. I might say that I don't know, officially, that the thing exists. If we as a force kept records, especially in this age of computers, of individual foibles of no criminal significance, the *New Statesman* and such would lose their marbles. But I see no harm if a private individual wants to do it for his own amusement. And I've been grateful for Mosley's journals more than once.'

'I do believe, Grimshaw, that you're actually glad you have no one but Mosley to assign to this case. And now there's something else. Chief Inspector Marsters: when are we going to get him back into general duty circulation again? I must say I'm finding it difficult to nail him down on his actual progress in this Hartley Mason business.'

'I don't like the smell of it either, sir. But if only a quarter of what Marsters suspects is true, it's something we've got to face up to. Managerial crime – '

'I know. But I wake up sweating cold in the night, dreaming that Marsters has overstepped it. We mustn't have overkill: and yet we either ram it home or leave it alone. Hartley Mason is a partner in the most respectable firm on this flank of the Pennines. Old William Fothergill would turn in his grave at the slightest hint of what Marsters believes.'

'I know, sir. But Mason isn't one of the family at Fothergills. And one does hear rumours from time to time that there are some in the family boat who don't care for him.'

'Rumours, Grimshaw! I'm sick and tired of rumours. You're getting as bad as Marsters.'

Mosley could not remember her name, but he did know the approximate date and, strong-mindedly steering past fascinating digressions and forgotten side-tracks, he finally put his finger on a sub-paragraph headed: *Farrington, Sandra.*

Sandra Farrington had come to Bradburn High School in September, 1962, straight from college, supercharged with a brand of sociology distinguished mostly for its indignation, of which she had assimilated mainly the slogans, and which she had had the pragmatic sense to suppress during her interview with the Governing Body. She it was who had become Brenda Thwaites's mentor during that last year at school, at a time when the girl, utterly disillusioned by everything she saw, at whatever level she looked, might possibly have lacked the resolution to assert herself, had she not seen confirmation of even her most whimsical rebel ideas mirrored in this deliciously anti-authoritarian figure, who nevertheless spoke, because she was a teacher, with the voice of formal authority.

Mosley, picking his way through his pages, located Miss Farrington at the stage, a year or so later, when she had walked off the Speech Day platform in protest against the positively elitist ambitions of the headmistress's report. The headmistress, no less of a pragmatist than she was, had skilfully provoked Miss Farrington over the next few months, to the point at which the girl had resigned, rather than waiting to be dismissed: which might have brought trouble from her professional association. And although politics, ideologies and religion may not be considered when making appointments to the public teaching force, it was remarkable with what consistency over the next few months she lost posts to other candidates when she applied for work with neighbouring authorities.

So she got married – the *so* was Mosley's interpretation in his pinched pothook notes. She got married to a man called Francis Dereward Tudor Balshaw who, whether or not he initially shared her views on the vices of the establishment, was nevertheless for remunerative purposes the promising executive servant of a monopoly that traded according to accepted market practices. He was on a month's notice, with a preferential company mortgage on a house of nicely gauged prestige. His young wife had to respect company rituals if she wished remuneration, mortgage and prestige to continue. Mr F.D.T. Balshaw became effectively anchored. Mosley wondered which of the conflicting elements in his wife had prevailed.

There had been no more diary entries about the

Balshaws after 1965, but after false runs through the telephone directories of several dormitory conurbations, Mosley finally ran them to earth on a large open-forecourt estate south-west of Rotherham.

He went there himself. Beamish had telephoned a negative report, and was now heading south though still north of the border. Mosley, dismissing his taxi out of sight of his destination, entered the open-forecourt estate, not turning aside to ruminate on its vandalized almond trees, its up-and-over garage doors or its wrecked telephone kiosks. The avenues were named after culinary herbs, the closes after gastrophiles. It was in Escoffier, leading off Marjoram, that he came to Evenlode, the domain of the Balshaws.

The garage doors were up and over, and in the space beside their second car he spotted the electric mower and plastic lawn-sprinkler that were all part of Sandra Balshaw's linkage with the bourgeoisie. He also noticed, from their car-stickers, that they had been to Interlaken, Dubrovnik and Antibes.

And Sandra was mercifully at home, now a buxom woman of – yes, he had it precisely – thirty-seven, in denim slacks, a woven leather belt and hair entirely concealed beneath a double triangle of printed nylon. She seemed embarrassed at having been caught unprepared – and at first surprised at the nature of his interest.

'Brenda Cryer – I've seen her name in the papers, of course. A horrendous case. But of course, I know nothing at all of the woman.'

'But as Brenda Thwaites?'

A furrowed brow and some seconds of internal rummaging were needed before even that produced an echo.

'She's not the same one! Well, fancy my knowing her! Well, hardly knew her, of course. Just one year, with me on one side of the fence and her on the other. Yes: I do remember her – just. But I don't know in what way I can possibly help you. She was a kid in her last year at school, and I was a kid in my first year beyond the pale. I only *taught* her – or was supposed to.'

There were ornamental beer steins from Munich and Mittenwald, a straw donkey from Fuengirola, a reproduction Aristide Bruant poster and any number of small silver cups and trophies for badminton.

'You didn't ever hear from her again? You didn't correspond?'

'Heavens, no! I wasn't that sort of teacher.' She laughed at the incongruity of the conception. 'The less said about my teaching career, the better. I didn't influence anyone.'

'In that case, I don't think I need take up any more of your time.'

'I did meet her once after we both left the place, though.'

Mosley clapped his hands together once, and left her to talk.

'Before Francis and I were married – just before. He was working at Rangate, in the North Riding, at Brooker and Ponsonby's, and I'd gone over to be taken out to lunch. And I saw her – well, I wouldn't have recognized her: it was she who saw me. She was coming out of a factory, with a whole host of other girls, all in beige nylon overalls. "Miss Farrington!" she shouted to me across the street, and I had to stop, and she expected me to know who she was, and I didn't. And when she told me, at first I couldn't remember. Her name meant nothing to me at all. And then, when it gelled, I could hardly believe it. She'd been quite an attractive girl – immature, but full of vivacity, reaching out, looking for something, as I suppose we all were in those days. But now! Well, the one thing that struck me most about her was the smell. She was working in a small concern – not one of the major suppliers – that made brake and clutch linings out of some sort of fibre. It stank sickeningly. It clung not only to her overalls, it must have been deeply absorbed in her pores. She was wearing no make-up, and looked as if she had been sweating all morning. She had lost flesh and the haggardness of her face gave her a mean look that I didn't associate with her at all. Her fingernails were misshapen and dirty and split, and her hands – she had slender fingers – were oil-stained and chapped. We only spoke for a minute or two. I was late for my date, and she told me there was a small caff she wanted to get to – she even mispronounced it like that, deliberately, I think to underscore what she'd come down to – a caff, that she wanted to get to before the barm-cakes ran out. That was the one thing that most sticks in my mind – her aggressiveness, a sort of outlandish enjoyment, a perverse pride in the mindlessness of the work she was doing – and the equally mindless company that she was stuck with. I remember thinking to myself: is this why we teach them Keats and Mallarmé, why they learn the law of diminishing returns and the memoirs of Tocqueville and Engels? And that was the last I ever saw of her, Mr Mosley, from that day to this.'

'I suppose you'd even have difficulty telling me the name of the firm she was working for?'

'What would you expect? I saw its signboard once, fifteen years ago. I doubt whether I even read it then. But I'll tell you what – ' Her expression brightened. She would help if she could. 'Francis will know. He drove daily down that road for two years.'

'When will he be home? I'll ring through.'

Seven

So there was nothing more to do that day, and it was D+2 before Mosley could get up to Rangate. And first there was Beamish to pacify.

'I might say, Mr Mosley, that our Scottish colleagues would have been only too happy to pull that chestnut out of the fire for us – or, rather, let us know by return that there was no chestnut.'

'No, well. It's happening all the time,' Mosley said cheerfully.

'Not to me. Not in my own division, it isn't.'

'No, well. Better luck next time. I have in fact another little chore for you, if you would be so kind.'

'Kindness itself,' Beamish said, in a tone whose implications, he feared, went unnoticed.

'A question, then: when is the toothache not the toothache?'

'When it's ajar?'

Something was happening to Beamish. He thought it might be the onset of madness.

'Put it another way, then,' Mosley said. 'If a woman with no teeth complains of toothache, what does it amount to?'

'Hypochondria?' Beamish tried.

'Could be, but I think not. Mrs Thwaites, Senior, has no teeth. She also consistently has toothache. She had it at home, before she went to the nursing home, she had it in the nursing home itself, and she had it at home again after her daughter had brought her back. On her bedside table at

Jackman's Cottage I found a half-used bottle of oil of cloves. And as she'd hardly be rubbing that into her dentures she must, I surmise somewhat uselessly, be rubbing it into her gums. Now what does that suggest to you?'

Sergeant Beamish at least appeared to be giving it some thought.

'Delusion,' he said at last.

'I think not. I think an uncut wisdom tooth – which is not my imbecilic idea of a joke. A lot of people suffer from them – including seventy-odd year olds. Probably it has become impacted into the bone, and ought to have been taken out years ago. But Mrs Thwaites appears to have developed a fear of the dentist. Perhaps she had a rough time when the last of her molars made way for her dentures. The merest suggestion of dental attention produced a false relief, of the sort that I believe is called psychosomatic.'

'So?'

'So Mrs Thwaites comes to live with her daughter, who is far too strong-willed to let her mother get away with dental cowardice. Old Mrs Thwaites has to be sent away to have the thing attended to – perhaps doesn't even know where she's being taken. But it's a rotten bit of oral surgery at any age, and definitely not so good in your seventies. It needs a general anaesthetic, probably stitches afterwards, and a few days' recovery time. So Brenda Cryer gets two birds with that stone. She gets her mother attended to – and clears the deck for the man who is coming to murder her. Which is where you come in.'

Beamish did not look as if he thought that a stimulating chore was about to be handed to him.

'Find the dentist who extracted Mrs Thwaites's impacted wisdom tooth, and find out where she was sent to convalesce.'

'I may have to ring every dentist in the United Kingdom.'

'It would take just as long with a computer,' Mosley said unprovocatively, 'by the time you had programmed it. But

I'll tell you this: I'll bet Brenda sent her mother to her own dentist, the one who last treated her. So you'll not only find the old girl – you'll discover where Brenda was living before she came back.'

'It will still be a long job,' Beamish said.

'I expect you'll find some way of narrowing it down. What's the word everyone uses these days: a rationale?'

Mosley's next visit was to Superintendent Grimshaw's office, where he cast a typescript down on the desk. After thirty years' experience, Mosley still typed as if the order of letters on the keyboard was a constant source of surprise to him.

'Well – that's out of the way.'

Grimshaw looked at him for one second as if he might, after all, be delivering a miracle.

'Kettlerake,' Mosley said. 'Hens. Thirty of them.'

'Thirty hens, Mosley? That is a substantial contribution to the division's loot-retrieval sheet.'

'Thirty hens mean a lot,' Mosley said, 'to five families who keep half a dozen each.'

Only then did he set out for the North Riding.

Eight

Rangate was a grey and rectilinear desert of trading estate: soft drinks, non-ethical drugs, baby buggies, mixed pickles and office sundries. It was possible to see the factory one wanted, its signboard impudently challenging a couple of streets away, and still not be able to find the right combination of intersections. There was not even a challenging signboard, however, for a well-spring of brake and clutch linings, because this no longer existed. It was after all fifteen years since Brenda Cryer had last sweated out her working day with the brake linings entering into her soul through her pores. Passers-by hurried on, unwilling to protract conversation with this middle-aged imbecile whose secular happiness seemed to depend on the discovery of a dried-up source of malodorous fibres, no longer on the estate map. Mosley stood and contemplated the asymmetrical wilderness of staff car parks – the Spruce Greens, Venetian Reds and Daytona Yellows – and reflected that even if he found the concern in its full, evil-smelling productivity, his chances of pinpointing the Cryer connection were necessarily slight. But any other approach must surely promise slighter hopes still, and he was never one to be put off by considerations that others found impenetrable. He asked a security guard at a frontier-post, a Pakistani dustman and an old woman with a grandchild in a pram. And he finally learned from a council surveyor with a theodolite that the firm had been taken over at the height of its prosperity, dismantled and sold as a development site before the laws against asset-stripping had been strengthened.

Mosley stood in the middle of the road, abused by lorry-drivers leaning out of their cabs. He looked, idly at first, at a group of girls in mob caps and nylon overalls of imperial purple, who were just coming out of the gate of a factory that provided a portion of the world with its requirement in fishermen's floats. He hurried over to speak to them, earning further opprobrium from a cylindrical load of newsprint whose approach took him unawares.

'I wonder if you could tell me if there's a caff anywhere near here where a man could get a barm-cake?'

They were an unproariously happy bunch, raucous, uninhibited and made-up in a variety of styles suggestive of latter-day sirens: Mosley noticed that most of them were young married women. They heartily begged him to accompany them, and he toddled along with them – *toddled* is an apt word for his gait in their sprawling company – with a great deal of shrieking laughter, the apparent implication being that one or the other of them – perhaps even an *ad hoc* alliance – was going to rape him before they arrived at their destination.

Amid this invigorating escort he arrived in a very few minutes at an older part of the settlement, the nucleus of the original village, which possessed a church, two pubs, a war memorial, a mobile fish and chip shop and a small bakery, round which other cohorts were gathered in nylon overalls of clashing hues. Connoisseurship of barm-cakes, a yeasty type of roll, apparently demanded that they be eaten hot from the oven, and the parturition of the midday batch at this establishment had been timed to a nicety for years. The small loaves were cut laterally in two by the consumer, and served as vehicles for sandwiches either of potato chips, or of thick slices taken from the interior of a pork pie. Thus lunched the young working married women of Rangate.

Mosley was patient. And eventually, from management

and assistants more intent on purveying barm-cakes than on helping improbable policemen with their enquiries, he came away with the single piece of material information that the one person between Trent and Tees most likely to help him was Jessica Makepeace. He also carried away with him a variety of unsolicited views. The common thread that ran through them all was that Old Jess could be difficult, even dangerous to handle.

It was well into the afternoon before Mosley had run her to earth – a wispy, wiry and shrunken woman in her seventies, who for the inside of her lifetime had been a supervisor at Crawleys. Yet her spirit had not been exhausted by long years of handling fights, jealousies, strikes, sit-ins, handbag and cloakroom pilferers, husband-thieves and boyfriend slanderers. She scanned Mosley's features in a manner that confirmed the tales he had been told of her: her intolerance, her singleness of mind, the indestructibility of her opinions once formed. What was odd was that after that first moment of terrifying assessment she seemed to take to Mosley. And Mosley took to her. It was as if two soul-mates had suddenly discovered each other, their common ground a shared view of humanity. Old Jess put her kettle on within five minutes of Mosley's entering her house.

'Brenda Bryce? I remember her. And she's the same person as this Brenda Cryer – ?'

Mosley reconfirmed the truth.

'I remember her well. One of the best workers I ever had. Such a good worker that at one time I thought I would have to get rid of her.'

Mosley's eyebrows requested expansion of the paradox.

'It was a disruptive influence, you see, having someone on the shop-floor who actually seemed to be enjoying the work for its own sake. It upset people, having someone there who was not trying to dodge the column all the time.'

'It seems to have been anything but enjoyable work.'

'That's the whole point. It was revolting. I remember one

married couple who broke up because the woman, who worked for us, wouldn't change her vest before she went to bed. If her husband happened to wake in the night, the smell made him have to get up and vomit. She said she'd tried most things, and this was the best kind of birth-control she knew.'

'And this was the kind of company in which Brenda Bryce took pleasure?'

'Not exactly. I can't say she ever made a friend here.' Jessica Makepeace used *here* as if she were still working for the firm. 'There were all sorts of upsets, not because she couldn't get on with people. It was because they wouldn't get on with her. The work was a sort of drug to her: something she was hooked on. You see, you could tell, right from the outset, that she was a young woman with something that had to be put far behind her. I don't mean something to forget: it was some experience stronger than that, something she had to wipe out by a sort of personal self-violence. Hard work alone wouldn't have done it – at least, I don't think she thought so. It had to be rotten, stinking, soulless work, in rotten, stinking, soulless company. It was as if she'd put herself on trial and come up with a sentence of penal servitude on herself, the only thing that would clear her. It was obvious to anyone who looked at her for twenty seconds that she was a girl who'd gone through something – something not to her credit: but perhaps a good deal less to her discredit than what she was tormenting herself with. I didn't ask questions. In my job, you learned not to. The answers came to you – if they were going to.'

Old Jess had no cakes to offer, and her idea of afternoon tea was thick and thickly buttered slices, cut from the loaf and served up with jam from the jar.

'And all the time she was here, she was working like a steam-engine, trying to qualify herself for something better. Evening classes: shorthand, typing, accounts, even company law. There was not an evening in the autumn and winter when she hadn't a class of some sort or other, and the study she did on the side was nobody's business. I used to ask her why she didn't ask for a transfer to our own office – I could have fixed that for her in a jiffy – and then she'd have had better company and a chance to get in some practice with typewriters and things. But she had the idea – and I think after all she was right – that if you went in at the bottom, that's where you were likely to stay. The way to the thin end on top of the pile was to go in at the top – not try to clamber through all the opposition inside. Besides, with the piece-work rates she could get here on overtime, she was better off on the floor than she would have been at a desk. She was saving like fury, hardly spending a penny on herself.'

'Things might have been set fair for her, then.'

'Are things ever set fair for anybody? I think she had more staying power than any other girl of her age that I ever came across. But that wasn't enough.'

'She didn't stay the course?'

'She took the exams at the local college, but she said that was still not good enough. She'd been saving like mad – to get to London, for a year in a private residential college, a place with a name, something to juggle with. Her argument was that if she went there with the back of the work already broken, she'd have every chance of coming out on top. She was going to be satisfied with no less.'

'She had her eye on a top job?'

'I don't know quite what it was that she pictured – right-hand woman to a cabinet minister, something like that, I imagine. An indispensable: one of those who do all the real work – and have all the real influence.'

'In other words, she thought big.'

'But not beyond her capacity. Brenda could have gone on to big things. I always said so.'

'And obviously, you were closely in her confidence.'

'No.' Jessica Makepeace was categorical on the point. 'On one evening, and on one evening only, she loosened up and talked to me. We'd had one of our shop-floor crises, but a worse one than usual – and as usual she'd been at the centre of it, through no fault of her own. It all happened because it had leaked out through someone in the office that she had A levels – something she'd always kept dark from the others. When that word went round, you'd have thought she'd spent the last eighteen months boasting about her intellectual superiority, whereas in point of fact I've seen more swank in a school-leaver with one CSE on his record. But this triggered off something that was just waiting to be detonated. They accused her, not only of giving herself airs, but of coming in where she didn't belong, of stealing some other working girl's employment from her. They hated her for being different, even though she never laid claim to be. And this time she was terribly upset about it, that was what took me by surprise. She was in such command of herself in all the other difficulties she'd hemmed herself round with. And here she was, looking as if she was going to go under – for something that, candidly, didn't matter a damn. I asked her round here for an evening – something I've never done before or since for one of our work-force. And that evening, just for once, she talked to me. She needed to.'

Somewhere behind a lifetime of keeping brake and clutch linings in production, Jessica Makepeace had come from a family home, with her favourite radio programmes, cinema memories of the thirties, albums of holiday snapshots. There were framed portraits of relatives about the room: uninformative, unoutward-going faces, each with its secret range of aspirations and disappointments.

'That's how she came to tell me about her marriage. We knew, of course, that there'd been one, because she always wore a ring. That, I think, was all part of the self-torture – a reminder. Also, it did at least make some casual men think twice before bothering her. I don't think she told me the whole of the truth: only part of it. I don't know how much you know about Brenda's background, Mr Mosley?'

'It would be safest to assume I know nothing.'

Old Jess looked at him with a sudden shaft of suspicion.

'If you are putting me through some sort of test, Mr Mosley – '

'I am not.'

And, oddly enough, she accepted that without further question.

'She'd got married too young to some man her family didn't approve of. I never did hear her call him by his first name. And suddenly, on the train, not an hour from home – they were on their way to the Canaries – she caught sight of him, from an angle, and suddenly asked herself, what had she done. She couldn't explain it, she knew she just couldn't stand him, couldn't bear to be tied to him for life. The way she put it, he was suddenly, shockingly, sickeningly the same as everyone else. So she simply got off that train, and never set eyes on him again. Myself, I think there must have been rather more to it than that. Something must have triggered it off. But that's how it went. Once her mind was made up – for no matter what slender reasons – I mean slender from the ordinary person's point of view – nobody was going to unmake it for her. Unfortunately, I believe she'd be obstinate to the point of silliness, rather than give way. I'd a long talk with Brenda Bryce that evening, Mr Mosley, and though I thought she was silly in a lot of ways, I had great admiration for her.'

'But she went on and kicked over the traces again?'

Jessica Makepeace refilled their tea-cups: a rich, orange brew, that would have gladdened the heart of Nurse Palmer.

'The little bit of bother in the workshop settled down, as these things always do. The women found some other way of relieving their boredom. Brenda took her local exams, came to the end of her evening classes, didn't register for any new subjects, and I began to think it wouldn't be long before she told us she'd be moving on. But the trouble was that she felt pretty flat with her studies behind her. Her evenings were empty. The pressures were off. Someone, some girl at the next bench, tried to persuade her to come to a works social, and to everyone's surprise Brenda said yes, it was time she moved in on a fresh world. She went to that social, and met a man there. And that, Mr Mosley, put an end to a lot of big thinking.'

'You mean,' Mosley said, 'that she went off with him? Did she get a divorce? Was he a married man? Did she leave the district? Did she shack up with him, here or elsewhere?'

'I can't tell you a thing, Mr Mosley. She gave in her notice, worked it out, went away.'

'Where did she live, here? Flat-sharing?'

'She had various living arrangements while she was at Crawleys. It took her a long time to settle down. She had the same sort of difficulties in digs as she had in the factory. In the end she came to some arrangement that lasted. She shared with two or three other girls. But they weren't ours, and I've no idea where you would find them.'

'In Rangate?'

'Somewhere the other side of the by-pass, that's all I can tell you.'

Beamish laboured under persistent difficulties. He was a man who still had to stabilize his attitudes, both towards others and himself; but he was no fool. The nagging suspicion had already formed in his mind that his assignment covering the dental records had something in common with his trip to Edinburgh: it was a way of getting him off Mosley's shadow. But he also had a persistent niggle that there might be more than a molecule of sense in it. The dental explanation was a hunch on Mosley's part – but not unfeasible. If it were true, then the man who broke it could be within a step of breaking the whole case – perhaps even of breaking it before his own inspector could reach the scene. Sergeant Beamish therefore applied himself with characteristic industry to a survey of dentists.

It was, at first contemplation, a discouraging prospect. The Yellow Pages listed two hundred dentists in this region alone, some of them working in partnerships, which meant multiple records. He hopefully considered the fact that the list of dental technicians was shorter, but it was by no means certain that new dentures would have to be made after the extraction of a wisdom tooth. Maybe some time would have to elapse before the old lady's gums were ready for a new fitting.

Then Sergeant Beamish remembered something from his own last visit to a dentist. There had been a form to fill in before treatment could be started, and it had had to go to some kind of executive council for ratification.

Beamish turned from the Yellow Pages to the directory proper and there, after a number of false trails, he found the number of the Area Dental Officer, who was able to put him on the right track. He began a more viable round of telephoning.

The degree of helpfulness and alacrity of response varied, but three quarters of the way through the morning he struck a clerk who actually turned up the name of a Mrs Nora Thwaites on an index-card: in East Yorkshire, somewhere along the coast, in a large village north of Scarborough.

He checked – not that he needed to – that Mosley was still away from HQ; and he went to see Grimshaw. Beamish's contempt for those set in authority over him extended to Grimshaw, but he kept that opinion to himself. Grimshaw, whether by his just deserts or not, was a power in the land.

And Grimshaw looked at him with close interest. Could it be that in their so far slight association, Mosley had already taught Beamish something?

Grimshaw listened with diplomatic appreciation to Beamish's account of his dental researches, which did not omit reference to the acuity of mind that had put him in touch with the executive councils.

'So what you are suggesting is that I should authorize you to go off on your own to some Yorkshire fishing village?'

'I am quite sure that it would be Inspector Mosley's intention for me to follow it up at once, sir.'

'It is equally possible that he might want to follow it up for himself – where *is* Mosley, by the way?'

'Rangate, sir.'

'What the hell is he doing in Rangate?'

'I don't know, sir. He didn't say.'

'Or when he would be back?'

And Beamish made the most of it. 'The impression I gathered, sir, is that Rangate might lead him even deeper into Mrs Cryer's past.'

'It might be fatal to underestimate Inspector Mosley's sense of direction, Sergeant.'

'I am sure, sir.'

'I think perhaps you had better go as soon as you can to Ember Bay, Beamish. See if you can locate Mrs Thwaites. See what state of mind she is in. See if you can find any trace of Brenda Cryer in the locality. See what she was up to up there, and if possible get the colour of her local associates, without talking to them too much, in case you cut across any ploys that Mosley might have going.'

'Yes, sir.'

'And report by phone direct to me, if Inspector Mosley is still not available, the moment you have something concrete to offer.'

'Sir.'

The relative density of his use of that word had never been so great as within the last five minutes.

Nine

Beamish enjoyed driving to Ember Bay because of the mental processes that accompanied the journey. It was a reasonably safe bet that the murder of Brenda Cryer was connected with the circles in which she had been moving just prior to coming home. And even if these were unconnected with the immediate vicinity of Ember Bay, there must have been some correspondence between her and the dentist who had treated her mother, something that would put him safely on her trail. Moreover, the dentist was almost certain to know where the old woman had been taken to convalesce; and that would almost certainly be in some place where even more vital information about Mrs Cryer would be forthcoming.

Mrs Thwaites herself, of course, was a more dubious prospect. The general picture was of a confused mind, but surely even senile dementia took some cognisance, albeit ill-defined, of the environment through which it passed. Mrs Thwaites might not know who had driven her from Parson's Fold to Ember Bay; she could hardly be expected to have noted down the numbers from the registration plates of the vehicle in which she had been carried. But there would be something, surely, some vital if misunderstood impression, that an alert and dedicated detective-sergeant could trace from woolliness to precision. He might even be so vivid in his reconstruction of events that he could persuade the old girl into a rare moment of clarity in which she would tell him all. Sergeant Beamish's view of the immediate future of Sergeant Beamish was a roseate one as the Yorkshire miles swept under his bonnet.

Ember Bay appeared to consist mainly of two uneven stacks of slate roofs that climbed the flanks of an inlet some half a mile across. The resort was served by two roads – one from the south leading in and one from the north leading out. The one from the south, which Beamish was following, was signposted with roadworks, of which the only evidence was a solitary standard of temporary traffic lights, burning arrogantly and long-windedly red. Beamish waited dutifully, the only vehicle in sight, for what must have been five full minutes. He then decided that if the law must be served, the law had to be broken. He drove through the Stop sign and encountered a lorryload of scrap coming over the brow of the hill opposite him. There was an exchange of views in which he came off the worse, being linguistically more of a purist than the lorry-driver. He reversed back to where he had been, the light now having improbably gone to green, only to return abruptly to red (without an intervening amber) for its next five-minute stint before Beamish could let in the clutch. Thus he arrived in Ember Bay in a state of mind that might conveniently be summarized as rattled.

Ember Bay was a former fishing village that had taken unto itself a colony of seaside painters, another of potters, and the minimal amenities of a holiday resort, without expansionist hopes of containing them. Its streets and public places were all lavishly framed in multiple yellow lines and its one-way traffic system was unintelligible to the most intelligent of strangers. Even Sergeant Beamish, brainwashed by a police driving course, was on his way out of Ember Bay by its northern egress before he realized that he had put the operative town centre behind him.

He eventually found the dentist, whose receptionist asked him immediately for the number on his medical card. She was a woman of his own age, distinguished both by her extreme good looks and her bad temper. She looked as if her hell was populated by people who did not know the numbers on their medical cards.

'We spoke on the phone,' he said, 'on the matter of your patient Mrs Thwaites.'

'Mr Hatton cannot see you until after hours.'

'I understand that. I do not need to see Mr Hatton at this stage – in fact perhaps not at all. All I need is the address at which I can contact the patient.'

She scribbled petulantly on the back of an appointment card.

Outside again, he found that his car had not only been boxed in, but also issued with a ticket by a female traffic warden in harridan's black stockings who implied that his warrant card only exacerbated the offence. Somewhere behind the ranks of closed-out-of-season restaurants, shuttered spade-and-pail shops and the empty racks for the deployment of comic postcards, must lie the sea itself, its presence now attested by the lugubrious and frequent but nerve-wrackingly irregular boom of a distant foghorn. The address scrawled by the receptionist needed research.

It turned out to be a house in a Regency terrace on the northern arm of the Bay: a quieter part of the community, this, approachable only up several hundred steps. There was a certain dignity here, a peace interrupted only by a single game of hopscotch on the pavement. The house was occupied by an exuberantly welcoming elderly woman called Mrs Reynolds, who, although a retired nurse, did not usually take convalescents into her home, but sometimes did so to oblige. This she told him as she relieved him of his coat in the hall. She was one of those women who cannot meet a stranger without an autobiographical preamble.

'Your friend is looking forward to seeing you.'

'She is not exactly a friend.'

But Mrs Reynolds had preceded him up the stairs, two treads at a time, with such speed that she missed this. Beamish further classified her as a one-way conversationalist: she was too busy talking to listen.

The house smelled of moth-balls, fire-lighters and paraffin heaters. As they approached the sickroom, a distinctly hospital smell began to win the day. Mrs Reynolds went straight in, going through the motion of knocking as she opened the door: characteristic number three – she was a woman who liked to observe, however perfunctorily, all the forms.

'Here comes your friend!'

She seemed intent on convincing both sides in advance of the glorious sentimentality of this reunion.

Mrs Thwaites was sitting up in bed in sprightly fashion, her hair ribboned in two bunches that stuck out in absurd fashion at the sides. Beamish thought that he had never seen anyone less suggestive of senile dementia. She beamed on him as he entered, a smile of friendship that must surely have rounded off Mrs Reynolds's day; a smile ruined only by its absolute toothlessness. Her eyes were very much alive indeed – and glad to be so. She said something – quite a long sentence – which emerged only as the lapping of her tongue over vacant gums, further muffled by flabby lips with a tendency to fall inwards. Beamish did not understand a single syllable of her speech, so looking vexed, she repeated the whole statement.

'She says if she'd known how smoothly it was all going to go, she'd have had it done years ago.'

The voice came from the far side of the bed, where the interpreter was seated: an uncomfortable-looking, disgustingly familiar creature, himself the perfect picture of senile decay: Mosley.

And that was impossible. There were no means by which Mosley could possibly have picked up the trail here.

'Show the sergeant your cavity,' Mosley said, and his way with old women was so effective that Nora Thwaites understood him before Beamish did. She opened her mouth moistly and he had to approach, peer down into the red, fleshy depths, and utter admiration for what he saw there.

'Nice, clean job he's made of it, hasn't he?' Mosley said. Beamish agreed and backed away.

'I had the stitches out yesterday,' Mrs Thwaites said with pride. 'It didn't hurt at all. I'd always thought it was a painful business, having stitches out.'

This time Beamish grasped enough of the sounds she made to put her meaning together along the lines of probability. A conversation with her, on strictly commonplace topics, might not be wholly impossible.

'Now tell Sergeant Beamish the story you told me about Albert Boardman and the root-cutter,' Mosley said.

Mrs Thwaites grinned sheepishly. 'He doesn't want to hear that.'

'He does, you know. He's come a hundred and twenty miles in his motor, just to talk to you – haven't you, Sergeant Beamish? So he doesn't want to miss your best stories.'

But a change seemed to have come over Nora Thwaites. The light of life in her eyes had unaccountably been replaced by a wildness – a mixture of fear, distrust of those about her, and an impotent anger at the impossibility of being understood and believed. 'All I know is, I've been sitting on this hillside for the last six hours, waiting for some conveyance to pass. How'm I going to get back home once the light starts to go?'

She seemed to have turned against Mosley now, and looked imploringly at Beamish. 'Young man – can you get me a conveyance?'

Mrs Reynolds, who had made no sign of being prepared to leave the room, now stepped forward and gave them the benefit of her professional experience. 'She gets mixed up, now and then,' she said.

And Mosley stood up, went to the bedside and looked down at the old woman with a sort of maudlin lovingness. 'Now listen, my dear. I've got to go down into town to attend to some business. Sergeant Beamish has come a long way to talk to you. I want you to be a good girl, and answer him nicely and properly. Tell him everything he wants to know.'

'All I want is a conveyance.'

'Yes, well, when I get back, I'll see what can be done about that. Perhaps the Sergeant himself will take you home in his motor. It all depends on how nice you are to him – how co-operative. You know what co-operative means, don't you?'

And Mosley was out of the bedroom before Beamish could head him off. He was halfway down the stairs before the sergeant had reached the head of the banisters.

'Inspector, where are you going? Hadn't we better make some arrangement about meeting again?'

'I'll be about an hour and a half, I expect,' Mosley said. 'And then I'll come back here. You get what you can out of the old girl in the meanwhile.'

Mrs Reynolds followed the inspector downstairs. Alone on the landing, Beamish looked back at the half-open sickroom door, and for the first time since joining the force, felt a nausea for most things connected with it.

It was two hours before Mosley came back. By then, Mrs Thwaites had mercifully fallen asleep and Beamish was sitting downstairs, listening to Mrs Reynolds, in a fireside chair at the hearth of the old-fashioned, cast iron, black-leaded kitchen range.

Mrs Reynolds was by no means loth to talk, but Beamish doubted whether he had got anything out of her that she would not already have told Mosley. He had learned, for example, how she had come to know Brenda Cryer. But the odd thing was that until Mosley's visit, she had not known that Brenda Cryer was dead. Mrs Reynolds did not take a newspaper or listen to news bulletins; the news, she said, always depressed her.

She knew Brenda Cryer because on Fridays, her shopping day, she always took her morning coffee in the lounge of a small hotel down in the Bay where Brenda had been the receptionist for some years. As often as not it was the receptionist who served the coffee, probably even made it herself behind the scenes; it was that sort of hotel. And Brenda was that sort of receptionist – the woman, in fact, on whom the whole place probably hinged: who had had oversight of chamber-maids, who spotted breakages and failures of gadgets, and had them made good by handymen, who kept an efficient reservation-list, who hired and fired staff, banked the takings, scanned the cook's orders and produced immaculate accounts when the absentee landlord showed periodic interest.

'I don't know how they'll manage without her,' Mrs Reynolds said. 'She needed a change, I suppose. I should have needed one before I'd been there a fortnight. I don't know how they manage to keep the place open. That's why it's so popular with me and my friends for elevenses. There's never a crowd, not even in season.'

'Did she tell you her reason for leaving?'

'Oh, no. It took us all by surprise. And she's going to be missed. If you ask me, she ran the place.'

'You don't know where she used to be before she came here?'

'No idea. She was the pleasantest soul – but she never talked about herself.'

'People didn't try to question her?'

'Why should they? We're not all policemen, you know. She wasn't the sort of person you'd think of asking personal questions.'

'A little forbidding, perhaps? A little toffee-nosed, even?'

'Not on your life. Nothing could be further from the truth. But dignified – though not at all in an off-putting way.'

'Did she ever behave as if there was something in her past that she wanted to hide?'

'Not in the least. Why should she? Sergeant – she's the

one who's been murdered, isn't she? You're talking as if some sort of blame attaches to her.'

'I was thinking of her associates. In cases like this, it's very often someone fairly close to the victim who is the culprit.'

'I couldn't say about that.'

'Who were her particular friends in the town, for example?'

'I don't know that she had any special ones. The Bay View didn't give her much time. And I never heard her complain about that. She seemed to like work – a lot of it.'

'She had no men friends?'

'Not to my knowledge. Of course, there were some who liked to play up to her, especially men travelling away from home. But she knew how to keep them at arm's length without offending them. If someone wanted to flirt, she didn't mind if that kept them at the counter for another round of drinks. She knew how to scotch it if things looked like going too far.'

'Did she never go away for a holiday?'

'Once a year. The hotel generally closed down for three weeks in October. Then she used to go away on her own: an organized tour, as a rule – Majorca, Capri, Crete. Sometimes she stayed in England: the Lake District, the Scottish Highlands. We used to laugh about it – what a change it was for her to stay in someone else's hotel.'

That was the tenor of the conversation with Mrs Reynolds. The retired nurse knew only what she had seen on the surface, and had never seen any reason to doubt – saw, indeed, no reason to doubt now – all that Brenda Cryer had allowed to be known about herself. The friendship between Mrs Reynolds and Brenda had not been deep. Brenda had known that once or twice – to oblige – Mrs Reynolds had taken in uncomplicated patients to nurse in her home, perhaps to give relatives a break. Brenda had written from Parson's Fold to ask if she would take her mother for a week to tide her over a nasty but not uncommon bit of dental surgery. Mrs Reynolds had obliged without expecting anything she could not handle.

'Of course, the old lady's not clear in her mind. But I'm accustomed to that. I had seven years on a geriatric ward. It's only a question of humouring them.'

'And who actually brought her here?'

'It was done through a car-hire firm, with a hired agency nurse.'

'You don't know which car-hire firm, or where they came from?'

'I asked the driver in for a cuppa, but I didn't plaster him with questions. I keep telling you: I don't ask many questions. I took it for granted he was from somewhere near Parson's Fold.'

Whatever he put to Mrs Reynolds, the answer fell always short of being usefully informative. Beamish was at bottom sufficiently fair-minded to admit to himself that it wasn't Mrs Reynolds's fault. She knew – or thought she knew – only what Brenda had intended her to know.

Beamish was relieved to see Mosley, which was something that he could not previously have forecast. The inspector was in that general state of contentment with society at large which was the only mood in which Beamish had ever seen him. He did not announce how he had spent the last two hours, but there was no sign of excitement to speak of success, nor of despondency to suggest disappointment. They walked down the broad stone steps leading to the heart of the place, and Beamish said he had better ring his wife to let her know how late home he was going to be.

'A good idea,' Mosley said. 'Why not err on the side of accuracy and tell her that you will not be home at all? I propose that we should spend the night in a hotel.'

'*The* hotel?'

'An interesting place,' Mosley said. 'I am curious to see your reaction.'

Bay View was situated in a side-road two right-angles

removed from Ember Bay's miniature harbour. Its title's only claim to veracity lay in the fact that there were two small attic windows – of rooms occupied by less favoured members of the domestic staff – from which a glimpse of distant waves might be had when sea-mists permitted.

'I fear that they have no night porter,' Mosley said, 'but they have lent me a key. I fear also that we are too late for an evening meal, for which indeed we would have to have given notice at lunchtime. But I have ordered sandwiches. They do have a bar, which they will open on request, if the barman can be found, which I fear tonight will not be the case. The grille is raised really only for the sale of aperitifs before the meal. The house is only a few days removed from its annual closure, and therefore business has been encouraged to run down. The only other guest beside ourselves is a traveller in trawlermen's cables.'

Mosley inserted the loaned key in the lock and let them in. Only a single pilot light was burning, casting melancholy shadows over the entrance hall and lounge. There was a strong smell of stale beer and the air had been tainted by years of cigarette smoke.

'It seems fair to assume that the house has a merrier air in high season,' Mosley said.

'It seems popular enough with Mrs Reynolds and her friends.'

'For the very fact that it fails to attract the crush of holiday-makers for whom it nominally caters. I am informed that sometimes, during the school holidays, the house is full. But it has become a joke among the staff that no one has ever been known to stay here twice, except hard-bitten commercials, who appreciate a bill made out for twice the amount that they have actually spent. I am also informed that the place was cleaner, tidier and more brilliantly serviced before Mrs Cryer handed in her resignation.'

Mosley switched on a lamp on one of the tables and they saw that sandwiches had indeed been left out for them – the thickest wedges of sandwich that Beamish had ever been offered, though cut so unevenly that they had a curiously tapering effect. The depression made by a large thumb was still visible in one of the rounds, and lace-like fringes of discoloured ham-fat hung over the edges of the crusts. Two glasses had also been provided, together with four small bottles of beer, but no means of opening them. Beamish had an opener attached to his combination pocket-knife, but before he could bring it into action, Mosley – with a degree of dash and sophistication that astounded his sergeant – opened his by bringing it down smartly across a corner of the table.

'Well now: let's have your report, Sergeant. How did you fare with old Mrs Thwaites?'

'Inspector – it's no use. What sort of information do you expect to get from her? Was it just a joke, leaving me like that? She's in an advanced state of mental decay.'

'But with lucid moments.'

'Who the hell can tell where, when and if she's ever being lucid?'

'I admit that it's difficult. I didn't do too well with her myself. That's why I was anxious for you to try your hand, unhindered by me.'

'An entire waste of time,' Beamish said.

'I challenge that, Sergeant. She's the only evidence we've got of several important aspects of the case.'

'*Evidence*? How can you possibly think of putting a woman like that into a witness-box? Or even of taking a statement from her?'

'I don't mean evidence for the court, lad – or even a document on the file. I mean evidence for your ears and mine: perhaps even the identity of the murderer, no less. Once we know that, our task will be tangibly easier. We shall then know what other, more presentable evidence we'd better be looking for.'

'How can she possibly know the identity of the murderer? She left Jackman's Cottage two days before

Brenda was killed. At least I was able to check that date with our dear Mrs Reynolds.'

'True. But she must have had some awareness of the men who came visiting her daughter on previous days. If I'm any judge of character, a much more acute awareness than it would suit her to reveal. She would have seen them, heard their voices, some of the things they said. Perhaps even exchanged a few senile hilarities with them.'

'And got it all mixed up for the rest of her life. She leaps thirty years every few seconds, Inspector. During the time when I was making an honest effort to dig something out of her, she tried to send me once to rescue a sheep that had fallen into a chasm. She mistook me for someone called Bert, with whom she appears to be pursuing a vendetta to the death. And then she thought I was her son, and told me what a bloody fool I'd been to marry a woman from Ribblesdale.'

'Exactly. She is a mine of highly specialized information.'

'And the spine's fallen off the book, and the unnumbered pages have fallen all over the floor. And there isn't an index.'

Mosley chuckled delightedly, in a manner that Beamish saw as yet a new facet of him.

'Very apt, Sergeant. A mixed metaphor, following my reference to a mine – but very vivid. As you say, there are a lot of loose leaves lying about, and we're going to have a testing time, reading them all.'

'Well, for God's sake don't ask me to read them. I made no headway with her at all, and I'm never likely to. And before you tell Superintendent Grimshaw that that's mutiny, do you mind if I submit a written memorandum on the point?'

Mosley looked hurt. 'I'm sure it needn't come to that sort of pass, Sergeant. You and I don't know each other. I don't know where your aptitudes lie. There may be somebody, somewhere who would have a way with someone like Mrs Thwaites.'

'Well, it isn't me.'

'We'll say no more about it, then. There are a few other jobs I'm going to ask you to do.'

Beamish heard this with a marked sense of the ominous.

'A spot of burglary in an hour or so, for example, if you'd care.'

Beamish said nothing.

'And thank you, lad, for looking at her cavity. Very proud of that cavity is Nora Thwaites. I thought it might just have tipped her sympathies in your favour, if you'd said the right thing about her cavity.'

Mosley rolled fat from the crust into his mouth in the most repulsive manner. 'Let's change the subject. What do you think of this place? Are you struck by any anomalies?'

'About its being open to the public at all, do you mean? About its remaining in business?'

'This is not the best time of year to be here, of course. And obviously, it's suffering from the withdrawal of Brenda's touch.'

'The withdrawal of somebody's.'

'Brenda's: the opinion is shared by the town generally. I think we can say that, six weeks ago, Bay View was in better condition than it is now.'

'It could hardly have been in worse.'

'I'll agree that some of the guide-books would be sparing with their stars. So what's that suggest to you?'

'That the British public is always ready to meet a con-man halfway.'

'That wasn't what I had in mind. I was thinking of Brenda's state of affluence.'

'Do we *know* anything about that?'

'We know that she came back to Parson's Fold giving every impression of being well off. A relative judgement, of course, dependent upon the poverty of the observer. But enough to impress her brother, who definitely thought she was well-heeled. She told him she was better off than he is – and he accepted that. And Donald Thwaites may be fighting a losing battle with the hags on his perimeter – but I respect his assessment of economic matters.'

'So – where is this leading us?'

'To two questions. Firstly, the source of her income. Bay View?' Mosley looked over his shoulder at the long shadows in the corners of the shabby lounge. 'Even when a hotel like this is going like a bomb, the bonuses that come the way of the receptionist are not overdone. Tipping by working-class guests during a Yorkshire Wakes Week is finely calculated. This place is owned by a syndicate – faceless out-of-town men who are happy to stay out of town, as long as the dividends keep rolling in. This lot even seems happy enough when they aren't. Since Brenda left, they have put a manager in: a manager, if you ask me, whose job is to preside over its final run-down. There have been managers before, while Brenda was in residence; and she managed them – from behind her reception desk. That is town talk, and I accept it.'

Mosley borrowed Beamish's knife to get into his second bottle of beer.

'And she was here eight years – eight years, remember – those eight years of her we'd lost, when we first started on this. For eight years, she didn't go out much, she can't even have seen a great deal of daylight. She had the sort of annual holiday that can be had by any sensible factory girl who looks after her funds. Eight years! Now why does a thoroughly attractive, pre-eminently capable young woman put up with a dingy existence for eight years? For one of three reasons, I suggest. She may be in love with work for its own sake, using it to kill something, including time. She may have some sentimental sense of loyalty to the institution for its own sake. Or somebody may be making it worth her while.'

'It's only that last that makes sense. But I can't think of any earthly reason why anyone should willingly overpay her for running a place that's perpetually in the red.'

'Then that is something on which we are clearly going to

have to concentrate. Eight years!'

Mosley seemed to be taking Brenda Cryer's lot to heart with a deep reserve of human sympathy.

'That's a long time for a woman blessed with free will, who's shown plenty of other evidence in her life of willingness to make up her own mind – and cut off her moorings when she fancies; and who is more than capable, on all the surface evidence we've seen, of making her own way.'

'I don't usually quote poetry,' Beamish said, 'but didn't someone once say something about: *Better to reign in Hell than serve in Heaven?*'

'I don't know: did someone? Eight years!' He seemed obsessed by the prospect. 'I said she had eight years unaccounted for – but don't let's underestimate some of the other gaps. How little we know of her! We know she sweated it out in Rangate from '63 to '65. From about '72 we have her here, the faithful lieutenant of an anonymous out-of-town syndicate. In '65, when she was twenty, she met a man at a works social – and walked out of the world of brake linings. So what was she doing from then till the age of twenty-seven?'

'I suppose that's going to be my next assignment,' Beamish said, his tone not revealing what would be his attitude if it were. The case was beginning to involve him, and although he could not have said when that started to happen, he was now closely listening to Mosley.

'I'm hoping that's going to be one of the things that will, as it were, spew sideways out of the machine. We're going to do a spot of burgling in an hour or so's time, and there's no telling what will come of that. Because there's one more puzzle that I can't see any answer to so far –'

'In my rough notes there are several –' Beamish began, but Mosley went on without seeming to hear him.

'If we accept the reading that Brenda Cryer did reasonably well for herself, what has she done with it all? Where is it? In some deposit account? Invested in the syndicate? In jewellery, real estate, even? Where, even, are her consumer durables? From the few pieces she brought with her to Jackman's Cottage, she'd keen tastes in art and music. So had she no Hi Fi equipment? No prints, books? That's why we're going to feloniously enter her room, presently – the room she had here. I want to find out what, if anything, she left behind; or, to put different terms to the same question – whether she intended to come back when the stint with her mother was finished.'

'You bewilder me,' Beamish said. 'I must say, I thought –' But he did not develop that line, which he saw in mid-stream had got away to a bad start. 'What I'm trying to say, Inspector – you've said an awful lot in the last ten minutes. But doesn't it all start from some pretty confident suppositions?'

'It's got to start somewhere,' Mosley said.

'Yes – but we've got to keep testing the bottom with the plumb-line, haven't we? Now I would have thought a more profitable line would have been her current men friends.'

'I dare say it would. And I'm hoping they'll be spewed out of the other side of the machine.'

Beamish looked at him with interest, not unmingled still with an oblique sense of pity. The old man was not such a fool after all – in his woolly-minded, hit-and-miss, unsystematic, uninformed way. He sat there now, solemnly and eagerly propounding his theories, rather like an old-time insurance man trying to persuade a poor family of the virtues of a cheap industrial policy. Mosley knew a lot about men and women and their motivations – as men and women and their motivations used to be. But had he a clue, for example, of how men and women comported themselves now that the liberating sixties were nearly two decades away?

And then it was uncannily as if Mosley were reading his sergeant's thoughts.

'My mind isn't made up yet,' he said, 'about Brenda's attitude to men. We know she's had at least one unhappy experience with a man, from which she escaped by simply escaping, if you see what I mean. I think there was probably at least one other such soul-searing episode – possibly two. But she hadn't turned her back on men. In a sponge-bag in her bedroom in Jackman's Cottage, she carried an emergency contraceptive kit. I couldn't tell whether it had been used since she had come back to the Fold: I don't think it had. From the encrustation at the mouth of the tube, I'd say it hadn't been used in the last week of her life, at any rate. But that isn't my main point. What struck me was the nature of the method she used: not the system of a woman who was always ready for it: the system of a woman who could quickly make herself ready if need be. Occasional only, in other words. Though whether to oblige a man, who for some reason or other had better be obliged, or whether so as not to miss an opportunity that she fancied herself – that's something I can't at this moment answer.'

'No, Inspector.'

'Well, don't sit there gawping at me. The people back in my foothills may lack the technology for which your Q Division is famous, but we are not without some know-how. Do you know I once retrieved a woman's handbag, containing two pounds, four shillings and sixpence – the whole case turning on a French letter found behind a rabbit-hutch?'

'Amazing,' Beamish said.

'Well, bed, then.'

Mosley got up, assembled the litter of their supper on the tray and carried it over to the apron of the bar-counter outside the grille.

'But I thought you envisaged –'

'Bed noisily, Sergeant. Up again quiet as mice. I'll see you on the landing outside my door, in stockinged feet, at half past midnight.'

The old man headed for the stairs, but turned back on his heel. 'A point I think I ought to make: you were talking earlier on about submitting written memoranda. I'm not fond of that way of looking at things.'

'Please forget that, Inspector – I –'

'No. Let me make myself plain. What we are about to do would undoubtedly be considered illegal in Q Division. In my division, left hands and right hands don't always work off the same circuit. If you wish to be excused from the impending operation, all I ask is that you do not know that it has even taken place.'

'Oh, no – I'm with you, Inspector.'

'You see, I have my reasons for doing it. I could get a warrant for the asking – even at a few minutes' notice at this time of night. But I do not wish it to be known which way my interest is turning. I do not wish that to be known at this stage either in Ember Bay or in the spiritual home of any faceless syndicate. They think I am a doddering old fool, and I find that a useful image.'

'Yes, Inspector.'

'Even the Assistant Chief Constable thinks I'm a doddering old fool – and there's no need for you to say, "Yes, Inspector" to that.'

'No, Inspector. But there is one thing I would like to know.'

'Well – if I happen to know myself –'

'How did you find your doddering old way to Ember Bay an hour ahead of me?'

Your doddering old way: Beamish never actually crystallized it out, but it was at that moment that he first knew he was beginning to like Mosley.

'Ah,' Mosley said. 'Friends at court, you see. I happened to think that it would be no bad thing, once in a while, to report progress. There is nothing so confusing as a man who breaks his own lifetime habits. So I rang through to Bradburn when I'd finished at Rangate. And Grimshaw not only told me where you had just left for: he pulled strings at Rangate and had transport laid on for me.'

Beamish suppressed any visible or audible reaction. There were things in this life that just weren't fair.

Ten

At twenty minutes past twelve, Beamish pulled a sweater over his shirt and tucked the bottoms of his trousers into the tops of his socks. At twenty-nine and a half minutes past, he opened his bedroom door. Half a minute later, Mosley opened his.

The corridor was dimly lit by a single dirty, unshaded bulb at the far end. The floorboards, under cold, cracked, brown linoleum, were uneven. Subsidence of the foundations years ago had given a tilt to parts of the house which produced a strange feeling of drunkenness. There was a single, irrationally chosen picture slightly askew on one wall: the Isle of Man – an etching of Peel Castle in the sort of storm in which Wordsworth once saw it.

Mosley knew precisely which way to go, which room had been Brenda Cryer's. Beamish did not ask him how he had come by the information. He was getting used to the marches that the old man stole, his quasi-miraculous efficiency when the present sort of brainstorm was on him. Napoleon, it had been said, preferred lucky marshals. If Mosley had been one of them, there might have been no retreat from Moscow.

They went up a half-flight, on to another short landing where there was no light. Mosley found a switch and pressed it and a bulb fused with a loud click and a blue flash. Mosley uttered a four-letter word followed by a two-letter one, then produced a pencil-torch with whose discreet light he found the door they wanted. About them, the hotel was full of the idle noises of the night: a lavatory with a worn ball-cock washer, the wheezings and knocking of the bizarre patchwork plumbing, a pattering and slithering of mice on linoleum. Beamish did not know what tail-end of staff the hotel still housed, what basic cooks, porters and under-managers might be snoring in cells somewhere in the honeycomb. The rooms on either side of Brenda Cryer's might be occupied; there might not be another soul in this wing.

Mosley had produced some tool from his pocket with which he was attending to the lock. Beamish could not see what it was; probably the old man had an obstinate jealousy of that sort of secret: a basic range of skeleton keys, probably, maybe filched from the kit of some felon years ago. He put his ear down close to the keyhole, listening sensitively for the reponse of wards and tumblers. The lock did not seem amenable to immediate persuasion.

'Let me have a go.'

Mosley made way for him at once. There was something out of the ordinary somewhere, no obstruction in the mechanism, a smooth motion of tumblers in either direction, but still the door remained locked.

Then footsteps entered the corrider at an angle below them, outside their own bedrooms, the unevenness of gait resulting from something more fundamental than the mere tilt of the floor. Mosley puffed out his cheeks and blew air out slowly through his lips. Beamish looked at him, as if asking for instructions.

'If he comes up here,' Mosley whispered, 'we'll just have to face it out.'

And he was coming up here. A shoulder brushed against a wall, a leather sole missed the edge of a tread, then tired muscles started hauling the man's weight up the half-flight.

'Hullo!'

Friendly enough, anyway – and, apparently, utterly unaffected by coming upon an obvious crime in the commission. Beamish diagnosed the dealer in trawlermen's hawsers, clearly awash with North Yorkshire bitter, clearly capable of little more than finding his way to his own bedroom. But that was evidently a feat which he had often enough achieved against an impediment similar to tonight's.

'Wasting your time there,' the rep said. 'She's gone. Went five or six weeks ago.'

'Oh, aye?' Mosley said, equally friendly.

'Aye. Made a difference to this bloody place.'

'I suppose it has.'

'You'll not find her in there, you know. And even if you did, you'd not stand a chance – not a couple of dead-beats like you two. I mean, she'll let you buy her a gin – and then hide it under the counter while you're not looking.'

He managed to strangle a belch, swallowing with dramatic nausea.

'I don't know why I drink this bloody stuff. I shan't half suffer for it tomorrow. She's not in there, you know. She's been killed.'

'Oh, aye?'

'Aye, it were in t' paper. So you'll get nowt there.'

Beamish was concealing Mosley's skeleton keys in the palm of his hand.

'Well, I'm goin' t' bed. I'm not stopping up half o' t' neight talking to you two silly buggers.'

He turned on his heel and Beamish prepared to catch him as he swayed at the top of the half-flight.

'It's double-locked, anyway,' he said to them over his shoulder. 'T' key has to go round twice. It's t' same wi' all t' staff bedrooms here. That's to protect their bloody virtue.'

He reeled perilously, noisily, but magically protected down the half-flight. Mosley and Beamish heard someone come out of a bedroom a landing below, speak to him. They stood frozen in darkness. Speech was resonant beneath them. The newcomer to the scene was obviously conducting the drunk to his room. Then he too went back where he had come from. The descant of the plumbing prevailed again. The mice, who had taken shelter, returned to their theatre. Beamish gave the tumblers the second pressure that they needed.

And then, after Mosley had quietly closed the door behind them, they found themselves in what was clearly one of the best bedrooms in the house, give or take the taste in interior decoration. It was a corner room, spacious, with a big bow window that commanded a view, if not of the Bay, at least of a roofscape with fanlights and cowls that might delight some kinds of surrealist. Even the decoration was not all that unacceptable, better than was to be found elsewhere in the hotel, reasonably recent, though scuffed by the moving away of furniture, and bearing the inevitable scars and faded rectangles, the cobwebs and chippings of a room that has been cleared.

One of Mosley's bed-rock questions was answered as soon as they were fairly in the room: when Brenda Cryer had moved out of here, she had moved out for good. The bed was stripped down to its interior-sprung mattress. The wall-to-wall carpet was gone, leaving only the rucked-up underfelt. The co-axial cable of a television aerial came in through a window-frame and lay in idle arcs round the skirting-board. Very little of furniture was left: a chest of drawers of a useful size, but that needed work on its veneer, a small writing-table with one of its castors wedged level over a folded cigarette packet. There had been pictures on the wall – more pictures than had eventually appeared in her bedroom at Parson's Fold.

'Well, that's something we now know. When she left here, it wasn't temporarily.'

Mosley went and opened one drawer in the chest after another, even examined the dates of the newspapers with which they were lined, found nothing, apparently, that stirred him.

'So what do we do next?' Beamish asked him. 'Get in touch with the syndicate?'

'They're the last people in the kingdom that we get in touch with. We don't betray any interest in that syndicate until we know a good deal more about them than we do at the moment. We don't approach them from a position of strength: it has to be omnipotence.'

Mosley found a metal wastepaper bin, emptied its contents on to the writing-table and went through them: screwed-up paper tissues bearing cosmetic smears, a cigarette packet of the brand she had been smoking at Jackman's, an empty tube of the sort of contraceptive jelly that she seemed to favour.

'One always lives in hope that they've left something behind that they meant to take with them.'

He brushed the waste back into the bin with the side of his hand, opened one of the drawers in the table, seemed to be having difficulty as it jammed, did not rest until he had pulled it out altogether. Then he reached in with his hand and brought something out. After he had examined it, his features were suffused with seraphic pleasure.

'Something left behind, Sergeant: for instance, the old snap-shot that's fallen behind the back of a drawer.'

It was a colour photograph, amateurishly posed, showing a summer afternoon tea-scene in front of the conservatory of a country house. It was a stone-built house, and from the corner that was visible, seemed to be a sizeable one. Behind it there was a back-cloth of low green hills, a deciduous coppice, an obtuse angle of distant roof. In the middle distance was an end of neatly trimmed box hedge.

An elderly gentleman was sitting at the tea-table, in front of him a china tea-service that one could see, even at this level of photography, to be a family possession of some quality. There were a plate of scones, jam in a server that looked to be of sterling silver and a Dundee cake with one slice cut from it.

The man was in his late seventies at least, exceptionally well preserved and groomed without blemish. He looked kind, happy, above all distinguished – and proud to be in the company that he was keeping.

Brenda Cryer was standing behind him, the only other person in the photograph; though one noticed that the table had been set for three. The picture had probably been taken about ten years ago – she would be about twenty-five, a great contrast to the photographs of her corpse that Mosley and Beamish had seen, with a bloom of maturity in her that was nourished by contentment and security. Her arm was about the gentleman's shoulder – and not as a casual gesture; not blatantly, vulgarly claiming proprietorship, either – but with love; pride, too.

'Well, now, Sergeant – this ought to be a job after your own heart: tomorrow's target. Find out for us where that house is.'

'Oh, yes, that will be right up my street.'

A good deal had happened to Beamish within the last couple of hours. He could not have pictured himself treating Mosley to this ironical banter – except perhaps as safety-valve nastiness for his own relief.

'Where do you reckon that line of hills is? Barrow-in-Furness? Just as obviously the Weald, I'd say. Or do I mean the Wold? No: it's Somerset for certain –'

Mosley was standing by wearing an expression of somewhat idiotic expectancy.

'Of course, it's the stonework that will have the last word. So obviously Yorkshire – or Derbyshire – or Northamptonshire. Or do you think it could possibly be in the Cotswolds? This will be child's play compared with an old woman's wisdom tooth. All I've got to do is get in touch with the estate agents' executive council.'

'You might try the advertisement pages in back-numbers of *Country Life* for 1971 or 1972.'

'We can't know, can we, that it was ever up for sale?'

'Oh, yes, we can. You see, I know it was round about then that this gentleman died. And presumably this property went up for sale. And Brenda Cryer, I wouldn't be surprised, came sadly down in the world. She came here.'

'You are a man for taking mighty leaps, aren't you?'

'I rather regard these as gentle paces. Though I can't be sure of the month of his death. I shall have to look in my journal for that.'

'You are building up the drama very neatly, Inspector Mosley. At what stage are you going to tell me who this gentleman was?'

'Oh, yes, that might be of considerable help to you. He was William – I can't remember his middle name – William Fothergill: of Fothergill, Fothergill, Foster, Sons and Fothergill. He was senior partner for very many years, and it was rumoured that he had a love-nest somewhere – and a young mistress who was somewhat coveted by the few who had been privileged to set eyes on her. Though the story went that she wasn't interested in letting her eyes stray. Maybe they were too firmly fixed on the main chance. Maybe no man had ever treated her quite as old Fothergill did. Incidentally, William Fothergill was the man her father had worked for since the day he'd left school.'

Eleven

'Has something got into Mosley?' the Assistant Chief Constable wanted to know. 'I saw him this morning leaving the office – not actually running, but walking relatively briskly, his chin thrust out like the bow of a snowplough, his chest expanded and his arms swinging as if to a march-step. Oh, and he had a new hat. I could swear he was wearing a new hat. The same shade and style as he has worn since the young Anthony Eden first popularized the model, but I am prepared to stand by my judgement that it was brand new.'

'Very probably, sir. There have been other small symptoms suggesting that Mosley has got his teeth into the Cryer case. I'm sorry that I cannot give you any details. Mosley is always reluctant to produce interim reports that he might be expected to live up to. What impresses me is that Beamish, equally uninformative, seems to be sharing his confidence.'

'Beamish? How is Beamish standing up to this new release of avuncular energy?'

'My fingers are crossed, sir. They seem to be firm friends. I wish I could feel certain that it is going to last.'

'I wish I could share your confidence in Mosley. And how much confidence have you honestly got in Sid Marsters these days?'

'Marsters, sir, is still groping his way through a dark tunnel. He has one of the most unenviable quests that has ever been undertaken by this force.'

'He started it.'

'I know. And he believes in it.'

'And do you?'

'Invariably, sir – for two or three hours after hearing Marsters on the subject.'

'The Chief's been up to London, had an Old Boys' Act session with someone near the top in the DPP's office, showed him the papers in their unfinished state, tried to get a tip or two on the blow of the wind.'

'And?'

'Was told to go for Mason hammer and tongs. The man's obviously a villain, that's what the DPP's right-hand man said. Get him busted. He did also add that if there's the merest haircrack of a loophole in our case, he wouldn't be in our shoes for a fortune. Does Mason suspect that we're on to him?'

'Marsters says he can't possibly.'

'Get Marsters in here at three this afternoon, will you? And drop by yourself.'

It was true that Mosley had bought a new homburg: within a minute or two of the outfitter's opening time. It was also true that he was walking smartly, holding the upper part of his body with military pride. What the Assistant Chief Constable had not noticed, for he had seen Mosley only from behind, was that he was even wearing a new tie, one that combined sobriety with a *soupçon* of *élan*. He rather thought that it was his immediate impact on Fothergill, Fothergill, Foster, Sons and Fothergill that would decide whether he would get a toe of his boot inside a partner's office at all.

He had one contact, and one contact only at Fothergill's: a now elderly maiden clerk who had been trained by Brenda Cryer's father in his own image. Miss Harrison was a thin, dithering woman of limited imagination, fierce loyalty and ferocious discretion, who combined copy-typing with reception, and at the same time acted as ballast to the potential high spirits of certain younger members of the clerical team. She was presiding in her draughty corner when Mosley went in, shortly after buying his new hat.

'I'll tell you what it is, Lilian. I want to have a quiet talk with one of the partners – one of those with his roots in the old days.'

'That doesn't leave many.'

There was in fact only one Foster left of the Sons, and for that reason he was still thought of, at forty-five, by some people as a youngster. No Fothergills remained at all. It was not publicly known how much it cost to buy one's way into the firm; but the probationary period was long, and several were known to have left early.

'I might need to take a little time over it, too,' Mosley said. 'It would be better not to have too many interruptions; and I'd like to get it over in one go.'

'It won't be easy, today of all days.'

But all days were today-of-all-days in Lilian Harrison's crisis-ridden life. She lived on crises as other people are compulsive doodlers.

'There's no one in yet, of course, only Mr Parnell – and he hasn't been with us a year yet.'

'No. He wouldn't do.'

'You'd better come back at a quarter past ten. I'll see what I can do for you after morning conference. Am I allowed to know what it is about?'

'Brenda Cryer.'

'Yes.'

She looked at him without emotion, without even a hint that she saw the mesh of complexities that must lie behind this. Mosley knew very well that Lilian Harrison could tell him more of what he wanted to know than could any of the partners. But he also knew that the only form of interrogation that would have persuaded her to divulge a secret of the firm was not available to the police forces of civilized countries.

He duly reported back to her at ten thirteen and she

permitted herself the ghost of a lip movement, meant to be the hinted smile of success.

'Mr Hartley Mason will see you. He's free now. He can give you half an hour.'

'Which is his office?'

'Mr Jonathan's old one.'

Jonathan Fothergill had died in 1957. Mosley knew the way up the gloomy stairs. Fothergill, Fothergill, Foster, Sons and Fothergill were, as a firm, acutely contemporary-minded, but they cultivated crepuscular gloom and a decor of Dickensian untidiness, their establishment redolent of pink tape, japanned deed-boxes, wax seals and bound statutes. It put the frightener on some clients, gave confidence to others – and also created a deceptive atmosphere of sloth and dawdling-wittedness in which action took place behind the scenes at a sometimes incredible speed. For example, a lot of capital had been multiplied – their own and that of selected clients – in the years of development booms, always legally, but with a smart eye for the critical moment.

Hartley Mason had always been looked on as a slightly enigmatic, slightly controversial acquisition of the Fothergills and Fosters. Hints of uncertainty at top desks had even seeped out into the town. But he had been Mr William's own protégé, brought in about seven years before Mr William died. One of the main reasons for the ripplets of discontent had been Mason's preference for the criminal side, which was something that Fothergills had had little to do with, except on those rare occasions when long-standing clients had found themselves in usually accidental trouble. It was not only that the firm's volume of criminal defence seemed to increase – as did their involvement in legal aid cases – relations with learned counsel developed along well-worn grooves, and a good deal of this sort of business started to come in from far outside the immediate neighbourhood. Hartley Mason put conspicuous energy into cases with which some of the senior partners would rather not have been associated. But Mason's position with the firm, consolidated during the uncertain years by old William himself, had now become unassailable. And Mason did not limit himself to being a link between his clients and their barristers. He had become interested in criminology as a social science – and more particularly in the rights of the depressed classes with whom he had to deal, both before and after conviction. He wrote papers for left-wing reviews on abuse of the Judges' Rules, on procedures after arrest and on the privileges of long-term detainees. No one doubted that Hartley Mason was one of the country's best brains in his preferred specialism, and he rapidly became known as a Prisoner's Friend on a national level – and among professional offenders of broadly-based notoriety. He may not have been popular among his immediate associates, but even they did not slander his professional rectitude. That was left for Chief Inspector Marsters to stir up; but Mosley did not know about that.

He did not greatly care for Hartley Mason. Mason had once dealt with him very snidely in the witness-box (over an affair in which a teenager had been stealing mildly erotic garments from clothes-lines) but both men were too big for this occasion to be remembered when Mosley accepted a leather chair in Mason's office now.

There was a time when the vogue-word for Hartley Mason would have been whizz-kid. In his early twenties, his precocity must have been insufferable to many – though not to a few like William Fothergill who, when he spotted exceptional talent, could be exceptionally tolerant. Hartley Mason was not forty, and had carried with himself to that age not only the reinforced habits of insufferable precocity, but also much of the exuberance of an adolescent well aware of his abilities. Even his rounded features, under his crisp-curled hair, had a youthful, almost puerile appearance – which was belied by the bands of fat under his chin and about his neck. He smiled at Mosley, and Mosley knew better than to assume that this was a propitious signal.

'And what can I do for the Criminal Investigation Department?'

By way of an answer, Mosley simply produced from his wallet the snapshot of Brenda Cryer and William Fothergill at tea and laid it on Hartley Mason's blotter the right way up for the lawyer to see.

'Ah-ha! I rather thought we might find ourselves up against this.' If Mason was to any extent shaken by what he saw, he concealed it jocularly. 'It has nothing to do with what happened to the poor woman, of course, but I rather thought you might happen upon it in the course of your enquiries. I can see that at first sight, this might appear to complicate your investigation no end – though I can assure you that there is no need for that. I know you will think I am speaking from self-interest. And I cannot pretend that my partners and I will be delighted by the shade of publicity that this is likely to attract. And I hope you do not doubt that I will only too gladly tell you all I can.'

'You were closely in Mr William's confidence over this liaison?'

'I was the only one in the firm who was – though I fancy that one or two of the others had their notions. Old William needed a go-between in the early stages.'

'Then perhaps you can tell from what *milieu* she moved into this country mansion – and in what circumstances she moved out of it into a sleazy hotel in Ember Bay.'

'It was not all that sleazy, Mosley – not in its heyday, when Brenda had the place under her thumb.'

So Hartley Mason was well abreast with the latter part of her life, and was taking no trouble to cover up that fact. He was putting on an image of bold, unembarrassed frankness from the start.

'And it certainly wasn't a country mansion.' Mason looked again at the photograph. 'Though I can see how you come to think so. *I* took this, by the way. Yes: this corner of the wall, the suggested grandeur of the garden: I'm glad for your sake that you didn't have the job of trying to trace the place from this. Actually it's rather a twee little cottage, south east of the Lakes, in a fold that's a sort of *hors d'oeuvre* for the Dales. That's a region that's a bit bleak, you might think, for some people's tastes, but old William had it snug – oh, my God, yes. It was equipped with every work-saver known to the Sunday supplements, and with deep-freezers stocked to withstand a post-nuclear dearth. And as for discretion: the newest office-boy had an idea he was going off somewhere, often for longer than a weekend. But there wasn't a soul who knew the whereabouts of it. By this time, of course, old William had more or less withdrawn from routine work, though he still had the final say in house policy, senior appointments, capital investment, and that sort of thing. However, I'm taking things out of their proper order. It will be far better if I stick to the terms of reference you've so usefully given me. Do smoke, by the way. Please don't feel anything but at your absolute ease.'

Mason took and cut a medium-sized cigar with the rituals of a connoisseur. Mosley preferred a somewhat moistly fuelled little bulldog pipe.

'From what *milieu* did she move to William's love-nest? From the bed-sit quarter of by no means the most salubrious sector of Leeds. I don't know how much homework you've done on her. She'd made a hopeless marriage, let's be frank, while she was still a schoolgirl. And then she'd had a flash of insight: not only the perspicuity to see things as they were, but also the guts to pull out – even at the thirteenth hour. She retreated to a no man's land called Rangate, where wholly admirably – and wholly wrong-headedly – she pursued career-girl plans under cover of squalor and dejection. I'm not sure why. I fancy she felt she had to do some sort of penance. I think she also wanted to teach herself the hard way what it really was like at the bottom. She was a bit of a dreamer, you know, more so in her early years than latterly. Anyway, what's the point of theorizing? That's what she *did*. I don't think she enjoyed what she was doing, but in some perverse way she enjoyed the image of herself doing it. By the way, I know most of this from hearsay. I didn't have more than half a dozen extended conversations with the woman in my life, and the last of those was years ago.'

He paused to flick away a speck of ash from Mosley's pipe, which had somehow strayed on to his blotter.

'Anyway, she got through the self-inflicted sentence, to all intents and purposes achieved what she set out to achieve. She'd saved up her fees and maintenance and was about to register at a prestigious private secretarial college. I wonder if they'd have taken her? And what she'd have done if they'd contrived some way of showing her the cold shoulder? The question didn't arise, because she never applied. At the crucial moment, she met this man Cryer – I think it was at a works social. And whatever lessons she'd set out to teach herself, she hadn't learned them. Perhaps she wasn't vouchsafed a second flash of insight; or maybe this time it was too much of a bore to pay attention to it. Are some women made to fall into the same trap over and over again? What was it about Brenda that made her fall crazily, scatter-brainedly in love with the sort of man who was the worst sort of medicine for her? Maybe, in the star-spangled stage, it's the attraction of contrasts. Be that as it may, she married Cryer. Bryce had divorced her *in absentia* – she hadn't, of course, defended the suit. They went and lived in Leeds: he was a travelling rep for something highly esoteric and universally unwanted in the machine-tool line. They bought a spec estate semi on mortgage – her savings providing the deposit. And life must have been hell in that corner of Roundhay as they belatedly got to know each other.'

Mason's words sounded strong, but his sense of participation was minimal.

'There were, as they say with such abandoned fairness in the romances, faults on both sides. He turned out to be a compulsive gambler, had no sense of financial responsibility, hadn't even the acumen to make plans, let alone stick to them. When major accounts came in, it was almost a question of drawing out of a hat which one to pay this month. The mortgage repayments were a standing order on a joint account – she'd even been blind enough to fall for that – and the obvious happened. The bank had to stop payments to the building society. She was working – semi-skilled clerical – and then it was the escape from the honeymoon train all over again: the impulse, the brain-storm, the instinct for self-disfigurement, call it what you will. She'd pulled them out of more than one hole, then she suddenly discovered, despite an ultimatum, that he'd run up some other insane debt that he knew they had no hope of clearing. So she threw up her work, said she'd rather be destitute than type invoices eight hours a day, in the company that that entailed keeping, just to grub-stake an idiot.'

Hartley Mason looked cynically across his desk.

'I long ago learned not to lose sleep over trying to analyse human motivations. I don't know what makes men and women do the things that they do. Enough for me that they bring me an income by doing them. Maybe she hoped that a really cold douche might persuade him; it certainly persuaded her. After a few days' first-hand acquaintance with destitution, she left him: hence the bed-sit. A new job, an attempt at incognito, a new loss of identity. And this time she was the one who started exploring divorce. She made an appointment with a city solicitor, was in the waiting-room when old William came out of the inner office; he'd been paying a personal call about some top-level urban development. Of course she recognized him – she was the daughter of his own managing clerk, remember – and something about the way she was looking at him made him look twice at her. Then he, too, remembered. It was some years, you'll understand, since he had seen her.

' "Don't I know you?" and the usual sequences. And he was struck.'

Hartley Mason embarked on a new phase, a sense of

involvement that might or might not have been sincere. 'I dare say you knew William Fothergill.'

And Mosley had; not, naturally enough, from the same angle or at the same depth as Hartley Mason had – but enough, rightly or wrongly, to have been impressed by him.

'He was a remarkable man. I'd go as far as to say a wonderful man. It goes without saying that I am prejudiced: he was my sponsor in Bradburn, and I don't know where I might have fetched up – or foundered – without him. But people who did not know him intimately did not know how sensitive he was – or what uncomplaining suffering he had gone through: he had been a widower for fifteen years. And he was struck by Brenda at first sight – I mean, of course, at first adult sight. And let's be frank: she was a striking woman. This photograph here says it all; or most of it, anyway. She'd still not pulled out of the bad times, that day William met her in Leeds. That was in her face, and there was something about it that gave her added depth and appeal. Old William was struck; and he took her out to dinner that evening.'

Mosley sat back in his chair as if the rest hardly needed telling.

'He had me do a little discreet checking up on her, which is how I come to know as much about her as I do. I know that sounds a bit mean, a bit mercenary, perhaps: which is one good reason why he farmed it out, instead of doing it himself. And then he propositioned her: not as a potential mistress, though there was a strong understanding that that was the way it might go, if it suited both sides. She was to be his housekeeper-companion, in a secluded retreat he had acquired not all that long ago. He was a contemplative man, he was courteous, he was tired – and he had been lonely for a very long time.'

Mason sounded more deeply involved with William Fothergill than he did with Brenda.

'I must give Brenda credit for a good deal of uncertainty at first, though, for all practical intents, she was on to a good thing. William wasn't likely to last more than another ten years at the most; she'd still be a presentable woman when her responsibilities to him were done. She'd lost her taste for suburban domesticity – and she found William sympathetic, fascinating company – a man who knew how to treat a woman. The projected settlement was not only handsome, it could not have been drawn up by more reliable hands. Sex wasn't an overriding consideration. If it happened, it happened – and let's hope it did, for both their sakes; I can't tell you whether or not. I did some of the negotiating behind the scenes. William leaned over backwards to avoid overbearing persuasion, but I knew what he went through while she was making up her mind. I must say it was a relief to me when she agreed to a trial month on a strictly housekeeper basis. You must take my word for it: it went on from there to become the sort of idyll that they both deserved. Old William adored her. She had never been treated properly. Only two things spoiled it.'

Mason looked at Mosley as if challenging him to say what they were; but he avoided such parlour-games.

'There came a day when William hadn't been back to Bradburn for nearly a month. There were documents that required his personal signature – a re-investment of maturing bonds. There were rumours about what sort of private life he was leading – some of them not very kind, but you'd be surprised how many people near to him took pleasure on his behalf. No one knew who the woman was. Only two people in the office knew the whereabouts of his hide-out. I was one of them, but this wasn't generally known, because William thought it best to keep dark the part I'd played in the affair. The other was Brenda's father, who had the address under lock and key, and could use it in emergency on authorization from one of us. No man could have been a safer depository. and it was he who took the papers for signature – because I was nailed down by a long court hearing. I thought it utterly safe to send him, because he was the last man on earth to bruit it abroad that it was his daughter who was involved. That was how I saw it: I did not know that he would take it the way that he did. There were quirks in his character that I did not know – and that I probably would not have understood if I had. The discovery that Brenda was his master's mistress was more than he could support. Loyalty to the one and the disgrace of the other were a conflict he could not resolve. I suppose most men would have come to terms with it in time: but not Arthur Thwaites. He had been brought up in a narrow school. His life's comfort had been a simplistic morality. His attitude to servant-master relationships was virtually feudal. He had been suffering from high blood pressure for some years, and he had a stroke when he got home from that trip. It was a hideous business.'

'I can imagine. Did –?'

'Did what, Inspector?'

'Did Brenda's mother ever get to know what he had discovered, up in the Dales?'

'I don't know, Inspector. There were things that it was no part of my life to go into. And there was worse to follow – for Brenda. The liaison in that little cottage lasted about seven years. When William Fothergill died – mercifully it was not at the cottage, it was on one of his infrequent cross-country trips – she sat it out in solitude for a couple of months, waiting to hear news from us. It fell to my ultimate lot to take it to her: that despite promises and assurances, there had been no ultimate settlement drawn up by old William – and certainly no trace of anything on our files. Yet this was something he had insisted on handling himself: he would not even trust it to me. It defeats me still, as it defeated me then. It cannot possibly have been insincerity. He was far too experienced a man to have left ends loose. He was not the one, certainly, to hesitate to think about his own demise. He left Brenda high, dry and penniless – without title even to the articles of furniture about her, which had undeniably been gifts. I was devastated – the more so because the tidying-up of all this – if that's what you can call it – somewhat naturally devolved on me. There was nothing – but nothing – that I could do for her. Her only hope was from his own son and daughter – who had never even formally met her – and they saw no reason why they should make any gesture.'

'She must have been flattened.'

'Indeed, I began to despair for her. This was her third devastating experience of men. But, being Brenda, her spirit revived. That was where Bay View at Ember Bay came in. It was a vacancy she had seen in the press. I knew about it, because she asked me to act as reference. It was a post for which she had no qualifications – and yet every qualification. She had common sense, energy, taste. She could type and keep books, get the best out of people. And by the grace of God, that was the way the syndicate saw her when they interviewed her. I might say that few candidates for any job were backed by the sort of reference that I wrote for her behind the scenes.'

'So why did she leave Bay View?'

'I don't know. I didn't stay in touch. I looked in on her just once, when I had my own family up in Scarborough – and the hotel was going like a bomb. She was busy eighteen hours of a summer day – and loving it. Well, sir: I've omitted a lot. Damn it, I've *forgotten* a lot – but there you have the bones of the story. I dare say you're bursting with questions – but just at the moment – '

He looked at his watch. Mosley stood up. The internal phone on Mason's desk gave the sketchiest tinkle, as if it was a matter of sheer luck that the hammer had contacted at all: Lilian Harrison, letting him know that his next appointment had arrived.

'He can come up at once.'

Mason smiled at Mosley: an indication that he had said all he was going to say about Brenda Cryer, that his interest in her was over. Mosley moved to the door, opened it. Mason had made no move to show him out of the room. On the landing were bare wooden tables, loaded with papers roughly tied up in manilla folders. Most of them must already have been there when Mosley first joined the force.

Heavy feet started to climb the stairs: the next man, with the next problem – something perhaps that was going to affect the pattern of his life, cost him maybe half his savings or more.

The newcomer turned and went back down the three treads he had already climbed, to let Mosley come down. In the gloomy recess at the bottom, Mosley felt strong fingers clasping his arm – and an angry whisper: 'What the blazes are you doing here?'

It was Chief Inspector Marsters, florid, blustering and anxious.

'Duty call,' Mosley said, like a password.

'Who've you been to see?'

'Hartley Mason.'

'And what case are you on that needs take you to him?'

'Brenda Cryer.'

Then Lilian Harrison was speaking from her draughty desk, so placed that it commanded several corners. 'Mr Mason *is* free, Chief Inspector.'

Twelve

Chief Inspector Marsters was trying to say something – something that came up against an impediment in his speech from which he did not usually suffer. Eventually he managed to produce it. 'Mosley!'

There were three of them in the Assistant Chief Constable's office. The ACC himself was like a man in an earthquaked building who is waiting with crossed fingers to see how much of it is going to fall on him. Detective-Superintendent Grimshaw, by nature and empirical persuasion a conciliatory man, was doing his best to hold himself in reserve, knowing that Marsters would take any premature attempt to placate him as an insult.

'Mosley! For eight months now I have been waiting in the shadows, flicking a fly across the waters over Hartley Mason's head. I have moved from covert to covert, never rustling a grass. Last night I sat at my desk from the smaller into the larger hours and orchestrated the final approach down to a development for every variation.'

Did the man think he was fishing, or composing a bloody symphony?

'I had worked out the optimum order in which to play my hand. I knew just what I was going to keep to myself, just how I was going to throw him the crumbs, just how one little thing was going to lead to a slightly bigger one until the trap was sprung. You've got to understand, Tom – one detail out of place, and Mason was alerted. And Mason alerted meant Mason lost. In that half hour, Mosley had not merely alerted Mason: he had taken him on a conducted tour of half the points I was building up to make – without, I may say, understanding the implications of a single one of them. Not only had Mosley warned him off – he had constructively rehearsed him through his defence against every finely balanced point that I was about to make. It was as if a trout had suddenly stuck its head out of the water and asked for a Greenwell's Glory instead of a Gold Butcher. Hartley Mason sat there openly preening himself on the luck of the gods. "May I refer you, Chief Inspector, to a statement I made less than ten minutes ago to a colleague who appears to be several stages ahead of you?" '

The Assistant Chief Constable sat wishing that Marsters would have a stroke and be done with it. There would be an untidy few minutes while they carried him from the carpet to the mortuary; but at least a period of calm would follow.

'Oh, I don't know,' Grimshaw said smoothly. 'We have to remember that this *is* Mosley's first murder. And you have to take your hat off to him: he has moved.'

'He has blundered!' Marsters said.

'Be fair, Sid. Most of the time with Mason you were talking about completely different matters. You'd guessed there had to be a woman in it somewhere, acting as go-between. I'll give you your due – you even thought it might have been old William Fothergill's fancy-piece. But it took Mosley to tell us who she was.'

The veins in Marster's temples looked dangerously close to final rupture.

'You knew there had to be a report centre somewhere –a safe house. It took Mosley to go toddling across Yorkshire in a straight line to Bay View.'

'And he doesn't know why!'

Marsters was saved from apoplexy by suddenly going the other way; he came near to tears.

'He knows who she was, but he doesn't know what she was doing. He knows where she was, and he doesn't know why.'

The Assistant Chief Constable looked from one face to the other, wishing that Grimshaw would wave a magic wand.

'We could, of course, always tell him,' Grimshaw said mildly.

And that did it. Marsters overcame the temptation to weep. 'Splendid! So why not take the affair entirely out of my hands and make the whole issue over to Mosley? Why not give him a direct line to the Director of Public Prosecutions? Why not absolve him completely from having to make any reports to us? We shan't lose any sleep over what we don't know about, shall we? And as for me, what better use could you find for me than prowling round hen-houses and warning kids who pinch sweets from Woolworth's?'

The Assistant Chief Constable closed his eyes and appeared to be devoted to silent prayer.

'I've been looking over your crime reports, Jack,' Grimshaw said, 'and murder is all very well. It makes a change for us all, once in a while. But we mustn't neglect our main reason for existence, must we?'

Mosley, in the one chair in Grimshaw's office in which he never felt at ease, looked at his superior with a face that could not be said to bear any expression whatever.

'What I am getting at, Jack, is that your bailiwick doesn't seem quite to have that untroubled air we have come to associate with it. Don't think I am being critical. But to a mere reader of morning reports, there are things going on up in your cloughs and dales that would not have been going on a fortnight ago. Unsolved crimes: a whole crate of tangerine oranges spirited away from a pavement display in Lower Spritwell. The word *HOAR* – spelt as if it referred to an overnight frost – printed in weed-killer on a council-house lawn on the Bracegirdle Estate. And geese, Jack: twenty-five of them, vanished as if some Pied Piper had led them overnight into a hole in the flank of Lanthorn Hill. Can it possibly be true, we have asked ourselves in this office, that a whole flock of bloody geese has been driven from the very nerve-centre of Jack Mosley's patch?'

'I expect someone is thinking ahead to the Christmas trade,' Mosley said. 'As a matter of fact, I was on my way up there when you sent for me.'

'That's what I hoped I would hear: first things first. The Chief sets great store, you know, by some of the less showy aspects of our commission. That is why he has decided, in his wisdom, that he would like you to concentrate on all the bits and pieces that are outstanding in your area. Try and produce a clean sheet in the next forty-eight hours.'

He waited for Mosley to ask the question; but Mosley could treat his superiors exactly as he treated his suspects. He remained silent.

'He has asked me to take general oversight of the Brenda Cryer affair, and Chief Inspector Marsters will be looking after an important lateral issue. We feel that this will relieve you of anything that might interfere with your own work.'

Mosley gave Grimshaw the full effect of his round, baby eyes.

Grimshaw looked away. 'You will understand, of course, that Marsters and I have to steer our way through some dangerous shoal waters. There are certain things, with which I need not trouble you, that are very delicately poised. It would be only too easy, with the best will in the world, for an unintentional fringe-movement to upset that poise. I hope I am not talking in riddles, Jack. There are times when a police force, like an intelligence service, must work on the need-to-know principle. Therefore I must ask you, if you do happen across anything that you think might have a bearing on the Cryer case, to do nothing about it – nothing at all except to inform me. You know you can always get me on a direct line.'

Mosley did not even nod.

'There is just one other thing, Jack – and I am sure it will come as another great relief to you. It will no longer be necessary for you to carry the additional burden of Sergeant Beamish. An excellent man in his own way, of course, but apt to become bored and restless over weed-killers and tangerine oranges. So we shall be retaining Beamish to help us.'

Mosley went straight not to Lanthorn Hill, but to Piper's Fold, to Mumper's Farm, whose tenant, 'young' Neddy Sladburn, he had made several unsuccessful attempts to contact over the last few days.

Mumper's was another example of the failed intake: a squat little stronghold of farmhouse, scarcely bigger than the average labourer's cottage, that had sheltered various unrelated generations who had starved slowly on the proceeds of the half-reclaimed moors above. Neddy Sladburn – known as 'young' at forty by everyone in the Fold – was not starving. It was true that he farmed: he had fifty sheep at large on the hills. He had a dozen hens, one cow and a sheepdog. His income came from his other occupation – definitely considered youthful by the people of Parson's – as a breaker of old cars. There were always a dozen or so of them littering his yard, much to the anger of the District Council, who had been refusing him planning permission to operate his trade for years, prosecuting him, giving him notice and final notice, harassing him with clerks, solicitors' letters and bailiffs. Neddy, for his part, had produced appeals, counter-appeals, committees of enquiry, last-minute stays of execution and ambiguous rulings by the Ombudsman: a perpetual state of running warfare in which the one feature that remained constant was the assortment of double-decker buses, old baker's vans, Ford Prefects and rusting old station-wagons that were visible on his hillside for a radius of many miles. The odd thing about Neddy was that he appeared to make his living without any visible diminution of his stock-in-trade:

he never seemed to part with an old vehicle. What he did was to study, with a phenomenal memory and a genius for economic forecasting, the desperate pleas that appeared in the smaller advertisements of the trade press. Neddy Sladburn asked – and apparently got – astronomical prices for such unconsidered trifles as a handful of obsolescent screws, an out-of-date coach-bolt, a superseded radiator-cap, a discontinued line in exhaust manifolds, or a still serviceable gasket for an engine of which the wide world contained only one other working example. But it was not for mechanical succour that Mosley now called on him: Neddy Sladburn had also been Brenda Cryer's – then Brenda Thwaites's – boyfriend, in the far-off schooldays before Charles Bryce had accelerated into her life in a red sports car.

'I've been wondering when you'd be coming.'

Neddy Sladburn withdrew himself from under a chassis from which he was retrieving cross-members that might have been made of platinum for the price he was proposing to ask for them.

'Well – actually – '

'Come in the house. Have a cup of tea.'

Neddy Sladburn ran a bachelor establishment. The sentimentalists of Parson's Fold liked to believe that at nineteen he had been so aggrieved by Brenda's treachery that he had vowed never to take up with another woman. He took Mosley now into a house that had certainly not had the benefit of a woman's hand during Neddy's twenty years' tenure of it. He was a man whose demands upon his environment were as little as his expenditure on it. He took things as he found them – and let them remain so. And Mosley was quite unaffected by the sugar-sack curtains, the tray of drained sump-oil that for some obscure reason had been brought indoors, the stained brown enamel mug out of which he was presently happy to drink his tea.

'Aye; it were a bad business. And if I can help you lay hands on the bugger that did it – '

'I was hoping you'd feel like that about it,' Mosley said.

'You can say what you like about her. She never harmed a soul in the world bar herself.'

'I was thinking about geese,' Mosley said.

'Geese? What geese?'

'Lanthorn Hill. Last Thursday night. Jimmy Pendlebury's.'

'Lanthorn Hill? That's fifteen miles away. I've not set foot up Lanthorn Hill for ten years – nor set eyes on Jimmy Pendlebury for longer than that. How could I tell you anything about geese on Lanthorn Hill? I was thinking you'd come to see me about Brenda Cryer.'

'Geese,' Mosley said, obsessively, but without emphasis. 'I've been taken off Brenda.'

Neddy considered this piece of intelligence with perplexity verging on alarm. 'Who's on the Brenda business, then?'

'Tom Grimshaw.'

'That daft bugger? I don't mind telling you, Mr Mosley, anything you want to know. In fact I've been waiting my chance. But Tom Grimshaw will have to whistle for answers.'

'Marsters is with him,' Mosley added casually, as if to secure the point.

For a few seconds, Sladburn hid his face in his capacious and oily hands. 'Well, I suppose somebody thinks he knows what he's doing. And I dare say you'll pull it out of the bag for them in the end, same as you have done before. I don't think, looking back, that it would have worked out all that well, me and Brenda; but I was very fond of her. Very fond.'

He allowed himself a moment of sentiment, gazing unseeing at his meal-table, on which the remains of his breakfast occupied such space as was not taken up by an old-type magneto he was stripping.

'I don't suppose it would have worked out. One of us would have had to change, and what I know of her, it wouldn't have been Brenda. I was a couple of years older than her, you know, and we'd always used to travel together on the bus, while I was still at school. And then, after I left, if there was ever anything on in the village – a dance, or one of the old vicar's barbecues – the pair of us would go together. Sometimes, of a Saturday or Sunday, we'd go for a walk; over the Beacon, or else across into the Trough. Her parents didn't reckon me, of course, which made Brenda keener than ever to come out with me. She was like that, even as a kid. And we used to have the most God-awful rows. I mean, it was one long slanging-match. I don't think we ever agreed with each other on a single mortal thing. That was the joy of it: we could say any mortal thing to each other – and did! – and still be together at the end of the day, and fixing up a trip to the pictures, down at Bradburn, next Saturday. It was relaxing, that's what I'm trying to tell you. We knew each other inside out, that's the truth of it – and we weren't afraid of telling each other. "Why don't you clean yourself up, Neddy," she'd say. "You really are bloody disgusting. Look at your fingernails. I don't know why I allow people to see me out with you." And I'd say, "You're not the only one who's taking chances that way, you toffee-nosed bitch. I've barely a friend left in Parson's Fold since I started walking out with thee. They all think I'm trying to get into t' New Year Honours List or summat." Aye; happy days, Mr Mosley! Then she had to take up with that fellow from Goosnargh, cracked on he was an artist. Just because he had that two-seater, that's what I thought it was at first. And when I heard they were getting wed, I thought at first my mind would shear a cotter-pin.'

He looked at Mosley for a moment of simple and uncontrived confession.

'I allowed myself the luxury of feeling hurt, Mr Mosley.'

A cat climbed on to the table and began to lick his breakfast plate. He did not interfere with it.

'And I don't know how long it took me to realize that of

course there couldn't have been anything in it for Brenda and me. For one thing, I know I'm a dirty bugger, and that's only the beginning of it. All the same, when she came back here, when she brought her mother home from that place where that half-baked bloody paint-merchant and his wife had sent her, I thought to myself, well, I'll go down and see her. And that wasn't because I'd any thought of taking up from the old days.'

Neddy laughed; not a very convincing effort to show unconcern for himself and his life.

'Just because we'd been old friends, and I thought she'd still be good for a laugh: and perhaps another bloody good row. Well: I did go down there. I went there several times, if the truth is told – but I only saw her the once. Because every other time I went, she had somebody with her; I'm not beyond a bit of window-corner peeping you know, or listening. And once it was her brother and his wife. And my God, were those three having a barney! Hammer and tongs it was, and I tried to make out what it was about – I always did have the reputation of being the nosiest Parker in the Fold – but some voices carried better than others and I never really got hold of the thread of it. But it was her brother who'd somehow or other got her goat. And this wasn't comic stuff, like the pair of us used to come out with, up in the hills. This was hate, Mr Mosley. This was the sort of hate that gets into some people's lives – and then they end up on hearth-rugs with bullets through the back of the neck. It was something he'd done, and I don't know what. Or, rather – it was something he hadn't done; something he ought to have told her and hadn't. "I'm not blaming my father at all," she said. "He just couldn't help it. He never did me a scrap of good in his life, so I wouldn't expect him to spoil his record on his death-bed. What he did was all he knew how to do. There are some people, and you'd be among them, I suppose, who'd say it was all I deserved. But you could have told me. If only you'd told me!" And Donald Thwaites said something I didn't catch –

something soft and self-satisfied, like the man is. And that got her worse on the raw. "Don't you go making excuses like that," she said. "Where do you think this is that we live? The middle of the flaming Sahara?" '

Neddy Sladburn had regenerated a good deal of emotion in the telling of this. There were red spots burning over his cheekbones.

'Well, other times I went, and she had visitors. And I don't know who they were: different men. Well: that was her affair, wasn't it? But this particular evening, I'd left it fairly late on, thinking that would give her the chance to bed her mother down, and there's a car standing out in the lane. So I'm round to my usual corner of window. And there's a voice that I recognize, though it took me a long time to place it. It was only when he moved so I caught sight of his face that I knew who it was. Three guesses, Mr Mosley?'

'I'm only supposed to be here about geese,' Mosley said.

'Bugger you and your bloody geese! I'll tell you who it was. It was Hartley Mason: that smooth operator that joined Fothergills ten years ago. I knew him, because the police put him up to prosecute me a couple of years back. They always point a solicitor at me, knowing my habit of speaking up for myself. And he threw the book at me: tread gone on two tyres, no windscreen washer fluid, faulty contact on tail-lamp, no MOT certificate and a jagged edge on the bumper that they reckoned was a danger to other road-users. It was a car I'd just bought; I was driving it home. Anyway; beside the point. Why I'm telling you this is that Hartley Mason and Brenda were having a worse row than I'd heard with her brother, perhaps not as rowdy, but dead icy. Danger-signals; and again that feeling came to me – Brenda was into something that was out of my class: not just a family quarrel. And not a woman breaking it off with a man. This was something nasty, Mr Mosley. "I want out," she said. "And when I say I want out – I'm out." Good old Brenda! That's the way she always talked – and did things. And I think Mason knew it too, because after a bit, he stopped trying to persuade her. "Well, you disappoint me," he said. "And if ever you change your mind, you know there's always a niche for you." And she said, "Yes, well, I might always take you up on that, but somehow I don't think I will. But if it's a favour you're wanting to do me, I'd like you to set Matty Pearson on to something for me – something right up his street." Who's Matty Pearson, Mr Mosley?'

'Oh, an enquiry agent. The Fothergills have kept him in business for years. This is all very interesting, Neddy – but it isn't taking us any nearer our feathered friends.'

'Oh, to hell, Mr Mosley. Will you stop talking about those blasted geese? I haven't finished what I'm telling you. Do you want to hear it or don't you?'

'Seems to me I just can't help hearing it.'

'Well, I did go back to see her. And it wasn't at all like I'd expected. I won't say we were right back where we'd started, because that wouldn't be true. And in any case, we'd both learned too many lessons since those days. But we were glad to be with each other, if you see what I mean. We weren't putting the clock back – but we were looking back at an old clock – together. And I saw she was looking away from me. And I thought, hell fire, can't she stand the bloody sight of me? – I'd cleaned myself up no end, Mr Mosley. And then I spotted it. She had tears in her eyes, and didn't want me to cotton on. We talked about everything under the sun, and odd things that had happened where there wasn't much sunshine. And we didn't have a row. God, that's just come to me! We didn't have a row! But she said to me suddenly, "Do you still love me, Neddy?" And it wasn't a question that meant what it said – because we both knew by now what love is and what love isn't. But it was meant to be leading somewhere, so I let it lead. "Well, will you do something for me, Neddy? Will you turn your hand to a little burglary for me?" And I said, "Now look, I don't know how you think I've spent all these years out of your control –" Hell fire, Mr Mosley, you don't think *I* nicked those bloody geese, do you?'

'I know very well you didn't, Neddy.'

'Small mercies, then. So I said to her, "I might now and then have overdone the profit margin on a pair of car-door sills. But burglary – no. I've always regarded that as a bit on the specialized side." And she said, "I don't think this is a case that calls for very great skill, Neddy. In fact, I've thought of several little ways in which it can be made very easy for you. As they say in the trade, I would set it up for you. I think there might not even be much in it. It's information I'm after, not loot: even negative information." And what she meant by that, I don't know. I was too busy thinking to myself, does she want me to break into Fothergills? Because that's where Edward Sladburn, Esquire, Mister, draws his line. Even for Brenda. Then she said, "I want you to insinuate yourself –" that's the word she used, Mr Mosley – "I want you to insinuate yourself into the Old Rectory." But what I was supposed to go there and look for I never did find out, because that's the moment for another car to draw up outside. And she let Hartley Mason in. So I just said to her, in a loud voice, like, "You obviously need a new clutch. I think I know where I can put my hands on one for you." And I'm off into the night.'

'Yes, Neddy.'

'Well, doesn't all that interest you, Mr Mosley?'

'Not as much as certain of God's creatures that I don't know whether I dare mention again.'

'You want me to go slogging up Lanthorn Hill, to find out who swiped Jimmy Pendlebury's geese? Doing your job for you, and not for the first time?'

'No, Neddy. I don't think there's much point in going up Lanthorn Hill. Jimmy's geese were the only things up there worth stealing, and they've gone. I want you to do a bit of strategic planning for me. Just imagine you're the mastermind behind an outfit that's on to a good thing:

getting poultry direct from the producer to an uninquisitive wholesaler. You're working this district. Where are you going to strike next?'

'Ah!'

'I hope the problem interests you, Neddy.'

'In the abstract, Mr Mosley. That's another word I learned from Brenda – twenty years ago. But what about all those other things I've told you about her?'

'Oh, I dare say I might pass them on to Tom Grimshaw – if I come across him.'

Thirteen

Mosley did not often start his working day in the central office, unless he had been sent for – and not always even then. It was something more than a headquarters, a hub of communications, intelligence and executive resources; there was primeval humanity at work here, as well as the autonomic nervous system of the force. It was a world of latrine rumours, of whispers behind cupped hands, of esoteric references to the high and mighty in trouble. Mosley had been known to go for a fortnight without ever setting foot in the place.

The sight of him therefore at twenty minutes to nine, making an unparalleled series of telephone calls, ticking off items on what looked suspiciously like an ergonomic progress chart, and referring constantly to the Ordnance Survey map, was one which aroused anxious curiosity in several already troubled hearts. To Marsters and Grimshaw, doing their best to creep in without his seeing them, the sight of Mosley operating as advanced an instrument of technology as a telephone was in itself cause for concern. Mosley undoubtedly controlled one of the most fruitful bucolic spy-systems in the history of detection, but it was rumoured that contact was mostly by smoke-signal.

Grimshaw could therefore not resist the temptation to pass down by Mosley's desk and extract heavy humour from his basic fears. 'I'd been hoping to see you with goose-down in your hair by now, Jack.'

Mosley looked up at him with eyes slightly bloodshot. 'Golden egg coming up,' he said, gathered up his papers into the old wartime respirator bag that was his executive briefcase and left without extending further courtesies.

Things had begun to move the previous evening, when he had received a visit at his home from Neddy Sladburn, driving a pick-up truck that looked as if it had been put together from remnants of his stock-in-trade which he could not have offered to the most specialized of buffs.

'Been doing a day's unpaid work on your goose-rustlers,' Neddy said. 'And I don't like the look of it. Foreigners.'

'Foreigners?'

'Well – visitors.'

'How far afield?'

'Sheffield.'

'Bad,' Mosley agreed. 'How did you get on to them?'

'They'd been up Lanthorn Hill that same morning: Cortina Estate, G registration, Sheffield Post Office stamp on the licence. Made out they had a radiator leak and went to Jim Pendlebury's for a can of water. That's when they must have cased the joint.'

'Aye.'

'And there's another thing – about Brenda – '

'Oh, aye?'

'It didn't come back to me yesterday until after you'd gone. You remember she'd asked Hartley Mason to do her a favour? She said she wanted a job doing by a man called Matty Pearson – '

'Matty Pearson, that's right.'

Neddy Sladburn's eyes narrowed.

'You look as if you know him.'

'We've come across each other in our time.'

'And aren't all that fond of each other, I dare say?'

'Oh – Matty can be handled.'

'Well, she wanted him set on to her brother, that's what I've remembered. *Set on* to him. Those were the words that she used.'

Mosley left the office, with Grimshaw still looking down at the space he had vacated at his desk. He made his leisurely way round to the Bracegirdle Estate and stood and contemplated a pocket handkerchief of lawn where a moral libel – or, at least, a moral statement – had been etched by a moving finger writing in weed-killer. It took him an hour to clear up the matter. Number 37 was occupied by a young married woman with two children who called her *Mummy*, but who said *Daddy* over the fence to the man who had moved in next door, in replacement for a man who had moved up two Avenues and a Close to live with a woman called Deirdre, whose husband had gone across the road to cohabit with Sandra, whose man had turned out to be a homosexual and was now shacked up with an Italian waiter on the far side of Bradburn. It was a simple matter of mental arithmetic to see that this chain-reaction had left one woman unrequited. Her name was Kim, she had four children and a diabetic mother-in-law, and she it was whose moving finger had writ. Mosley assumed that she would be bound over to keep the peace.

He spotted a milk-tanker on its way back to a distribution centre at the foot of one of the dales and organized himself a lift to Lower Spritwell, where he applied himself to the loss of a tray of oranges. This gave him a great deal of trouble: the most exhaustive cross-elimination of movements in the village street proved stubbornly unproductive. A short chat with the headmistress of the village school drew forth only an unfeigned faith in the innocence of her flock; and, once intuitively impressed, Mosley was not given to labouring an approach. It began to look sadly like an inside job, always, in Mosley's experience, the most melancholy of unfoldings. And he was at a loss to see any motive for it in the present case. Why should Peter Morridge, a shopkeeper of the old breed, either steal from himself or falsely pretend that he had been robbed? Or why should his female assistant – no fly-by-night, a widow in her depressed mid-sixties – soil her fingers with a deed that must surely have left her with a well-nigh impossible problem of disposal?

Mosley postponed further consideration of citrus fruits until after his lunch, a pork pie consumed from the palm of his hand in a discreet corner of the churchyard. He then paid a visit to the telephone kiosk, for which he appeared to have furnished himself in advance, to judge from the large supply of coins which he marshalled beside the slots before consulting his list of numbers. He made precisely the same number of calls as he had made earlier from the office, and, indeed, to precisely the same acquaintances – who included four rural constables, one vicar, two licensed victuallers and an old lady who lived alone. One reply was so fruitful that he forthwith abandoned any further immediate attention to the straying of tangerine oranges.

For he was faced with an affair that was going to need planning, reconnaissance, persuasion, co-ordination, briefing – and strenuous nocturnal exercise. He would need the assistance of, he calculated, preferably three and ideally four physically well-developed members of the uniformed branch. Their detachment to his command would have to be authorized. The inevitable objections of their operational superiors would have to be overruled. The task-force would have to be assembled, transported, instructed and deployed. Mistakes, misunderstandings and mechanical breakdowns would have to be taken in his stride, if not in the stride of those specifically employed to rectify them.

The report which suddenly activated Mosley had come from the old lady who lived alone, who was notorious for walking her poodle whenever anything of interest seemed likely to break in her home village of Cresset, and who had become Mosley's firm friend ever after he had eased her over a completely misguided complaint that she had once made about a non-existent Peeping Tom who she believed had been spying on her ablutions from under her eaves. Mosley had always found her one of the most rewarding agents in his network, for amid her copious irrelevancies and capricious digressions the salient facts were always somewhere to be found, needing only the arts of an experienced interpreter.

In the present instance the crisp precision with which he had briefed her had done much in advance to shear away surplus material. It was perhaps inevitable that she believed that the newest young doctor in the group medical practice had been spying on her with binoculars from a high fork in an ancient beech tree. But, this apart, she was clear about the Cortina Estate car – G registration, and remainder of number-plate obligingly noted – which had lingered briefly in Cresset this morning. It had apparently mistaken its route, for it had proceeded only a few yards up the Giggleswick Road when it had stopped, attempted a reversing manoeuvre on the grass verge and become bogged down, its offside rear wheel digging itself deeper in with every revolution.

The driver had had to get out to go to a farm, Isaac Jowett's, to borrow a spade with which to extricate the vehicle. Isaac Jowett had, for the last two years, been fattening turkey-poults, what was known as running them on, on experimental sub-contract to a large-scale purveyor in Wakefield.

Mosley spent a large portion of the afternoon with the old lady who lived alone. He admired her home-made jams, and she had a propensity for producing home-made wines of epic potency at unorthodox drinking hours which it would have been tactless to have discouraged. He made diplomatic notes about all her manifold recent causes for alarm and left her before first dark to survey the theatre of tonight's encounter.

As compared with Neddy Sladburn's, Isaac Jowett's was a real farm, with modern machinery in evidence and the shed that housed the turkeys both visible and audible from the road. There was also a large metal skip containing the mortal remains of such sickly or over-pacific young poults as had failed in the struggle. Keeping this to leeward, Mosley approached Isaac Jowett, who appeared to believe that a battery of shotguns manned by himself, his sons and grandsons would be preferable to the time-consuming and ultimately unreliable processes of the law. Mosley was eventually able to decide on a course of action and – what was basic to it – the best use of ground. There had to be an area in which the thieves would be allowed to work unmolested until such time as they had burdened themselves with evidence against them. There had to be cover behind which the forces at Mosley's command could wait for the whistle; and there had to be scope for a pincer-movement which would turn attempted retreat into self-sacrifice.

Mosley decided all these elements in battle and set off for the rendezvous with his troops. These transpired, thanks to various urban priorities which obtruded themselves at the critical moment, to consist of one village constable, the incumbent of Cresset itself, a man within a month of retirement, in whom the beacon of ambition had burned down to a mere memory in the ash. Mosley posted him in a hedge-bottom from which, if not actually asleep, he might be able to observe the parking of the rustlers' transport. Himself, he went into the cover he had already chosen, a dense and thorny thicket from which he could see the main door of the turkey-house and the cinder-track leading up to it.

There were certain crimes, Mosley had always considered, in which the risk and physical labour were so great, the chances of discovery so probable, the discomfort so appalling and the rewards so uncertain that they could surely only be committed by romantics in love with misdemeanour and suspense for their own sake. Among these he counted the stripping of lead from exposed heights, the puncturing of strongholds with aging and unstable explosives and the acquisition of works of art which could not under any circumstances be displayed. As he settled down in his bed of thorns, with a growing suspicion that a wind of change was now blowing over the canister of carcases, he now added the purloining of livestock to his list of incomprehensibles.

The hour-hand of his wrist-watch pushed up towards eleven. Ground-floor lights continued to burn behind the windows of the Jowett residence. He pictured three generations of Jowetts keeping their own counsel about his admonitions, the working parts of their shotguns clean, bright and slightly oiled. At a quarter past eleven the downstairs lights were extinguished and three upstairs windows showed pale yellow rectangles. At a quarter to midnight they were still showing. A motor vehicle drove at modest speed through the village, changed into low gear and cruised slowly past the entrance to the farm, picking up speed after inspection and driving off in the direction of Giggleswick. At least there was some hope that they would have wakened PC Hunter; but he wished he had a runner whom he could have sent to tell the Jowetts for God's sake to get their heads down. At a little after ten minutes past twelve he was alerted by an at first indefinable variation in the ongoing noises of the night. This was not a weasel. It was not an owl taking off from a branch. It was not a mouse among dry leaves: all the leaves, like his ankles, the turn-ups of his trousers and the inside of his coat-collar, were wet. He pricked up his ears; but the car was coming back again down the Giggleswick Road and its engine played havoc with the local noise-to-signal ratio. Again it slowed down, but this time on brakes alone, not more than notionally. Again its driver must have taken note of the vigilance of the Jowetts, and again he drove off for more time.

But then Mosley heard again, and this time much nearer at hand, the anomalous sounds that had disquieted him not long ago; and wishful thinking could not dispel the only reasonable explanation. Someone was approaching him from behind. Of course, poachers were not unknown in the history of Cresset; nor were nocturnal fornicators or even the allowably enamoured. But this man was making too much noise for a poacher, yet taking too much care over his fieldcraft for one on his lawful occasions. There was a long pause, a patient suspension of movement, after every brush against a twig, every pebble set rolling. Once there were the unmistakable sounds of the man falling and Mosley could picture a heel losing its grip down the greasy slope of an unseen bank. There was a longer silence after that set-back; and in that interval the last of the Jowetts' lights suddenly went out. Mosley braced himself for action – but action on two fronts, he knew, lay outside his potential. He strained his ears afresh for any indication that the car was approaching.

He judged that the other oncomer was now not more than ten to fifteen yards behind him. There was a chance that he might even pass him in the dark and vanish on an oblique course towards his own business. But Mosley knew that this was unlikely. He himself, in order to permit rapid emergence, had avoided the more impenetrable parts of the thicket and was in the line of any man choosing a moderately carefree line of progress; Mosley had heard no evidence that the stranger was hacking his way with a *parang* or *yataghan.* And indeed, a second or two later, the new arrival had reached him. There was a sudden over-dramatized whisper.

'All right. Don't panic. It's me.'

'How interesting.'

'Sergeant Beamish. I gathered I'd find you in this neighbourhood. I want to talk to you about the Cryer case.'

'Ah. No time quite unlike the present.'

'They've put me on an aspect of it that's more up your street than mine.'

'Sh!'

But whatever Mosley had heard was lost on Beamish –

who nevertheless respected the silence until Mosley spoke again.

'False alarm. They may not come back.'

'Bit thin on the ground, aren't you?'

'Your arrival has increased my reserves by a hundred per cent.'

'At your disposal. We'll get your bit of business out of the way before I go into mine.'

'Thank you.'

'Though you'd better not let Marsters or Grimshaw know I've been helping you.'

'Or even associating with me, I suppose?'

'It's not quite like that, Mr Mosley.'

'Sh!'

This time there was no mistaking it. It was not an isolated noise. It was the let's-get-it-over-with orgiastic outburst of a faction who were resigned to the inevitability of noise at this juncture. It came from the very far end, the blind side of the poultry-house, and it issued from lusty young turkeys awakened and pounced on pell-mell, from tearaway young turkeys escaping into the night, from less star-blessed young turkeys confined in sacks and carried over men's shoulders, from the pounding of those men's feet across a field, from the running-up of sash windows and the firing out of them of double barrels and from the haphazard showering of lead shot over corrugated iron roofs.

Beamish made to press forward out of the thicket.

'Don't be silly, Sergeant. We don't stand a chance. I took them for lazy men who'd be bound to park here, where they surveyed the ground this morning. As it is, they got tired of waiting for the sandman to clobber the Jowetts. So they switched to the back approach. Which means they've half a mile cross-country run to their nearest parking-point. And we don't stand an earthly.'

'We can alert mobile patrols.'

'We also have their car number and the Sheffield police can search them for feathers in the morning. That's what

I'm settling for. Now what's all this about Brenda Cryer?'

'This seems hardly the best of places to talk.'

'What time is it?'

'A quarter to one.'

'Pubs won't be closed yet,' Mosley said. 'Not in this part of the world. Let's try the Anchor at Padbolt.'

Fourteen

'Marsters,' Beamish said, 'got his first inkling from a grass about two years ago. Not a super-grass, either. Just a bottom-of-the-dredger copper's nark, who hadn't got personal experience of what he was talking about, who'd got no backing for his word, and whose evidence would have raised hollow laughter in any jury-room.'

They had gained admittance to the Anchor, whose landlord had expressed the most inhospitable disgust at the sight of them. He had only just got rid of his domino school and between one and two in the morning was ready for bed. But he understood the last-ditch menace in Mosley's eye – a look such as he had never seen in the old man's eye before – and he resignedly stoked up the fire for them.

'Do we consider we're on duty?' Mosley asked.

'Absolutely not,' Beamish said. 'I've been warned you'd come plying me with questions about the Cryer case – which you haven't. And I've been told not to unbuckle a thing.'

'We'll have a couple of pints of best bitter, then. And then you can leave us to it, Joe Mycock.'

'Marsters's tip-off wasn't evidence,' Beamish said, 'and well he knew it. But it rang true. It was the sort of yarn an experienced copper believes. And Marsters put it away in the back of his mind, took it out now and then, gave it a dusting and looked it over. And it gathered strength as time passed. There were middle-of-the-road villains who were getting silks to their defence; bottom-of-the-barrel screwsmen who were going to work in strange company; wives of men who'd gone down still buying new furniture; men who were coming out to a spot of well-heeled leisure after they'd finished their time; bent coppers who were very choosey where they were doing their favours. There was nothing you could prove – above all else, there was nothing you could prove. But there were a lot of things that could be explained away if you played with the idea that somebody with a lot of money, and a lot of brains, and a lot of contacts, was organizing the aristocrats of the trade. It had to be somebody, too, who was enjoying the game, getting a kick out of tweaking well-chosen noses. I don't give Marsters much credit for spotting that Hartley Mason might fill the bill. If you ask me, it wouldn't have occurred to him if Mason hadn't wiped the witness-box rail with him in some quite insignificant case. It was police-court stuff, the pettiest of possible larcenies, and Mason got Marsters's man off on a technicality that made Marsters look a berk. It was only through childish malice that Marsters tried to see if he could fit Mason into this role of hypothetical manager: which was why he wasn't listened to in high places when he first started going on about it. But the odd thing was that Mason did fit – if you looked at him from the right angle. And what ultimately clinched it – and won Grimshaw over to Marsters's side – was a sort of dog-that-didn't-bark syndrome. You remember that chap Palfrey, who was sprung out of Aston, and they never did get to the bottom of it? The strange thing was that Hartley Mason had acted for him often enough in the past, had got him off a time or two – but hadn't represented him on the charge that he'd just gone down on. There could, of course, be plenty of possible reasons for that. But then Marsters hunted out another case. A little tyke breaker-and-enterer at Manchester Crown Court put up a QC who was quite out of his class, got acquitted. And he'd just sacked Hartley Mason, too – though in the past he'd always come running to him when he was in trouble. Marsters's theory was that

Mason was getting rid of characters he didn't want to be associated with – but he was still pulling the strings behind the scenes.'

Mosley went behind the bar to the pumps and topped up both their tankards.

'Marsters followed up those lines. He watched where Mason was acting – and who he was ditching. And that very nearly splintered the theory, because Mason was too smart to be consistent. He dropped some, carried on with others. Marsters calls that a randomization of alibis.'

Mosley looked neither surprised nor complacent. He might have been a child, grown old before his years, who has suddenly been told that he is in a new world – and can see nothing different in it.

'Of course,' Beamish said, 'this all fitted in with Mason's existing image: the conceited junior partner of the long-standing firm. He was the one who first brought Fothergills into crime in a big way. It was a local trade at first. Then it spread over the north-west and into Yorkshire. Then he started picking up national figures. And what a cover he had! Solicitors aren't allowed to advertise, but Hartley Mason kept his name in front of the people who mattered to him: letters to the press, papers in professional periodicals, correspondence with MPs that got questions asked in the House. Mason on prison reform; Mason on the handling of suspects in police custody; Mason on deaths in overnight cells; Mason on diminished responsibility; Mason the canvasser of new legislation on the accountability of Chief Constables – Mason, in fact, the national prisoner's friend. Which he also was in a lot of ways that he didn't advertise.'

Beamish was still young enough to be excited by a current case. Mosley did not stir. He did not look as if anything had ever moved him in his life.

'Marsters says it was like an army: an army that's owned by its field-marshal, a man who does his own staff-work. Mason has a vast intelligence department, an interlocking and cross-checked knowledge of money movements, of wage lifts, of art markets and outlets – and especially where money, blackmail or a fiddled privilege can buy one: prison warders, senior police, wallies on the beat, security guards, transport managers. He has his own technical services, an encyclopaedic knowledge of the right man for the right job. Sweaty and Jock, putting something together in Sunningdale, Berks, don't have to worry about who's going to get into the safe, who's going to do a spot of steeplejacking over the roof, what they are going to drive away in, who's going to buy the loot, what sun-drenched beach they're going to celebrate on: not if they've been admitted to Mason's élite. Above all, if they need to be capitalized, and Mason approves of the ploy, then they've no worries in that direction.'

'And can Marsters prove any of this?'

'What do you think? The more he dug around, the more convinced he became – yet he could still find nothing that they'd act on upstairs. So he changed his approach. Instead of trying to get at the warp and weft of the overall picture, he decided to follow up one case in depth, with all its ramifications, however trivial. And he found another parallel with a well-run army: the troops have to have confidence in the welfare arm. *When the enterprising burglar's not a-burgling, not a-burgling,* he has his wife and kids to think about. He might have the odd stretch to serve, either because he's unlucky or because the system has had to sacrifice him for some tactic or other. That has to be made worth his while. More important, he's got to know, while he's inside, that the little woman is getting better supplementary benefits than the government pays. In other words, there has to be a domestic back-up system, a left hand that might not know too much about right hand's activities, but that every man-jack in the ranks knows that he can rely on.'

Beamish took a draught of refreshment.

'Policemen need the odd stroke of luck as much as

anyone else, and Marsters suddenly had one. There was a receiving and disposing ring based in Preston on which he'd done some of the fringe work. And one of the men who went down was a man called Frank Humberstone. Not much to reckon with. There are Humberstones doing bird all over the country, and not one of them ever amounted to much.'

'I had one up on my patch, once. I did him for pinching a crate of lemonade from a cricket pavilion.'

'That sounds like an average Humberstone operation. Anyway: Frank Humberstone went down, and about a month after the trial, Marsters caught sight of Mrs Humberstone, going into Fothergills. He loitered, because he was curious: the Humberstones lived in the Wirral, which is a long way from Bradburn. And Mrs Humberstone was visibly upset – a woman whose tether-ends were showing. She was arguing, volubly, with that gaunt woman at the reception desk: it didn't look as if she had an appointment – and she wasn't going to wait for one, either. But she did manage to get shown upstairs. The pattern was an interesting one – and familiar. Up to three years ago, Hartley Mason had invariably been Humberstone's mouthpiece. For this latest case, there'd been a change. Yet it was to Mason that Humberstone's wife turned when, as was obviously the case, there was some sort of trouble. Women!'

Beamish suddenly sounded like a man who'd had troubles of his own in that department.

'There has to be a weak link in every chain. No wonder management consultants have started interviewing executives' wives. I suppose you can't expect a woman in married quarters to have the same respect for the sergeant-major that her husband has. And that was another good reason, Marsters argued, why Mason would keep his welfare wing well screened off from the Operations Room. He kept a close eye on Mrs Humberstone, for the short time she was in Bradburn. She wasn't upstairs with Mason for long, came out evidently dissatisfied, even talking to herself under her breath. She went straight to the railway station and bought herself a ticket to Scarborough. Well: Marsters couldn't follow her there, but he got on the blower and asked Scarborough to run her to earth if they could. But they missed her. Marsters could really sniff the battlefield cordite now. He'd been keeping close tabs on Mason, and Mason was taking two or three winter weekend breaks a year over in Scarborough. But Scarborough was as far as Marsters had ever accounted for him. It took you to lay the trail to Ember Bay.'

'No – you,' Mosley said. 'You're the one who chipped out the dental records.'

'You got there first,' Beamish said, not unruefully. 'Anyway – Marsters sees it all now – or thinks he does – thanks to what you've unearthed. Hartley Mason knew Brenda from the time she was ministering unto old William – maybe he was even having it away with her on the side. When old William dies, leaving her unexpectedly destitute, all Mason can do is commiserate. As a lawyer, there's no help he can give her. Even an *ex gratia* payment is out of the question, due to cross-currents in the firm, and resentment by the Fothergill offspring. Then he suddenly sees an opening for her. She is a superb secretary; she probably did quite a lot of right-hand woman work for old William during those years in the Dales. She's seen her share of low life and has been neither contaminated nor thrown off-balance by it. She has roughed it and survived. She's been too badly let down in her time to take any more dicey chances with men. She has no love for the establishment. She's a soft spot for down-and-outs. She's got to support herself – and she's damned if she'll ever rely on another man. What better welfare officer – with a genuine but not over-trodden seaside hotel as her cover? A hotel that can be at once report centre, transit camp and safe house?'

'Possible,' Mosley said.

'You don't sound convinced.'

'I don't know, one way or the other. Has Marsters thought of everything? Are men perfect in this underworld Utopia of Hartley Mason's? Is there no such thing as disloyalty? What does he do when a Humberstone is just plain stupid? Suppose he doesn't approve of this Sunningdale job: are Sweaty and Jock going to go it alone? Suppose he likes the job, but doesn't think Sweaty and Jock are the ones to do it? Suppose some peterman is asked in to do a combination for them, and casually slips twenty thousand into his own inside pocket?'

'Marsters thinks Mason had a percentage contingency margin to cover human weaknesses.'

'Surely. But what if Mrs Humberstone thinks Sweaty's wife has had more than her share of holidays in Benidorm? Suppose Sweaty falls for an inducement, and grasses on Jock? These things need discipline from time to time. Even Hartley Mason needs a heavy mob.'

'Who's to say he hasn't one?'

'His reprisals would have to be memorable, if he wanted to keep the peace in his kind of empire. If it were my case, that's where I'd be moving in from.'

Beamish nodded appreciatively.

'That's what Marsters thinks, too. He thinks that Brenda was what you call a memorable reprisal. What's more memorable than murder? What's going to shake an army more than the knowledge that a Corps Commander has just had his? Brenda wanted out. Perhaps she just wanted a change. Or maybe there was another memorable reprisal, somewhere, which she'd heard of and didn't like the cut of. What better cover for her than to go home and nurse her own mother? That is the gospel according to Marsters. Marsters doesn't like you, by the way.'

'That's his privilege.'

'You stole a march on him for which he'll never forgive you. He had finally got authority to go and confront Mason. There were a lot more bits and pieces that I haven't mentioned to you – disconnected grounds for sus. He still didn't know about the Brenda connection, because he'd had no reason to rummage in William Fothergill's private life. He didn't know about Ember Bay. Yet you'd been chatting to Mason about those things two minutes before Marsters went into his office. He's convinced that you put Mason on his guard. Mind you, it's only in his hysterical moments that he suggests that may not have been an accident.'

Mosley did not seem outraged by the insinuation.

'I'm telling you this,' Beamish said, 'to show you frankly where I stand. I changed my mind about you, over in Ember Bay, you know.'

There was something almost schoolboyish about Beamish's step-by-step self-justification.

'I was impressed by what you dug out of Bay View. I liked the cut of your jib when we were burgling. I was impressed by the way you handled old Mrs Thwaites. I'm impressed by the grip you've got over this private bloody wilderness of yours. And I want you working with me. Marsters doesn't seriously think you're one of Mason's satellites. Grimshaw, if that's any comfort to you, refuses to listen to him when he talks like that. But they are in agreement to keep you out of things, just in case – and I'm quoting them – you mess something else up.'

Mosley was not offended.

'So they've given me the job of tapping the gossip in Parson's Fold – even of going over for another session with old Mrs Thwaites. You'd do both jobs better than any man they could turn to.'

Mosley showed neither pleasure nor irritation at this effusive and naive expression of confidence, so out of place between professional colleagues that Beamish would have been branded a crawler in some company.

'Mind you,' Beamish said, 'if you feel at all uneasy about conflicting with higher authority – '

Mosley laughed heartily.

'The key question, to which they want an answer tomorrow, is whether Hartley Mason was one of the visitors that Brenda received at Jackman's Cottage. If they can establish that, they feel that they'll have case enough to have him in and talk to him till he's tired.'

'They'll trip up if they do,' Mosley said.

'You talk as if you know something.'

'No more than anyone else would, who'd given his mind to it.'

'Well – what about it? If we were to bump into each other, by accident, in Parson's Fold, do you think you could have found time to chat up a few of your old friends?'

'*Quid pro quo.*'

'Anything you like.'

'I've a case I'd like taken off my hands.'

'If I can possibly fit it in.'

'It won't take you long. Only a crate of bloody oranges. To tell you the truth, it's beginning to get on my wheel. I suppose I'd better get off now and ring night-duty at Sheffield and get them looking for turkey-feathers.'

He said nothing about his conversation with Neddy Sladburn; did not mention that the car-breaker had met Mason at Jackman's.

Fifteen

Mosley, as they parted that night, had been difficult to nail down about the details of their meeting the next day.

'Oh, some time between ten o'clock and half past two,' he said, so seriously that he seemed to mean it.

'Where, then?'

'Somewhere around.'

Ten o'clock seemed well advanced in the day to a man of Beamish's energies: time to dispose of the small affair of the Spritwell oranges. By half past nine, having followed up every lead that Mosley had given him, he was beginning to doubt his own sanity. Alice Renshaw, the elderly assistant who had had charge of the greengrocer's shop since it had opened at eight, looked upon every question he asked her as a slight upon her honesty. The shopkeeper, Peter Morridge, who arrived at a quarter to nine, bringing in the day's supply from a wholesaler on the back seat of his family car, was a vague, repetitive and dogmatic man who by now thoroughly regretted having reported the theft in the first place. He and Mrs Renshaw answered questions in operatic duo, with long explanatory digressions in which no issue was simple. Beamish asked to see the original invoice for the fruit, which suddenly could not be found. The day of the loss, it seemed, had been a heavy one for Lower Spritwell, greengrocery-wise: there had been a hamper made up for a raffle prize at the Pigeon Club; a bedside basket to go up to the hospital. Beamish wandered into the village street, where there was no lack of informants: only a lack of information. Beamish, struggling hard not to be abrasive – for all these villagers were surely Mosley's friends – began to feel that he was losing his touch.

He drove down to Parson's Fold, the Spritwell oranges no nearer to accountability than Mosley had left them. And in Parson's Fold a very opposite spirit prevailed from the tangled helpfulness of Spritwell. Here people were not falling over themselves to answer questions. There did not even seem to be any people. There were no comings and goings this morning. The pub was not yet open. The wooden bench round the oak tree was unoccupied. Kitchen doors were shut, their panels conveying an impression of prolonged domestic coma. Women were not gossiping; there were no women in evidence. The children had been bussed off to school. And those of pre-school age, whom one might expect to have found playing with dangerous farm machinery and sucking their fingers on dunghills, appeared to have been locked into cellars and coalholes. Somebody with a good pair of eyes and a faultless memory for his number-plate must have spotted Beamish while he was still dust on the horizon.

At least the peace of the village assured him of an uninterrupted session in Jackman's Cottage, a dream which had so far been denied him. And even in his wave of admiration for the inspector, he had not forgiven Mosley for the cavalier fashion in which he had despised the scientific evidence on the spot. Beamish loved scientific evidence – though even in the enlightened home-ground of his Q Division, he had not so far made his name by inferring miracles from it.

He stood now in the living-cum-sickroom and steeped himself in the thought that this was a room in which murder had happened. A room in which murder had happened was not quite the same as a room which had not witnessed a killing. In the more reasonable type of ghost story, the explanation was sometimes put forward that, in some way not yet accounted for, places could register emotions and energies, playing them back at random to visitors with the right grade of sensitivity. Beamish stood for some seconds to see what vestiges of recorded distress his own sensibility could pick up in here. The result was akin to switching on a record-player during a power-cut; or maybe he had the wrong type of stylus. This was a sickroom which had been untidily vacated. It was a living-room in which no fire had been lit for the last ten days – with autumn eroding the days and a chill – an early frost, even – staking a claim in the nights. It was a room in which no one had flicked a duster since before the killing, in which objects had been moved, drawers unpacked and repacked by policemen with other work to hurry away to. Nevertheless, it was a room in which murder had been done – in the presence of these armchairs, those pictures, those china ornaments.

Fainter than before Mosley had trampled over it, there was the chalk-line that marked where the body had lain. Beamish studied it systematically. Given the woman's weight and height and the pathologist's record of bruises sustained in falling, it should be possible to work out the position in which she had been standing when the shot was fired. Beamish got out the photograph of Brenda Cryer's body, lying *in situ.* Both the lie of the corpse and his own interpretation of her fall suggested that she might suddenly have swung round, have turned her back on her killer. So where had he been standing? Behind her – when her back was towards him. That was so obvious, it had to be bloody silly. Though even the obvious, he told himself, was worth thinking over at this stage. *At this stage?* Wasn't it high time they pushed on a stage or two?

The medical report had attested what any layman who could bear to look would have seen with his naked eye: that the little bijou pistol had been fired only an inch or two from the nape of the neck. So he had been in the same room as her; so he was probably someone whose presence had not unduly alarmed her: she had probably been talking to him at the time. So why had she turned round to enable him to shoot her? Had he played some puerile *What's that?*

prank on her, and she had swung her torso? And his fingers had perhaps already been clasped round his pistol, perhaps in his trousers pocket. He had held it an inch from her cervical vertebrae and fired.

Could it have been otherwise? Was that in question?

Beamish got out Forensic's report and read it again – the first time he had read it in the actual room, though he knew it by heart from office perusal. They all knew it by heart from office perusal – Grimshaw and Marsters, and everyone with a shred of suspected specialism in his make-up to whom it had been referred for an opinion. It had not been referred for Beamish's opinion. Beamish had had to ask to see it.

It was a careful report, exhausting all the available evidence. Dust had been analysed from the soles, welts and laceholes of Brenda's shoes, from the hems and seams of her slacks. Scrapings had been taken from her fingernails, her scalp and the holes pierced for her ear-rings. Comparisons had been made with garden soil, mantel-dust and beatings out of the upholstery. And the only thing that was proven to the point of certainty, forensic scientists being the positivists that they were, was that Brenda Cryer had lived in Jackman's Cottage during the period in which it was already known that she had. Beamish did his best to prevent himself from becoming disenchanted with Forensic; of course, science had its limitations – though that was no excuse for Mosley's ignoring it altogether.

At opening time, Beamish went across to The Crumpled Horn. At opening time The Crumpled Horn opened, and those gentlemen who were always there were there. Unlike the outdoor village, they did not treat Beamish to silence. They treated him as if they knew him well, admired his record and wished strength to his arm; and they skilfully avoided saying anything that was worth his hearing. One old fellow called Arthur Blamire left his pint, saying that he was nipping back home for a minute or two to put a light under his potatoes.

Beamish knew – and with fear – that once he had compromised the line that he had come to the village to pursue, then that line was compromised. This was a morning, it seemed, for the elegantly obvious; once the damage was done, it was done. Beamish hardly dared make a start: a rare attitude for him. Then, like a learner making his first dive, he dived.

'Everywhere I go, I keep hearing stories about visitors calling on Brenda Cryer, when she moved back to Jackman's – '

And such a blunt introduction produced a silence at first, a sort of community concussion.

'Everybody seems to know about it,' Beamish said, 'yet no one can name names.'

'Aye, well, there used to be an old saying about that,' someone put in at last. 'Something to do with pack-drill, if I remember correctly.'

Beamish realized that they had to be put at their ease. 'No one's saying anything about pack-drill. We're not going to arrest the first person we know to have gone in there. But somebody could tell us something – if only we knew whom to ask.'

It sounded appallingly weak. They chewed it over – and to them, apparently, it sounded appallingly sinister. No one could think of anything to say at all. They were trying, of course, to make Beamish himself name a name, thereby undermining himself irrevocably.

'If only we could speak to someone who'd set foot in there – '

'Like the milkman?'

'No, of course we know what he has to say. Someone – well, someone who might have used his eyes. Someone you wouldn't perhaps have expected to call there.'

And then a man in a corner laughed. 'Shall I tell you what I think? I reckon it's old Arthur Blamire you ought to be talking to. He's in and out of here like a jack-in-the-box, always reckoning to have something to put on the hob or take off it. Maybe he fancied his chances up at Jackman's.'

'Or else it was Stevie Pollitt.'

Gross and universal laughter. Beamish did not know who Stevie Pollitt was, but it was clear that he was either the village idiot or some decrepit elder statesman. He was surprised that with the woman not long dead, there should have been this willingness to lapse into crude humour about her. It suggested two things: firstly, that there was at bottom a standing contempt for her reputation; secondly that they were solidly unwilling to commit themselves on the side of authority.

Then Arthur Blamire came back.

'Just the man we want, Arthur. Your ears been burning, have they? Your name's being taken in vain, Arthur.'

And Blamire looked round their faces with puzzlement and anxiety; an unintelligent and lonely old widower.

'You spend more time crossing the road than you do either at home or in here, Arthur. The detective wants to know who you saw visiting at Jackman's.'

'What – while Brenda was there?'

Goodness knows why else he thought Beamish might be interested.

'Oh – I can tell you who that was.'

And Beamish looked at him with a hopefulness that seemed to be shared by everyone in the room.

'I said to myself – I'd nipped back home, you know, because I had to keep pulling the chain, because of a worn washer in the ball-cock – I said to myself, now I wonder who's that, gone up there?'

He seemed to regard that as answering the question.

'And who was it?'

'Her brother,' he said, 'and his wife.'

Beamish gave up. At eleven o'clock he left the pub, decided to retreat back to Jackman's, where he could at least sit down. But as he was crossing The Pightle, he saw a tractor approaching, driven by a wild-looking man with a long-outgrown basin-cut sticking out all round from under his hat. Behind the tractor was a trailer, and in the trailer sat Mosley. He waved with great pleasure at the sight of the sergeant.

'Can we go up to the cottage first?' he asked as he got down. 'I've thought of one or two things that I didn't do justice to, last time I was in there.'

So they went up to Jackman's and it looked for some time as if Mosley was doing precisely what Beamish had done: weighing up niceties of evidence to which he hadn't paid much attention before.

'You don't happen to have the forensic report on you?'

Beamish produced it and Mosley studied it, apparently with growing perplexity. But he did not communicate any of his findings, either about the report or the room. Instead he said, 'Mind if I take another general look-round?' and went through each of the other rooms in turn. Beamish heard him go upstairs, and presently he reappeared, carrying an armful of old clothes.

'Some people are strange, aren't they? I mean, they had this place up for sale, and yet they still haven't cleared all the drawers and wardrobes. I can understand them holding on to the stuff while the old girl was still living here – she was probably as sentimental as hell about it. But this is a good coat – '

Mosley laid a heavy dark overcoat over the arm of a chair. It was not new, but it had not been worn often. There was also a narrow-brimmed bowler hat, of the quality that is the hallmark of a certain fastidious type of professional man; and a faultlessly furled umbrella. When old Thwaites was made managing clerk, he knew precisely what image to step into.

'And this, I imagine, is the sort of thing that a devoted family might give a man on his sixtieth birthday.'

This was an expensive and fashionable executive briefcase.

'You'd have thought, wouldn't you, that young Thwaites would have taken this for his own use? But I suppose there's some sort of sentimental barrier there, too.'

Mosley went through every pocket and compartment in the case, but the thing had been efficiently cleared. There was one postage-stamp of pre-decimal vintage.

'Does this tell us anything?' Beamish asked.

'It tells us about a certain attitude to death; about an unwillingness to face up to it – even to think about it afterwards. Possibly we shall be told that young Thwaites simply did not have time to dispose of his father's effects – that he kept putting it off till next week. There are other things up there, too. Perhaps it was the old woman who insisted on hanging on to everything – and after she went, they never got round to it.'

'I don't see that this can possibly be relevant.'

'Everything's relevant, Sergeant, that tells us anything about anyone. Anyway, I want to hang on to these few things myself for the time being. All right – don't look so worried – I'll give you a receipt for them.'

'I'm not very good at riddles this morning, Mr Mosley.'

'Hat, coat, umbrella, case: I've got a use for these things, if the murderer takes the line of action I think he will.'

'This is beyond me.'

'It shouldn't be. Have you sorted out those oranges for me yet?'

Beamish groaned.

'All right, Sergeant, let's pay a call. I'd like to get my feet inside the Old Rectory again.'

So they walked together past the lawn that could have competed with an Oxford quadrangle. But Beryl Thwaites looked rather less academic than the Vice-Chancellor of an ancient university. She had on a vast and shiny plastic apron bearing the reproduction of a historic poster advertising an apparently pre-Raphaelite soap. Her hair was wrapped in a drab cloth, her nail-varnish was palpably unrenewed and she had deployed in her spacious entrance hall the not inconsiderable range of accessories that went with her vacuum cleaner. Her pretence that she was not displeased to see them came a little belatedly.

'I'm sorry. You've caught me on a bad morning. I'm having a spring-clean. Donald has gone to Ember Bay to fetch Mother. We are fixing up a downstairs room for her. We are not going to let her go back into any of those horrible homes.'

'You mean, your husband has taken a day off from work?'

'He has more than a day owing to him, Mr Mosley.'

'That I don't doubt. Well, in that case, Mrs Thwaites, I wouldn't dream of trespassing on your time.'

'Oh, but if I can be of any help – '

'No, really.'

Mosley turned on his heel and Beamish's feet were on the verge of following his example when the inspector had a second thought.

'You could help me on one little point if you would.'

Mrs Thwaites looked all readiness.

'Who is the Company Secretary at your husband's works?'

It was a simple little question, in casual enough tone, and although Beamish could not see what bearing it had on the case, he did not miss the effect that it had on Mrs Thwaites. She did not actually catch her breath, she did not markedly blush: but it was clearly a question that she neither expected nor relished. Her lower lip lost its discipline for a second.

She looked first sharply at Mosley, and then away from him. 'You mean one of the personal secretaries?'

'No: I mean the Company Secretary – the board's right hand.'

'Why, that's Pauline Murray, wife of one of the directors.'

'Ah, yes. I could have got that out of one of the standard directories, of course.'

'Why, what – ?'

'Oh, it's nothing, really – just a thought. I wonder if you'd allow me to use your telephone?'

And Beamish thought that this was just an excuse to get their feet into the house, so that Mosley could ask any questions he wanted to, irrespective of what he had said about not hindering her.

But all he did was to ring up Murray and Paulson's, work his way round their switchboard to somebody helpful, and make an appointment to see Mrs Murray an hour from now. And as soon as he had put the receiver back down on its rest, he dialled again, a number which Beamish was surprised to see he carried in his head. But the nature of the call that he made was more than a surprise: it was a positive shock.

'I want an appointment, please, to see Mr Hartley Mason – but not in his office. I'd like to meet him in his home – or anywhere else he would care to suggest. This evening: yes – that would be fine. Drinks before dinner: that is a very civilized way of doing business.'

Mosley put down the receiver again as if challenging Beamish to point to any irregularity.

'My God,' Beamish said as they walked back along the drive. 'I'm not supposed to have brought you here. I'm not supposed to have whispered a word about the case. If Marsters finds out you've been talking to Mason again – '

'Oh, he'll find out. He might even in the long run have cause to be grateful – though I doubt if he'll have the manners to show it. You're right, though: it wouldn't do for him to find out too soon. That's why I made the appointment in Mason's home.'

'And he was ready to see you – without throwing up difficulties?'

'Of course. Don't you think he *knows* that the pincers are closing?'

'Well, this is something I think I'd better not know about, old friend. If you don't mind – '

'As you wish. I'd have thought, though, that Marsters would have preferred you to come with me. To keep me on the rails, so to speak. And, of course, to fill him in on what's been happening.'

Beamish unlocked his car, the passenger door first.

'You're a clever old bugger, aren't you? I wish I could be certain you're not overstepping it this time.'

'You wanted to know whether Mason was one of those who called on Brenda at the cottage. That was your brief, wasn't it?'

'Yes. But we don't seem to have moved any nearer to that simple issue.'

'We will. We'll ask Mason this evening, shall we?'

'And another thing I don't understand,' Beamish said, 'is where's the sense in the Thwaiteses bringing the old woman back to live with them?'

'Do you mean the sense in it – or the reasoning behind it?'

'Call it anything you like; it doesn't add up. The Thwaiteses can't stand the sight of her, nor she of them. Their home-life, their social round, for whatever that's worth, are going to be wrecked. And can you see Beryl Thwaites being nice to her?'

'No,' Mosley said. 'Life's going to be hell all round.'

'What, then?'

'You haven't grasped what makes the Thwaiteses tick.'

'Illusions – and not the sort that would appeal to any normal person.'

'On the contrary: the commonest clockwork spring behind most human actions, Sergeant – public opinion. Their image – not what people see of them, but what they think people see of them. They got by before, when the old girl was in The Towers, because everything just went quiet. Distance and oblivion, so they thought, so they kidded themselves, were saving them from public disgrace. But now there's been all this publicity, they can *see* the fingers pointing. And short of moving out of the village altogether – which would make fatal inroads into capital – they've simply got to do the right thing. They've got to be seen to be doing it. What is more – '

Mosley slewed round in the passenger seat and peered down a side-road; they were making a right-hand turn. He did not back-seat drive, but one would have thought that he did not trust his driver.

'What is more, Sergeant, that's why Brenda Cryer is dead.'

They went to Murray and Paulson's: it was by no means as easy to find parking space as it had been when Mosley had cycled in after working hours. Reception staff had clearly been alerted to expect them, and they were shown at once to Mrs Murray's office. It was the one whose door had stood slightly open when Mosley had come away from his first talk with Thwaites. It was the one through whose window a woman in heavy plum-red costume had been watching him as he tested his tyre-pressures with his thumb.

Mrs Murray was not wearing plum-red this morning. She was in off-white slacks that clung tightly to her fat thighs, emphasized without exaggerating the protuberance of her overfed buttocks. Her hair had been disposed of into a hasty French roll and she was wearing a blue ceramic brooch on a chain over a beige sweater in heavily ribbed knitwear. A far from comely woman; and no sign that she had ever been or desired to be one. Presumably she had at some time meant something to her husband. Presumably, from a different angle, she still did, for her shelves were up to date with Company Law, Trade Year Books, EEC Directories. Her command of the economics of small paint-trading was probably empirical, unadventurous, inelastic – and fundamentally sound. Murray and Paulson probably owed it largely to her nagging insistence on a few safe principles that they continued to exist on the perimeters of profitability.

'I don't know, gentlemen, in what respect you think I might be able to help you.'

'A quick answer to an unexpected question,' Mosley said, making the most of the enigma, though in a casual and entirely unsinister tone.

'Please ask me your question.'

'I just wondered whether you had noticed, during the last week or two, that someone has been following you.'

The question was certainly unexpected, and it certainly hit her. But she suppressed all but an initial revelation of the shock; presumably she had learned to keep her aplomb during what passed for sticky moments in the family board-room.

She laughed in the most humourless and unconvincing manner. '*Following* me? You mean men with their hat-brims pulled down over their eyes? Men leaping into taxis when they see me cross a road? This is a paint-factory, Mr Mosley, not a cover-plant for germ-warfare.'

Mosley seemed not to hear this at all. He simply sat waiting for an answer to his main question. When it became obvious that she hoped to ridicule it away, he became quietly solemn. 'I'm afraid this is not a joke, Mrs Murray. It is a long story and, alas, not compounded of fancy. It could have lamentable consequences. That is why I want you to think hard, and see if you can remember anything unusual.'

She thought – or pretended to think. 'Somebody following me? It seems so improbable. And yet – '

'And yet, Mrs Murray – ?'

'Well, no – there can't be anything in it. Two or three mornings last week, when I was leaving home to come here, there was a green van coming out of a side-road. And I noticed it again, a time or two – oh, just in the traffic, when I was coming home.'

'A green van?'

'The sort of thing a man might have bought tenth-hand. Dark streaks where a tradesman's name had been roughly painted out.'

'Did you catch sight of the driver?'

'Not at all. What is this about, Mr Mosley?'

'I don't think you need worry yourself, Mrs Murray. This is as we expected, and we have it in hand. But there is one more question – '

'Please ask me anything you like.' She looked bewildered. 'Anything to get this kind of thing off my shoulder.'

'I would like to know whether you have been away at all, on business trips, with Mr Donald Thwaites.'

'What are you getting at? What *is* this, Mr Mosley?'

There was no doubting her disturbed state now.

'I am not getting at anything. I just want to establish a yea-or-nay fact. Have you been away at all, on business trips – ?'

'I don't see of what possible interest it can be to you. But yes, I have.' She was not sheltering behind anger. 'He and I – and, I may add, a duenna from the typing pool, went to Cologne last March, in connection with a tender that is only just now coming to fruition.'

'You were away long?'

'Three nights, two working days, if you need to know.'

'Your husband did not accompany you?'

'He is managing director, Mr Mosley, and the works manager was down with a bug at the time. And if you are suggesting – '

'I am suggesting nothing. I have put a simple question of fact and you have answered it.'

She was summoning up kinetic forces inside her, like a clock that knows noon is approaching. Mosley thanked her, and they came away.

'Ghastly woman,' Mosley said, as they got back into the car. 'Though capable of getting and giving satisfaction, one is compelled to conclude. A man would need to be married to someone like Beryl Thwaites to look for adulterous relief there. God: I wonder what Murray's like?'

Sixteen

Hartley Mason might have been expected to have risen to at least a modest country property. He lived, in fact, on the outskirts of Bradburn, within walking distance of his office, in a largish post-Second War house set in largish though manageable grounds. They were indeed very well managed: a mature shrubbery, with exotic specimens, a grass tennis-court for his adolescent offspring, a loggia overlooking fishpond and fountain. But Mason was not a man who retreated to weekends of expansive leisure. He had a houseful of books – working books – and Beamish was impressed by the evidence of work in progress: a large stack of manuscript on a desk, with two works of reference open and a stack of others waiting with pages marked. Mason was evidently a man who improved all his shining moments.

Moreover, he was unexpectedly quite delighted to see Mosley.

'And may I say, Inspector, how much I appreciate your discretion in coming out here? There has been at least one official visit too many at the office. Malignant observers are beginning to invent things. What can I offer you gentlemen to drink?'

And, 'No,' he said, when the soda was tickling the Scotch, 'much as I admire zeal, perspicacity and unshackled imagination, I fear that your colleague Marsters is embarrassingly assiduous. And he is, I suspect, unaware of your present visit?'

'Quite so,' Mosley said, the archaism not strange from his lips.

'Not that I would have much difficulty in refuting the absurd charges which I fear the Chief Inspector is about to frame – but it would be a bore and a great waste of time to have to do so. The attendant publicity would not go down well with some of my partners. What is more, I fear that he is about to unearth something that I would far rather not have exposed to the broad light of day.'

'That I can well believe,' Mosley said, though with no sense of accusation.

'May I ask what put you on to it, Inspector?'

'You know there are things that I would not dream of asking you, sir – '

'You can always *ask,* Inspector.'

'Well, in that case, you wouldn't mind telling me, perhaps, what sort of a job it was that Brenda Cryer wanted you to set Matty Pearson on.'

'Now how on earth can you have got on to that? Don't tell me: it was that damned second-hand car-dealer. He had the look of an eavesdropper. Well, Inspector Mosley, I must simply remind you of the privileged relationship enjoyed by solicitor and client.'

'Yes, sir. I respect that. I will withdraw the question.'

Silence: and the potential of the interview seemed suddenly spent.

'Of course, sir, if you don't care to tell me, I dare say that Chief Inspector Marsters will be asking you the same question. Tomorrow, I wouldn't be surprised.'

Mason showed the hint of an appreciative grin. 'You're not suggesting that Marsters doesn't yet *know*?'

'I don't see how he can,' Mosley said innocently. 'His enquiries haven't taken him as far as hillside car-breakers yet.'

'You really are a bastard, Mosley. Didn't I once tell you that in open court?'

'Not in so many words, sir. But if you follow the way I am

thinking, by being frank now, you might be able to save yourself a good deal of – what's the vogue word? – aggro? – in the comparatively near future.'

'You can call Marsters off?'

'Hardly that, sir.'

Mosley seemed to derive no end of amusement from the suggestion.

'But when I lay things on the line, sir, I dare say he will call himself off.'

'Or be called off by the Chief Constable?'

'That might happen *in extremis.* I always think these things are best done on a family level.'

Beamish had to fight not to wriggle. It was the nearest he had ever stood to stage-wing corruption. He had heard stories, of course, but had never had reason to suspect his own top corridor. And as for Mosley – !

'All right, Mosley. You have to win. Matty Pearson, as you know, is a private eye to be reckoned with. Let us say I have put him in once or twice to cut case-work corners for me.'

In fact, ninety per cent of Pearson's work came from Fothergills.

'I can't quite remember how Brenda came to know about him. I expect his name had cropped up some time when we were yarning.'

Oh, yes? How many briefings had Pearson had in Bay View?

'She wanted me to set him on to her brother.'

Mason was holding his glass at an angle, looking into it as if he could see fairy pictures.

'A squalid business – just about as nauseatingly uncompelling as anything you could think up. Donald Thwaites was supposed to have done some hotel-corridor tiptoeing with his boss's wife. The thought of that pair together is about as repellent an image as my mind could boggle at. Be that as it may, there are supposed to have been high jinks in Germany, and they sometimes stay late at the office: passionate panting behind the paint-pots. Never mind the sordid tableaux. They must need each other pretty badly. Or shall we say, each needs someone. All Brenda wanted to be able to do was to taunt him. He always took such a high-minded view of her own little side-histories. I don't know whether you've picked up Brenda's high sense of fun – especially when there's a neat twist of poetic justice in the tail.'

'And Matty Pearson delivered the goods?'

'Enough of them.'

The interview closed a few minutes after that.

Hartley Mason stood up to show them out. 'One thing occurs to me, Mosley. If you want a little evidence that will help you to convince Marsters, I dare say I can put you on to something.'

'That might be very helpful indeed.'

'Call at the front desk late tomorrow afternoon. I'll have something waiting for you.'

Beamish hardly felt able to talk to Mosley as they came away.

Seventeen

There was the rest of the day to kill; above all else, Mosley put it firmly into words, it was to be killed out of reach of headquarters. He himself disappeared into his hill-country, mumbling about the activities of mice in the absence of cats. He recommended Beamish to have a mechanical breakdown, preferably off the public highway. He suggested an abandoned quarry in which his car might be concealed.

But Beamish was to rematerialize at first twilight. He was to park his car in Parson's Fold, pointing the right way to be driven off without hindrance. He was to proceed to the Old Rectory, was to contrive to get and keep the three Thwaiteses in one room, and was to concentrate on questioning the old woman.

Beamish did not jib verbally, but his face was expressive.

'Go on!' Mosley told him. 'You're capable of holding the Thwaiteses in conversation, I hope. *Invent,* man! You'll get nowhere in this job if you can't keep the drama going.'

'But what am I to talk to the old woman *about*? Last time, we talked about rescuing sheep out of holes, being stuck out all night on the moors and flagging down passing conveyances.'

'In that case, tell her about other phenomenal sheep-rescues you've pulled off. Keep going out of the front door to see if a conveyance is coming. Above all else, keep her mind centred on the old days. Talk about her husband. Admire the man. Regret the passing of such prudence and decency. Adopt a reactionary attitude. Be on the side of the ancient battalions. I want her mind, such as it is, dwelling on a vanished security by the time I get there.'

'And when will that be?'

'I'll be along.'

And Mosley vanished hillwards to the empire of his capering mice before there could be any argument. It was in a state veering on misery that Beamish realized that he must either comply or abjure any further co-operation. And at the stage which things had now reached, that was out of the question. It was remarkable how firmly Mosley had him in the palm of his idiotic hand.

Beamish idled an afternoon away out of sight. As the light began to fail, he drove leisurely – an astute observer might have thought reluctantly – down to the Fold. He parked his car tidily under the oak, crossed The Pightle and strode, assuming an air of purpose at last, down to the Old Rectory.

Donald Thwaites came to the door to him, in broken-down maroon bedroom slippers and a formless cardigan, his clouded eyes peering out at the figure framed in the dusk. Beryl Thwaites had also advanced into the hall, unable to quell curiosity – and either not bothering to, or incapable of hiding her exasperation when she saw who their visitor was. The mother had not been put to bed yet, but was swaddled in rugs only a few feet in front of a blazing log fire, into which she was staring as if unaware that anyone else had come into the room.

'There are one or two little points I want to run over – mostly matters for confirmation or elimination.'

And Beamish had in fact worked out a programme of innocuous questions with which to get going, until such time as he saw the chance to bring Mrs Thwaites Senior into the conversation. But after a few minutes, he wondered whether this was going to be possible at all. She simply sat looking into the flames; perhaps she thought someone was roasting a sheep.

'Now you say that it was on the evening of the 17th that you had supper at Jackman's Cottage. I would like you to cast your minds back – '

Where the hell had Mosley got to? Three quarters of an hour plugged solidly by. Beamish decided to give him another ten minutes by the mock-ormolu clock.

'You heard rumours of male visitors to the cottage. Did any of the rumour-mongers advance theories about the actual personalities?'

The Thwaiteses must have suspected by now the repetitive purposelessness of it all. And still the old woman was present only as a blanketed hulk. Then suddenly there was a racket outside the front door: not a knocking or a ringing at the bell, but a veritable assault, as if someone were actually fighting the timbers. Then knocker and bell were attacked simultaneously. Thwaites and his wife looked afraid; even the old woman became aware that something was going on, looking from the fire into the body of the room for the first time.

Beamish went with Thwaites to the door. Thwaites opened it, and standing there was an angrily gesticulating man whom even Beamish did not at first recognize as Mosley. Mosley was wearing old Arthur Thwaites's narrow-brimmed professionally modish bowler, carrying Thwaites's rolled umbrella and birthday-present brief-case and wearing Thwaites's heavy, dark overcoat which, being on the long side for him, gave him a ridiculous and seedy-looking air.

But he carried this off by the sheer aggression of being unaware of it.

'Does a man have to wait to be let into his own house?'

And he came, blinking, appearing to totter slightly, in through the middle of the room.

'Arthur!'

Although the others, once the first shock was over, were not under any illusion, the old woman seemed completely taken in. Mosley put his hand to his forehead, stood still, looked as if he were about to reel.

'Donald – get a chair for your father. Can't you see he's not well?'

And such was the compelling nonsense of the scene that Donald Thwaites actually did this – moved an armchair in the direction of Mosley.

But Mosley, as Arthur Thwaites, had other things on his mind. Clumsily, snatching, he tore open the brief-case, brought out a large brown envelope and drew from it a handful of typescript.

'Just look at this – the shamelessness of it – to think that my daughter – '

He thrust the papers into the old woman's lap. Her eyes flickered over the lines as if she were reading them. 'Donald – just look at this – ' She stretched out her arm, holding the documents out towards her son.

Thwaites took them, glanced briefly, then showed that he, at least, was refusing to take any more part in the pantomime. There was a light akin to frenzy in his yellowish eyes.

Mosley took two strides across to him and seized the papers from his hand. 'Well – so much for that!' And he threw the sheets into the heart of the fire, where they curled up one by one as the flames took the edges and corners. Mosley now put both hands to his head and began to sway.

'Cut it out, Mosley!'

Donald Thwaites had been pushed as far as he was going to allow. And as if obeying a parade-ground instruction, Mosley at once reverted to his proper self.

'But I didn't go far wrong, did I?'

'What's the point, anyway?'

'As you say – what's the point?'

Mosley turned to Beamish. 'When Arthur Thwaites visited his employer in a North Yorkshire property, he made the discovery, shocking to him, that his daughter was old William's mistress. And old William had meant this to happen. He had made a generous settlement on the girl, and he was convinced that a sight of that settlement would be a neutralizing comfort to anyone as steeped in the reliability of the law as his chief clerk. And one of Arthur Thwaites's duties that afternoon was to bring the documents back to the office and file them away in old William's personal file, in William's personal safe. But William had sadly misread Arthur. He must have known about the narrowness of his attitudes and the limitations of his outlook – but he probably just didn't believe that they went as far as they did. Arthur Thwaites's daughter had her rewards still to come: and her father threw her title to them on to the fire. And you, Donald Thwaites, having read through those papers, watched him do it. You, Beryl Thwaites, had the greatest satisfaction in knowing that your sister-in-law would never be in a position to outdo you.'

Mosley swung round on Thwaites, and it seemed to Beamish that his indignation now was no mere acting.

'That was what your sister never forgave you for. Because you *knew;* and if only you had told her, she could have had the will drawn up again, have seen that it was properly safeguarded. But there's a streak of poisonous righteousness in you, Thwaites. As I say, Brenda never forgave you. Why should she? And when she found that she had it in her means to blackmail you, she had no second thoughts about it. She was going to give you hell. What chance would you have now of a seat on the board – even of keeping your present job – if certain facts were made known to the Managing Director? What chances, even, of finding another job, when the hard core of your experience has been nothing more up-to-date than Murray and Paulson's?'

Mosley let his eyes wander over to Beryl Thwaites, who was looking on now with fear, but without understanding.

'Do I have to go into the details in full, here and now?' Mosley asked.

Thwaites closed his eyes. It was as if everything had shut down on him. He was too lost and too tired to fight back at this clutch of circumstance – one of those criminals unable to carry anything off beyond the first heat of impulse.

'The trouble is,' Mosley said, 'it's been thought all along, though in fact never put in words, that a lady's handbag pistol belongs in the world in which your sister spent much of her adult life. In fact, nothing is further from the truth. Anyone can get hold of a gun these days, if he really wants to. I don't care particularly how you came by it, Thwaites. I do want to know where it is now.'

Thwaites's shoulders moved involuntarily, but he said nothing.

'Come on, lad: be the son of your father. Let's have chapter and verse.'

'What's the use?' Thwaites asked, of no one, as if he were asking permission of the universe to make a decision. 'It's all finished. If you'll take me down to the lab, Mr Mosley – away from these people – I'll show you where the gun is.'

The next morning, Mosley was early at his official desk. Also early at theirs were Grimshaw, Marsters, the Assistant Chief – even the Chief himself.

'This is a remarkable story,' Grimshaw said, 'and he doesn't seem to want to contest it.'

Mosley looked up from a long and tortured letter he was reading. It was from a greengrocer in Lower Spritwell and it had to do with invoices, raffle-prize hampers and a sudden influx of gifts to patients in hospitals. It also had to do with instructions misunderstood by his assistant and a temporary shortage of supply. The apologies were even more elaborate than the explanations. What it all boiled down to was that owing to a series of misunderstandings, there never had been a crate of oranges.

'Before you go and lose yourself up there among the bilberries and heather, Jack,' Grimshaw said, 'would you mind getting four sacks of rotting turkeys off our backs? The Sheffield police have brought four men in overnight, also four sacks of carcases, still in their feathers, and still undrawn. Oh, and a sack or two of geese, that have been even longer deteriorating. At present they've been put out in the transport yard – hence the lack of congestion in one particular corner this morning. I gather your rustlers are playing it with buttoned lips at the moment – and asking to have Hartley Mason for their defence.'

'Which is why,' said Chief Inspector Marsters, who also seemed to have come into the room, 'I propose to take this case out of your hands, Mosley. I can't think of four sacks of turkeys as managerial crime, but one thing might lead to another, and you will not be on hand to lead it anywhere else.'

Mason was asked to come in. He took one look at the poultry-fanciers – among whom Mosley at once recognized an old friend – and said he was sorry, but he could not take them on.

'But I am claiming help under the Humberstone Foundation,' said the one Mosley knew, who seemed to provide most of the brains and eloquence of the team. 'Freddie Humberstone was my mother's cousin.'

Hartley Mason sighed, looked at the poultry-thieves with pity – and at the policeman with a sort of conspiracy.

'I am still hoping that this will not get too much publicity. Freddie Humberstone was an incorrigible but remarkably successful rascal who came and went through prison gates with sickening regularity in the forties and fifties. His wife, a patient, faithful and ever hoping woman died while he was doing his last stretch and Freddie had a *crise de conscience* in which he not only vowed to go straight evermore, but made a substantial investment, the interest on which has to be applied to the deserving dependants of men serving custodial sentences. It provides them, if not actually with luxury, at least with a few little extras. I am an executor of the scheme – an office, I might say, which is a mixed blessing. There is nothing illegal in its operation: it is a charity, albeit a highly selective one. Every case it has organization, I'd think.'

'Not so small that I didn't know a thing or two of what documented. The books are audited annually. You will recognize Mrs Cryer's hand in the ledgers. I am sorry that this has come to light. If the fund were too widely known, the amount of claims on it would be an embarrassment. I have to give far too much of my time to it as it is.'

'But what about my blood relationship,' said the spokesman-rustler. 'Doesn't that give me a prescriptive right – ?'

'No, sir. Our founder was a man of some wisdom, who hoped that as many as possible of his kin would see the light earlier in life than he did himself. Therefore, in case of repeated offences, I am given discretion to withhold support from the funds. In such cases, I am always ready to compensate for over-zealous prosecutions, misapplications of the sus laws, and so on; but as far as I can I respect the recorded wishes of Frederick Lonsdale Humberstone.'

Marsters had not the grace to conceal his unhappiness. 'I suppose you can give me some proof of this so-called foundation?'

'You shall see the foundation deed. The files are copious, and it will take you a week to do them justice – but they are at your disposal.'

Marsters turned away brusquely. 'I want to see those papers, Mason: every last sheet of them. And Mosley – you'd better get down to your feathers.'

'We've met before,' Mosley said. 'On the landing of a hotel at Ember Bay. There were people on the premises who understood that you were a traveller in trawlermen's chains.'

'But there aren't any trawlers in Ember Bay,' the man said.

'There are along the coast, so you were on a safe ploy – with a reasonable excuse to stay at Bay View. What were you – some sort of messenger? Pretty small fry in the handled, every penny it has spent, has been faultlessly went on. Any chance of a deal, Mr Mosley?'

'Not with me, brother.'

'What about your mate?'

'What would you have to tell him?'

'A few jobs that were done in the old days. And that Mason's a bastard: picking and choosing. It never used to be like that. You could rely on the firm. Charitable foundation? Of course the books are in order. They *have* to be, see? That's the cover – that's never been needed before. A few years ago there was a lot going on; and if you needed help – with a job, I mean – you knew where you could get it. That side of thing's gone to pot, since Mason took charge. Why do you think Brenda pulled out? Mason's too clever by half, makes too much noise, has too many big bloody ideas. Old Fothergill, now – you never heard much of him. He was dedicated, dead quiet. Life was different when he and his lady-love were running things. I remember being sent up to their place in the Dales once – '

'You've plenty to say, mate, that's evident. Can you prove any of it?'

'Get your pencil out.'

Mosley knocked respectfully on Marsters's door. Marsters looked over his desk, his eyes irritable and fatigued.

'What now?'

'I've struck a difficulty with these turkey people.'

'Go and tell Grimshaw about it.'

'I think it might be more up your street.'

Marsters stared at him, uncomprehending.

'What I mean is, I think you could be where you want to be by lunchtime. There's a chap down there who has it in for Mason. He'd be worth having a go at while he's still on the boil.'

Marsters cast aside the file he was squinting at. 'All right – I'll give it a try. And Mosley – from now on, stick to things that you understand.'

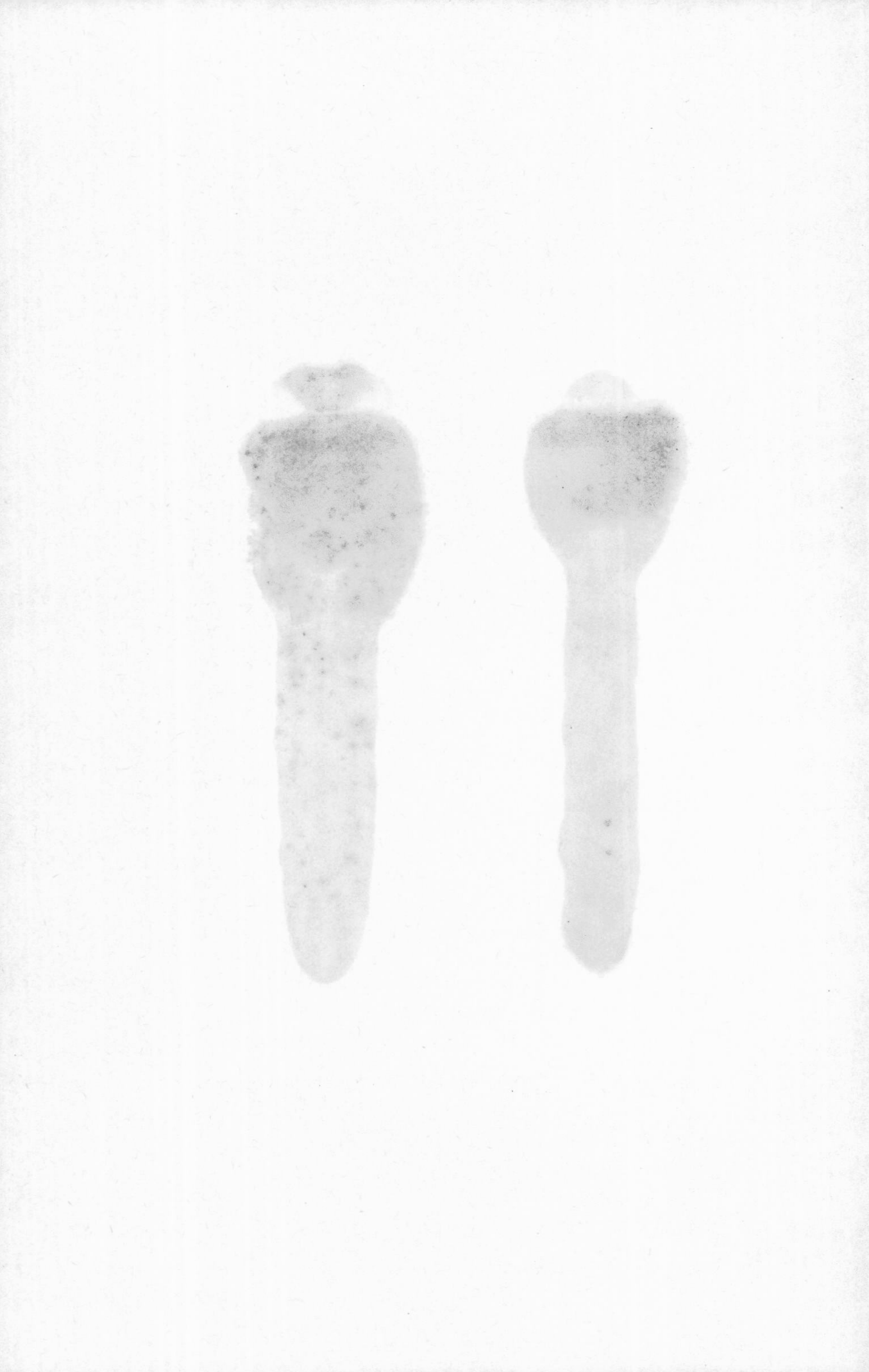

The Butler's Revenge

Also by Margaret Powell

Non-fiction

BELOW STAIRS

CLIMBING THE STAIRS

TREASURE ABOVE STAIRS

MARGARET POWELL'S COOKERY BOOK

MARGARET POWELL'S LONDON SEASON

SWEET MAKING FOR CHILDREN

MY MOTHER AND I

MARGARET POWELL IN AMERICA

MARGARET POWELL'S COMMON MARKET

ALBERT, MY CONSORT

MARGARET POWELL DOWN UNDER

MY CHILDREN AND I

SERVANTS' HALL

Fiction

A WOMAN WAITING

MAIDS AND MISTRESSES

THE HOUSEKEEPER

The Butler's Revenge

Margaret Powell

LONDON
Michael Joseph

First published in Great Britain by Michael Joseph Ltd
44 Bedford Square, London WC1

1984

ISBN 0 7181 2273 9

British Library Cataloguing in Publication Data

Powell, Margaret
The butlers revenge.
I. Title
823'.914 [F] PR6066. 093/

ISBN 0-7181-2273-9

Filmset by Alacrity Phototypesetters, Weston-Super-Mare
Printed and bound in Great Britain by
Billing & Sons, Worcester and London

Chapter 1

Mrs Edith Stewart came into the sunny breakfast-room punctually at nine o'clock with an expression on her face — never very amiable at the best of times — indicative of utmost annoyance. This had no visible effect on her husband; he had long since ceased, through habit and inclination, to take an interest in his wife's appearance or conversation.

Her eldest daughter, Eleanor, after one quick glance at her mother, hastily resumed eating. She always started at 8.45; a vague idea that her father liked to see at least one member of his family when he came down to breakfast was her reason for being earlier than the rest of the family.

'Henry,' said his wife, 'what do you think has happened?' And without waiting for a reply she continued, in a very indignant voice, 'Carter has given in his notice, and before breakfast too! Really, servants have no consideration these days. My dear mother's butler would never have done such a thing, he was the essence of loyalty to our family. You remember him, Henry? James Merton, who kept the staff in order. He was a perfect butler.'

Mr Stewart looked up from his newspaper long enough to say, 'Well, there are other butlers, I suppose,' and then added, 'Cook as usual has left bones in this kedgeree. I do wish you would make her understand that I don't expect to start the day half-choked with fish-bones in my throat.' His contribution to the conversation finished, he promptly retreated behind his newspaper.

'Why is he leaving, Mother?' timidly enquired Eleanor.

'It is utterly ridiculous. He said he is going to Sydney, in Australia, to help his brother run a hotel. What sort of an hotel can there be in a place like that, I would like to know?"

'What would you like to know, Mother?' said her son, Edward, who had just entered the room.

Mrs Stewart, whose meagre stock of affection was centred on her son, managed a weak smile. 'Carter has given notice because he wants to work in an hotel in Australia. Did you ever hear of such a notion? I'm sure he has never been further than fifty miles from London; he is used to civilisation.'

'Mother, this is the nineteen-thirties, not the eighteenth century. Australia has made progress since we sent our convicts out there. And its climate is considerably warmer than it is here. Anyway, Carter's not indispensable. One can always engage a butler, I suppose — especially if you offer high enough wages. Where's Elizabeth, still in bed?'

Mrs Stewart pressed the bell and when the butler appeared she frostily ordered him to send the parlourmaid to tell Mrs Markham that breakfast was on the table.

Just then, Elizabeth, the youngest daughter, and obviously enceinte, opened the door.

'Good morning, everybody,' she said, but receiving no acknowledgement from the head of the house, added, 'Good morning, Father.'

Mr Stewart lowered his newspaper and surveyed his youngest daughter with a somewhat sardonic eye. 'Good morning, Elizabeth. Though you are thirty minutes late it is, I suppose, a pleasure to have your company for a few moments before I leave for the office. Since your brother left the University, and your husband left you here, breakfast has become like a railway buffet.'

Elizabeth and Edward exchanged glances and began to laugh, which Edward quickly suppressed as his father turned a glacial eye on him.

'Have you decided, Edward, just which of the professions will have the benefit of your estimable services? It is now a year since you left university and it does seem to me you have had time enough. Or am I supposed to support you in idleness indefinitely?'

'Oh, but Henry,' began his wife, 'Edward is going — ' but where and when he was going was unheard by Mr Stewart, who had left the room.

'The Old Man gets on my nerves,' muttered Edward. 'Always on at me about work. Just because he likes to spend eight or nine hours a day in an office he seems to think that it's good enough for me.'

'You should not talk about Father in that way,' remonstrated Eleanor. 'Where would we be without him?'

'I suppose you'd be where all old maids go,' replied her brother cynically. 'Unless you think that at twenty-nine there is still a chance of Sir Lancelot riding by.'

Poor Eleanor's eyes filled with tears as her mother laughed at this sally and she hastily left the room.

Mrs Stewart had a certain contempt for her eldest daughter because, in spite of all the money lavished on her 'coming out', Eleanor had not managed to become engaged during her London Season. Truth to tell, no amount of clothes and attention could make poor Eleanor into a beauty, and her plainness was accentuated by a retiring disposition and absence of 'social chit-chat'.

Fortunately Elizabeth had not disappointed when it was her turn to 'come out'. Marrying into a high-class county family, she had recently returned from Bengal — where her husband's regiment was stationed — to be at home for a certain event.

Mrs Stewart was fond of relating, at great length and detail, the marvellous success of her own 'coming out'. 'I had a wonderful year,' and her hard features would soften into a complacent smile. 'I was presented at Court and the dear Queen smiled at me, and I went to dances and balls and I had five proposals.'

Her children could not but think that if their father was the best of the five, either there was a great dearth of handsome romantic young men that year or their father had considerably deteriorated. For, looking at the portly, heavy-jowled and partly bald man they could not visualise him dancing the light fantastic and squiring the debutantes at tea-parties.

Malicious acquaintances hinted that Edith Brewston had mistaken the financial standing of Henry Stewart; that she must have thought merchant banker synonymous with merchant prince. Certainly she often complained about her household; saying that in her home they'd had a butler and two footmen — not just a butler and a parlourmaid — and two gardeners, not just one.

With Mr Stewart's indifference to his less exalted status, it was poor Eleanor, always at home, who had to be a silent listener. For Mrs Stewart had no desire to hear that she lived a comfortable existence, that there were countless families worse off. What did Eleanor know about society? Twenty-nine years old and not married, or ever likely to be.

Rising from the breakfast-table she decided that Eleanor must go to the registry office and find another butler. What a nuisance it was, Carter leaving after six years. Her mother's servants had stayed for years; when they did leave it was only because they were to be married. But then they were country servants with ideas of loyalty to the 'big house'. They were not always asking for a rise in wages or more time off. In London, where there were so many large houses with staffs, servants felt free to change at any time. One simply could not expect below-stairs to consider their employers, and with these thoughts Mrs Stewart went to find her eldest daughter.

Chapter 2

'Well!' said Mrs Trouson, 'You did it then, Mr Carter. What did Madam say when you told her you were leaving?'

Mrs Trouson, the cook — the Mrs a courtesy title only — was a somewhat short and well-proportioned female in her early fifties who liked to think that she was motherly. That was not how Grace, the kitchenmaid, regarded her, but then Grace had been brought up in an orphanage, so perhaps had experienced a dearth of mothers to compare with Cook.

'She was properly taken aback, Mrs Trouson. She said to me, "Why do you wish to leave us Carter? By next month you will have been with us six years and Mr Stewart was going to raise your wages." They are always going to give one a rise, Mrs Trouson, when it's too late. You and I know that it's like getting blood out of a stone to get more money from them above-stairs, even if you went down on your bended knees.'

Cook, whose rheumatics precluded her from any such activity, and in any case thought that bended knees were strictly a Sabbath proceeding, nodded her head in agreement, adding, 'It's five years since I entered Madam's service, I wonder if she'll offer me more money when I've done another year? Between ourselves, Mr Carter, the wages in this establishment are not of the highest. Not that I under-rate myself, the place suits me and Madam knows better than to interfere. Once a day to give her orders for the meals; after that she never enters my kitchen without permission.' Sharply, to the kitchenmaid, she added, 'Are you here to listen to conversation or to help me and learn a few things? Start on the scullery, Madam will be down in a few minutes. Young girls, nowadays, Mr Carter, have no idea what work is. Sixteen that Grace is and only just started in service. When I was her age I'd already been working for four years.'

Grace had worked as laundrymaid in the orphanage until she was sixteen when, expressing a wish to learn cooking, had been sent out to start from the bottom as a kitchenmaid.

'Ah well, Mrs Trouson, coming from that orphanage Grace didn't have your advantage, of a family life. You have to make allowances.'

Cook, taking slight umbrage at the implication of strictness, uttered shortly, 'If it comes to that, Mr Carter, when I tell her off it's for her own good. I'm sure I try to be a mother to her.'

The butler, whose private opinion of the cook's motherly qualities were only to be aired the day before he left the house hastily smoothed her down by saying, 'Madam doesn't know yet that Alice is also leaving, that we're going to be married. Wait till she knows that she's got to find a lady's-maid as well as a butler! She'll raise old Harry. I pity that poor Eleanor—Madam will start on her as though it's her fault. Oh, I can hear her coming down right now.' And the butler quickly slipped away.

'Good morning, Cook,' Mrs Stewart greeted her.

'Good morning, Madam.'

'I suppose you have heard about Carter leaving? I'm so vexed. Perhaps Brown will not get on with a new butler.'

'Oh! I expect she will Madam. Maud's a good parlourmaid, she knows her duties.'

'Such a ridiculous notion Carter has of going to Australia. He has no knowledge of the country, it's not in the least like England. What is your opinion, Mrs Trouson? Don't you think that he's making a mistake?'

Cook, knowing full well that, unless her opinion coincided with that of Madam it would not be welcome, temporised, murmuring, 'It is a long way away, Madam. I suppose Mr Carter wants to see his brother.'

Later that morning, just before the elevenses cocoa, Cook asked the butler if he was going to let the staff know about himself and Alice.

'Yes, Mrs Trouson, it doesn't matter now we are leaving. Apart from you I kept it quiet because I didn't want the young ones giggling and gossiping all over the house.' And he proceeded to break the news when all were gathered.

'Well I never, Mr Carter. We had no ideas like that about you and Alice. I congratulate you both. I'm sure Mrs Trouson and I feel it won't be the same here when you are gone,' said

Lily, the head-housemaid, endeavouring to look appropriately serious.

'It's ever so romantic,' giggled Flora, the under-housemaid, and then gazed with some apprehension at that austere person, the butler.

However, Mr Carter, from his position as potential bridegroom, was feeling benign and actually smiled at Flora. In truth, Mr Carter, fifty years of age, large of girth and scant of hair, felt that he was in the prime of life and that his engagement to Alice Beach really did constitute a 'romance'.

'Where is Alice?' asked Cook.

'I saw her go into Madam's boudoir. I expect she was giving in her notice,' and Lily laughed, adding, 'It's going to be a case of "look out for squalls this morning". I was engaged once. I thought he was ever such a nice chap. He was a postman where I used to work in the country, and he played cricket in the village team,' Lily smiled reminiscently.

'What happened?' asked Flora. 'Did you break it off?'

'Well, let's say it was a sort of mutual arrangement. He was keen on express delivery while I preferred slow bowling. Here comes Alice now.'

Alice Beach, a rather angular female with mousy-coloured hair had, at forty-five, resigned herself to a spinsterish existence. Until she was forty, as the only daughter, she had cared for two aged and crabbed parents until, death removing both within two years, she was left with two hundred pounds and the need to earn a living. Now five years later here she was, to her amazement, engaged and shortly to travel to Captain Cook's country.

'Well, Alice,' said Cook, 'we all know the good news and offer you our congratulations. We'd like to know too what Madam said when you gave in your notice. Was she very angry?'

Alice, her usual sallow complexion changing to a somewhat unbecoming pink, tittered, 'Oh dear, she certainly was. At first she couldn't seem to understand why I wanted to leave. Then she tried to dissuade me by pointing out that I had no idea what kind of life I'd have; that Australia was a primitive country compared to England. At the end I could see Madam was furious with me. I reckon it's as well I won't need a reference when I leave.'

'Don't you let her bully you, Alice,' interrupted Lily. 'If she tries on any of that caper you stand up for yourself. It's not as though you'll need to look for another post.'

'I stood up to Matron at the orphanage,' said the kitchen-maid. 'When she threatened me I told her that when the Society lady came round I'd make a complaint about the way I was treated.'

'What's a Society lady?' asked the under-housemaid.

'Never mind who or what she is,' sharply interposed the cook. 'Are you going to get on with your work, Grace Taylor, or do you want to request an interview with Madam to complain of your treatment in the basement?'

With a barely-smothered giggle Grace departed to the scullery where she could be heard vigorously pursuing black beetles around the brick floor.

The housemaids going upstairs and Mr Carter and Alice disappearing, presumably to indulge in personal attentions, Cook was left with the parlourmaid.

'I wonder what sort of butler will be here, Mrs Trouson? I do hope he's a nice man, it makes such a difference. In my last place the butler was always making nasty jokes and I know he used to drink the Master's whisky.'

'Don't worry about it, Maud; it will be a month before it happens. I suppose Madam will be lamenting and complaining about the servants during her At Home tomorrow. Ah well, it will give her something to talk about. Don't you think so, Mr Carter?' she said as the butler came into the kitchen.

'You are right there, Mrs Trouson. That Mrs Nash will look in for sure and she can't keep servants for love or money. I reckon it's on account of that husband of hers, he's too free with his hands and too tight with his money. Why only last week, when I was having a quiet drink at the Mariner's Arms, Mr Hinton—he that used to be chauffeur to Mr Nash—was telling me,' but just then Grace came into the kitchen, Cook gave him a warning glance and the tale was never told.

'I expect Miss Eleanor will be sent to the registry office to find a butler and lady's-maid. She is put upon in this house, that's for sure, and she's such a nice person. Yesterday she knocked on my kitchen door as polite as you please and said, "I'm sorry to disturb you, Mrs Trouson, but Mother says there will be two extra for dinner tonight and will you cook another bird?" She may not have her sister's looks but she's got a lovely disposition. What a pity she never married.'

'Well, there is still time, Mrs Trouson,' said the butler, with a complacent smile. 'Look at me and Alice.'

'In my last place the cook wanted to marry the butler, but he wouldn't have her,' said the parlourmaid, with a singular lack of tact as it was rumoured that the cook had 'been sweet' on Mr Carter.

'Come along, Maud, we've all the silver to clean, it's Madam's At Home tomorrow,' said Mr Carter, and with that the butler retired to his pantry thinking that never in this world would he have wanted to marry Mrs Trouson. She was certainly a good cook but a man needed more than a bit of food in his stomach. What was in his bed was equally as important. Horace Carter pursued this theme with his crony, Fred Penfold — Lady Farron's butler — as they sat in their sacrosanct seats in the Mariner's Arms. But although Fred nodded acquiescence, inwardly he thought: there's not much to choose between Alice and the cook as regards looks. For my part I'd sooner be in bed with the oversize cook than a bag of bones like that Alice. At least the cook would keep me warm. But a man's better off without taking on any female for life, once he gets spliced he's not a free man any longer.

Chapter 3

'Eleanor,' said her mother at breakfast the following morning, 'you must go to the registry office to find a butler and a lady's-maid. Impress on Mrs Hunt that I don't want some flighty young girl, I need a thoroughly experienced woman. Somebody about forty years old. Seymour can drive you there as I will not require the car this morning.'

Mrs Stewart's insistence on a middle-aged lady's-maid owed more to knowledge of her son's frivolous nature than her own inclination. Edward Stewart, having few of the outward qualities that appealed to girls of his own class, nursed his ego by condescending to badinage with females of the lower class. Lily, the head-housemaid, needed to keep a sharp eye on Flora who, at twenty, was flattered that Master Edward took notice of her. Similarly, Mr Carter kept an eye on Maud, though she was far too sensible to respond to amorous advances from one above-stairs, knowing full well that 'them above' felt immeasurably superior to 'them below' stairs.

Edward Stewart's four years at the University seemed to have left him singularly ill-fitted for work in any form and particularly in his father's business. His doting mother explained to friends that 'dear Edward was looking around for a suitable venue for his talents'. Tactful friends forebore to ask in which direction did Edward's talents lie; while others, asking this question from the mistaken notion that they might be able to help, quickly discovered that 'dear Edward is so independent he wants to do everything on his own initiative.'

'But Mother,' he now protested, 'I need Seymour to run me down to Guildford. I have to see a fellow I know. Eleanor can take a taxi surely, there are plenty of cabs in London.'

'Of course, my dear, you can have the car; it will make no difference to Eleanor.'

Mr Stewart looked up from his newspaper and, fixing his son with a cynical eye, said, 'There are also plenty of trains that go to Guildford. Eleanor is to have the car and that's an order.'

Poor Eleanor, the recipient of this benevolence along with a malevolent look from her brother and a severe glance from her mother's frosty eye, though grateful for her father's consideration, would have preferred to remain unnoticed. Fortunately — Edward sullenly leaving the room, followed by his father, and Elizabeth coming in — the conversation became centred on the coming event and the subsequent installation of a nurse. How would she get on with the servants, and would Elizabeth be coming into the drawing-room for the At Home?

'No, I think not, Mother. I don't want to listen to old Lady Farron describing harrowing details about her seven *accouchements*, or little Mrs Symmonds talking about the "sweet little stranger coming into the world". Personally, I find the whole business boring in the extreme. One loses one's figure, cannot wear pretty dresses or accept invitations to dances, and all because one's husband wants a son and heir. It is a pity that Eric couldn't be the one to have the baby as he has such an urge for a son to add to his illustrious family tree. Fortunately, he doesn't yet know that one child is my limit.'

'Elizabeth,' exclaimed her mother, in a scandalised voice, 'how can you talk in that dreadful way? Children are blessings from heaven.'

'Is that so, Mother?' answered Elizabeth, not in the least abashed. 'Father never gives the appearance of being thankful for his three blessings.'

'Now, Elizabeth, you should not speak about your father in that manner. He loves you all but he has many business worries to contend with,' said her mother in a tone of mild reproof. And, in answer to her son who, now that his father was no longer in the house had asserted his right to the chauffeur's services, 'No my dear, you had better go by train. Your father has said that Eleanor is to have the car today and it is better not to go against his wishes.'

With a furious glance at his sister Edward departed, while Eleanor, feeling that she was to blame, murmured to her mother, 'I don't mind taking a taxi; Edward hates travelling by train.'

'Then why did you not say so to your father? What is the point of telling me now, when it's too late?' and Mrs Stewart turned a cold eye on her daughter, adding, 'Hurry and get ready, there are several things I require and I have no time to go out on my At Home day.'

Mrs Stewart invariably asserted how exhausting were her monthly At Homes, though as she was never involved in the actual preparations for this event there was no reason for her to feel tired. The cook and butler felt exhausted, perhaps with reason, as the former had cakes and scones to make and the latter to prepare the elaborate silver tea-service. After lunch Mrs Stewart retired to her bedroom to rest before visitors arrived at four o'clock, her equanimity not enhanced by the news that Eleanor had been unsuccessful at the registry office; no butler was prepared to work for the wages she was offering. Really, servants in London were intolerable in their demands for high wages and liberal outings. As Alice helped her to change into a fashionable tea-gown, she was reminded again of how vexatious it would be to find another lady's-maid as competent as Alice. Really, one would have thought she would know better, marrying and leaving England at her age.

An idea occurred as Alice was doing her hair, and she said, 'Beach, I wonder if Chambers would like to become my personal maid? When you are off duty, she is very quick and competent in looking after me. I could engage another head-housemaid. What do you think?'

'I'm sure I don't know, Madam. Lily has never mentioned that she'd like a change. I could ask her, I suppose.'

'No, leave it to me, Beach.'

Later that afternoon Mrs Stewart, while the butler and parlourmaid were out of the drawing-room, discussed the servant problem with her friend, Lady Farron.

'Two of my servants are leaving,' she lamented, 'and to go to Australia of all places! Carter has been here for six years, and I'm sure this is an easy situation. We are not entertaining every day of the week, and on his free afternoon he is allowed out until eleven o'clock. The servants even have a bathroom. It is so unsettling when servants leave; it puts ideas into the others' heads that maybe they could "better themselves", as they so peculiarly express it.'

'I know just what you mean, my dear,' said Lady Farron. 'Why, only the other day Penfold, my butler — a most superior type of man — said to me —' but just then Carter came into the room with more hot water for tea so the topic was hastily changed to discussing the theatre. After he'd gone Lady Farron continued, 'Penfold told me that Higgs, my hall-boy, had got the between-maid next door into trouble.' In a whisper Lady Farron added, 'The girl is going to have a baby and she is only sixteen. My hall-boy is seventeen. Of course Penfold dismissed him instantly, and without a character reference and the girl was also dismissed. Really, one would think that in their spare time they'd have something better to do. I have always said it was a mistake to make education compulsory for the lower classes.'

While Mrs Stewart wondered what connection this sordid tale had with her own butler leaving, Eleanor, a silent and unwilling listener, thought, why is education to blame? It's far more likely that because such young servants have to work so many hours, when they have leisure the ordinary human emotions are too much for them to cope with. But Eleanor, fearing her mother's sarcastic tongue and knowing that her opinions were of no account, remained silent.

'Did I hear that you would soon be needing a butler?' enquired Mrs Trentham, a rather fat lady who had consumed a large amount of sandwiches and scones before she made any conversation. 'I know of one who is looking for a situation. That is, I don't know him personally but I know his parents. They used to be in service with a family that are friends of mine. The man's name is John Barrett.'

'Oh, do get him to come here for an interview, I much prefer a personal recommendation,' exclaimed Mrs Stewart and then, a few gentlemen arriving — mainly to collect their respective wives — the conversation changed to intellectual subjects, theatres, balls and other social events. Before the departure of the fat lady, Mrs Stewart managed to glean a few details about John Barrett, though no definite information about his reason for leaving his recent employment.

At dinner that evening the topic of this possible butler was discussed until Mr Stewart exclaimed irritably, 'Engage him then, Edith, if he ever turns up. So long as he knows how to look after my clothes I don't care why he is looking for a post.' This remark enabled his wife to yet again inform her family that her dear father had had a valet; Menton, the butler, had not expected the care of his master's clothes to be added to his duties. Menton had known the value of his place.

Mr Stewart took no notice for, having heard all this on numerous occasions, was impervious to such comparisons. Eyeing his son he enquired if the journey to Guildford had produced any definite advantage, such as an opening suitable for a person of his undoubted talents. It would not do for Edward to forget all that specialised knowledge he had acquired at the University.

Inwardly fuming with rage — as he relied on his father for support he did not dare show anger — Edward muttered that the chap he hoped to have seen was abroad.

'Ah! what a pity Edward. I suppose he is not on the telephone so that you need not have had a wasted journey? And trains are so uncomfortable. You did travel by train, Edward?'

'Yes, Father,' muttered his son, with an angry glance at Eleanor.

'And you, Elizabeth, have you had a busy and exciting day helping your mother entertain her élite circle of friends? Telling them about your wonderful life in India where servants are thick on the ground and one doesn't have to search for a butler?'

Elizabeth just giggled at this sarcasm, for as a married daughter no longer under her parents' jurisdiction, she felt no obligation to perform household tasks.

'What about you, Eleanor, my dear? I suppose your time has been fully occupied as usual by your mother's request. Shopping and doing flowers, handing tea and cakes to the At Homers, making polite conversation; what would your mother do without you?'

'I do not understand you, Henry,' fretfully interposed Mrs Stewart. 'You seem to imagine that Eleanor is treated as a kind of drudge. She does no more than I do and I also have the responsibility of running the household every day. I am sure that Eleanor does not consider herself ill-used. What else would she do all day if she did not help me?'

'Perhaps Eleanor would like more time to devote to her painting; I think she has talent,' and Mr Stewart smiled at his daughter.

Poor Eleanor, happy to hear her father's praise, but not strong-minded enough to disagree with her mother, was saved by the sound of the telephone and the butler's entrance to inform Mr Stewart that he was needed to answer the ring.

With Mr Stewart's departure Edward angrily declaimed that he was absolutely fed-up with being at home and the butt of his father's idea of humour.

'Just because the Old Man had to work for a living he seems to think that's all a chap needs. Dash it, Mother, anybody would think I left university five years ago instead of one. Lots of chaps I know are travelling abroad, financed by their parents.'

His mother's placatory answer was interrupted by the butler's entrance to say that Mr Stewart had gone to his club.

Eleanor, pleading a headache, retired to her bedroom, followed by her sister; Mrs Stewart and Edward, drinking coffee in the drawing-room, continued to discuss his misfortunes and the intransigence of his father, and the servants below aired their opinions while having supper in the servants' hall.

Chapter 4

'What do you think, Lily,' asked Alice Beach, 'I do believe that Madam is going to ask you to take over my duties when I leave and she'll get another head-housemaid — or perhaps promote Flora and get an under-housemaid.'

'Flora is far too young to take on the responsibility,' observed Mr Carter. 'Don't you think so?' he asked, turning to Mrs Trouson.

Lily, while inwardly thinking, what's it got to do with old Horace, he won't be here when Alice goes, said, 'The question doesn't arise, Mr Carter. Nothing would make me be Madam's lady's-maid. I see quite enough of her as it is, without having to dance attendance when she comes back from a ball or the theatre. Besides, I hate needlework; it's bad enough having to mend the house-linen, but looking after Madam's clothes would be worse. I used to be a parlourmaid but even then I had to darn the tablecloths and napkins. What a fiddly job that was; Madam expected the darns to be almost invisible. I like being a housemaid as much as I like work at all. One hasn't got to wait on them at table.'

'But you've got to carry all those scuttles of coal up to the bedrooms, and I hate all the dust when one is making beds and all that turning down of beds at night and putting hot-water bottles in. And it annoys me to see what luxury they sleep in compared to us.'

'Too true, Maud. I expect they think that by the time we get to bed, we're tired enough to sleep on a plank.'

'There was a right old to-do in the breakfast-room this morning,' said the parlourmaid. 'That Edward was in a real wax just because he couldn't have the car. He looked at Miss Eleanor ever so nasty and so did Madam. Miss Eleanor never said a word, she never does. I reckon she ought to stick up for herself a bit more. They all put on her.'

Cook thought to herself, Horace really shouldn't let the young maids gossip about their employers and what they say above stairs. It's all right for us older ones, we know when to stop. A butler should exercise more authority than he does. I wouldn't let my Grace tittle-tattle about them above. But as her kitchenmaid was never in contact with 'them above' the prospect of her discussing their goings-on was very remote.

Now Cook spoke sharply, 'Go and make the tea, Grace, you don't have to listen to everything that's said here; it doesn't affect you. You get your wages and outings and enough to eat; it's a deal better than the orphanage, I'll be bound.'

'Do you think so? Grace,' asked the irrepressible Lily, 'is being here better than in the orphanage?'

'Well, I always got enough to eat there and we had jam every day and I didn't have to work so hard. We stayed in bed until seven o'clock; here I have to be up at five-thirty to light the kitchener. At the orphanage they had gas-stoves and a boiler for hot water.'

Cook, somewhat incensed that her kitchenmaid should compare the merits of private service and an orphanage, motioned Grace in the direction of the kitchen. Mr Carter, in an endeavour to placate Cook, described how the fat lady had consumed a large number of Cook's cakes and scones and that Maud had overheard her telling Madam that she knew of a butler who was seeking a situation.

'Though come to that, Mrs Trouson, if he is a fully-trained butler, he should have no difficulty; it is not so easy as all that to get one of us. I was talking to Lady Farron's butler in the Mariner's Arms and he told me that he was offered nearly double in wages by an American who was a guest in the house.'

'Did he accept? I would have done,' said Robert Seymour, the chauffeur.

'Certainly he did not,' answered the butler with some hauteur. 'Fred Penfold would never work for them Americans. Especially after being in titled service. He knows his worth.'

'Well, you're going to work for them Australians,' interposed the chauffeur.

'That is quite different, Mr Seymour. The Australians are really British, and besides I'm not going into service there, my brother runs a hotel. I shall be working for him.'

'Well, I hope Alice knows what she's letting herself in for out there. Them Australians are a matey lot; the men get together and the women don't get a look in — or so I've heard.'

'As my wife, Alice will be treated with respect,' loftily answered Mr Carter, while Robert thought what a pompous ass the butler was and how he'd soon get taken down a peg out there and told where to get off.

'In my last place one of the servants came from Australia,' said Lily, 'and she was always getting into trouble, because she would call Madam by her name — instead of saying Madam. Millie said that in Australia there's no class system at all. Jack's as good as his master.'

'I have always thought what a silly saying that is. If it was true, why isn't Jack the master? Anybody with sense would prefer to be,' and the butler looked at Cook for approval.

'In this country, even shop-girls think they are better than us,' said Lily.

'Because they think it, that doesn't make them so. They have to work for their living, the same as we do,' and Cook gazed around the table as though waiting for a chorus of assent.

'At least shop-girls have a handle to their name and a lot more free time than we have,' interposed the under-housemaid. 'They can stay at a dance until it's ended. They don't have to tell their partner, it's nine-thirty now and I must leave. Neither do they have to tell him that it will be another week before they are free to see him again. Of course in that time he's got fed-up and found another girl. Who can blame him?' and Flora gave a derisive laugh.

There was a pause, then the butler, in a severe voice, said, 'Flora Little, not only is it not your place to air your views unasked, we upper-servants stand *in loco parentis* to you. If you were at home I'm sure that your parents would not let you gallivant through the streets at all hours of the night —'

'You can hardly call wanting to stay out a bit later than ten o'clock gallivanting,' muttered Maud.

'— and no decent young man would respect a girl like that, let alone think of marrying her.'

In the silence that followed this moralising Cook nodded her head in approval. It was a matter of doubt whether she at any time had been given an opportunity to gallivant; but if so, time had successfully eradicated all traces of an erstwhile frivolous disposition.

To help Flora — though she seemed in no way distressed — Lily changed the subject by saying, 'The nurse is coming next week, she's having the spare bedroom next to Miss Elizabeth's. Flora and I have got to get it ready today. The happy event is supposed to be in about ten days.'

'That's a thing I object to,' grumbled Cook. 'Why must Mrs Markham come here to have her baby? Why couldn't she have gone to her husband's parents? They have a larger house and the old Nanny is still there; she could have looked after the child.'

'I agree with you, Mrs Trouson. And it will make more work for Maud and me. The nurse will expect her meals served in her room. She'll think herself above the servants' hall, I'm sure,' Lily said.

'I'll thank her not to come into my kitchen with any hoity-toity manners and telling me what she wants for Miss Elizabeth. I take my orders from Madam and nobody else. Except Miss Eleanor,' Cook added, 'she is always so kind and thoughtful. Why, only the other day when she came into my kitchen Miss Eleanor said, "Mrs Trouson, you sit down and rest your feet, I know it must be hard for you to stand on this brick floor all day." And she made me sit down at the kitchen table. When Madam comes down to work out the menus she expects me to stand all the time while she is there.'

'At the orphanage we all had to stand up when Matron came into the room, she was ever so strict,' volunteered Grace. 'And we had prayers every morning before breakfast. I thought we would have prayers here too. I thought they always did in domestic service.'

That Grace, thought Cook with exasperation, takes too much on herself for a kitchenmaid. I'd have thought an orphanage girl would have known better than to air her unasked-for opinions before her elders. Just because she has no parents, Horace Carter seems to think I should overlook her faults. All the more reason in my opinion to correct them. Who else will? It is no concern of a kitchenmaid's whether Madam does or does not have prayers.

In fact, Mrs Stewart would have liked to see the entire staff assemble for prayers. In her old home all the servants, with Menton at the head, had assembled in the hall, marched into the morning-room and knelt down — at a suitable distance from the family, of course. Her dear father had read the Collect and every day a different piece from the Bible and then the servants had filed out to resume their various duties. Prayers gave them a good start to the day. But Mr Stewart had given a determined refusal to preside at this ceremony, saying, 'If the servants feel in need of the deity's intervention on their behalf, they can supplicate him in their own rooms.'

It had to be admitted, albeit reluctantly by his wife, that Mr Stewart was a Laodicean and attributed none of his good fortune to the 'One Above', but his own abilities and business acumen.

Ignoring her kitchenmaid, Cook added, 'If Miss Eleanor ever married she would be such a kind mistress to her servants.'

'It's a big "if",' said the chauffeur. 'Why doesn't she make a bit more of herself? Smarten up, go out more, give up being so meek to her mother. She's so quiet; she never gets noticed in a crowd. Why, my wife was saying the other day that —' but here Mrs Trouson, who disliked the chauffeur's wife and considered it an impertinence for her to pass remarks about 'The Family', rose from the table saying it was time they all went to bed.

Grace and Flora shared one of the attic bedrooms, and ill-furnished and unheated as it was, Grace considered it a great improvement on the orphanage. There she had slept in a dormitory and had no chest-of-drawers or cupboard for her clothes.

'Isn't that Mr Carter the last word?' said Flora. 'In "loco parentis" indeed. I bet he once heard the word used above stairs and ever since has aired his knowledge at every opportunity. He's certainly loco and I'd have to be very hard-up for a man before I'd pick on him. Still, I suppose at Alice's age she's lucky to get the chance.'

'Oh, he's not so bad, Flora. The hall-boy at Number 26 told me that the butler there is a holy terror and footmen never stay long because they can't stand him. I hope we don't get a butler like that when Mr Carter goes.'

'Grace Taylor, do you mean to tell me that you have a boy-friend and never said a word about it until now? Well, you are a sly one, I must say, and you only sixteen.'

Grace, blushing furiously, protested that she'd spoken to him only a few times, he wasn't a boy-friend.

'At least he knows you're in service,' gloomily remarked Flora. 'At the Palais last Wednesday, I met such a handsome chap. He'd got brilliantine on his hair and he smelt ever so nice. He asked me for a dance and he was ever such a good dancer. He even bought me a lemonade in the interval and wanted to see me the next night. But when I had to tell him that I wasn't free until next Wednesday — because it's not my Sunday off — of course he wanted to know why and I had to tell him I was in service. I could tell, Grace, that he was thinking, "she's a skivvy". I shall tell lies next time a chap seems to like me, I'll make out that I have to look after my invalid mother. Or perhaps I'll say rich uncle; what do you think, Grace?'

But Grace, mindful of her early rising, was already asleep.

Chapter 5

'Henry, John Barrett is coming this morning at ten o'clock; do you want to interview him?'

'Who is John Barrett and why on earth should I want to see him?' irritably replied her husband.

Mr Stewart's disposition, never at its best at breakfast time, was further exacerbated by the arrival of his first grandson and the subsequent disorder of the household. And as he was far from gratified to become a grandfather with its connotations of old age, Mr Stewart was feeling aggrieved.

He repeated, 'Who is John Barrett?'

'Henry, I did tell you about him. He is the butler that Mrs Trentham recommended as seeking a situation.'

Mrs Trentham — irreverently designated the 'fat lady' below stairs — had not exactly recommended John Barrett, but merely mentioned that she knew of him.

'Well, that is certainly more than our son is doing,' Mr Stewart caustically remarked, as his son, obviously attired for a day of leisure, entered the breakfast-room.

'Good morning, Father,' Edward said, and busied himself collecting his breakfast from the sideboard.

'Good morning, Edward. And how are you? I heard you come home around two o'clock this morning. I suppose you were seeing another chap about finding you an opening suitable for your talents?' and Mr Stewart laughed at this sally, while Edward maintained a sullen silence and Mrs Stewart hastily interposed her question about John Barrett again.

'I have no time to waste interviewing domestics, Edith, I leave it to you. Who is that starchy-looking female I passed on the stairs this morning? Has our staff increased without my knowledge?'

'Of course not, Henry. She is the nurse for Elizabeth. She'll be here only a month.'

'Only a month, living at my expense, like everybody else in this family. I except you, Eleanor,' with a smile at his daughter, 'for you seem to be required to wait on everybody here.'

'I'm sure Eleanor does no more than I do,' protested Mrs Stewart. 'You have no idea, Henry, of how exhausting it is to run a household.'

'I thought I was paying a staff to do that. What are the servants doing; or do I employ them for show?'

With that he departed. Mrs Stewart and Edward were obviously relieved, while Eleanor, feeling her brother's hostility, murmured that she wished to see the baby and went upstairs.

'Really, Mother,' angrily exclaimed Edward, 'Father is the limit. Why cannot he leave me alone? I have a good mind to clear out and never come back.'

But he knew, and his mother also, that he would not 'clear out', he was too fond of a life of ease and comfort.

'Why don't you pay a visit to your aunt Bertha, Edward? You would be very welcome there, and your cousins would love to see you.'

'What! Go and bury myself on that isolated and bleak Scottish moor? And Agatha and Agnes are absolute frumps. Why, they must be forty if they're a day. I'd sooner put up with Father's sarcasm. At least I see him only at breakfast and dinner.'

'Well dear, do try not to irritate your father, he does work very hard.'

She forbore to add that the sight of his son's apparent inability to work contributed to her husband's ill-humour.

'Carter,' she said, as the butler came into the room, 'I have rung the bell five times.'

'I did not hear it, Madam. I was in the wine-cellar putting aside the wine for dinner tonight.'

'Could not Brown have answered the bell?'

'I will mention it to her, Madam.'

'A Mr Barrett will be coming this morning at ten o'clock; shew him into the hall. At eleven o'clock a Miss Collett will call, I'll see her in the drawing-room.'

'Very good, Madam,' said the butler, with the air of one to whom such matters were of little importance.

'I shall not be sorry when Carter goes,' said Mrs Stewart. 'He is becoming almost insolent now that he is leaving domestic service. He will find that waiting on a lot of hotel guests is far less satisfactory than waiting on people in our position in society.'

'Well, Mother, as Carter will not need a reference I suppose he feels independent. Who is coming to dinner tonight?'

'A couple of boring men and their wives, Edward, who now and again your father insists I shall invite to dinner. During the meal the men will discuss nothing but politics, arguing about the respective merits of Baldwin and MacDonald and where they made mistakes. I often feel like saying, "if you know so much, why are you not in Parliament?" After dinner the conversation will be about the Stock Exchange, business and money, while your father's old port will go round the table considerably faster than it does at my dinner-parties. Of course, I shall be expected to entertain the ladies while we are drinking coffee in the drawing-room. Though Penelope Courtland will probably monopolise the conversation. She is one of those dreadful socialistic females who, ever since women were granted the vote, imagine that they are just as capable as men when it comes to running the country. Just because Lady Astor is in Parliament, Penelope Courtland thinks that all women should strive to make their voices heard. Can you imagine, Edward, she addresses meetings of working-class women, urging them to use their vote; not just sit at home while their husbands go to the polling-station. The other day I heard that she was involved in a most vulgar situation — I cannot tell you the nature of it — but what can you expect from a lot of poor, semi-literate women in Whitechapel.'

This incident that Mrs Stewart thought too indelicate to relate happened when Mrs Courtland was exhorting her audience of working-class females to: 'Stand up for yourselves, let your husbands know that you are women with a purpose.'

Up from the audience rose a hefty female wearing a moth-eaten jacket and a man's cap — probably irritated with the la-di-da accent of the speaker — who shouted in a rancorous voice, 'Gorblimey, after 'aving six kids my bloody 'usband knows what my purpose is. To be there when 'e comes 'ome from the bloody pub on a Saturday night so's 'e can get me in the puddin' club with another bloody kid.'

After that, amid screams of laughter, the meeting broke up in disorder.

Edward commiserated with his mother's coming ordeal, hoping thereby to extract a few pounds to supplement his monthly allowance. There was a certain golden-haired and petite shop-girl from Selfridge's who, to misquote Lear, 'Gave some honey and took plenty of money.'

Having 'obliged', Mrs Stewart descended to the basement to give Cook her orders for lunch and listen to her suggestions for the evening meal. Then she retired to the dining-room in readiness to receive the prospective butler. She hesitated whether to delegate this task to her eldest daughter, but decided that Eleanor would not be firm enough in the matter of references. When, punctually at ten o'clock, John Barrett arrived, Mrs Stewart quickly opened the dining-room door; she did not altogether trust Carter — he might say a derogatory word about the situation. Carter certainly said a great many things during the servants' midday dinner.

Chapter 6

'There he stood, on the doorstep, as easy as you please, for all the world as though he was a friend of the family,' Mr Carter sounded very indignant as he continued, 'And then he said to me, "I'm Mr Barrett," and walked by me into the hall as large as life. Then Madam came out of the dining-room and said, "Good morning, Mr Barrett," and that's all I heard.'

Mr Carter had hovered in the hall for some considerable time, hoping to overhear the conversation from the dining-room but unfortunately the voices were too low.

'I said to myself, Mrs Trouson: Mr Barrett, is it now? You'll soon find out if you work here that the Mister will never be used by them above stairs. Why, even you, Mrs Trouson, are known as "Cook" to them.'

Mrs Trouson, always quick to assert the value of her position, took umbrage at this remark.

'I would have you know, Mr Carter, that "Cook" is my own choice. When I came here Madam asked me whether I wished to be called by my name, or "Cook". But I told Madam that I expected to be treated with respect by the other servants and would be Mrs Trouson to them.'

'I don't blame you,' said old Daniel Oates, the gardener. 'There's too much of this familiarity goes on nowadays. Why, when I'm at Mrs Salford's — I goes there twice a week, same as here — her young whippersnapper of a footman has the cheek to call me young Danny; and me getting on for seventy! What I say, Mrs Trouson, is don't let them sit on you, you stick up for yourself.'

Cook was not appeased by Daniel's rambling remarks, they bore no relation to the subject as exemplified by her. She had never in her life been 'sat on'; furthermore she considered that Daniel Oates, who came only two days per week, had no sort of right to discuss her or the Family.

'What did he look like — John Barrett, I mean?' asked the

headhousemaid. 'Was he old, young, dark, fair, bald and with a squint? We all want to know.'

'Whatever he looked like, he couldn't be a patch on my Horace,' said the butler's intended, smiling at him tenderly — or, as Lily thought, sloppily.

'Well, I must say, he was fairly good-looking, about thirty-five to forty I reckon. But, I don't know, I can't put my finger on it, to me he seemed not quite straightforward. I wouldn't altogether trust him with young girls.'

Mrs Trouson frowned at this, and then pointed out that the only girl here under twenty was Grace, adding, with a dark look at her kitchenmaid, 'I can't imagine that she'll have anything to worry about.'

There was a giggle from Grace who appeared to think Cook had paid her a compliment, thus entitling her to speak.

'If you ask me — ' Grace began, to be interrupted by Cook saying, in a withering voice, 'I must be deaf, I didn't hear anybody making an enquiry of you.'

Grace was in no way abashed. Presumably during her years in the orphanage, she had heard such remarks on many occasions.

'I saw that Miss Collett this morning,' said the parlourmaid, 'I wonder if she is going to be Madam's lady's-maid?'

'Yes, she is,' said Lily. 'Madam told me so just before I came down. Sooner her than me, I say. Madam said her name is Miss Dorise Collett.'

'Dorise, is it then?' and Horace Carter gave a satirical laugh. 'All I can say is, if her name is Dorise, then I am Horise.'

'Whatever do you mean, Mr Carter?' asked the under-housemaid, mouth agape.

'I mean, Flora, that her name no doubt, is Doris. She's put the "e" on to make out she is somebody, French perhaps. What is she like, Maud?'

'I reckon she's about fifty, Mr Carter, and she is ever so thin, as though she never gets enough to eat.'

'Well, that will be remedied if she comes here,' remarked Cook, complacently. 'I will say, Madam is not mean when it comes to food.'

'Pity she doesn't spend a bit on making our servants' hall

more comfortable,' complained Lily. 'That brown paint and lino gives me the creeps and as for those wicker chairs that used to be in Madam's bedroom: bits of the cane stick into me every time I sit down, they're only fit for a jumble sale. You should see the servants' hall where my friend Etta is cook. It's got wallpaper instead of brown paint and a carpet on the floor and proper chairs and all the servants have ever such nice bedrooms.'

'How do you know?' asked Cook sharply, She felt it denigrated her position if another cook had better conditions in which to work.

'Because my friend took me up the backstairs to show me her room. It's all done in pale green and she's even got a bedside lamp.'

'I prefer to sleep in the basement,' said Cook. 'All those stairs to climb would just about wear me out.'

But Lily, with singular lack of tact, pointed out that her friend Etta was only twenty-one, so quite capable of running upstairs. This information so incensed Mrs Trouson — who always maintained that it took years of learning before one could become an experienced cook — that she retired from the servants' hall to her bedroom.

'You've properly upset her ladyship,' said the gardener, with a grin, 'you and your friend Etta being a cook so young; really put the old girl's nose out of joint.'

'Has she got a kitchenmaid?' asked Grace.

'More than that,' whispered Lily, with a quick glance in the direction of the cook's bedroom, 'she's got *two*.'

'Cor, fancy that! I bet I'll never be a proper cook. Mrs Trouson says I'm too heavy-handed and I peel the spuds too thick and make the cabbage all watery.'

'Never mind, Grace,' consoled Daniel, 'you've got a nice name. Did they give it to you at the orphanage?'

'Oh no, Mr Oates. I was four years old when I went there with me two sisters after me Dad died. My three brothers went somewhere else.'

'That was very sad, Grace,' said the butler, 'your father could not have been very old. Did he have an illness or was it an accident?'

'It was the drink, Mr Carter. Me Mum and Dad was always having rows 'cause me Dad was always in the boozer and he spent all his wages on beer and one Saturday night he got into a fight and fell down and hit his head and got done in, me Mum said. She told us it was a "happy release".'

'Weren't you sad at leaving your home?' asked Flora.

'No, I wasn't, 'cause we got enough to eat in the orphanage and I had my two sisters. We never saw our Mum again 'cause she went off with a bloke what came from Ireland and she never came back.'

Grace, suddenly realising that this opportunity to relate her misfortunes was due to the absence of Cook, and fearing her re-appearance, hastily rose and began to clear the table.

Mr Carter also rose, remarking unnecessarily that it would not be long before he and Alice would be far away from this servants' hall and he hoped that Mr Barrett — that is, if Madam engaged him — would fit in with them all.

Mrs Stewart had engaged John Barrett, though it was doubtful whether she would have done so if she had known the real reason why he'd left his previous employment. From the time that he was twelve years old women had taken notice of John because he was so handsome. Thick brown shining hair, greenish eyes with long lashes, regular features and a slim figure, all combined to make John Barrett feel that he was certain to become a somebody in life.

Unfortunately, the brains inside that handsome head were mediocre; so there was no question of further education. He left school at fourteen. Born ten years after his two sisters — both of them now in domestic service — his parents could not understand how they had produced such a problem child.

Mr and Mrs Barrett had been butler and upper-housemaid respectively in the very same country mansion where their own parents had once worked. So when 'their lady' was in need of a hall-boy they thought it a splendid chance for their son. He certainly made the most of his chances; his handsome face and engaging manner netted him many tips from departing guests, especially so the ladies. It was just misfortune that the butler, with no claim to physical charms, should have strongly resented the unequal distribution of largesse, so John had to go.

In two years he'd had no less than four similar situations and with the money he'd saved he took elocution lessons. He had visions of becoming the romantic hero in a musical comedy.

His sisters, who loved him and were also flattered to be seen with such a presentable male, contributed a large part of their wages towards the cost of his stage training. But, eventually, it transpired that not only could he not sing, he had no talent for acting either. Being strongly averse to hard manual work, John drifted back to domestic service becoming, in turn, footman then butler.

He invariably caused trouble with the young female staff, so frequently changed his situations; either at his own request or by those above stairs. His last dismissal was occasioned by giving — and receiving — amorous glances to the young daughter of the family. This so infuriated the lady's-maid — to whom John had given more than amorous glances — that she informed Madam her butler wasn't to be trusted in the same house as a young girl.

After living on his parents for three months John Barrett, presenting highly commendable but forged references, was now engaged by Mrs Stewart.

Chapter 7

Certain it was that John Barrett would feel no amorous inclination for Mrs Stewart's prospective lady's-maid, Dorise Collett. She was five years younger than the parlourmaid had estimated, but years of caring for her ailing and querulous mother, sitting for hours in a hot and airless bedroom reading to the invalid, had sallowed her complexion, stooped her shoulders and stifled her individuality.

Dorise Collett had been a contented and healthy lady's-maid, reasonably well-liked by the other servants — though rather too much of a church-goer to have their full approval. Most servants considered that as their free time was so circumscribed, and their opportunities to sin so limited, they were in no real need of moral instruction.

But, when Dorise was thirty-five, her widowed mother took to her bed, and announced that it would not be long before she left it to be transported to her grave and from thence to be wafted to those regions 'where your dear Father has gone'.

Her married son, whose wife Ivy had not liked her mother-in-law even when she was mobile, now made it extremely plain to her husband that she had no intention of being saddled with a bedridden old woman. He must write to his sister and point out that as the only daughter, it was her duty to leave domestic service; return home and look after her mother. This he did, adding as a consolatory thought, 'it will not be for long, Mother is very frail, she says she longs to join our dear father.'

If that was true, Mrs Collett must have decided a great deal of preparation was needed before she joined in spiritual harmony with a husband whose physical demands had generally been unwelcome and borne with silent fortitude.

For ten years Dorise stayed home, her life bounded by her mother's room, the public library, the Post Office, shops and — her one comfort and solace — the church.

There were times — and these increased during the last year of her mother's life — when Dorise longed for her to die, to have silenced for ever that complaining and opinionated voice. Then, filled with remorse at such unfilial thoughts, Dorise would hurry to her church, kneel down and silently seek forgiveness.

When her mother finally 'passed over' the few remaining friends who came to the funeral whispered to Dorise that 'it was a happy release'. Uncertain whether they meant the happy release was for her, or her mother, Dorise gave a vague reply and plied them with cake and sherry.

Her sister-in-law, who had already made a mental inventory of the contents of the house — refused to join in with the muted lamentations. Over the years, paying her weekly duty visit to her mother-in-law, she'd had to listen to Mrs Collett's complaints and aggressive arguments that invariably ended with her assuming a martyred expression and muttering, 'So long as I'm wrong.'

So now Ivy whispered to her eldest daughter, 'When it's time to put a stone on grandmother's grave it should be inscribed "Right at last".'

A month later, Dorise, looking and feeling years older than when she had left domestic service, returned to it, though not without some fears. Would she remember all the duties of a lady's-maid, would she get on with the other servants?

As to the latter question, it was being discussed in the servants' hall during their supper — the last supper that Mr Carter and his Alice would eat in domestic service. They were leaving the next day.

Mrs Trouson would not be altogether sorry to see the back of Mr Carter. She had often become exasperated when forced to listen to his interminable accounts of life in Australia, and his reading aloud from a travel book which described the climate, natural scenery and the people as though it was a land of milk and honey. In Cook's opinion no country in the world could hold a candle to Britain. But when she voiced this sentiment in the servants' hall, the chauffeur said disparagingly, 'And what about all the destitute who are out of work? What sort of life have they got? Empty pockets, empty food cupboards, queuing for a paltry dole. Of course their plight doesn't affect us, immured as we are in this basement. You can't even wave a flag for our royalty now that the king has abdicated and popped off with that American woman. 'Course I know you thought his father was the salt of the earth.'

'Lord knows why,' interposed Mr Carter. 'He didn't do anything special that I know of.'

'How can you say that?' indignantly exclaimed Cook. 'What about his visits to the front line during the war? He didn't have to go.'

'So he didn't; but he got back all right, which is more than a million or so others did,' answered the butler, laconically. 'Anyway, Alice and me won't be sorry to shake the dust of Britain from our feet — though we'll miss our friends of course.'

Mrs Trouson, with that air of superiority, which had so often exasperated the butler, said, 'Well, I'm sure Mr Carter we all wish you and Alice well and I'd be the last to throw cold water on your plans, but what I do say is, that it doesn't do to be too optimistic just because you're leaving service. It stands to reason that a new country like Australia, all those thousands of miles from Britain, can't possibly be the same as living here where there are Lords, Dukes, Earls and other aristocratic and old-established families. They have nobody out there to look up to.'

Mr Carter, who was becoming more and more incensed as Cook spoke, now burst forth, irately, 'What do me and Alice care about royalty and aristocrats? What have they ever done for us? Ill-educated and poor, we are less than the dust to them nobs. "The working class" they say, with their noses in the air, "understand nothing of the finer things of life. So let us work them all the hours God made and when they're too old to work there's always the workhouse or the infirmary." I know what poverty is; it made my father a violent man, killed my mother through slaving away at the laundry every day and half-starved us children. Many's the time we've gone to school with only a cup of milkless and sugarless cocoa in our stomachs and we've walked along the gutters looking for apple-cores and orange peel. I know things are a bit better now — for those who've got a job — but we're still nothing. My brother tells me, and he should know, that out there everybody's got a chance if they're willing to work.'

An uneasy silence followed this diatribe, so unlike Mr Carter's usual mode of expression. Then he added, in a milder voice, 'Australia might be thousands of miles from Britain but that didn't stop them from coming to Europe to help us win the Great War.'

To change the subject Lily said, 'It seems strange to think that tomorrow evening, two different people will be sitting round this table. Well, I suppose the lady's-maid will have her meals down here. One place where I was the lady's-maid was French and she expected to have her meals served in her room. Mind you, she was ever such a smart girl, like the picture of those Paris Midinettes that I saw in that book of Mr Edward's.'

'Paris what?' asked Flora.

'Midinettes. I think they're sort of shop-girls.'

'If Miss Collett doesn't want to eat with us then she'll go hungry,' averred Mrs Trouson. 'It's bad enough having to send up meals to that nurse, it's certainly not going to be done for a lady's-maid.'

'In my last place,' said the under-housemaid, 'the lady's-maid and the governess had their meals in the housekeeper's room.'

'Well the question doesn't arise here,' said Mrs Trouson, tartly, 'as we have no housekeeper or governess.'

'Just as well there is no housekeeper here,' interposed the chauffeur; he was having supper preparatory to picking up Mrs Stewart from the theatre. 'Where my wife used to work the housekeeper was a real tartar. Even the butler was nervous when she was around.'

'I can assure you, Robert, that no housekeeper, be she ever so bossy, would intimidate me. As a highly-trained butler I consider myself equally as good as a housekeeper. She —'

'The same goes for me,' interrupted Cook, not to be outdone in the matter of laurels. 'An experienced cook, as I am, is always in great demand. She can get a place at any time. At a pinch one could manage without a butler, but a high-class cook is not to be come by every day.'

Mr Carter, considerably affronted to hear his position thus denigrated and, now that he was leaving, careless of disharmony in the servants' hall, was quick to reply. 'Well of course, there are high-class cooks, and just cooks. Personally, I don't think an establishment of this size would employ a really high-class cook. For one thing, they wouldn't pay the right wages.'

For a few minutes there was a tense silence. The other servants glanced surreptitiously round the table as they waited for the explosion.

Mrs Trouson, fixing the butler with a stony glare, exclaimed — her voice squeaking with rage — 'I have never been so insulted in my life. Let me tell you, Mr Carter, I have been in situations where the likes of you could never be! When I was in the service of Lady Monleigh — where I had two in the kitchen — the butler there was a *real* butler with a footman and hall-boy under him. He knew the value of his position and never hob-nobbed with the under-servants. I have cooked for the highest in the land,' and with that, Mrs Trouson rose up from the table with all the dignity allowed by her short stature. Turning to her kitchenmaid she said, 'Grace, you can bring me a cup of tea in my room.'

When she was gone, the butler said, with a satirical laugh, 'Cooked for the highest in the land, eh! I expect he was a steeplejack.'

Alice laughed loud and long at this sally, but Lily, Flora and Maud managed to restrain their mirth. They were not leaving for Australia so it was politic to keep on the right side of the cook.

Mr Carter, carried away by his success in routing the cook, now proceeded to relate a tale of the previous cook, the one before Mrs Trouson.

'Irish, she was,' he said, 'as Irish as a bit of shamrock. Her name was Mrs McGinnis and for sure she liked a drop of gin. Whenever she'd had a drop too much she'd talk about the departed Pat McGinnis. "He was a lovely man," she'd say, "and he had the face on him that would turn one to water inside for all that he worked in the fields. On our wedding night I climbed up the ladder to our room and lay in the old feather bed that me

Ma had given to us, and I blew out the candle. I could hear the hens clucking below when that Pat crept into the bed, as stark as the day he was born. 'What's this then?' he says, feeling me flannelette nightgown, 'off with it! What's this then' he says, feeling me vest, 'off with it'. I can tell you, girls, that there feather bed never had such a pummelling as it had on that night." Ah,' said Mr Carter, 'that Mrs McGinnis was as different as jam and jalap from Mrs Trouson.'

'What happened to her?' asked Maud. 'Did she leave?'

'She didn't leave of her own accord, Maud, she was summarily dismissed by Mr Stewart. One evening she got drunk on a bottle of port and started banging the pots and pans around and singing a bawdy song at the top of her voice. We could do nothing with her, neither could Madam when she came down to see what was the matter. So we had to get the Master down and when Mrs McGinnis saw him she scrambled up from the floor where she'd been sitting, threw her arms round the Master's neck and warbled, "Oh you lovely man," over and over again.'

'She never did, Mr Carter!' exclaimed Lily. 'Whatever did Mr Stewart say?'

'It wasn't so much what he said, Lily, as what he did. He rang the police, got them to take her away for the night and then, although he was dressed for dinner, he went straight upstairs and had a bath.'

'Whatever for, Mr Carter?' asked Grace, open-mouthed.

'For the simple reason, Grace, that he couldn't bear to be touched by the drunken cook. The suit had to be cleaned before he wore it again.'

'I think Mr Stewart is a man who doesn't like to be too close to anybody,' said Lily. 'I have never seen him so much as give Madam a peck, or Miss Elizabeth. Miss Eleanor is the only person he seems to care about.'

'Pity his son doesn't take after him,' said the parlourmaid. 'He knows better than to try the old "come on" with me, but he's got a leery look.'

'Ah, that reminds me,' said the butler, 'I was walking up Oxford Street this afternoon when who should I see on the other side of the road but Master Edward with a young woman. They were walking arm in arm as large as life. She looked ever so common, with a silly little hat perched on her brassy-looking hair; mincing along for all the world as though she was a lady. I wouldn't give such a one house-room. She wasn't a bit like my Alice,' Mr Carter added, with a fond glance at his intended.

I bet she wasn't, thought Lily. A person like Alice, even if she was several years younger, wouldn't be that Edward's type; she looks far too respectable. I do wish Mr Carter hadn't upset the cook. It's all right for him and Alice, they'll be gone tomorrow, but the rest of us will have the job of smoothing her down. I hope the new butler isn't one of those pompous types, like the new butler in my sister's place, Claud Gander. Claud, what a name to give a son, sounds like a nancy boy! Perhaps his parents hoped he'd have artistic tastes.

'As Madam and the Master are out I'm going round to the Mariner's Arms for half an hour,' said Mr Carter. 'I want to say good-bye to my friend, Fred Penfold. Master Edward won't be back till midnight and if Miss Elizabeth or Miss Eleanor should ring, you can tell them I've gone to the post, Maud.'

In their accustomed seats in the Mariner's Arms, Mr Carter expatiated about his two forthcoming ventures; getting married and leaving England. He spoke about the business of getting to Australia as though he was a pioneer prepared to pave the way for others to follow, and was not too pleased when the landlord, overhearing the conversation, remarked, 'But it won't be no hardship to you, Horace. You've got your brother's place to go to. You'll be all right. Ain't that so, Fred?'

The Mariner's Arms was a popular public house with the menservants who lived in the vicinity. These had always respected Mr Carter and his friend Mr Penfold and any stranger who was sitting in their seat was made to feel an alien. But Bert, the landlord, with no experience of life in 'good service' looked upon his customers as working men, like himself. Mr Carter strongly deprecated Bert's habit of referring to him and his friend, as Horace and Fred.

So now, ignoring the landlord, Mr Carter said, 'I shall miss you, Fred, we have been friends for so many years. I wish you were coming with me.'

Fred Penfold from the age of twelve had spent all his life in the homes of the élite and wealthy, and had no desire at all to leave domestic service. Now that he had risen high enough to be a butler to Lady Farron, where he had a comfortable room, good wages and liberal free time, he considered he was living in clover.

'I'm too set in my ways to change, Horace,' Fred said, ''sides, you've got your Alice. I could hardly tag along with the two of you.'

A rather similar conversation was heard later on in Lily's bedroom where the five females had congregated.

'Cheer up, Alice,' said Lily. 'You look as though you're going to be buried, instead of married.'

'I shall miss you all,' said Alice, almost snivelling. 'I wish you were all coming with me.'

'I don't think your Horace would care for that. Besides, what would we do in a country like Australia? From all accounts they don't have domestic service out there.'

'You would all find husbands, that's what,' said Alice. 'Horace's brother says there's ever so many more men than there is women.'

'I don't particularly want to get married,' said the under-housemaid. 'It's not all romance and roses like you read of in magazines. Not for people like us it isn't. In my Mum's wedding photograph she looks so pretty and smiling, but by the time she'd had eight children — I was the last — Mum had become an old woman. She lost her teeth — and had no money for false ones — her face was all lined, her feet were splayed and full of corns and her hair was grey. And Mum had become hard; I don't remember her ever cuddling or kissing us. I'm sure the reason was she always had to work and worry to give us food and some kind of clothes. My Dad was a house-painter and there was never enough work, especially in the winter, so Dad often got the sack with just an hour's notice.'

'I reckon those magazines should print a few stories like that,' commiserated Maud, 'and not always fairy-tales — 'cause that's what they are — of pretty girls and handsome young men falling in love and living happily ever after. Look at Grace here. Not much in the way of romance about her Mum and Dad. I remember —'

But Maud was interrupted by Alice saying she must get her packing finished and get to bed.

'I reckon Alice was a bit narked about us running down married life,' said Maud later. 'I suppose if you are going to be married in a few days you don't want to listen to a lot of talk against the idea. 'Sides, for all that, I'd get married if anybody decent asked me. Anything to get out of service.'

'Do you think old Horace really did see that Edward with a common-looking girl?' asked Lily. 'I'd have thought he'd have more sense than to be seen in public with such a one.'

'Well, Mr Carter did say the other day that he had to brush some yellow hairs from Master Edward's suit. But she's probably only some fly-by-night that he's having a bit of fun with. Good luck to her if she can get anything out of him,' and laughing, Maud departed to bed as did Flora and Grace.

Chapter 8

Edward's 'bit of fun' was likely to prove very expensive. For, when Mr Carter observed them in Oxford Street, the 'bit of fun', Norma Parks by name, had just informed Edward that she was pregnant.

On hearing this most unwelcome news, Edward was both furious and fearful. His strongest inclination was to ditch this yellow-haired lady-love there and then, but there were no flies on Norma.

With her superficial good looks she'd had the pick of the male shop-assistants, but Edward was the first 'gentleman' to fall for her charms and she was gratified by her conquest. Nevertheless, before she let herself be persuaded to lose her virginity, she had ascertained that Edward was an only son, that his father was strict and, even more important, just where he lived. Norma was taking no chances; she wasn't going to be left in the lurch like her friend Cissy.

In the shabby hotel room where Norma had first 'given in', she and Edward were now having an extremely acrimonious conversation. Not for Norma the tears and wailings of a rejected woman; Norma was prepared to make trouble unless something was done for her in the way of financial help.

'Surely you can take something to get rid of it?' said Edward sullenly. 'A girl like you, or your friends, must know of pills or things like that?'

'What do you mean, "a girl like me",' screeched Norma. 'I'll let you know I was a perfectly respectable girl until I met you. You seduced me and now you can pay.'

'You cannot get blood out of a stone. I have no money,' angrily protested Edward. 'All I have is an allowance from my father and I have spent that taking you around, fool that I was.'

Edward's passion for Norma had instantly died from the moment she'd told him she was expecting his baby. 'And how do I know it's mine?' he added. 'There have been many evenings when you refused to see me; probably because you were with some other idiot like me.'

'That's an absolute lie,' squealed Norma. 'And I can tell you, if I fancied another fellow, he wouldn't have been a bit like you. You ain't no love's young dream, and that's no lie. If you ain't going to marry me — '

'Too damn right I'm not,' interposed Edward.

'Then I want enough money to get rid of the brat, and that will cost a pretty penny. I'm not having no back-street abortion, like my friend Cissy. She ended up in the hospital and nearly died.'

'I tell you I have no money,' hissed Edward, 'and no means of getting any either. There's nothing I can do about it. You shouldn't have got yourself into such a situation.'

'Is that so? You've got some nerve. You're the one who was supposed to be taking precautions. Who was it whispered so softly, "Let's risk it for one night, let us be as nature made us, like Adam and Eve". Yes, you can turn red-faced now, when you have to listen to such slop. I should have known better. Adam and Eve, you said! I should have remembered what happened to them. I'm telling you: get me the money or I'll ask your father for it,' screeched Norma, all trace of the genteel shop-girl eradicated.

Inwardly groaning at the necessity of calming down this belligerent female, Edward promised that he would get the money as soon as possible.

'I'll give you a week and that's the limit,' said Norma. 'I'm not waiting until it's too late nor you ain't going to get away with doing nothing. I know where I can find a doc, but it costs money.'

Poor Edward slept badly that night. He well knew what his father would say if he heard about Norma. Though undoubtedly he would pay her off rather than have unpleasant publicity, nevertheless the resultant effect would be to make his son's life hardly worth living.

So his entry into the breakfast-room the following morning certainly bore no resemblance to a sunbeam. Fortunately for Edward, Mr Stewart had already left for the City, leaving his wife and Elizabeth much relieved by his departure.

'I don't know why Father should be so grumpy about Nurse and the baby,' complained Elizabeth. 'It's not my fault that Eric's leave is postponed for a month. Such a nuisance for us when we had taken a furnished house for six months. What's the matter with you?' — to her brother — 'You look as though the worst has happened. Are you starting work?'

But Edward was not in the mood for raillery. Giving his sister a sour look as he collected his breakfast from the sideboard, he muttered, 'This coffee is cold.'

'Well, ring for Carter to bring some fresh,' advised Elizabeth, 'if you have enough strength to press the button.'

Carter, duly appearing and receiving the order, departed with the air of one to whom a matter of hot coffee was beneath his notice.

'Thank heaven I won't have to look at that fellow's face after today,' said Edward, peevishly. 'He always looks at me as though it's only as a great favour he waits on me. Who does he think he is anyway? He won't find many gentlemen in Australia.'

'Perhaps he's had enough of gentlemen,' answered Elizabeth — who was addicted to needling her brother — and left the room before he could think of a suitable retort.

Some five minutes elapsed before Carter reappeared with the coffee and Edward said, sharply, 'What took you so long?'

'More needed to be ground, sir.'

'Why isn't enough done to start with?'

'I am sure I don't know, sir. It is Mrs Trouson's responsibility. The kitchenmaid grinds the coffee. I will inform her of your complaint,' and with that Carter prepared to leave the room.

'That's all right, Carter,' hastily interposed Mrs Stewart, 'I will speak to Cook myself.'

After Carter had gone Mrs Stewart admonished her son, saying that she could not have Cook upset, it was bad enough that two of the staff were leaving.

Now that he and his mother were alone, Edward, red-faced and almost stammering in his embarrassment, told her, in as few words as possible, of his predicament. Of necessity, he managed to insinuate that he had been led astray by an experienced and designing female who would certainly cause trouble unless money was forthcoming.

Mrs Stewart listened in silence, her face expressing in turn, consternation, disgust and then commiseration for her dear Edward.

'Oh Edward, how could you? And a common person like that too, a shop-girl. Probably the child isn't yours.'

Edward forbore to point out that it would not have happened with a girl of his own class.

'How much money does this person demand?'

'She wants two hundred pounds.'

'Two hundred pounds!' exclaimed Mrs Stewart. 'Impossible! I cannot ask your father for that amount and I have little money of my own. You father pays for everything but he wants to see all the bills before he settles them.'

At the thought of his father's cold contempt and searing remarks if he knew of his son's sordid affair, Edward shuddered.

'I could ask Eleanor to lend the money to me; she would not enquire why I needed it,' his mother said.

'Ask Eleanor? How could she lend me the money? She has only her allowance from father.'

'Eleanor has the ten thousand pounds that Aunt Sophie left her. You must remember; I wrote and told you, about two years ago.'

'Why on earth did Aunt Sophie leave the money to Eleanor and none to Elizabeth and me? I used to be one of her favourites.'

'That was when you were a small boy. After you grew up and refused to visit her — saying she was a tedious old lady — she changed her will. Eleanor went abroad with Aunt Sophie, remember, and paid frequent visits to her country house. Aunt Sophie said that she was like a daughter to her.'

'Oh yes, Eleanor would be,' said Edward with a sneer. 'She's had a lot of practice at being a daughter, and a spinster daughter she will remain; for it's certain she'll never get a husband.'

Edward's dislike of his eldest sister partly owed to jealousy because of his father's obvious preference for her; and partly because her meekness and goodness — qualities he could not, nor desired to, emulate — caused him intense irritation. As did the thought of being indebted to her for help, even though she would be unaware that the money was for him.

Mrs Stewart, with a promise that she would approach Eleanor at the earliest opportunity and — her only reproach — that he should not have let such a person know his real name and address, left the breakfast room.

Edward thought, what does Mother know about it, married to a man like Father? Of course Norma was a common little bitch but she had more life in her than any of the members of this house. Look at Father, nothing but business; Mother twittered around with her At Homes and afternoon calls; Elizabeth, indifferent to her child, interested only in flirting with the officers; Eleanor — but here he ceased to think and moodily went upstairs, giving a sour glance at the butler as he passed him in the hall.

'Six years I have been here,' said a resentful Mr Carter to his parlourmaid, 'six years and never had a complaint from Sir about my work nor time off, apart from what I was entitled to. Yet that young whippersnapper hasn't even got the manners to shake my hand and wish me well in a new country.'

'Never mind, Mr Carter,' consoled Maud, 'in a few hours you won't be beholden to any of them. You'll be a free man.'

'Thank you, Maud. I hope you get on all right with the new man — what's his name? — Barrett. You've been a good parlourmaid, a big improvement on the couple of flibbertigibbets I had to try to train before you. One stayed six months and the other a year but they just were not domestic service types.'

Maud hardly knew whether to take his opinion of her as a compliment implying as it did that she was staid and reliable. However, she was gratified to receive, 'from Alice and me', a present of six embroidered handkerchiefs. Mr Carter's leave-taking of the cook was of the briefest. Mrs Trouson's umbrage had by no means abated and, without an apology from the butler, she had no intention of overlooking his derogatory remarks of the previous evening.

Nevertheless, Horace and Alice departed to quite an ovation

from the rest of the staff. Supplemented by a few of the regulars from the Mariner's Arms, they stood on the pavement outside the basement vigorously waving as Horace and Alice rode away in a taxi. Afterwards, in the servants' hall, they naturally discussed the imminent arrival of the new butler and lady's-maid, until Cook, still considerably ruffled, sharply called Grace into the kitchen with the information that it wasn't for a kitchenmaid to talk about upper servants, and she was sure that Maud had enough to do getting the drawing-room tea on her own.

Chapter 9

'Brown,' enquired Mrs Stewart, 'has the butler arrived yet?'

Maud, red-faced from the exertion of carrying the heavy silver tea-tray from the basement to the drawing room, told Madam that Mr Barrett and Miss Collett were having tea in the servants' hall.

'Very well, Brown. I rely on you to show him where everything is kept. It is a simple dinner this evening, just the family, and we are dining early as Mr Stewart has an appointment.'

Down in the basement John Barrett was not only entertaining and charming the cook with an account of his — largely mythical — career. He was also laying on the flattery.

'Your name, Mrs Trouson, is so unusual. How do you spell it?'

The cook spelled her name and John Barrett added, 'Do you know, it seems a French name to me. Are any of your ancestors French, Mrs Trouson?'

Cook, the bristly hairs on her upper lip quivering with pleasure at thus being singled out said, 'I have an idea that my great-grandfather came from France.'

'Funny that she's never mentioned it until now,' muttered Lily to Flora.

Mrs Trouson added, 'My grandfather had an old drawing of a cottage and I remember he once told me it was where his father lived before he came to England.'

'Perhaps that accounts for you taking up cooking as a profession, Mrs Trouson. All the best cooks are French. It was probably in your blood.'

Lily thought, profession is it now? Cook had gravitated to it through the usual ways: scullerymaid, kitchenmaid and then cook. Lily did not dare catch the chauffeur's eye for fear of laughing at this high-falutin' 'profession'. But Robert Seymour, the chauffeur, who had already taken a dislike to the new butler — partly because he was so good-looking — gave a derisive snort.

'You might as well say, then, that I was related to my previous employers, their name was Seymour. Or old Daniel here to Titus Oates.'

'Or the butler where my sister is housemaid, to a male goose,' giggled Lily, 'for his name is Gander.'

Receiving a disapproving glance from the cook, Lily hastily said to the chauffeur, 'Wasn't it rather awkward you having the same name as your employers?'

'Well, it meant that they couldn't call me by my surname, the same as they did with the other servants. They had to call me Robert.'

'In my last place we were all called by our Christian names,' said John Barrett; naturally omitting to mention that it was partly because he did the same with the daughter of the house which had led to his dismissal.

'Well, I can assure you that you'll be Barrett here. You can forget all about being a person, you'll just be one of "them below stairs",' and the chauffeur gave a cynical laugh. 'My sister, who fancied herself as a singer, used to warble those comic songs of Gilbert and Sullivan. One of them, I don't know which one, went something like, "We'll all equal be, the Earl, the Marquis and the Duke, the groom, the butler and the cook." What a hope, we're about as equal as duke and dustman.'

'I consider myself just as good as them up there,' stated John Barrett. 'Just because they were born into money and position doesn't make them any better than us.'

'I agree with you, Mr Barrett,' said Cook, her features relaxing into what passed for a smile, 'and you certainly can speak in just such a way as they do.'

'Ah well, I was at school until I was sixteen,' and John Barrett, with a serious expression and in a grave voice, proceeded to relate yet another mythical story of his high-class parents sudden financial misfortune and his own subsequent withdrawal from further education.

The females below stairs were surprised to hear these revelations, but surprise was mild compared to the astonishment Mr and Mrs Barrett would have felt, could they have heard their son describe them as high-class and dealing in high-finance.

Amid the silence that followed, the lady's-maid, Miss Collett, timidly enquired what Madam was like: was she very fussy, adding, 'It is a long time since I have been in service; I do hope that I don't make a lot of mistakes. One does forget the duties.'

Cook, who was relieved to discover that the lady's-maid would not be one of the 'uppity' types, reassured her by saying, 'Don't you worry, Miss Collett —'

'Oh, do call me Dorise,' interrupted the lady's-maid.

' — You'll manage all right, and I'm sure that Lily will help you for the first day or two.'

'Dorise is an unusual name,' said Lily.

'Well, my two grandmothers' names were Dorothy and Lettice and they both wanted me to have their Christian names. So my mother compromised by calling me Dorise. I hated the name at school.'

'My friend's name is Henrietta,' said Lily. 'She hated her name too and was happy when it was changed to Etta. But now she thinks Henrietta is a posh-sounding name.'

'Ah, that reminds me of when I was a kid in our village school,' chuckled old Daniel Oates. Cook, well aware that the gardener's reminiscences often bordered on the bawdy, ordered Grace to the scullery to start on the vegetables.

'There was this pretty gal in our class and I was fair taken with her black hair, rosy face and plump little legs. Her name was Rosie Lumb. One day, in the class, it was just before I left school so I was about twelve years old, I had the cheek to write her a poem. "I loves your hair, I loves your face, the sight of you makes my 'eart race. But most of all, dear Rosie Lumb, I loves your little b . . ."' but before he could finish Cook hastily interposed, 'That's enough, Mr Oates, we can guess the rest.'

Old Daniel continued to chuckle and the chauffeur gave a hearty laugh. But Mr Barrett looked disapproving of such vulgarity.

'Are we allowed to have a friend to tea on a Sunday?' the butler enquired.

'Yes, we are,' answered the parlourmaid, 'but we're not allowed to ask a boy-friend in, but as none of us have got one, that's no hardship. Unless,' turning to Dorise with a smile, 'you have one in the offing?'

'Oh no, dear me no,' and Miss Collett blushed at the very idea. 'In fact I have no friends at all who live in London.'

The butler, looking around at the staff in the servants' hall, thought, there's not one of them that I fancy. I wonder what they are like up there? So far I have seen only Mrs Stewart. I wonder what the old man is like?

He was soon to find out that to Mr Stewart, the chief recommendation of a butler was his ability to care for his master's clothes. Noting with approval that Mr Stewart had no less than twenty suits as well as three evening suits — after all he might want to borrow one for an evening as he had done in his previous place — Mr Barrett laid out the clothes in meticulous order.

Meanwhile, Mrs Stewart was in Eleanor's bedroom with a trivial excuse about the baby, but in reality to ask for a loan of two hundred pounds. She did feel, in view of her marked indifference to her eldest daughter, a certain embarrassment but as she had assured her son, Eleanor promised to procure the two hundred pounds as soon as possible and asked no questions about the need for it.

Before they assembled for dinner Mrs Stewart managed to let her son know the money would be forthcoming. Edward felt little gratitude towards his sister; after all, what did a spinster want with ten thousand pounds? Just imagine how he could have made use of the money.

'Where is Elizabeth?' enquired Mr Stewart.

'She is not coming down to dinner, Henry. She is still in delicate health.'

'What do you mean: "delicate health"? Elizabeth was well enough during breakfast. As far as I am aware, she has not been ill, merely enlarging the family, at our expense too.'

'Really, Henry, how can you say such things? Elizabeth got up far too soon in my opinion. When I had our children I laid in bed for three weeks afterwards.'

'I believe the women in India get up within a matter of hours after having a baby,' diffidently remarked Eleanor.

Her mother was just beginning, out of habit, to refute this

statement when she recalled the two hundred pounds. Edward however answered, in a cynical voice, 'Oh! Indians, they are not white people, they are not like us.'

'Indeed,' said his father, 'and that makes them less sensitive I suppose? They are certainly different to you in that most of them work if they can.'

Edward relapsed into a sullen silence and fearful thoughts of his father's wrath if he discovered the mess his son had got into.

Eleanor asked to be excused from dessert as she had a meeting to attend.

'A meeting?' exclaimed her mother sharply. 'Now? What kind of meeting? You cannot go out on your own at this time of night. Your father needs Seymour. Why is the meeting so late?'

Endeavouring to answer all these queries Eleanor said quietly, but surprisingly firmly, 'It is only eight-thirty, Mother, and I can order a cab there and back. The meeting is late because the working-class men and women have to work long hours and cannot get there earlier.'

'Eleanor,' cried Mrs Stewart, 'the speaker is not that awful Penelope Courtland? All she can talk about is socialism and women's rights and how we all ought to vote. For heaven's sake keep away from such a person.'

'Edith,' interjected Mr Stewart, with a heavy frown, 'Arnold Courtland is one of my friends and I am sure would not let his wife behave in any way that was objectionable. Besides, Eleanor is nearly thirty' — poor Eleanor winced at this — 'and quite capable of taking care of herself. In any case I do not require the car until nine o'clock; Seymour can take Eleanor first.'

Thanking her father and giving her mother and brother a hasty goodnight, Eleanor departed, to be followed soon after by Mr Stewart.

Drinking coffee in the drawing-room, free from the need to suppress their ill-nature, Mrs Stewart complained, 'Your father was annoyed because of my remarks about Mrs Courtland. He may consider Arnold Courtland to be his friend but your father doesn't really know his wife. In my opinion, no objections by her husband would have any effect on Penelope

Courtland. She has an *idée fixe* about "a woman's place", that is her favourite expression. She seems to think that women are oppressed, but I have never felt oppressed. I run this house' —or the staff do, thought Edward—'and I consider that a full-time occupation. Mrs Courtland has these meetings and tells the women, and the men too, that they are over-worked, under-paid and that together they can better conditions. Don't you think it absurd?'

Edward, to whom the working class hardly existed, so consequently was bored by this monologue, merely nodded.

His mother needed no encouragement to continue: 'I am sure it is asking for trouble to rouse up that class of people and give them ideas above their station. In the long run it will do them harm. They will lose their respect and loyalty for their employers. My parents were so kind to the poor villagers. In the winter they helped them with coal and blankets and the poor were always so grateful. I am astonished at Eleanor getting mixed-up in that sort of thing. She has never even mentioned Mrs Courtland's name to me!' and Mrs Stewart ended on an exasperated note.

'Well, Mother, as Eleanor has no hope of ever finding a husband, she probably envisages herself bringing comfort to other plain and boring spinsters; sisters in misfortune, alternately bewailing their lot and denigrating the male sex. There's not one of them wouldn't get married like a shot if she had the chance.'

Then, thinking he had done his duty long enough, Edward departed leaving his mother either to continue the conversation with Elizabeth or remain alone in the drawing-room. Elizabeth, while always interested in discussing men, had no interest at all in social problems so, ringing the bell for the parlourmaid to remove the coffee tray, Mrs Stewart settled down to write letters, while below stairs they ate their supper and discussed them above.

Chapter 10

'Mrs Trouson,' said the butler, 'that was a splendid shepherd's pie. Some cooks make them too dry. In my last place the staff called it a resurrection pie because it seemed to be composed of meat that should have been interred long ago.'

'That wouldn't happen in my kitchen, Mr Barrett,' answered Cook, gratified at this praise of her cooking. 'Only the best beef or lamb is minced and never the two together. Madam may not pay the highest wages, but I must say she is not mean over the food.'

'Madam remarked during dinner that the Ragout of Chicken was delicious and Mr Stewart had two helpings.'

'Yes, he always does,' said Cook, with a complacent smile. 'It's a very old recipe, given to me many years ago by a Scots cook when I was a kitchenmaid. She took a fancy to me.'

Old recipe my eye, thought the head-housemaid. Old Mother Trouson got it out of Mrs Beeton and just changed one of the ingredients. Took a fancy to you, did she? Well, it's a sure thing that this butler isn't going to, for all his honeyed tongue.

'How did you get on with Madam, Dorise?' asked the cook.

'All right, thank you, Mrs Trouson. I found that, in spite of being at home for the last ten years, it all came back to me. I had no difficulty in doing Madam's hair. Miss Eleanor said she didn't need my services, she always does her own hair.'

'Ah! Miss Eleanor wouldn't trouble anybody,' said the cook. 'She's always that kind and thoughtful.'

'They don't seem a very compatible family,' said the butler; then, sensing that Cook did not grasp 'compatible', he added, 'They didn't talk much to one another. Most of the conversation was between Mrs Stewart and the son.'

'It would be, 'cause she dotes on him,' said the chauffeur, who was waiting to collect Mr Stewart. 'For my part, I can't stand him. When he's allowed to have the car — which isn't very often, otherwise I wouldn't be working here — it's: Seymour drive here, Seymour drive there, as though I was a ruddy bus-driver. *And* he wants to take the wheel, but I tell him my orders are that only I am to drive. I can see he gets that ruddy mad, but he isn't the boss.'

Cook, annoyed at the chauffeur's strong language, but deeming it politic to let it pass for fear of hearing worse, said, 'At least, Mr Seymour, you do get away from the house, you have your own flat. And you get the whole day free every Sunday, which is more than we do.'

'I have driven a Rolls-Royce,' said John Barrett. 'What a splendid car that was; everybody envied it.'

'Have you really, Mr Barrett?' chorused Grace and Flora, showing their admiration for a butler who had actually driven a Rolls-Royce.

The chauffeur, who had already summed the butler up as a 'big-mouth', and was sceptical about his claim to be a driver, now enquired where, and when, had he driven this car, for there weren't all that many of them around.

But John Barrett was too old a hand at weaving fantasies to be caught out. With great aplomb and laughing, he said, 'Oh! I don't mean that I was a chauffeur — though I was taught to drive by one. No, it happened at Goodwood. My gentleman with two friends was going to the races and I went also — to serve them the picnic lunch. All went well until just before we were ready to leave. Then Williams, who was standing on a box to get a better view, slipped, fell on his arm and sprained his wrist so badly that he was unable to drive. You can imagine my gentleman's surprise when I volunteered.'

'That I can,' was Mr Seymour's enigmatic reply, which the butler wisely ignored.

'When he knew that I could drive the car, he took me abroad with him touring on the Continent — he had titled friends living there. The chauffeur was furious and gave in his notice. He was stupid because it was a good situation and there were two other cars in the family. My employer treated me as an equal; which I consider I am.'

'How could you be equal,' said the chauffeur, sarcastically. 'Weren't you just a chauffeur, valet and general handyman?

Did you have the same accommodation, eat at the same restaurants, meet his titled friends? I bet you did not. Just because you can speak more like them up there doesn't make you one of them. You might like to think you're equal, but they certainly don't. To them you, and all of us, are just "the servants". Of course there are good and bad employers, but even the good see nothing wrong in us working all the hours there are while they have unlimited leisure,' and without bothering to say goodnight Mr Seymour left to collect his employer.

In no way disconcerted by this oration — in fact, completely ignoring it — Mr Barrett said to Cook: 'Have you been here many years, Mrs Trouson?'

'Five years, coming up for six, Mr Barrett. They aren't a bad family to work for. Madam doesn't interfere with me once we have settled the meals. Master Edward came down once and started talking to my kitchenmaid — the one I had before Grace — and a flighty piece she was too — but I soon sent him packing. I know his kind only too well.'

Inwardly consumed with mirth at the very idea of Mrs Trouson ever having the opportunity to 'know his kind', Mr Barrett replied, looking suitably serious, 'You are so right, Mrs Trouson, one cannot be too careful where young girls are concerned.'

'Of course Miss Eleanor is different from the others,' said the cook. 'She will come into my kitchen — but never without asking — and sit down just as though she was in her own room. And she'll talk just as though it was you and me talking. Once she told me about her "coming out", and how she disliked the whole business of balls and parties, and how when it was Miss Elizabeth's turn she loved all of it.'

'Well, I expect it was different for Miss Elizabeth,' said the head-housemaid. 'She is not bad-looking and no doubt had a choice of partners at the dances. And she managed to get married which is more than Miss Eleanor did. Course, she's got a kind nature but that don't make no odds to young men. A kind nature isn't exciting and it doesn't lead to a walk up the aisle like a pretty face does.'

Cook gave a sniff of disapproval. 'A pretty face doesn't

last for ever and if you ask me—' which I don't, thought Lily '—I think Miss Eleanor would make somebody a good wife.'

'Ah, Mrs Trouson,' said the butler, sententiously, 'probably you are right, you know Miss Eleanor's character. Nevertheless, at her age, to be plain and penniless means that she is unlikely to ever become a wife.'

'But Miss Eleanor is not penniless,' interposed the parlourmaid, 'she has ten thousand pounds.'

'Ten thousand pounds,' echoed Mr Barrett, astounded to hear this. 'Are you sure? How do you know?'

'Because me and Mr Carter heard them talking about it one evening during dinner. I think an aunt or somebody like that left her the money. Mr Stewart was ever so pleased but we could tell that Madam was that cross because Miss Eleanor had the money. But she's never nice to her.'

'Why does she stay with the family, then?' queried the butler. 'With that money she could afford to rent a place of her own.'

'Whatever do you mean, Mr Barrett?' exclaimed the cook. 'Leave her family, live on her own, a young girl like that; she could never do such a thing! Why, she would be unprotected and people would talk.'

'Twenty-nine's not all that young,' said Lily, 'but of course Miss Eleanor would be too timid to do something so daring and Madam would certainly put the kibosh on any such idea. For all that she's so sharp with her, she'd never do without Miss Eleanor to run her errands and help with her At Homes. Madam could never get Miss Elizabeth to do half of what her sister does.'

'You are right, Lily,' said Cook, 'and what I want to know is, when will that stuck-up nurse be leaving? She comes into my kitchen, rustling and scratching in all that starched get-up and in that plummy voice of hers says, "Is Miss Elizabeth's breakfast tray ready?" as though this was a boarding-house or something. Anyway, it's getting late, I'm going to my room. Goodnight Mr Barrett, goodnight everybody.'

Later, upstairs in the attics, the five females congregated in Maud's bedroom.

'Isn't he just so handsome,' breathed Flora, 'and doesn't he talk posh. Just the same as them upstairs. Clark Gable's got nothing on him.'

'Except money,' said Lily dryly, who knew that the 'he' referred to John Barrett.

'I wonder if all those things that he told us really happened,' said Miss Collett. 'He does seem to have had a lot of adventures. It is strange that he is still only a butler.'

'Only a butler!' echoed Maud. 'Don't you let Mr Barrett hear you thus lowering his position. Some butlers think they are the cock-of-the-walk below stairs.'

'He wouldn't have much chance of thinking that with Cook around,' said Lily. 'She might have taken a fancy to him but that wouldn't extend to letting him come the old acid over her. She's boss in her kitchen; isn't that so, Grace?'

'Oh! Mrs Trouson is not so bad,' said the kitchenmaid. 'When it's my time off she often gives me money to go to the pictures. There was a girl at the orphanage who went out to be a kitchenmaid and she came back because the cook was a horrible woman and threw things at her.'

'I nearly married a butler,' interposed Miss Collett. 'In fact I was already stocking my bottom-drawer. He wasn't good-looking like Mr Barrett, but I fell in love with him from the first time I saw him.'

'Why didn't you marry?' asked Lily, 'Did you change your mind?'

'No, he did,' but Dorise smiled as she spoke, adding, 'My mother and I went for a holiday to Bournemouth and Ronald, my fiancé, came for a week. We stayed with my mother's sister, but Aunt Vera wasn't a bit like Mother. She had five daughters and they were always having friends in and dancing to the gramophone. Rita, the eldest, was such a pretty girl, full of life, all the boys competed to dance with her. My mother said Rita was fast and would come to a bad end, but Mother was wrong. For my Ronald fell in love with her and she with him; they got married and now they have three children and run a small hotel. Mother was fond of saying, "The wages of sin are death", every time Ron and Rita's names were mentioned, but of course they hadn't sinned; only fallen in love.'

'You must have been very upset and miserable,' commiserated Maud. 'You could have sued him for breach of promise.'

'Oh! I'd never have done that, Maud. What would have been the use? Ronald would have hated me and so would've my cousin. He wouldn't have come back to me. After about a year I got over it, but I have never fancied another man in that way.'

'My Mum always said never trust men until you've got the wedding ring on your finger,' said Flora.

'It's not always the men who are to blame,' said Lily, laughing, 'and not even a wedding ring will keep some husbands or wives on the "straight and narrow". When I was a kid there was a woman next door to us who left her husband and a pack of kids and went off with the tallyman. Never turned a hair, she didn't. Mind you, he lost his job, 'cause he didn't dare show his face round our way afterwards, so he couldn't collect the weekly dues, and the women spent the money and got behind with their payments. My Mum said to Dad, "Fancy Sal going off with that tallyman at her age," and my Dad said, "More bloody fool 'er. She'll find that one bit of bloody stick ain't no different from another." My Mum was fit to burst with laughing. Now I look back on it I don't blame Sal going off. Her old man had a foul temper, was as squat as a toad and a face on him like a steamroller had gone over it. And all those kids he gave her; I suppose Sal thought even the tallyman would be an improvement on her old man.'

Amid the general laughter, Flora said, 'I reckon men are all the same, they're all after one thing. Last week on my time off I went to the pictures with a chap I'd met at the Palais. His name was Ken and, honestly, he seemed ever so nice and quiet. Yet all the time in the pictures I had to hold his hand to protect myself against its wanderings, and it was such a lovely film; that sheik one with Clark Gable. What some fellows expect for a quarter of toffees and a one-and-sixpenny seat is enough to make you give them up. I wouldn't go out with that Ken again —not that he asked me to,' and Flora giggled, in no way abashed at this lack of romance.

'While Ronald still cared for me,' said Dorise, with a reminiscent sigh, 'he used to say such romantic things. He couldn't say I was pretty, for I was never that, but he said my hair was soft and silky, my skin so smooth and that my high-cheek bones made me look patrician. Ronald was fond of that word, "patrician", he was always bringing it into the conversation. And yet he fell for Rita. She was pretty but there was certainly nothing patrician about her.'

'Obviously, Dorise, your Ron was like a lot of men; easily seduced by a pretty face,' said Lily dryly, adding briskly, 'Come along we must get to bed.'

Just before Grace dropped off to sleep, Flora whispered, 'Isn't that Mr Barrett handsome, Grace? I could just fancy him, couldn't you? I wonder what he's thinking now; I wonder if he's thinking about us. It seems strange him being only a butler; why, he's handsome enough to be a film star like that Ramon Novarro. Don't you think so, Grace?' But Grace was already asleep.

Chapter 11

Mr Barrett was certainly thinking, but his thoughts were not centred on the staff; far from it. The butler was thinking of Miss Eleanor and her ten thousand pounds.

John Barrett's good looks and charm had given him considerable success with women, and not always women of his own class. There had been a certain Contessa who would have taken him back to her native Italy; fortunately he'd discovered before it was too late that she had no money other than the amount the Count provided. Then there was old Mrs Hemslow, who'd taken a fancy to him. What a sweet old lady she was, and so generous. Assuredly he would not have accelerated her departure from this life as her relatives had almost insinuated before they removed her to a nursing home. If only he had money; a man like him should have money. How he hated being a nobody, having to obey orders, answering bells, hearing, 'Barrett do this; Barrett do that'. Waiting on 'them' at table, people who were no better than him apart from their wealth. John Barrett never admitted it was his lack of application and talent that kept him below stairs; no, life itself was against him, had cheated him. Ten thousand pounds she had, eh! Properly invested it was a nice little sum. Of course, Miss Eleanor was no beauty, but she had a kind face and had smiled at him — which was more than any of the others had done. He would start his campaign at breakfast tomorrow morning ... and Mr Barrett drifted off to sleep.

He was unaware that breakfast in this household was far from a propitious time to start anything, the atmosphere being generally charged by Mr Stewart's aversion to conversation and Edward's ill temper. This morning a slight change was caused by Elizabeth announcing that the nurse wanted to leave next week, and whatever would she do? She couldn't possibly manage Baby on her own.

'Well, I expect there are others of the species,' said Edward sourly. 'Nobody's indispensable.'

‘I have an idea,’ said Mrs Stewart. ‘Why not ask Eric’s old Nanny to come for a few weeks? I know she’d love to look after Baby. Furthermore, Nanny gets on well with Cook so that would be no problem.’

‘When can I expect to have the pleasure of my son-in-law’s company, Elizabeth?’ asked Mr Stewart, sardonically. ‘I suppose it will be before my grandchild starts to crawl around?’

‘Oh, Father, I did tell you. Eric will be here in another two or three weeks.’ Turning to her sister Elizabeth said, ‘I hear that you have taken up the cause of the meek and oppressed, and actually went to a meeting of them. Personally, I cannot say that I have found the working class particularly meek; they seem well able to air their grievances, real or imagined.’

The butler, who had just entered the breakfast-room bearing hot coffee, undoubtedly heard the tail-end of Elizabeth’s speech. He glanced at Eleanor, who gave him a faint smile; the butler construed it as a sympathetic one.

‘Was Mrs Courtland there?’ enquired Mrs Stewart.

‘Yes, Mother, the meeting was arranged by her; she is on the committee of the F.D.W. organisation.’

Mrs Stewart was just going to make a scathing remark about Penelope Courtland when she recollected her husband’s stricture of the previous evening. Really, Henry was absurd; head buried in the newspaper, never contributing to the conversation except to find fault.

However, Edward, in his customary rancorous voice, said, ‘F.D.W., what’s that supposed to mean? Or is it some kind of secret society? Let me guess. Perhaps it stands for, Follow down wind. I’d certainly not want to be down wind from some of the great unwashed,’ and he gave a derisive laugh.

Eleanor answered quietly, ‘F.D.W. stands for a “Fair Deal for Workers” and you, Edward, would probably be one of the “great unwashed” if you lived in a tenement slum with no hot water or bathroom, no indoor sanitation, and no money to improve conditions.’

Mr Stewart lowered his newspaper — yes, thought his wife, resentfully, Henry can always speak if it’s for Eleanor — gazed at his son with an enquiring look, then, turning to his daughter, said, with elaborate irony, 'My dear, you should take advice from your brother. After all, who should know more about workers than he does? Never having done any work himself he is able to study them objectively, as it were; he need not become involved in the sordid business of earning a living. Am I not right, Edward?'

His son's face turned red with anger but he remained silent, knowing full well that to speak would only result in another dose of his father's caustic tongue. Poor Eleanor thought: oh dear, I do wish father would not antagonise Edward, it makes him so ill-tempered and annoys Mother. He means well, I know, and he's so kind, always trying to help me. Some fathers would object to a daughter becoming involved with the working class and unemployed.

In fact, Mr Stewart did not feel any great pleasure in knowing that his favourite daughter was taking up a 'cause'. A son of a wealthy family, he had never been poor or had to do manual work, and as head of a thriving concern he considered that he paid his employees an adequate wage with reasonable working conditions. Beyond that he had no desire to know anything about them. Showing concern for workers invariably led to demands for a rise in wages. He hoped that this 'concern' was just a passing phase with Eleanor. Pity she's never married; never would now, he supposed. What a fool his son was, lounging about the house all day and gadding around every evening. Well, he'd continue his allowance until the end of the year; after that if Edward had not found what he considered a congenial post, then he'd have to start in the business whether he liked it or not.

Mr Stewart, with a curt farewell, departed to the City, leaving a hostile son and a peevish wife at the breakfast table.

Elizabeth, impervious to her brother's lowering expression and her mother's openly-expressed annoyance, gaily announced that she was going to write to dear old Nanny Smith straight away; she was sure that her mother-in-law would not mind her coming to care for dear Baby.

'Since when has she become "dear old Nanny Smith"?' said Edward, sourly. 'You hardly remembered her existence until she's found to be of use to you.'

Elizabeth ignoring this remark and leaving the room, Edward turned his attention to Eleanor, and with a false show of pleasantry he enquired, 'And what is the great social reformer going to do today? Will she be shoulder to shoulder with the workers, marching in the vanguard waving a flag that proclaims, "Up the workers, down with bloated capitalists"?'

To his surprise, and to Mrs Stewart's also, Eleanor, instead of her usual timidity — even tears — answered firmly, 'It is not your business, Edward, to know what I am going to do. Sufficient to say that at least I am concerned with those less fortunate than us, which is more than can be said for you. I shall be at Layton Hall next Wednesday evening and you are welcome to come along; who knows, you might learn something?' As Eleanor left the room, Edward and his mother gazed at each other in astonishment. Was this their docile Eleanor who heretofore had never put forward her own opinion, who had always been self-effacing?

'Well, well,' exclaimed Mrs Stewart, 'this is all the result of becoming involved with that Penelope and her mania for women's rights and the condition of the lower classes.'

'You should forbid her doing such things, Mother.'

'Forbid her, how could I? Your father doesn't object and Eleanor is not such a young girl, she is nearly thirty. It is so vexing; whatever would Lady Farron say if she heard about Eleanor mixing with such people? If she must be a do-gooder, I am sure there are plenty of our own class in need of assistance. Anyway, and of more importance, Eleanor will give me the two hundred pounds this morning for you to pay off that dreadful person. I hope that will be the last of it.'

'Of course it will, Mother. I have finished with her after this and any more like her. I have learnt my lesson.'

'But has she finished with you? I don't trust that type of person. They are not like us, they have few, if any, morals.'

Mrs Stewart uttered this palpably false statement with all the effrontery of established rank and position — regardless of that fact that her son was equally to blame — if not more so. She added, tempering her admonition with a smile, 'I hope you really mean, my dear that you have finished "playing around". Find a nice girl of your own class; somebody like that sweet niece of Lady Farron's. Beatrice is such a pleasant girl, so good-tempered.'

Yes, and that is her only asset, thought Edward. She is about as exciting as a slice of suet pudding; in fact not unlike one with her pudding cheeks and currant eyes. Such a malicious thought affording him amusement he laughed aloud, then, in answer to his mother's enquiring look, said, 'You might as well propose Lady Farron's brother for Eleanor. He has —' but what he had was interrupted by the butler coming into the room to know if he could clear the table.

As they went up to the drawing-room Edward remarked to his mother that Barrett must be causing some flutterings below stairs.

'Whatever do you mean, Edward?'

'Oh, Mother! You must have noticed that he's devilish good-looking. Apart from Seymour — and he's married — Barrett is the only male below stairs, and five females are cooped up with him. Well, I suppose one must exclude Cook, she hardly rates as one of the female sex. Her virtue would be safe even if there were half a dozen Barretts below stairs.'

'Edward, I'm sure you are exaggerating,' said his mother, half-vexed to think that domestic harmony might be disturbed. 'I haven't noticed that he is any different from Carter. Anyway, I'll discreetly say a word to Cook; she will keep an eye on the young girls.'

Mrs Trouson, when she heard the 'discreet word' was firmly of the opinion that Mr Barrett was too much of a gentleman to lead young girls astray and that he would be looked up to and respected by the maids.

Mrs Stewart, while not altogether approving of the appellation 'gentleman' applied to a servant, nevertheless was reassured. In fact she need not have worried, for her butler's amorous inclinations were not stirred by his fellow servants. Facing Mrs Trouson at their midday dinner — and that's enough to cause one indigestion, thought Mr Barrett — he expatiated on the merits of the — purely imaginary — family where his capabilities as a butler had been much appreciated.

'They were such a happy family, Mrs Trouson. It was easy to see that Madam adored her husband and children. I may be wrong but that does not seem so here. At dinner last night and breakfast this morning there was no light-hearted conversation such as I heard while I waited at table at "The Moorings". And for Sunday lunch we servants were allowed a bottle of wine. What do you think of that?'

Cook slightly annoyed at hearing this implied criticism of the Stewart family answered, rather severely, that she did not approve of strong drink in any form. It was an artificial stimulant and invariably led to drunkenness and a general lowering of morals.

'When I was a young girl I was never allowed to be alone with a man. But now I see young couples sitting in the backs of cars, kissing and cuddling and standing in dark alleyways hugging each other, not caring who sees them. If you ask me, it's all on account of young girls drinking in pubs. Shameless, I call it.'

The butler's sardonic thought was that it would have needed a very dark alley before a man would have felt a desire to embrace the cook. Aloud he said, 'A bottle of wine is hardly strong drink, Mrs Trouson. Besides, only the upper servants were allowed to drink and as there were five of us it wasn't exactly an orgy. Not in the least resembling a Roman Saturnalia,' he added, laughing.

Cook, whose education had not included a study of ancient Rome, gave an audible sniff, while the under-housemaid, gazing besottedly at Mr Barrett, said, 'In the church my mother goes to there was a vicar whose wife left him because she said she couldn't put up with living in the huge, shabby and cold vicarage, and they couldn't afford servants. After she'd gone the vicar kept on drinking the sacrificial wine, and one morning at Communion he fell right over, my mother said, and had to leave the church. All because his wife went off,' Flora finished, with an apprehensive look at the cook.

'He could not have been a true believer or his faith would have sustained him,' remarked Mrs Trouson. 'We all have a cross to bear. I'm sure I have had many troubles in my life but I have always looked to the One Above for comfort.'

The chauffeur gave a sardonic laugh, saying, 'I expect the vicar found that comfort from the bottle was more readily available than comfort from above. Besides, if you are going to get drunk it must surely be an advantage to drink sacramental wine; not only had it been blessed, it cost the vicar nothing.'

The cook, frowning at such levity, was just about to change the subject when the gardener said, 'Ah! I can't see why a man takes to drink 'cause his old woman has skedaddled. When my Annie went I was fit to dance a jig,' and old Daniel grinned.

'Mr Oates!' chorused Lily and Maud. 'You never told us you had been married; you never even mentioned the name, Annie.'

'Well, gals, you never asked me. Yes, eighteen years I was wed to that non-stop talking and nagging female. Before we was wed, butter wouldn't have melted in her mouth, she was that sweet-talking and coy-like. She was pretty, I grant you that; the young men envied me, thought I'd got a prize—I thought so too in the beginning. But Annie wanted more money for clothes, she wanted me to take her dancing and in the pub. She nagged me to get a better job, work in a factory. I was fair fed up, I can tell you.'

'But what happened, Mr Oates?'

'What happened, gals? Well, I'll tell you,'—Mrs Trouson visibly shuddered in dread of hearing something 'not nice'—'Down at our local the landlord had a son; great hefty chap he was with a hairy chest on him like a bearskin rug'—giggles from Grace and Flora—'and, of course unbeknown to me, my Annie took a shine to him, and 'e to her. To cut a long story short they went off together one morning when I was out at work. My Annie left me a note saying that she was fed up with a bloke that was always grubbing in the ground for roots. By the look of him I bet she got a dang great root with that Fred Parkes and I was that glad to be shot of her,' said Daniel with a chuckle.

This story occasioned loud laughter from the chaffeur and smiles from all except the cook and lady's-maid; they silently disapproved of such vulgarity. John Barrett, sensing Cook's displeasure, rapidly changed the subject to talk of Miss Eleanor; knowing that Cook would not be averse to discussing her merits.

'Maud and I could not help overhearing that Miss Eleanor is

interesting herself in the plight of the workers and the unemployed. There are very few people of the upper class who have any consideration for the working class. Don't you agree, Mrs Trouson?'

'Indeed I do, Mr Barrett, but Miss Eleanor is an exception; she is such a kind person. Though I'm not sure if it's right for her to mix with that kind of people. Some are all right of course, but she might find a lot of riff-raff ready to make trouble for an unprotected lady.'

'Miss Eleanor is speaking at a big public meeting next Wednesday,' said Lily. 'She has a note pinned on her dressing-table to say she must be there by eight o'clock.'

Has she though? thought the butler. That's my evening off; I'll make sure of being there. Of course it won't be so pleasurable as dancing, but one has to suffer in a good cause — the good cause being my financial future and putting one over on them up there. Aloud he said, 'Where does Miss Eleanor go for this assembly, Lily?'

'A place called Layton Hall, but I'm not sure where it is; Bermondsey, I think.'

'Madam told me this morning that when the Nurse goes, Mr Markham's old Nanny will probably be coming, for a week or two,' interposed the cook. 'She must be nearly seventy; but she's a nice old lady, no airs and graces; we get on well. Some old people get cantankerous, but Nanny Smith is always good-tempered.'

'I once worked for a sweet old lady,' said the butler, with a reminiscent smile. 'She was very frail and continually rang the drawing-room bell because she wanted something or other. I waited on her practically hand-and-foot. When she was young she must have been very pretty.'

'I bet she wasn't any prettier than my friend Etta is,' said Lily, 'She is a —' Lily was about to say high-class cook but, mindful of Mrs Trouson, substituted, 'a cook now, but when she was a kitchenmaid, she was painted, wearing her uniform, by a real artist. One day her picture might be in the Royal Academy.'

'Is that so, Lily? Why don't you bring her to tea one Sunday so that we can form our own opinion. Eh, Mrs Trouson?'

Cook, with a wintry smile at Lily, agreed that a Sunday visit would be in order, knowing full well that as she had every Sunday afternoon and evening free — a privilege granted only to Cook — she need not be there to welcome this paragon of beauty and culinary skill.

Chapter 12

'Etta, I do wish you'd come to tea next Sunday, just for once. Mr Barrett is always asking me when will he have the pleasure of your company. Oh, he's so handsome Etta, like a film star, and he has such good manners. He's been with us three months now and Maud says it is much nicer being his parlourmaid than it was with Mr Carter. I don't like to keep on telling him all your Sundays are engaged.'

'All right, Lily, I'll call next Sunday to meet this celluloid hero. But, as you know, I have always said it's a waste of one's free time to go from one basement to another, just to meet a different collection of servants. I'd far sooner walk in Hyde Park or go to the cinema. As a matter of fact, I'd half-promised Angus that I'd go to a tea-dance with him, as it's not your free Sunday.'

'Etta, you're not still meeting that chauffeur? He's not good enough for you. What about that lovely fellow in the Palais a couple of weeks ago? He was real taken with you and I'm sure he's got money going by the way he was splashing it around. I thought you were going to meet him again.'

'Well, I changed my mind, Lil. Those fellows that we dance with at the Palais are not the type that would care about us as domestic servants. We have a bit of glamour dressed up for dancing, but if they saw us in our uniforms they'd get a shock; they'd think: oh, a skivvy.'

'That's not true about you, Etta. You look so nice, whatever you wear. Anyway, you'll come next Sunday? But,' added Lily, gloomily, 'don't expect to see a servants' hall like yours at Lady Moreham's. Ours is the usual type, brown paint, lino and rejects from above stairs. I didn't tell you, Etta,' continued Lily, brightening, 'our chauffeur's got his brother staying with him and he's ever such a nice chap. He's come down from the North because there's no work there — and the father and another son are out of work too and all living on the dole. It must be awful up there.'

'Not only there, Lil. My Dad had a long spell out of work and it was miserable at home. Luckily I was able to help with money. Which reminds me, it's my sister Vera's birthday next week; let's go up Oxford Street, look for a present and make eyes at the shop assistants — male, of course — and tonight we'll go to Lyons Corner House.'

The two friends went off arm in arm, giggling, one at least receiving not a few admiring glances. Lily, returning at ten o'clock, was at last able to inform the butler that her friend would be coming to tea the next Sunday.

During the last two months John Barrett felt that he had made some advance in his design of attracting the attention of Miss Eleanor. He had sat among the audience at Layton Hall, listening to and memorising some of the points made by the speakers — including Miss Eleanor. On the second occasion, arriving early, he had sat in the front row and struck up a friendly conversation with his neighbour, for the reason that when Miss Eleanor came on to the platform, she would see him there, ostensibly with a friend. During question time, armed with knowledge from the previous meeting, he'd stood up with a query about scandalous slum-housing conditions and received quite an ovation from the audience — many of whom were living in just such slums. Afterwards, he'd left the hall with the man who'd been sitting next to him; an heroic deed on John Barrett's part, for the man smelt as though he and a brewery were life-long partners.

The following morning, alone in the breakfast-room before Mr Stewart appeared, Miss Eleanor had expressed her great surprise at seeing him in Layton Hall among the working class and the unemployed. Obviously she felt it was not his milieu. But he'd been ready with his tale about befriending this poor man, Mr Hodge, who'd taken to drink because he couldn't get work. Clever as he undoubtedly was at spinning false tales, John Barrett forgot the anomaly of a man who had no money taking to drink — it was most unlikely that Mr Hodge had found a benevolent pub landlord. Miss Eleanor, whose recently acquired knowledge of the working class did not extend to their drinking habits, had praised him for giving up his free time to the service of others, and how clearly he'd put his point at the meeting.

John Barrett had subtly altered his voice for, without entirely losing his deferential air — he did not want to alarm Miss Eleanor — he'd spoken as though he belonged to a higher level than 'below-stairs'. Afterwards, he wondered what impression he'd made on her, did she really see him — apart from seeing him as a butler.

He would have been gratified to know that Eleanor's first thoughts were not of how kind it was of him to give up his free time, but of how good-looking he was, and how well-modulated his voice. Alone in her bedroom, she unexpectedly found herself blushing at the thought of how pleasant it would have been if a man of her own class had respectfully admired her — as she sensed that John Barrett did. Women friends she had who appreciated her kindness, good nature, even her paintings but, apart from her father, no man had shown any inclination to further an acquaintanceship. In sheer self-defence against pity, Eleanor had cultivated an air of indifference to the male sex, but privately she envied her sister's married life, especially now there was a child. And she thought what a sweet old person was Nanny Smith and how pleasant it was to be able to enter the nursery without that stern and starchy nurse showing disapproval if one so much as breathed on Baby.

Nanny Smith had quickly made herself popular in the servants' hall by bearing out Cook's observation that she 'did not put on airs and graces'. In fact, so well had Nanny Smith fulfilled Cook's expectations, she was even invited into the innermost sanctum, Mrs Trouson's bedroom.

Nanny Smith, now that her services as a Nanny were seldom required, with consequent loss of status, had taken up fortune-telling by cards — asserting that she had the 'gift'. Nanny made no attempt to elucidate why this mysterious 'gift' had taken so many years to develop; sufficient it was to know she had the power to divine the future. All the staff were eager to have their fortune told; even the chauffeur, who had been openly sceptical at first, succumbed to Nanny Smith's long and intricate method of laying out the cards. Of necessity, once one's long-term future had been prognosticated it could not be recast, but for possible imminent events Nanny told the tea-leaves; with emphasis on the fact that this was just a light-hearted occupation, not to be compared with her 'gift'.

Nanny's power of prediction was further demonstrated on the Sunday that Lily's friend Etta came to tea. Appealed to by the butler — who obviously admired Etta's good looks — Nanny read the cards and not only prophesied that Etta would go far in her profession before she married, but that she would in the near future receive a letter from overseas — and it would be from a handsome man.

Before Etta could restrain her, Lily had exclaimed, 'Oh Etta, that will be Lance writing to you,' and then told the staff that Lance, who now lived in Florence, was the artist who had painted Etta.

During supper that evening the butler remarked that one would have to go a long way to find a prettier girl than Lily's friend Etta, 'and she seems sensible,' he added.

'Oh, she is, Mr Barrett,' eagerly answered Lily, 'and so clever too. Although Etta is not much over twenty she is cook to Lady Moreham, has two kitchenmaids and a scullery maid. Her real name is Henrietta but she used not to like it, so we all called her Etta. That artist who painted her — a real gentleman he was — took a fancy to her, and though Etta would not admit it, I do believe she fell for him. But then he went off to Italy.'

Nanny Smith, who in the absence of Cook was actually allowed to sit in her chair, such was her prestige, remarked sagely, 'Perhaps it was for the best, Lily. That artist might have ruined your friend. Those kind of people are not the same as us, they haven't the respect for morals that we have. I remember, years ago when I was an undernurse, the mistress — I won't mention her name — created a sensation by leaving her husband to live with a painter in Paris. She had money of her own, but in no time this man had gambled it all away and I heard that eventually he deserted her.'

This sad tale produced a rather similar one from the lady's-maid, ending with the unqualified observation that above and below stairs was like oil and water, incapable of mixing.

John Barrett demurred saying, 'That is not always true,

Dorise. There have been many occasions in history when the aristocracy fell in love with, and married, a girl from the lower classes. Look at Lord Nelson and Emma Hamilton. She was only a blacksmith's daughter to start with. Or going even further back to the Old Testament, there was King Cophetua and the beggar-maid.'

'Fancy you knowing all that, Mr Barrett,' said the under-housemaid, admiringly. 'I've long forgot all I ever learnt in school. I was generally at the bottom of the class 'cause my Mum was always keeping me home. She said she could teach me all I needed to know for a job in domestic service. I sometimes wish I knew more.'

Dorise, ever ready with a quote from the 'good book', said, with a smile, 'You'll do well enough as you are, Flora. Ecclesiastes says, "He that increaseth knowledge, increaseth sorrow." '

When Nanny retired to the night-nursery the others also departed to their bedrooms. John Barrett told Lily that he would very much like to see her friend again. Did she think that Etta would meet him one Sunday?

'I don't know, Mr Barrett. I'll be seeing her on Wednesday and I'll tell her what you said.'

Lily, sitting on the parlourmaid's bed, said, 'I do believe Mr Barrett is fair taken with my friend. He wants to meet her on a Sunday but I don't know whether Etta will agree. She's funny that way, for ever since that artist painted her she's gone off ordinary chaps. She won't admit it but it's my idea that she hopes he'll come back to this country one day. He does write to her, but only very rarely.'

'I wish Mr Barrett would take a liking to me in that way,' said Maud. 'Sometimes, when I imagine him kissing me, I go all shivery with excitement. I been going with that Bill a month now but I'd chuck him up like a shot if I had a chance with John Barrett.'

'Maud, you never would! You'd regret it, that's for sure. Like Mr Carter said, I feel there is something not quite right about our butler; he's too good-looking to be true. Besides, Maud, think of the worry of trying to keep him for yourself only. All the girls would make eyes at him and try to flirt, you'd never know where you were. You take my advice and stick to your Bill; he might be only a hod-carrier but one is lucky to get a fellow at all with the shortage of men, and the glut of females. Especially a fellow with a job. I've been out with about six different fellows — one at a time, of course — since I finished with that postman, and none of them were any good.' Lily added, rather gloomily, 'The last one, a chap called Cuthbert — what a soppy name — I was properly introduced to. I met him at my aunt Fanny's and she said he was a decent fellow, belonged to the Y.M.C.A. and was a teetotaller — not that that aspect particularly appealed to me. But what happened Maud?'

'I've no idea, Lil. What did happen?'

'I'll tell you, Maud. That Cuthbert took me to the pictures and then into a café for a cup of coffee. He knew I had to be in by ten o'clock so at nine o'clock he suggested that we could walk through Hyde Park on our way back to the house. Well, if a chap belongs to the Y.M.C.A. you don't expect any hanky-panky, do you, but you'd be surprised, Maud. We'd just passed about half a dozen prostitutes — and I blushed I can tell you — when that Cuthbert yanked me into the bushes and started kissing me. His kissing was enough to damp anybody's ardour, wet enough to extinguish a fire. But after that he attempted to maul me. Was I mad at his nerve! I kneed him you know where and dashed away. I bet he needed more than a spot of arnica,' and Lily and Maud giggled madly.

'It reminds me of my aunt Susan,' said Maud. 'She's always on at me to get a regular fellow, get married and have a family. Yet I once heard her complaining to my Mum about how disgusting Ern was — that's my uncle. "Twice a week," she said to my Mum, "he expects me to 'do that' with him and I think it's horrible. And sometimes he takes so long and he says it's my fault 'cause I'm like an old sack in bed." And Mum said, "Men are all the same, Sue, we just have to put up with it." Have you ever wondered what it's like, Lil?'

'Of course I have, Maud. But I don't think it's so much fun for us as it is for the men. They even pay prostitutes to get it. Just imagine if we had the same chance. I'd choose somebody like our butler; he might be worth the money.'

'Lily Chambers, you are awful,' said Maud, laughing. 'Talking about men,' she continued, 'that Edward got a letter this morning and he was reading it in the hall. His face went all red and he looked ever so furious. He tore up the letter and put the pieces in his pocket. I wonder what was in it? Ill news of some kind for him to have that face on him.'

Chapter 13

The letter that Edward had received was the third from the same source; namely the once adored, but now detested, Norma. The 'common little bitch' as he labelled her, had written to ask, politely in the first letter, demandingly in the third, for more money, because since the abortion she had not felt well, was unable to work and so had lost her job. She needed money for a holiday to recover her health. She needed more money to buy clothes for the holiday. He was not to send it through the post, but was to write and assign a place to meet, otherwise she would call at the house.

Poor Edward cursed the day he had entangled himself with such a devilish female. He had no hesitation in making Norma's demands known to his mother; from her he would receive sympathy — it was not in her power to give more. But the very thought of his father finding out was enough to reduce Edward's bombastic outbursts to a sullen silence.

'I cannot ask Eleanor for more money, Edward,' said his mother, 'and even if I could, where will it end? The more you give in to that type of person, the more she will try to blackmail you.'

'But what am I to do, Mother? Suppose she did call here? You can imagine what Father would say. He'd as lief cut me off without a penny. It's rotten luck that Eleanor should have all that money; it's not fair. What can she do with it? She'll never have a home of her own or a family. I reckon Elizabeth and I are entitled to a share; we are a nephew and niece, too. How can anybody be certain that our sister didn't work on the old lady's feelings; persuade her that as a spinster, she'd need the money more than Elizabeth and me?'

For once Mrs Stewart defended her eldest daughter. 'I am sure that is not true, Edward. Eleanor was genuinely fond of her aunt and spent a lot of time with her. You would never go down there and Elizabeth had Eric. Anyway, how can this person do you harm? If she's had an —' Mrs Stewart tried to think of a euphemism for 'abortion'. The sound of the word was so sordid, so nasty and unclean, such a world apart from her own respected life. How could her son, with his upbringing and education, have possibly become involved in such a squalid affair? She went on, 'If that person had an illegal operation, she would of necessity have to keep quiet about it. You don't even know for sure if her claim was true, or if it was, that you were responsible. If she is threatening you, then you must threaten in turn.'

This advice gave no consolation to Edward. Weak-willed and vacillating, he knew himself incapable of dealing firmly with the situation. All his anger and resentment was centred on Eleanor. It was all wrong that a mere woman should be financially independent, and even more so when that woman was his unmarried sister. Ah! if only he had the money, he'd know what to do with it. He'd go abroad, get away from his domineering father who thought only of making money and considered that his son should do likewise. There was more to life for a young man than being cooped up for hours every day involved in business affairs. Like a refrain he continually thought, 'if only I had Eleanor's money', and in consequence was even more than usually antagonistic to her.

But Eleanor, immersed in her painting, her social work and a certain something — so tenuous as yet that she feared to acknowledge it even in her heart — was oblivious to her brother's animosity and her mother's usual indifference. Only her father, with his affection for his eldest daughter, noticed the change in Eleanor. She was still soft and gentle in her manner but she was far less vulnerable to unkind words and no longer was she so timid in voicing an opinion. In some way her father could not understand, Eleanor appeared younger and brighter. It must surely be that her friendship with Penelope Courtland, and subsequent involvement with meetings and committee work, had given Eleanor a new interest in life.

He would have been surprised, and certainly displeased, had he been aware that his own butler devoted his meagre free time endeavouring to improve the lot of the poor. Though not more surprised than anybody who knew John Barrett intimately;

self-interest, not philanthropy, had up to now been his prevailing characteristic.

The Mr Hodge who'd sat next to John Barrett at the first meeting was in reality a happily-married factory foreman who had never been unemployed. He and Mr Barrett had never met again, but Mr Hodge would have been astonished to know that this slight acquaintance had given him an imaginary life of hardship and misery.

John Barrett had found it expedient to retain Mr Hodge and represent himself to Miss Eleanor as a good Samaritan trying to help this unfortunate man. He had won her approval, for only last week, Miss Eleanor, descending to the basement with a message for Cook, had stopped by the butler's pantry to give him a sympathetic smile. Though she had not been able to speak to him — by reason of Cook's sharp ears — John Barrett knew that Miss Eleanor was thinking of how helpful he'd been at Whitechapel. There'd been a couple of rough and rude hecklers and Mr Barrett, with the assistance of another man, had ejected these toughs from the hall. Afterwards, her taxi failing to turn up, he had escorted her through the mean streets until he'd managed to hail a cab. He'd spoken to her as an equal, saying how much he admired her devotion to such a cause, and as she'd shaken his hand on saying goodbye, he'd given her hand a slight pressure. Miss Eleanor had blushed but shown no sign of displeasure. So John Barrett had reason to congratulate himself on how far he'd advanced in Miss Eleanor's estimation.

It was only natural that the staff wondered where the butler went in his free time and why he never discussed what he had done. For, domestic service being by its very nature an enclosed existence, as each servant in turn came back from her free afternoon and evening, the others were always keen to hear what she'd done, and where.

But the butler volunteered no specific information and to all enquiries gave vague answers that he'd walked in Hyde Park or been to a film — the name of which he couldn't remember — thus confirming Lily's opinion that there was something different about Mr Barrett.

Though she had to admit he'd been loquacious enough last

Sunday evening when he returned from taking Etta out. Of course Mr Barrett knew she would hear all about it when next she met Etta. It appeared that he'd taken Etta to tea at the Trocadero and then they'd gone to the cinema — and strangely enough Mr Barrett remembered the name of the film this time: it was Greta Garbo in *Queen Christina*.

'Last Sunday I was having my tea in very different surroundings to these,' remarked the butler as he sat in the servants' hall. 'It is so pleasant at the Troc, there's a three-piece band and one is served quickly — and with smiles.'

'Oh, it's the Troc, is it?' thought the chauffeur, satirically. I suppose that Barrett imagines himself as quite the man-about-town. I'm having tea — not at the Trocadero, at the Troc.

Aloud he said, merely to annoy Mr Barrett, 'For my part I'd sooner be here eating Mrs Trouson's delicious cakes. One does know that they are wholesome, which is more than can be said of those gaudy iced cakes they serve in the cafés.'

'The Troc is not a café, I'd have you know,' retorted the butler. 'It's a high-class restaurant.'

Mrs Trouson — who was gracing the servants' hall with her presence this Sunday, mainly because Nanny Smith was departing the next day — gave a gratified smile to Mr Seymour because he'd praised her cakes, and said, 'Ah! if you knew what went on behind the scenes at some of those places you'd never want to eat the food. My sister's boy, as nice a lad as you'd hope to meet' — he would be, of course, thought John Barrett — 'was working last summer at one of those seaside hotels. He wrote to his mother that it was as posh as you please in the reception and restaurant, but in the kitchens it was filthy with dirt and grease and black beetles were scuttling over the floor.'

'I've seen black beetles in the scullery,' interposed Grace, much to Cook's annoyance. Really, kitchenmaids nowadays had all the cheek in the world. When she'd been one, she wouldn't have dared to speak unless spoken to. Sharply to Grace she said, 'You may have seen one or two, every basement has them. But my kitchen is spotlessly clean, everything is well scrubbed.'

Yes, by me, thought Grace. My idea of heaven is a place

where there are no buckets, scrubbing brushes and hard lumps of yellow soap.

'I shall be sorry to leave here,' said Nanny Smith. 'It has been such a happy time to have a baby in the nursery to care for.'

'I consider it's time the parents came back,' said the lady's-maid. 'It doesn't seem right that they should stay all those weeks in Scotland, leaving their baby here.'

'I agree, Dorise; where is their parental affection, I'd like to know? No disrespect to you, Nanny,' added Cook, seeing a frown on Nanny's face. 'Nobody could have cared or given the child more attention than you have.'

Somewhat mollified Nanny allowed that Mrs Markham could not be described as a doting mother. She added, 'But I'm sure it's not Master Eric's fault that they have been away for so long. He was such a sweet and affectionate child — and so thoughtful too. I remember when he was about seven years old, he came into my little room while the under-nurse was cleaning the day-nursery. I was writing a letter and Master Eric said "Nanny, why haven't you got a proper table to write on?" "But I have, Master Eric, I have my dressing-table" I replied. "That's not a proper one, Nanny. I shall ask Mama." And sure enough, he did and Madam gave me a small table. She's always been kind to the servants, like her mother was.'

'In my opinion,' said Dorise, rather pompously, 'above-stairs get the servants they deserve. If they treat them fairly in the matter of wages and living conditions, then servants will react accordingly and give good service. It is not too bad here, though I admit I would prefer to be called Dorise, not 'Collett do this' or 'Collett do that'.

'Why can't we be "Miss" like shop or factory girls?' asked Flora. 'They are no better than us.'

'It's nothing to do with "better", Flora,' said Cook, rather severely. 'If you think about it, how could we be called "Miss"? For instance, there would be you and Lily being called Miss Chambers and Miss Little; while you would be saying as you do now Miss Elizabeth and Miss Eleanor. Think of the confusion? Of course,' Cook added, hastily, 'it doesn't affect me being known as Mrs Trouson because I don't work above stairs.'

All this stupid talk about above and below stairs makes me sick, thought the butler. To somebody like old Trouson or that Dorise, domestic service is the be-all and end-all of existence. But not for me it isn't, oh no. 'Yes sir, very good sir, Yes madam, very good madam,' is not going to be said by me much longer. Them with their 'Barrett this' and 'Barrett that', and the way they never really see you, as though you were an object, set in motion by clockwork. There's only Miss Eleanor that looks upon us as people. Even apart from her money, I'd like her — though not too far apart of course. Aloud, Mr Barrett said to Dorise, 'Would you class this servants' hall and our bleak bedrooms as good living conditions? Just take a good look at it. Why, even their lavatories upstairs are brighter than this.'

Dorise blushed to hear such a crude word as 'lavatory'. If it was necessary to mention such a place, she referred to it as the toilet, or the little room. As Dorise made no answer to the butler's adverse criticism, Mrs Trouson complained, 'I wish it wasn't so damp. I'm sure that's why I get rheumatism; coming out of a hot kitchen to sit here. I went to the doctor but he told me there's no cure. He said that he can't get rid of his own.'

'I wish they could find a cure for old age,' said Nanny Smith.

'There is a cure, Miss Smith, and a permanent one too,' said the chauffeur.

'What do you mean, Robert? A cure for old age? There can't be. What is it?'

'Death, Miss Smith. Death inevitably cures old age 'cause you can't get any older.'

But Nanny took umbrage at this flippancy, so the lady's-maid hastily intervened, saying, 'Next Sunday at my church there will be a faith healer. He is a marvellous man. An American, and he's cured ever so many cases that the doctors had said were hopeless. Perhaps he could help your rheumatism, Mrs Trouson?'

'Does a faith healer condescend to anything so ordinary as rheumatism?' enquired Mr Barrett. 'I thought they went in for the more spectacular conditions, like cripples or people mentally ill. Maybe he hasn't enough faith for them.'

'Indeed he has,' exclaimed Dorise, indignantly. 'But he is

ready to help everybody, rich and poor, it makes no difference to him. Our vicar told us that Mark Tenson, the faith healer, is like another clergyman who died about sixty years ago and wrote a poem, "Do the job that's nearest, though it's dull at whiles; helping when you see them, lame dogs over stiles."'

'Have you ever seen one?' asked the chauffeur, sardonically.

'Have I ever seen what?' said Dorise.

'A lame dog hanging about waiting to be helped over a stile? It would look peculiar to see even a fit dog hopping over.'

This occasioned laughter from Maud and the butler while poor Dorise was reduced to silence. Cook, who considered that all matters appertaining to religion should be rigidly kept where they belonged, namely in church, said to Nanny Smith, 'Have you noticed, Nanny, that Miss Eleanor seems different, though I can't put my finger on the difference. Perhaps she seems brighter, makes more of herself.'

'You are right, Mrs Trouson, there is a difference. Miss Eleanor comes into the nursery several times a day—she knows she's always welcome. She's more of a mother to that baby than Mrs Markham, and that's a fact. I too have noticed that Miss Eleanor makes more of herself. I do believe she used Mrs Markham's rouge, but it's the wrong colour for her. It looks more like the flush of fever than the bloom of youth. But I wonder why she is changing. It's not as though there is any sign of male interest.'

'Don't you be so sure of that, Nanny,' said Maud. 'At Madam's last At Home, the fat lady's son came to collect her and he and Miss Eleanor were talking for quite a while.'

'You can't mean Victor Trentham,' exclaimed the butler. 'I know a lot about him, he's a piece of no-good. Besides, he must be five years younger than Miss Eleanor, she'd never think of him in that way. And he hasn't a penny, bar what his mother allows him.'

'Well, Miss Eleanor has money and what's five years if you fancy somebody?' said the chauffeur. 'Anyway, Victor Trentham's no worse than that Edward upstairs. What does he do? Ruddy nothing but sponge on his parents and go to night-clubs to pick up girls. I wouldn't give him house room. You mark my words, there'll be trouble there.'

As nobody attempted to answer this statement, Nanny Smith offered to read their tea-leaves for the last time, and predicted nothing but good fortune for all of them. Mr Barrett, slightly perturbed to hear that Eleanor had shown an interest in that no-good Victor Trentham, thought: next Wednesday he'll be one of the guests at the dinner-party. I'll take particular note of him and Miss Eleanor. I wonder if he knows about her money?

Chapter 14

'Now then, Grace,' berated Mrs Trouson, 'there's no call to look so glum, just because you've had to change your free time. It's not as though you have a home to go to, so a Thursday must be the same as a Wednesday to you. Or do you expect Madam to ask you if it's convenient for her to have a dinner-party on a Wednesday?'

In fact, Mrs Stewart had noticed the kitchenmaid's rather sullen expression and remarked on it to Mrs Trouson, asking if Grace minded changing her day. Cook, knowing that Grace did mind, nevertheless answered, 'Oh no, Madam, she has nowhere special to go. She generally goes to the cinema and one evening's the same as another there.'

Mrs Stewart had proceeded to tell Mrs Trouson that there would be twelve for a dinner of six courses, adding that one of the guests would be an old and very dear friend, a professor. Mrs Stewart did on occasion utter a personal remark to her servants; she considered it made them feel that she took an interest in them as human beings, not just as her servants.

The butler, overhearing the cook reprimanding her kitchen-maid, said, half-laughingly, 'Perhaps Grace had a special reason for wanting this Wednesday evening? Didn't Nanny Smith foretell in the tea-leaves that Grace would shortly meet a dark stranger. It might have been this very evening that he'd have turned up? Can't afford to lose chances, eh Grace?'

But Cook, who disapproved of such flippancy, said, 'Now then, Mr Barrett, don't you go giving a young girl ideas. Grace is too young to be paying any attention to young men. She should be saving her money, get a bit in the Post Office to have at the back of her.'

'Not much chance of saving money on two pounds a month,' muttered Grace.

'What do you mean, Grace Taylor? You pay out nothing for board and lodging, of course you could save. Why, when I was your age I got only twelve pounds a year — *and* I managed to save half of it, too.'

Though Grace felt malevolent towards Cook, she knew better than to give a pert answer. But she thought, yes, and what good has it done you: frosty, fat and fifty.

Cook, feeling that she had done her duty in thus speaking severely to her kitchenmaid, said, in a milder voice, 'Anyway Grace, you will have help with the washing up tonight. You know Mrs Seymour comes in when we have a large dinner party,' and to Mr Barrett she added, 'I have an idea from what Madam said that there's some big-wig coming tonight, somebody to do with politics.'

'Ah! with such a distinguished family as this is, it's certain to be one of the high-ups,' said the butler, ironically. 'Now let me guess. Would it be Lloyd George? No, he's practically a nobody now. What about our new P.M., Mr Chamberlain? One can't get any higher than him.'

But, of course, no such distinguished company graced Mrs Stewart's table; the 'political man' being merely a back-bencher. Nevertheless, as an experienced hostess, Mrs Stewart had invited a mixed collection of people. Apart from herself, Henry, Eleanor and the back-bencher, there were Arnold Courtland and his wife, a cubist painter — a long way after Picasso — a barrister, a professor from the London School of Economics, Lady Farron and Mrs Trentham with her son. Inevitably the conversation turned to the recent events in Germany, the professor asserting that the fundamental traits in the German character were power, destruction and death. In Hitler they had found the right man to fulfil these three things. The barrister said that before long there would be no intellectuals left in Germany, while the painter protested that not all the Nazis were philistines, they supported modern artists such as Nolde. The back-bencher, endeavouring to impress on the company his privileged position as a purveyor of 'inside knowledge', supplied the information that there was more going on behind the scenes than was printed in newspapers.

Oh dear, thought Mrs Stewart, I do hope they are not going to talk politics all the evening, but she was even more apprehensive when, during a momentary lull in the men's conversation, Penelope Courtland, speaking to Julia Trentham, was heard to say: 'What working women need is more birth-control clinics so that they're not saddled with half a dozen children they cannot afford.' Lady Farron, frowning with distaste at hearing this outspoken remark, said, 'What the working class need is more self-control, and intelligence to realise it's all wrong to bring unwanted children into the world.'

Eleanor, who had not spoken up to now, said, 'But Lady Farron, although their children are not planned, when they do arrive they are not unwanted. They receive just as much love, if not more so, than the children of wealthy families.'

The professor, a dried-up little man whose wizened features and sparse hair gave the appearance of a person far removed from human relationships said mildly, 'What I don't understand, is how men and women who do hard manual work get the energy to produce so many children. Believe me, I envy them. My dear departed wife lost all interest after the third child. Maybe that's why I did so well with my mental studies,' the professor added, smiling.

'You have to remember, professor,' said the barrister, 'that most manual workers have low incomes and so cannot afford the pleasures that you and I take for granted. So, they indulge in a pleasure that costs nothing at the time. A kind of weekend bonanza — while I have to put up with *bona vacantia*.'

This occasioned laughter from all but Lady Farron, though actually it was only the professor who knew the meaning of the last two words.

The butler, carrying out his duties, nevertheless managed many a surreptitious glance at Victor Trentham and Eleanor, who sat next to him. It did appear to Mr Barrett that Victor paid Eleanor a great deal of attention, seldom turning to his neighbour on the other side. However it was some consolation to see that Eleanor shewed no particular signs of pleasure at this attention, and John Barrett was certain that, as he served her, Eleanor was really aware of his presence.

When the ladies retired to the drawing-room, the gentlemen, indulging in Mr Stewart's fine old port and cigars, very soon felt free to discuss the latest scandal in high society involving a prominent financier and a married lady of high birth and low morals. The back-bencher then volunteered the information that the Government preferred Bolshevism to Facism and that he knew a man who'd met Mussolini and said his face was like a balloon. When Victor Trentham suggested joining the ladies Mr Stewart demurred, saying, let them twitter a while longer; for, in common with most men, he considered that no female was capable of intelligent conversation.

In fact, conversation in the drawing-room was becoming rather tense; though it started mildly enough with Julia Trentham — who had mentioned Barrett as a possible butler — asking Mrs Stewart if he was giving satisfactory service.

'Oh, yes he is. Edward suggested there would be trouble with the maids because Barrett is good-looking, but Cook tells me there is nothing like that; they are respectful to him.'

'Apart from my hall-boy I have never had any trouble with staff,' said Lady Farron. 'They have all been with me years and would do anything for me. But last year I was staying with a great friend of mine and a terrible thing happened. One of the maids — I think it was the between-maid — a young girl of eighteen, Green her name was, had a baby in her bedroom and nobody knew that she had got herself into trouble. The kitchenmaid —'

'What do you mean: "got herself into trouble"?' interrupted Penelope Courtland. 'It was a man got her into trouble.'

Ignoring this, Lady Farron continued, 'The kitchenmaid found her on the bedroom floor in a pool of blood. Of course, my friend was disgusted at such immoral behaviour, sent the girl to a hospital and told her never to come back. And what do you think?' Lady Farron lowered her voice as though she was about to disclose a state secret. 'That girl was shameless; she went on the streets and became a prostitute.'

Lady Farron sat back in her chair after this disclosure of the depths of human iniquity as though in amazement that a girl, a maid in a highly respectable family, could sink so low.

Eleanor, while sympathising with the girl, said nothing, not wishing to antagonise Lady Farron or her mother, but Mrs Courtland said, sharply, 'Well, what did you expect her to do?

Did your friend give her a reference? Would you have given her a reference?'

'Indeed I would not,' said Lady Farron, obviously annoyed at the question. 'I wouldn't have such a creature in my house to corrupt the maids.'

Penelope Courtland snorted with indignation as she said, 'Then how was Green supposed to live? How could she get work without a reference? I suppose your friend would have been satisfied if her maid had taken to heart the song in *The Vicar of Wakefield* and, "to give repentance to her lover, and wring his bosom — is to die". As though the guilty lover ever does repent. Why would he, when all the blame and opprobrium is heaped on the woman?'

Silence followed this speech, though inwardly Mrs Stewart was seething with rage. The very idea that a woman like Penelope Courtland should upset Lady Farron, and even cause Mrs Trentham to look uneasy! Never again if she could help it and in spite of Arnold Courtland being a friend of Henry's, would she invite such a person to her house. Her anger was in no way alleviated by the entrance of the men, when Mr Courtland said jocularly, 'Well, have you all finished talking about hats?'

Later that evening, when the staff were having their supper, the guests, and a certain amount of their conversation, was as usual an interesting topic. Mrs Trouson was not over pleased that the chauffeur's wife was at the supper table; she considered that Mrs Seymour, having a home of her own, should have gone there as soon as she'd finished her washing-up duties. But Mrs Seymour reckoned she was under-paid; it was only because Robert worked for the Stewarts that she agreed to help on dinner-party nights. She thought, as she'd thought on many another night, that stiff-necked cook begrudges me a meal, but I reckon I've earned it. There was another extra person at the table, for Lady Farron's chauffeur was waiting to take her home, but Sidney West, unlike Mrs Stewart's chauffeur, 'lived-in', so he was in no hurry to leave one servants' hall for another.

Mrs Trouson had made a large beef casserole for the servants' supper, to be followed by an apple tart. When Mr West, after a liberal helping of the casserole, said he wouldn't have eaten so much if he'd known there was one of Cook's delicious apple tarts to follow, Mrs Trouson, unsuccessfully endeavouring to look modest, said, 'Well, Mr West, of course we don't eat like this every evening. But it's my opinion that when we have worked so hard for them above, we are entitled to a little extra in the way of food.'

'Especially as "them above" never give us any extra in the way of money, no matter how many hours we've worked,' said Robert Seymour, sourly. 'Don't you agree?' he added, turning to the butler. He did this merely to embarrass Mr Barrett, guessing rightly that the butler had reaped a few benefits in the way of tips but had no intention of disclosing this to the kitchen staff.

Mr Barrett, ignoring this remark, said to Cook: 'The dinner went well tonight, Mrs Trouson, and the saddle of lamb was perfection. The amount of food eaten by that Mrs Trentham is really something to see. Her jaws were going chomp-chomp all the time. When I served her with the lamb and Maud handed the mint sauce and redcurrant jelly, she took some of both. Did you ever know such a thing? No wonder she's so fat.'

'Yes,' added Maud, 'and she was ever so made up. Her face was all pink and white and her hair was sort of reddy, as though she'd been dyeing it.'

Cook, eager to hear what they talked about rather than what they looked like, said, 'Did the Member of Parliament disclose anything that we haven't read in the newspapers?'

'Not him, Mrs Trouson,' said the butler, scornfully, 'he was a nobody. I bet he was one of those who, once they've been elected to sit in the House of Commons, say nothing all the time they're there. But that Mrs Courtland properly put Madam out by — with apologies to you Mrs Trouson — mentioning birth-control clinics. Maud and I could see that Lady Farron looked disgusted to hear such a remark and she said that the poor had no right to bring children into the world if they cannot afford to keep them. Civilised people should have more self-control.'

'Well, her ladyship's not exactly a model in that way,' said her chauffeur, facetiously, 'though I suppose as she could well afford to support her seven she'd no need for moderation.'

'Well I wouldn't have fancied that Sir David Farron if he looked anything like he does now; not for all the tea in China I wouldn't,' said the upper-housemaid. 'He's got piggy little eyes buried in a mound of flesh and a corporation on him like the Dome at Brighton. Lady Farron could only have married him for his title and money.'

'A fair exchange for being allowed a poke in bed, I reckon,' said Robert Seymour dryly, and, to Mr Barrett's surprise, even Cook joined in the laughter.

But Mr Barrett was unaware that Cook, for the first time in her life, had been 'taken with palpitations'—like her dear mother. Dear mother had always taken a tot of brandy, then lain flat on the couch with her feet raised over the arm. Cook, the exigence of the dinner-party preventing a horizontal position, had perhaps overdone the tot of brandy. Grace was the chief person to benefit from this mellowness, for in the normal way Cook was not a pattern of sweetness on dinner-party nights.

'My mother brought up nine of us,' said Mr West, 'and she lost four at birth, so that made thirteen altogether. Dad died when he was seventy, but Mother's eighty-five and likely to go on living for ever from the look of her.'

'She must miss your father though,' said the lady's-maid. 'My mother in the last years of her life was longing to join dear father,' and Dorise looked suitably sentimental while omitting to mention how many years had elapsed before her mother decided it was time to join the departed.

Mr West laughed, saying, 'My mother's still got seven of us, some with families, living near her. She's got no time to miss Dad. 'Sides, Mum don't believe in all that stuff about meeting again in heaven. "There ain't no such place," she says. "Cause if there was, him up there would have looked after us a bit more and not let me see me kids half-starved for want of a bit of money."'

'Your mother must have had a hard life, bringing up that large family,' sympathised Mrs Trouson, 'but I suppose some of the daughters helped her. Was your father handy about the house?'

'Dad do housework! Not likely. 'Sides, Mum wouldn't have let him. Down our street any man who helped his wife was known as a "mop rag". We lived in a two-up-and-downer so there wasn't all that much housework. Dad was a docker and often got work for only two days in the week. Some of the men used to grease the hand of the boss — the man who said: "you, and you, and you, can work" — but Dad never would, said he'd see the b—— in hell first. After the strike — I think it was the year King George was crowned — things got a bit better. Dad's money rose to five shillings for a nine-hour day. Course there was still no guarantee of work, but if a man wasn't picked out for a job, he got eighteen pence. Anyway,' added Mr West, slightly embarrassed to have monopolised the conversation, 'all that's old hat now and I mustn't go on boring you.'

The staff, all excepting the butler, protested that they were not bored, his conversation had been most interesting. Mr Barrett, to whom the hardships of life — unless they happened to him — were matters of no interest, was just about to change the subject when the kitchenmaid, perhaps emboldened by Cook's mellowness, had the temerity to say, 'Mr West, I don't get five shillings a day even now, and I work more than nine hours. I only get two pounds a month. If you ask me — ' but Grace got no further, for Mrs Trouson, fixing a cold and disapproving eye on her, said, 'Grace Taylor, nobody has, or is likely to, ask for your opinion on anything; least of all on whether you are down-trodden and under-paid. But since you seem to think your services are not fully recognised, let me inform you that, as well as your two pounds a month, you are housed, well-fed and, if you keep your eyes open and use your brains, will eventually be able to cook. Mr West's father had to keep a wife and family on his five shillings a day.'

Poor Grace almost subsided into tears while Lily, ever sympathetic to the trials of under-servants, hasily said 'I often think there should be a domestic servants union so that we could bargain for better living conditions and wages. We ought not to have to be in by ten o'clock when it's our free afternoon and evening and we ought not to have attic bedrooms that are sparsely furnished, bleak, unheated and a bed either lumpy or hard as a rock. I know that by the time we get there we're too tired to care but that's not the point.'

'How could a union be organised?' said the butler. 'We all live so tightly enclosed. It's not like a factory where there are hundreds of workers all in similar positions. They can get together and organise a protest.'

'Not all servants would want to join anyway,' said the chauffeur's wife. 'Where my sister is an upper-housemaid, all the maids have been there years and they'd never dream of making a complaint. They have every comfort and liberal free time.'

'My friend Etta is in a good place too,' remarked Lily. 'Lady Moreham believes that as servants have got to live in their place of work, it should be as much like a home as possible.'

Mr Barrett's face clouded over at the mention of Etta, for he'd not been successful in his efforts to arrange another date. Although fixed in his determination of pursuing Miss Eleanor, he nevertheless was very much taken with Etta's good looks and air of self-sufficiency. He had suffered very few reverses from young women, who were almost always fascinated by his charms, but Etta appeared impervious to his handsome face and seductive voice. Not that Mr Barrett had any real feeling for Lily's friend, it was just that he couldn't understand why she rebuffed him. Surely a pretty girl like her didn't intend to stay in domestic service for the rest of her life? Was she waiting for a Prince to call with the glass slipper? Well, she'd wait in vain. Princes were not addicted to descending a basement in search of a true love.

Cook, her feelings still ruffled because she sensed that the staff felt sorry for Grace, announced that it was time the supper was cleared and the lights put out. Retiring to her bedroom she thought: they all feel sorry for Grace because she came from an orphanage. Yet she didn't come into service until she was sixteen and she couldn't have had a hard life there going by the way she is now. When I was a kitchenmaid I'd never have dared to voice an opinion to the cook or the upper-servants. If I'd ever had the nerve I'd very soon have been put in my place. I don't know what girls are coming to nowadays. They think of nothing but dancing and boy-friends and getting out of service as though it was some kind of prison.

Upstairs in the attics the staff, all except the lady's-maid, were enjoying their usual nightly chat. They did not intentionally ostracise Dorise, but somehow she did not fit in. Dorise's lady's-maid's duties caused her to be so frequently in Madam's company, that she now spoke in a more refined accent from the others. But it was her piety that gave them a feeling of constraint. They were reluctant to mention anything appertaining to sex and, after all, if they couldn't talk about boyfriends, or the lack of them, what was there to discuss? Dorise had hung several texts on her bedroom walls, one of which stated, 'Resist the devil and he will flee from you'. But as Lily said, 'One didn't need much power of resistance in domestic service; the opportunities to sin were so limited.'

So now Maud remarked, laughing, 'You properly upset Mrs Trouson tonight, Grace. I'm sure she reckons that it's a privilege working as her kitchenmaid, you shouldn't even consider the money.'

'I didn't mean anything against being here, Maud. It was just because Mr West said his father had five shillings a day; it made me think of my wage.'

'Mr Seymour's brother has got a job at last,' said Lily. 'He's working in a warehouse. The wages are not much but it's better than the dole. He's asked me if I'll go out with him. I wanted to say, you bet I will, not half, but of course it wouldn't have done to look too eager. He might have thought I was desperate for male company—he'd have thought right too.'

'Will you go dancing with him, Lil?' said Maud.

'Not on your life. What, go to a dance-hall where the girls outnumber the fellows by about four to one and maybe in a Paul Jones have some female nick Don from me? I'll watch it. We'll go to the pictures, the Roxy's got a romantic film on with Pola Negri in it. I could do with a bit of romance. The last time I saw Pola Negri I was with a chap I'd got talking to in a Joe Lyons teashop. He seemed ever so nice, asked if he could sit at my table, and when he was gone you know where, I asked the Nippy who'd served us if she'd seen him before. She said he was often in but always on his own. So I risked going to the pictures with him, after all he couldn't do much there. It was a lovely film and Jean Harlow — who'd just vamped the hero — was being passionately kissed when this chap I was with gave a terrific belch, I'm sure it could be heard a dozen rows away. I was fit to pass out with embarrassment, but this fellow — I never did know his name — just sat there as though nothing had happened. Talk about romance, I'd had it.'

Amid the general laughter Flora said, 'In every letter I get from my Mum she writes, "When are you going to get a steady young man and bring him home?" Where does Mum think I can find one? There's no clubs for the likes of us where we can meet the opposite sex. I wish I'd been born a man and then I wouldn't have to worry about getting married. For if I didn't want to, it wouldn't be taken for granted that nobody had asked me.'

Downstairs, in his basement bedroom, John Barrett gave no thought to Mrs Trouson or the rest of the staff. He was thinking about Miss Eleanor and the next meeting she would be attending. Somehow I must contrive to be alone with Eleanor, he thought. I know women and I am certain she is aware of me not as her parents' butler, but as a handsome, well-mannered and kind man, with the interests of the working class always in my heart. Little does Eleanor know that I don't care a hoot about the poor and unemployed; it's the Government's business to look after them. I wonder if that Victor Trentham knows about her money? I believe he does, because he's not the type to care for a woman who is thirtyish and plain. Nothing but money would attract a cad like him. I know all about that unsavoury business with the little chorus girl. His mother paid and hushed it up but I wouldn't wish a man like him on a person like Eleanor, she has a very kind nature: I'd be a better husband to her than that Victor Trentham ... And with ideas about ten thousand pounds the butler drifted off to sleep.

Chapter 15

Victor Trentham was aware that Eleanor Stewart possessed ten thousand pounds. Her brother, relating the tale of his misfortune with the shop-assistant, Norma, had mentioned it was his sister's money that had relieved him of an awkward situation.

Though Victor Trentham and Edward Stewart frequented the same rather sleazy night-clubs, they were acquaintances rather than friends. For whereas Edward was selfish, idle and weak, Victor Trentham was thoroughly unprincipled, immoral and considered all women fair game to be seduced. He was also heavily in debt and could squeeze no more money from his mother.

He thought Edward a fool for playing around with a shop-girl and even more of a fool for giving her money.

'How do you know that the brat would have been yours, or even that she was pregnant? A girl like that is capable of any lies to get hold of money. Two hundred pounds you gave her, you're mad. I'd have given her fifty and told her where to go.'

Edward protesting that the girl was a virgin, Victor gave a snort of derision, 'Girls like that can fake anything and you're not exactly a Don Juan in experience.'

And now Norma Parks was asking, nay demanding, more money, complaining that since the abortion she had never felt well and was unable to find work. Edward, terrified that she would appear in person at his home and not knowing how, or having the means to deal with her demands, approached Victor for help, with money if possible, if not, advice.

'Cannot help with money, haven't a bean, up to my ears in debt. Besides, the more you give her, the more she'll go on squeezing you. My advice is to tell your old man. He can't shoot you and he'll probably do for that harpy.'

'You don't know my father, Victor. He thinks he's God Almighty in the home, he'd probably turn me out of the house and cut off my allowance. No, I couldn't face him.'

'You know best, old boy. My old man popped off before I was old enough to leave prep school, so I never had to face a father's wrath.'

'Lucky for you I say. I'd sooner approach my sister. She's become so wrapped up in good works for the "deserving" poor that any day I expect to find her with a halo. Well, she can rescue me. After all, what good does all that money do for her? She doesn't need it; the old man will always look after Eleanor.'

Victor Trentham, who had designs on Eleanor and her money—though he would have preferred the latter with no strings attached—was far from pleased at the prospect of more of her ten thousand disappearing to help this fool of a brother.

Aloud he said, 'I tell you what, old man. Let me see this harpy. I've had more experience with her kind than you have. I know how to deal with them. Where had you arranged to meet? Point her out to me.'

Edward explaining that the following night he was to meet her in a pub, Victor arranged to go with him. As soon as Edward had pointed her out, he was to disappear and Victor would take over. He'd soon sort her out.

But, if Victor Trentham knew how to deal with her kind, Norma Parks was equally as well versed in the likes of Victor Trentham. Also, in anticipation of a belligerent Edward, she had brought reinforcements in the shape of her friend, Cissy. Cissy's experience of perfidious men had taught her to recognise the type and in Victor Trentham she saw a prime example.

When he introduced himself as Edward Stewart's friend and explained that Mr Stewart was prevented from coming through illness, Cissy Clegg quickly interruped, saying grimly: 'Friend, is it? Two of a kind if you ask me. I bet he ain't got the nerve to turn up. Mr Stewart, is he now? He was an Eddy when he seduced my poor friend, Norma. Look at her, a bundle of nerves, skin an' bone. How does your Mr Stewart think she can work, that's what I like to know? Don't come the old baloney about the money she's had; that's gone now.'

During this verbal onslaught Victor Trentham studied Norma Parks and became convinced that Edward Stewart was a bigger fool than he seemed. For how could he have become enamoured with a girl like that; her kind were two a penny. As for her being a 'bundle of nerves', that was a joke. There she sat for all the world as though she was beyond indulging in such a sordid subject as money, yet no doubt calculating how much she could hope to get.

Breaking into Cissy Clegg's diatribe and speaking directly to Norma, Victor Trentham said, coldly, 'And how much money had you in mind for your second blackmail attempt? Another two hundred pounds?'

'See here, Mister-whoever-you-are,' angrily retorted Norma Parks, 'I'll thank you to keep a civil tongue in your head and not make false accusations. A libel, that's what it is.'

'You're mistaken, it's slander.'

'What d'you mean, slander?'

'Libel has to be written, not spoken.'

'Well whether it's bloody libel or slander I don't care. All I say is, you watch what you're accusing people of.'

'Demanding money with menaces is blackmail.'

'What d'you mean, menaces?' interposed Cissy Clegg, scowling, 'My poor friend here is just asking for a little help until she gets on her feet again. There ain't no menace there that I can see.'

'Where is the guarantee that supposing, and only supposing, Mr Stewart gave you fifty pounds — you certainly wouldn't get more — you'd be content and not bother him ever again? If it was up to me I'd see you both in hell before I'd part with another penny — but my friend has a softer nature than I have.'

The two females were certainly intimidated by the barely-repressed ferocity of Trentham's voice and manner for, showing far less bravado than she'd started with, Cissy Clegg promised that if Norma got fifty — she was about to say one hundred, but one glance at his face deterred her — Eddy would never hear from her again.

Meeting Edward as arranged, Trentham gave as his opinion, that after one more payment, Edward would have nothing more to worry about; of that he was certain. But, he'd had to promise that trollop one hundred pounds. Edward should get the money and hand it to him to pay her off. That way he'd no need to see her again. For Victor Trentham considered that fifty pounds in his own pocket would be the right reward for being an intermediary. Left to Stewart's generosity, he knew he'd get nothing.

Edward looked gloomy at the mention of one hundred pounds. He complained, 'Where the hell am I going to find the money? Cannot get it from Mossy, I owe him seventy-five already. I'll have to swallow my pride and ask my sister for a loan. She will never get it back, but she won't know that. Anyway, thanks for your help, old man; I'll see you at the weekend and hand over the necessary.'

But Victor Trentham was not as confident as he made out to Edward that there would be no further demands from the erstwhile lady-love. He thought: left to herself, that Norma Parks could be frightened into silence, but that Clegg female egging her on is a hard case; she'll not give up easily. Besides, I don't want Stewart borrowing from his sister. Already two hundred has gone, now another fifty; how much more, and how often? I don't trust those harpies. I reckon with a little persuasive flattery I could get Eleanor to fall for me.

It was true that Eleanor, with her new-found confidence in speaking, had found Victor Trentham surprisingly interesting; mainly because he had a genuine enthusiasm for, and knowledge about, painting and the Old Masters. After the dinner-party Eleanor had rather shyly shown him some of her water-colours and he recognised that she had real talent. Her father had always been generous with praise, but Eleanor knew it was rather from affection than the ability to appreciate art. So to hear her work commended by one who understood painting was very gratifying and caused Eleanor to appear far more friendly towards Victor than normally so. It did not occur to her that on previous occasions he had extended the barest courtesy and had never mentioned his interest in art.

So, thinking of Eleanor and her money, Trentham, casting aside any nebulous ideas of friendship with Edward, decided to acquaint Mr Henry Stewart with the circumstances of his son's misfortune. After all, he reasoned, I am probably doing Edward a good turn, for he will never have the nerve to tell his old man and that female could go on asking for money ad infinitum. What a jelly fish the fellow is; it's more than likely that the brat — if ever there had been one — was not his.

Of course, Victor Trentham had no intention of a personal meeting with Mr Stewart. From Edward's description of his father's biting sarcasm and ill-temper, he could well imagine how Mr Stewart would receive any information about the misdemeanour of his son. No, he would send a letter, printed and unsigned. Nobody could possibly connect him with an anonymous letter. Certainly not Edward, grateful for his help with that woman.

So Victor Trentham decided on his plan of wooing Eleanor. He would take her to the Pre-Raphaelite exhibition and to the private showing of Crane's water-colours. He knew that when he wanted to do so, he could make himself very attractive to the ladies by giving them his special attention. He was certain of making an impression on a plain woman like Eleanor.

But what he did not know, and would not have believed if told it was a fact, was that a very different man from Victor Trentham, a man whom he had seen with his eyes but never really *seen*, a man so far beneath him as not to be given a thought, was, at this very moment, making a far greater impression on Eleanor Stewart than ever he could have done for all his intelligence and charm.

Chapter 16

So assiduous had Mr Barrett been in the way of attending meetings, so helpful in the matter of setting out chairs in the hall and on the platform that he was almost one of the committee. Fortunately, as the meetings were held on a Wednesday, Mr Barrett was able to attend, though occasionally he had to miss one because Penelope Courtland would be there and certain to recognise him as Mrs Stewart's butler.

To some extent, Mrs Courtland had lost her initial enthusiasm for helping the poor — whether they were deserving or not. For one thing, not all of them shewed appreciation of her efforts on their behalf. Ribald remarks were made, especially on the occasion when she said that a woman who did the same work as a man, should have equal wages. Furious denunciations of this arbitrary point of view broke out from the men, ranging from, 'you're bonkers', 'garn, get off the platform', to 'what about women taking our jobs, then? Ain't there enough bloody unemployed without you giving our jobs to a pack of women whose proper place is in the home?'

As Mrs Courtland afterwards explained to Eleanor, a working class man wants to keep his wife subservient and a household drudge, for only in that way can he assert a man's superiority to the female sex. So now Penelope Courtland's ardour was centred on the right of women to enter professions still closed to them, the right to promotion and of course, equal pay.

So, the very evening that Victor Trentham was planning his assault on Eleanor's ten thousand pounds, John Barrett, relieved to discover that Mrs Courtland was elsewhere, was wondering how he could further advance in his plan of making Eleanor aware that she was falling in love with him. When Eleanor was unaccompanied to the F.D.W. meetings it had become a habit for him to escort her through the streets until a taxi could be procured. Then, as they went through the park John Barrett would leave the cab, saying that he liked to walk around in the fresh air before returning to the basement. Of late instead of serious discussion about the meeting, Eleanor had seemed confused, started to speak, broke off, looked away from him and blushed if he accidentally touched her; in short, exhibited signs of being fully aware of his presence.

This evening, to John Barrett's considerable surprise and delight, when the taxi stopped to let him out, Eleanor asked if he would mind walking with her for a while. She had a slight headache, the meeting had been so noisy; perhaps the fresh air would cure it.

In the house she was of necessity compelled to address him as Barrett, but always away from her family she had called him Mr Barrett. Now, walking along the dimly-lit path, her hand resting lightly on his arm, John Barrett thought, is this the right time to speak, to call her Eleanor, to say I have fallen in love with her? Would she be alarmed and take offence, act the lady, be angry at my effrontery in aspiring so high? He was afraid to risk it, afraid he was premature. A few words at the wrong time could undo all his previous advantage, there was need for caution.

As they strolled along in companionable silence he wondered if Eleanor was thinking about him, or the rather rowdy element at the meeting, it had certainly got out of hand. He remarked on this to Eleanor and she said, softly, 'Thank you, Mr Barrett, for rescuing me from that horrible man who kept interrupting,' and when he protested that it was nothing, she added, 'Indeed it was, for a while I thought he was going to assault you.'

Without conscious volition on his part they sat down on a bench and Eleanor started to talk about her childhood and growing-up. She had so disliked going to parties and balls where one met the same people over and over again. Suddenly she murmured, 'When we are alone, I shall call you John and you must call me Eleanor. After all we are friends,' and with mock authority she demanded, 'Say it now John, say, Hello Eleanor.'

To John Barrett's mortification and chagrin, all his aplomb, all the pretty speeches he had rehearsed in the privacy of his bedroom, seemed to vanish. Instead of seizing the opportunity of declaring that she had long been 'dear Eleanor' in his heart, he almost stuttered, 'Yes, Miss Eleanor — I mean Miss, Miss, I mean Eleanor.'

The low laugh she gave on hearing this quickly dissipated any emotional feelings or embarrassment. Some time later, when he left Eleanor at a safe distance from the house, he held her hand in both of his as they said, goodnight John, goodnight Eleanor.

Descending to the basement he was surprised to find that the rest of the staff shewed no signs of retiring to bed.

'Hallo, why are you all up then? Has something unusual happened? Have I missed a world-shattering event?'

'Oh Mr Barrett,' cried the parlourmaid, 'there's been such goings-on upstairs, you'd never believe.'

'I certainly would, Maud. I'd believe in fairies if you told me they really existed. I'd believe there's a man in the moon and that pigs can fly,' and the butler laughed heartily.

What's the matter with the man, thought Cook. Is he drunk or something? There's a peculiar look in his eyes tonight, I wonder what he's been up to.

Aloud she said, her voice proclaiming a tragedy, 'The Master and Madam are very upset because Miss Elizabeth came here this evening.'

'What is upsetting about that? She has often been here.'

'She came with Mr Markham to tell the Master and Madam that, almost on the eve of returning to India, she doesn't want to go; in fact, refuses to go. Maud heard it all,' said Lily.

'How could you know all that, Maud? I'm sure they didn't talk in front of you.'

'They spoke so loudly, Mr Barrett I couldn't help overhearing. Mr Markham was ever so upset, Madam was crying and Mr Stewart was that angry with Miss Elizabeth, shouting that it was her duty to be with her husband. And Miss Elizabeth said such a dreadful thing because when Mr Markham said that he'd take the child away from her, take him to India, she said, oh ever so calmly, "Well that's up to you." It was just as though she doesn't care about her baby.'

'She probably knew it was just a threat,' said the head-housemaid. 'He couldn't take a young baby back with him. What would he do with him? Take him on the parade-ground, display him to the regiment?'

'He could get an Indian nurse, I think they call them ayahs,' said the lady's-maid, looking very concerned. 'But what a terrible thing, to leave one's husband, and both so young. She will regret it I'm sure. "Those whom God has joined together—" '

' "—let no man put asunder," ' finished Mr Barrett. 'What makes you think, Dorise, that there is another man?'

'Oh I don't think so, dear me no,' twittered Dorise. 'I was just quoting from the marriage service.'

'It's time we all went to bed,' interposed Cook. 'What goes on above stairs is not our business and we shouldn't sit here tittle-tattling.' To her kitchenmaid, 'You hear, Grace? No talking about this when you go to tea at the orphanage.'

'You are quite right, Mrs Trouson,' said the butler, gravely. 'The best way in which we can help is to go on as though nothing had happened.'

Upstairs, free from the restrictions of butler and cook, tongues were working overtime. Even the lady's-maid was not averse from joining in the talk.

'Mrs Trouson gets on my nerves,' said Lily. 'All this Master and Madam stuff, she's even got me copying her. We have to say "Madam" and "Sir" when we speak to them, but why can't they just be Mr and Mrs Stewart in the servants' hall?'

'I wonder if that Elizabeth has got another man?' said Flora. 'She's quite a pretty girl and full of life, so different from her sister.'

'I much prefer Miss Eleanor. She may be quiet but she has such a sweet nature. The other night, when I was waiting up for Madam to come home from that grand ball, Miss Eleanor said to me: "You look so tired, Collett, go to bed, I'll look after my mother. I'll tell her that I insisted you should go to bed." You wouldn't get such kindness from Miss Elizabeth.'

'Funny her going off her husband. He's not a bad-looking chap and they haven't been married that long. Perhaps her Eric is like my cousin Joe, a bit inhibited,' and Lily laughed.

'What does that mean, inhibited?' asked Grace.

'Well, my cousin Joe's kind of bashful. A bit slow in the uptake in bed — if you know what I mean. He got married about six months ago to an old school-friend of mine, Hilda, and when I asked her how she was enjoying married life, she made a face and said, "Joe's attitude to a sex-life is the same as his attitude to having a bath. He 'performs' once a week, on a Saturday night."'

There were giggles from Maud, Flora and Grace. 'There is more to marriage than that kind of thing,' Dorise demurred. 'Marriage is a union blessed by God; there is loyalty and companionship.'

'Oh for sure,' retorted Lily, 'but who wants to be half of a Darby and Joan when you have been married only a few months?'

When Dorise, looking pained, had drifted off to bed, Maud said, 'She's a fine one to talk about marriage, what does she know? And of course she must always bring religion into everything she says.'

'She's got a new text hanging in her bedroom,' said Flora. 'It's a picture of a kind of palace with two angels hovering above and the words underneath say, "Permit me to dwell in the heavenly dwelling".'

'Oh, I don't think she's ready for that yet,' Maud laughed, adding, 'At least her earthly dwelling is better than ours, she's got a carpet on the floor.'

Down in the basement the butler and cook, in their separate rooms, were thinking very different thoughts. Mrs Trouson was genuinely concerned over the misfortunes of above-stairs. She knew from experience that an atmosphere of discord above inevitably effected below-stairs. Servants wasted their time listening and observing instead of getting on with their work. Anything untoward above-stairs provided an endless source of interest to below. Even the smallest incident was blown up and chewed over out of all proportion.

But Mr Barrett gave the problem of Miss Elizabeth hardly a thought. He was filled with satisfaction at the progress he had made with Eleanor. He felt certain now that in the very near future he would cease to be a butler, cease to be a servant of any kind. Though Eleanor was no oil-painting, she wasn't all that bad-looking when she took the trouble to do herself up. That friend of Lily's was a corker, he must try to meet her again. How the young men in the Troc had envied him sitting at the table with a girl like Etta. And as he too drifted off to sleep he thought, I wonder if Eleanor will dream about me tonight?

Eleanor was a long way from dreaming about John, she was in fact, wide awake. The events of the evening outside of her home, coupled with the stormy atmosphere generated by Elizabeth inside, were not conducive to calmness and a desire to sleep.

Even now, when every thought of John filled her with delight, she could not envisage a time when they would be always together. Her whole life, the traditions of the family, were against such a idea.

None of the family, from as far back as one could trace, had ever married out of their class. There were several Lords and Ladies in the family tree, along with Sirs, esquires and plain country gentlemen. Eleanor, who was not without a sense of humour, smiled at the thought of an addition to the family tree, "Eleanor Mary Stewart — m. John Barrett, a butler". But naturally, in her mind she defended his position. He was not an ordinary butler like Carter had been. He had the appearance, speech and manners of a gentleman; it was not his fault that he had not been born into their class. But would she have the courage to say yes, if John ever asked more of her than friendship? Eleanor positively shuddered at the thought of her father's reaction; a Stewart marrying the butler!

Elizabeth and Eric had left before Eleanor arrived home, and her father gone to bed, but her mother, alternately fulminating against Elizabeth and finding excuses for her, talked on and on until Eleanor thought, rather bitterly: because I am the only person who will listen, Mother has said more to me tonight than in a week when she doesn't need me. If I now told her about John she would probably have hysterics, and as for Daddy — no, I could never hurt him so. But how I dread tomorrow. Why should my sister make such trouble? She has a husband, child and home, she should be satisfied.

Chapter 17

Breakfast the following morning, never a light-hearted occasion at any time, was positively funereal. At the head of the table sat Mr Stewart with a louring face and at the other end his wife, looking as though the end of the world was nigh. Edward, as usual, preserved a sullen silence while poor Eleanor, trying to be a peacemaker, met with no response.

'Henry, what shall I do about Elizabeth?' enquired Mrs Stewart, uneasily.

'Do about her! What do you mean do about her?'

'Well, she says that she won't go back to India with Eric — so where will she live?'

'Won't go back, won't go back,' exclaimed Mr Stewart repetitively, as though twice said emphasised his opinion. 'Of course she'll go back, Edith, she's the fellow's wife. She wanted to marry him, it was her own idea, she had a choice.'

'But Henry, Elizabeth says she hates India and military social life; it's too boring and so is Eric. She doesn't want to live with him any longer.'

Mr Stewart, red-faced and spluttering with indignation, rasped, 'Hates India, hates India? She didn't hate it when she came back. She was full of the joys of the social life and all the servants she had to wait on her hand and foot. What does she mean, "bored with him, doesn't want to live with him"? Your daughter is mad.'

Yes, his wife thought resentfully, it's always my daughter, or my son, when they don't meet with your approval. 'Henry, I think — ' but she got no further, for Mr Stewart interrupted grimly, 'If everybody who was bored decided to leave their partners, there would be very few couples left together in my opinion.'

Edward inadvertently tittered at hearing this, but receiving a furious glance from his father, hastily resumed eating.

'What about Eric's army career?' added Mr Stewart. 'How

can he go back to India without his wife? What would the General say? He'd want to know the reason.'

Eleanor said, rather timidly, 'He could say that Elizabeth's health would not stand the climate out there. That she had never been really well since having the baby.'

Her father made no reply at first then, rising abruptly from the table, he growled, 'Oh, settle it among yourselves, I wash my hands of the business. I suppose it counts for nothing that I spent a small fortune launching her into society and another small fortune getting her married. Who does she imagine will keep her now?' and with that he strode from the breakfast-room.

A strained silence followed his departure, then Edward said, 'What is Elizabeth going to live on, and where, if she doesn't go back with Eric? For sure the old man won't give her an allowance. Of course,' he added, maliciously, 'if she was like Eleanor, Elizabeth would have money.'

'Eric will have to support Elizabeth,' said Mrs Stewart, 'He cannot let his wife and child starve.'

'Don't be so melodramatic, Mother,' said Edward sardonically, 'there's no question of starving, but Eric can't be made to support Elizabeth if she leaves him without a good reason. What a happy home this will be if she comes here. Father's welcome will bear no resemblance to the welcome received by the prodigal son, so don't bother to fatten the calf,' and laughing, he too left — though not to work.

Alone with her mother, Eleanor fully expected to hear another long lamentation, but Mrs Stewart merely remarked that she did not know what Lady Farron would think when she heard about Elizabeth wanting to leave her husband.

'She may not find out, Mother, and in any case it's no business of Lady Farron's.'

'Find out? Of course she'll find out! If Elizabeth comes here we can't hide her out of sight. Yes, you can clear breakfast,' this to the parlourmaid who had just entered.

Later that morning, while the staff were having their elevenses of cocoa, bread and cheese, Maud said, 'When I went into the breakfast room to clear, Madam was saying something about Lady Farron finding out about Miss Elizabeth.'

'Oh, she'll find out all right,' said the chauffeur. 'If Pinkerton's employed her she'd be their best agent. Sid West, her chauffeur, swears she writes everything down in a little notebook.'

'Madam never said a word to me about it when she came into the kitchen,' said Mrs Trouson. 'And of course it's not my place to mention Madam's trouble. I feel sorry for the poor baby; he is going to be deserted by one parent — perhaps both if he goes to Mr Markham's mother.'

'Well he won't have to go to an orphanage like me and my sisters,' said the kitchenmaid.

Mrs Trouson, giving her a severe look, said sharply, 'There's no call for you to compare yourself with the baby. Your mother came from a different class altogether.'

'Ah, it reminds me of when I was under-gardner down in Somerset,' said the gardener.

Cook thought, irritably, why does any event that happens in this house always remind Daniel Oates of where he's worked? Two days a week he comes here and he seems to imagine it gives him a licence to say what he likes. And I'm sure he makes up half of it.

Daniel Oates, unaware of Cook's annoyance, went on with his tale of down Somerset way. 'Madam's youngest daughter, the prettiest gal you could set your eyes on, but a terrible flirt, married young Alec Welling, son of the Lord of the Manor. He worshipped the ground she walked on but that Isabella led him a fine old dance. Course, young Welling didn't think she meant any harm like, but they 'adn't been married above a year when she ups and elopes with the young chap what taught her to play the piano. That young Welling went into a decline like, wouldn't eat and he died of a broken heart.'

This sad story evoking no expressions of concern from the staff, Cook said, grimly, 'I see no comparison with what is happening here. There is no other man —'

'As far as we know,' murmured the chauffeur.

'— and I'm certain that Mr Markham will behave like a gentleman.'

'Is going into a decline not behaving like a gentleman, then?' enquired the chauffeur.

'You know what I mean, Mr Seymour,' coolly replied Cook.

'All I say is,' said the head-housemaid, 'if I was Miss Elizabeth I wouldn't come back here to live. With a couple of parents like them up there criticising and watching, she might as well be in prison.'

'Lily, how can you talk like that!' exclaimed the lady's-maid. 'I'm sure Madam will do all she can to make this a real home for her daughter.'

Lily gave an audible sniff and, as she explained later to her friend, Etta: 'I had a job to keep from laughing, that Dorise talks so daft. I felt like telling her to hang a few of her texts in Elizabeth's bedroom; especially the one that reads, "Resist the devil and he will flee from you".'

'What does John Barrett have to say about the goings-on?' asked Etta. 'Plenty I bet.'

'Well, that's strange, Etta; he seems to take no interest and makes no comment. Old Mother Trouson gives it as her opinion that Mr Barrett is too much of a gentleman to discuss the affairs of his employers. But I reckon that's all my eye and Fanny Martin. I can't help feeling he's got something on his mind, but what is it? Perhaps he's thinking of you, Etta. He often talks about how pretty you are.'

'He can forget all about me, Lil. Lance is coming back, I had a letter from him two days ago.'

'He never is, Etta! What, after all this time. When will he be back? Why is he coming? What does he say?'

'Hold on Lil, one question at a time. He's coming back partly because the friends who were living in his house in Chelsea are going to America, so Lance wants to arrange to sell the house, and partly because he is shipping over from Florence some of his paintings for an exhibition. He is going to stay with his friends next door to where he lived. I'll go to see him in about a month's time.'

'Has he mentioned in the letter about you meeting him again, Etta?'

'Well, he hasn't exactly arranged a time Lil, but I shall go round to the house.'

'Etta! you can't do that unless you are invited. Suppose he

doesn't want to see you? After all he's been away — how long is it now, must be four years.'

'Oh Lil, you are daft. Of course he'll want to see me. Why would he have written to me during those years if he wasn't intending to meet me again? I wonder if he'll think I'm different? Of course I'm older now and more sensible. I've read a great many books and gone to art galleries and museums so I know quite a bit about antiques and pictures. Anyway, don't let's talk about him now Lil. How are you getting on with Mr Seymour's brother — or is it all "off"?'

'It was never really on, Etta,' said Lil, moodily. 'Not what you'd call permanent-like.'

'Give him a chance, Lil, it's only a few weeks since you met him. You can't expect a declaration of undying love in that little time. At least he's got a job now.'

'Yes, I know, but I didn't see him last week 'cause he said it was his shift. But how do I know if he isn't having me on? He's moved out from Mr Seymour's place, gone into lodgings, and his landlady's got a daughter younger than me. You know what chaps are like — "out of sight is out of mind".'

'Cheer up, Lil. I say, why don't we go to that place for tea where John took me, the Trocadero. I saw a lot of women on their own there, it's a very respectable place. Course, it's not like Joe Lyons, you can't pick up a young man. I'll treat you as I'm quite well off for money. I will say that about Mr Munson, our butler. When we have a dinner-party and there's tips being given, he always hands me a share; not all butlers are so fair . . . Then we'll go to the Roxy — they're showing an old film, Douglas Fairbanks in *The Thief of Baghdad* — and when we come out of there let's go into that nice pub, The Crown, and have a couple of glasses of port. Let's live in style,' and laughing, the two friends went along, arm in arm, determined, if only temporarily, to forget about their respective love hopes.

Later on that evening in her bedroom Lily thought: after all this time Etta is still in love with that artist chap. How her eyes sparkled when she spoke about him coming back here. I can't think what she sees in him, he must be getting on for fifty. Course, he's got money but I'm sure he's not rolling in it.

'Sides, it's not because of his money that Etta is so soppy about him, I'm sure of that. Wish I had her good looks, those lovely eyes with sweeping lashes and her beautiful hair. I bet if I looked like she does I wouldn't have to worry about the landlady's daughter ... Who's that knocking on the door?

When she unlocked it Maud was standing outside. 'D'you always lock your bedroom door, Lil?'

'You bet I do. I wouldn't feel safe sleeping in my bed with the door unlocked.'

'Well, I don't know who you imagine is going to assault you in this house, or any of us come to that. 'Sides, wouldn't they start on Cook first, she's nearest? I pity any burglar that started on her, he couldn't know what had hit him.'

'What did you want Maud? Couldn't you have told me whatever it was before I went to bed.'

'No, I couldn't Lil, 'cause it hadn't happened then.'

'What on earth do you mean? What hadn't happened?'

'Well Lil, I'd undressed and I was just getting into bed when I realised I'd left my reading glasses in our sitting-room. So I crept down the backstairs and had just started to open the door into the hall when who should come out of the little morning-room but Mr Barrett. And he acted so funny, like. He peered to right and left, looked up the main stairs then swiftly went through the baize door to the basement.'

'I wonder what he was doing in there so late in the evening? Still, Maud, I can't see that it was important enough for you to come knocking on my door.'

'Ah Lil, you haven't heard the half yet,' said Maud, with barely suppressed excitement. 'Before I could close the door to go back upstairs — I wasn't going downstairs with him still around and me in my dressing-gown — who should come out of the room? Well, you'll never guess, Lil.'

'Come on, hurry up and tell me who it was.'

'Miss Eleanor, Lil. And she too gave a quick look round and her hair was all rumpled-like. Whatever does it mean?'

'Maud, you're not suggesting that our butler and Miss Eleanor were up to something?' said Lil, incredulously.

'Why were they in that room then, Lil? After all, Mr Barrett is real handsome and speaks so refined, like.'

'No, I can't believe there was something going on, Maud. Not with Miss Eleanor. Now if it had been her sister I wouldn't have been surprised. But Miss Eleanor would never stoop to familiarity with a butler. Anyway, Maud, let us keep it to ourselves and don't breathe a word in Mr Barrett's hearing.'

'Right-o Lil, I agree. But I'll keep my eyes open when we're in the breakfast-room to see if I can spot anything. By the way, while you were out this afternoon Mr Seymour and Cook had quite a shindy at teatime. It was Dorise that started it off. You know how she will bring religion into her conversation; she means well but it does get irritating. Well she was on about this faith-healer, how marvellous he is and how faith can move mountains when suddenly Mr Seymour interrupted her by saying, "Has he ever moved one?" "Moved what?" said Dorise. "Moved a mountain." "Of course not, why would he want to?" Mr Seymour gave a kind of jeering laugh and said, "Well, until his faith can move a mountain, spare us the eulogies." Poor old Dorise was upset and the tears came into her eyes but she never said a word. But Mrs Trouson did, several words in fact. She glared at the chauffeur and said, sternly, "Mr Seymour, no gentleman would speak so rudely to a lady. I suggest that you either apologise or in future have your tea in your home." '

'Did he apologise?'

'He did not, Lil. After telling Cook that he knew two other servants' halls where he was always welcome, that in fact he was doing her a favour in gracing ours with his presence, he slowly finished his cup of tea, removed the last piece of cake, and walked out. I didn't dare look at Grace and Flora in case we all burst out laughing.'

'Very funny, Maud, and now you just walk off to bed. I'll be fit for nothing in the morning.'

'Me too, Lil, and it's Madam's At Home day. Still I'll not miss any signs at breakfast I can tell you. Anything for a bit of life, upstairs or down, that's my motto. All right, Lil, I'm going. But I still wonder what was going on in the morning-room.'

Downstairs, in his basement bedroom, John Barrett—

unaware that he had been seen by the parlourmaid — was sitting on his bed thinking what a lucky chance it was, that hearing a slight noise overhead, and knowing that everybody had retired for the night, he went upstairs to investigate. He'd looked into the dining- and breakfast-rooms, then opened the door of the little morning-room, and found Eleanor sitting at the desk, apparently writing. He'd entered the room, closed the door — and even now he wasn't sure whether Eleanor came over to him or he moved over to the desk — but without conscious volition, he had his arms around her and they were kissing. He was pleasantly surprised that Eleanor, who presumably had negligible experience of physical ardour with the opposite sex, kissed him with considerable feeling. Then, without either of them saying a word, she had indicated that he must go. Now here he was, full of satisfaction that he'd reached a watershed in his campaign.

As for Eleanor, she was so bemused that she had only a vague idea of how she'd reach her bedroom. The nearest she had ever been to a love affair was as an eighteen-year-old, when she and Elizabeth had spent two weeks with Aunt Irene, whose eldest son, just home from university was, in Eleanor's opinion, like a Greek god. She promptly fell in love with him and he had seemed to like her company — he said that she was soothing. Alas, after meeting a Mademoiselle Lucille at the local tennis club, the Greek god Oliver shewed less and less inclination to be soothed, and as Eleanor could not compete with Lucille in looks or tennis prowess, she quickly faded from his life. But now she was older, a mature woman who'd accepted her plainness, her inability to enjoy the social whirl that so delighted her sister. She had not been unhappy for she had her painting, her father's affection and of late, with Penelope Courtland's help, she had found a new confidence in being able to speak for and help those low in the social scale. Never had she expected to find love; and have that love returned. Of course she and John could never marry; it was impossible to renounce her family. Above all, there was her father — she could not repay his kindness, encouragement and affection by such a rejection of all his values. He would never understand that in everything but high birth, John was a gentleman. Kind, thoughtful, gentle, well-mannered and ah, so handsome; how could she help loving him? She must be careful not to give herself away at breakfast, she thought, for her mother had a sharp eye.

Chapter 18

If the parlourmaid was expecting anything out of the ordinary to happen in the breakfast-room, she was disappointed; the only variation from usual being that after Mr Stewart had read his letters, instead of placing them by the side of his plate and going on with his breakfast, he rang the bell. When the butler appeared Mr Stewart said, 'Barrett, tell Master Edward that I wish to speak to him in my study.'

'Master Edward is not at home, sir.'

'Not at home so early in the morning. Where the devil is he, Edith?'

'He has gone down to Guildford for the day, Henry. He wanted to catch the early train. He said he would be back about six o'clock.'

'If he returns before I get home he is to wait for me. Give him that message, Barrett.'

'Very good, sir.'

'What is it Henry? Why do you want to speak to Edward? Has something happened?'

'Nothing that I care to discuss at the moment, Edith. You will know all about it soon enough.'

After he had gathered his letters and departed, Mrs Stewart gazed uneasily at Eleanor.

'I wonder why your father particularly desires to speak to Edward. Why couldn't he have spoken last night, after dinner? It must be something to do with one of his letters this morning.'

'I wouldn't worry, Mother. Father didn't appear to be angry. Maybe father has news of an opening for Edward.'

'I understand your father better than you do, Eleanor. I know what that cold silence can portend. He made all that noisy to-do about Elizabeth,' — more than a to-do, thought Eleanor — 'but that's over and your father will make no other objections if she wants to live here. But his silence is to be dreaded, for that is when your father is so angry he cannot even speak.'

'Well, Mother, apart from the fact that he is not working, Edward has done nothing to arouse Father's anger. Maybe it was a business affair that upset him?' and as Eleanor, unaware of any reprehensible action of Edward's, chatted on about the weather and her mother's At Home Mrs Stewart, who had never ceased to be uneasy about her son, became increasingly irritable and at last exclaimed, crushingly, 'You know nothing about it, nothing at all,' and angrily departed upstairs.

Eleanor, having often experienced her mother's displeasure, was not unduly perturbed, apart from wondering of what she was ignorant.

Below stairs, with the kitchenmaid banished to the scullery, the butler and cook were having a private conversation about the vagaries of them above.

'I could see that Madam was ever so worried when she came down this morning,' said Cook, 'As a rule, when it's Madam's At Home day she goes on about what sort of cakes and biscuits she requires; but this time I had to ask her and all Madam said — and I could tell she had something else on her mind — all Madam said was, "I leave it to you, Cook, you know what we generally have." I suppose she's upset about Miss Elizabeth.'

'I don't think it's altogether that, Mrs Trouson. I'm sure it's to do with Master Edward. When I answered the breakfast room bell this morning, Mr Stewart said he wished to see Master Edward in his study. He was right put out when I had to tell him that his son had already left the house to catch an early train. When he comes back my orders are to tell him he is not to leave the house before his father returns. I wonder what he's been up to,' and the butler displayed pleasure rather than concern at the possibility of Master Edward being in trouble

'Ah, Mr Barrett,' said Cook, lugubriously, 'the times are now so different from when I was a young girl. Then everybody knew their place, high and low. When I was a kitchenmaid, unless I was asked — which was rarely I can tell you — I would never have dared to offer an opinion to any of the upper servants. Nowadays' — this with a sharp glance in the direction of the scullery — 'people think they know everything and are fully entitled to say so. They respect neither their elders or their employers. I have cooked for some of the highest in the land' — what are you doing here then? thought the butler — 'and I can assure you, Mr Barrett, they were lovely people to work for. Except for me, all the staff were called by their Christian names, because m'Lady knew the servants would never become familiar. Yes, things were far different in those days.'

That afternoon some such thoughts were occurring to Mrs Stewart as, over the rattle of the tea-cups, she could hear snatches of conversation. Her immediate neighbour was talking of Hitler, comparing him to a modern Napoleon; further off she could hear birth-control clinics mentioned and old Colonel Locker in the far corner was trumpeting his opinion of the Spanish Civil War: 'all Fascists should be stood against a wall and shot.'

Oh dear, mused Mrs Stewart, dear Mama's At Homes were such pleasant occasions. We would talk about tennis-parties, picnics, Goodwood and Ascot, Paris and fashions. We were all so well brought up, so polite, we all moved in the right circles. We discussed the latest books from Mudies — Mama approved of Mrs Humphrey Ward, Rhoda Broughton and Mrs Henry Wood. Mama's principles would not let George Eliot into the house — Mama never knew I used to read her in secret. All one hears of nowadays is that dreadful Faulkner man or Hemingway, always writing about the bad side of life as though there was no beauty or love in the world ... But uppermost in her thoughts was the problem of Henry and Edward; she hoped fervently that Edward would arrive home before Henry. At five-thirty, when the last guest had departed, she told the parlourmaid that when Master Edward returned he was to go straight to the drawing-room.

Some fifteen minutes later, when he came into the drawing-room, she greeted him with a cry of relief, 'Thank heaven you are back before your father.'

'Why, what has happened? Has Elizabeth run off with the milkman?'

'Don't be facetious, Edward,' said his mother, sharply, 'I want to talk to you seriously. At breakfast time your father, as usual, received several letters, and after reading one of them he folded it up, put it back in the envelope, spoke not a word but pressed the bell. When Barrett apeared, your father simply said, "Tell Master Edward that I wish to speak to him in my study." He also gave a message to the effect that you were not to leave the house before he returned. What does it all mean? Have you got into more trouble?'

'Of course not, Mother, what a stupid question. How the hell do I know what the old man wants me for?'

'Edward, I forbid you to use such language in this house. You are speaking to your mother. And do sit down.'

With a muttered apology Edward sat down on the edge of the chair with the evident intention of leaving the room at the earliest opportunity.

'It's no use looking like that Edward. What about that girl, that Parks person? You have not had more trouble with her?'

Reluctantly Edward explained that the harpy, with the excuse that she'd lost her job and needed to convalesce before seeking another, had demanded more money—'I told you that's how it would be,' interrupted Mrs Stewart—and, having talked to Victor Trentham (God knows he's had women in plenty so he knows how to deal with them), Victor had met Norma, settled on a last payment of one hundred pounds and threatened her with what she would get if she ever asked for more. The money had not yet been given because Victor, who had agreed to hand it over, was out of town for a few days.

At the end of this unsavoury tale Mrs Stewart asked, 'Where did you expect to find one hundred pounds?'

Sullenly Edward admitted that he intended to ask Eleanor for it.

'Ask your sister for money!' exclaimed his mother. 'What reason will you give? You can hardly explain that the money is required to help a girl recover from an ab—miscarriage.'

'Eleanor won't ask why I need it, but if she does I shall say it's for a gambling debt. Anyway, now she's taken up with helping the lower classes, she can help this one. You can't get much lower than that female.'

'Oh Edward my dear, it is all so sordid. But do you think she has written to your father? Was all that in the letter this morning? Whatever will happen if your father knows about the business?'

'Why would she write to Father? She knows I'll give her the money eventually.'

'I don't know, my dear, but I feel so nervous,' and poor Mrs Stewart gave a heavy sigh. It was not only the sordidness of the affair; she, who had given her son as much affection as her wintry heart allowed, was grieved to discover that this affection counted for very little in his life. She thought, rather bitterly, we were all a comfort to Mama, but none of my children really care about me. Elizabeth couldn't wait to get married and leave home and Eleanor leads her own life, she cares only for her father. I believe he is really glad that Eleanor never married, will never leave home. Henry probably envisages her as being a comfort to him in his old age, like that Mary Jocelyn, in *The Rector's Daughter.* Mrs Stewart did not care to consider the indifference and rebuffs that Eleanor had received from her, she felt only a certain indignation at her husband's obvious preference for his eldest daughter.

While she thus sat and thought, Edward went to his room outwardly unperturbed, but inwardly feeling disquiet; knowing from past experience that any tête-à-tête with his father was bound to have unpleasant repercussions. As indeed did this when, some half-hour later, his father confronted him in the study with a letter in his hand, demanding to know what it meant, and was it the truth? He thrust the letter in front of Edward's face.

The letter, crudely printed on cheap paper, read: You may be interested to know that your son is being blackmailed by a young woman he got into trouble. Her name is Norma Parks and she lives in Kilburn.

Edward was stunned on reading the words. Who could have sent it? Not Norma surely, why would she after he'd promised her more money? Who knew about her besides Victor — he could be trusted. Could it have been that awful friend, that Cissy Clegg? From what he'd heard about her she'd meddle in anybody's business. But sending this letter would certainly not help her friend Norma.

'Well,' his father barked, 'don't stand there like a fool. Is there any truth in this disgusting stuff?'

Red-faced and stammering, knowing that it was useless to deny the accusation because his father would not let it rest, Edward had to confess that it was true.

Mr Stewart, contrary to his son's expectation, did not rant and rave; if anything he became quieter, though to Edward's apprehension, his father became more menacing on that account. He demanded a full account of the affair but, when Edward reached the two hundred pounds his father interrupted, 'Where did you acquire two hundred pounds?'

Weak-willed and lacking in morals, Edward yet retained some decency. He knew full well how invidious it would be for his mother if he admitted that she had borrowed the money from Eleanor. So he muttered sullenly that he had borrowed from a money-lender.

'On what security? My name, I suppose? And how did you propose to repay the money?'

'I have kept up the interest from my allowance.'

'Which ceases forthwith, I can assure you. A son of mine messing about with a common girl like that and getting mixed-up in a filthy abortion.'

After further execration of his son's conduct, Mr Stewart asked for Norma Parks' address, saying he knew her type, he'd soon put a stop to any further extortion. 'And now,' he proclaimed, with such a look and manner as would have intimidated even a more courageous person than his son, 'there is an end to the kind of life you have been enjoying. An end to race-going, dancing and night-clubbing. From next Monday you work in the business. You start at the bottom, you will get no favours, you will work the same hours as the rest of my staff. That's all I have to say. You can go now.'

While all this was going on Mr Barrett and Maud, putting the finishing touches to the dining-table, were conscious of footsteps pacing up and down in the study overhead.

'Whatever does it mean, Mr Barrett?' whispered Maud. 'Mr Stewart and Master Edward up there — do you think there'll be any dinner tonight?'

'As far as we know, Maud, there is no reason why dinner is

not as usual; Mrs Trouson has received no orders to cancel it.'

Mrs Stewart, alone in the drawing-room adjoining her husband's study was too agitated to remain still; she too was pacing up and down the room, though less forcefully than her husband next door. Would they never be finished, what had happened? Many times she quietly opened the door but however hard she listened it was impossible to hear a word of the conversation. At last she heard the study door open and somebody went upstairs. Was it Edward, or Henry? Softly she opened the door again just as her husband left the study. With an expressionless face he looked at her, spoke not a word and went up to his bedroom. She did not dare to follow him or to go to Edward's room but, consumed with longing to speak to somebody, she knocked on Eleanor's door and went in.

'Mother, what is the matter, are you feeling ill? Shall I ring for Collett?'

'No, I am not ill. I am upset about your father and Edward. They were shut up in the study.'

'But why, Mother? Edward and Father have had differences before this; it always blows over. You are worried about the letter Daddy received this morning; perhaps it was nothing to do with Edward.'

How dense she is, thought Mrs Stewart. Elizabeth would have realised by now that something more serious than a peccadillo was being discussed. I suppose Eleanor is so naive because she's had little contact with men. Then, feeling that she must be able to talk about the situation, she disclosed to Eleanor the reason why she had borrowed two hundred pounds and her fears that, once a girl like that got hold of money, she would regard Edward as a never-ending supply. Women like that had no scruples over ruining a man. Poor dear Edward had no experience of that kind of person.

Mrs Stewart expected her daughter to be shocked and express commiseration for her brother's misfortune, but Eleanor felt neither the one nor the other. As regards unwanted babies, she had heard many a lurid tale from some of the overburdened women at the F.D.W. meetings, and for her brother she felt only contempt. She thought, Mother considers no blame attaches to Edwad, she looks upon him as the victim, not the girl. Inevitably Eleanor's thoughts went to John Barrett, how different he was to such as her brother. John had respect for women . . .

Lost in such daydreams of John as would have made him smile at her ignorance, Eleanor had forgotten her mother's presence until, 'What do you think about it Eleanor? I am sorry I could not tell you the reason why I needed to borrow from you. But you will get the money back eventually.'

Why tell me now? thought Eleanor, I have no sympathy for my brother, I'm sorry for the girl. Aloud she said, 'It doesn't matter about the money except that I hope he gave it to the girl. Anyway, Mother, it is not certain that Father knows.'

Giving her a sharp look Mrs Stewart said dejectedly, 'I fear that he does and that is why he is so quiet. If it was his usual annoyance with Edward, we would hear your father's voice from the top of the house to the bottom. I must go and dress for dinner though I dread sitting through the meal.'

Retiring to her boudoir and ringing for Collett to dress her hair Mrs Stewart thought; Eleanor does not care in the least about her brother; she shewed no concern at all that he might be in serious trouble. And Mrs Stewart resented her daughter's unconcern, ignoring the fact that Edward had consistently shown dislike of his sister and belittled her artistic talent.

Shut in his bedroom Edward suffered almost a physical collapse after his ordeal. However, a liberal tot of brandy soon restored him and he began to reflect — though too late — on all that he could have said in his own defence. He thought, why does father have this paralysing effect on me? I am no longer a child, I should be able to retaliate. What a stupid man is father, a reactionary if ever there was one, like one of those Victorian papas who were models of rectitude and martinets in the home. Nobody has any affection for Father, I'm sure mother does not, they lead separate lives. Well, Eleanor does of course, but she's got nobody else to care about. Then Edward felt relief because the problem of that avaricious Norma was settled, his father would make short work of her ambitions. But who could have sent that letter to the old man? It couldn't have been Norma, not after she'd been promised another one hundred pounds.

Dinner was certainly a dismal affair exacerbated by the difficulty of appearing normal before the servants. Such conversation as there was when the butler and parlourmaid were in the room, was between Mr Stewart and Eleanor and included such innocuous subjects as her water-colours and the recent Pre-Raphaelite exhibition. When dinner was over Mr Stewart ordered coffee to be sent to his study, Eleanor—pleading a headache—retired to her bedroom and Edward and his mother to the drawing-room. As soon as Barrett had served the coffee Mrs Stewart, hardly waiting for the door to close, exclaimed, 'What happened? What were you talking about in the study? Was it the letter? I was so worried because your father spoke never a word to me.'

Edward started a recital of the conversation when his mother interrupted, 'But the money, Edward, the two hundred pounds. Does your father know it came from Eleanor?'

'Of course not, Mother. I told the old man I'd borrowed it from a money-lender. Father expects me to pay it back from the meagre salary I'm to have working for him. The old man was consumed with rage, and I shudder to imagine his reaction if he knew the money was borrowed from his pet.'

'So you are really going to work for the firm?'

'Got to, Mother, the Great Panjandrum himself has given the order,' said Edward, facetiously. 'The old man doesn't know it but I may soon be clearing out. Reece—the chap I went to see in Guildford—is starting up in antiques. He said there's money in it if you know the ropes, and he reckons he does, he's got the eye. There're dozens of country cottages full of old stuff and the owners have no idea it's worth money. Reece says, offer them a tenner and they'll think, "a tenner for Grandma's old china dogs, the man must be a fool", and in no time they thrust other objects at you. Reece will spot the bargains, and I will impress the rustics with my public school accent,' and Edward smiled, complacently.

His mother, her voice expressing some anxiety, said, 'But Edward, is it a legitimate business? How well do you know this man, Reece? Is he honest?'

'Of course it is legitimate, Mother.' Impatiently he got up from the chair thinking, parents are the limit, they live in the past. Life is different now, it's every man for himself.

'Edward dear, you are not going out this evening, are you?'

'Why not this evening, Mother? If I'm to be immured in an office from next week, I might as well use what little freedom I have left for pleasure. Oh don't look so tragic, I shall be home early tonight before the authoritarian retires.'

Ringing for the butler to remove the coffee tray Mrs Stewart enquired, 'Do you know if the Master is going out this evening Barrett?'

'I think not, Madam. He told Seymour that he would not require him this evening and when I removed the coffee tray, the Master said he did not wish to be disturbed.'

Mrs Stewart hesitated whether or not she should disturb him, but misgivings about her reception, especially when the subject was Edward, made her decide against invading Henry's sanctum. She wished that Elizabeth was at home; one could talk to her without feeling one was being judged.

Down in the basement the events above stairs were being discussed at great length, especially as the chauffeur was absent — Mr Barrett knew that he would not be subject to derisive remarks.

Supper over and cups of tea being handed round by Grace and Flora, Cook remarked, 'I wonder what really happened up there, Mr Barrett.'

'Something quite serious I fear, Mrs Trouson. Madam looked really upset at the dinner-table and the only conversation while Maud and I were in the room was between Mr Stewart and Miss Eleanor. Could you hear anything that was spoken in the study, Dorise or Lily?'

'I never heard a word although I was on the landing above,' said Lily. 'Madam opened the drawing-room door two or three times, I suppose she was worried about her precious Edward. I say, serve him right if he's in a bit of trouble. He's got no manners at all. Yesterday morning, when Flora was brushing the staircarpet and he wanted to come down, d'you think he'd pass her on the stairs? No, not him. Flora had to walk down to the bottom before he'd step on the stairs — just as though she had some contagious disease.'

'When I did Madam's hair this evening I was ever so

surprised,' said the lady's-maid. 'As a rule Madam never talks at all, except to say what she will wear, but this evening she said to me, "Collett, do you ever think of getting married?" My face went as red as a tomato and I kind of stammered, "Oh dear no Madam, nothing like that has crossed my mind."'

'What did Madam say to that?' asked Mrs Trouson.

'She looked at me quite hard and then she said, "Very wise Collett, very wise indeed." Wasn't it a strange thing to say? It's not as though Madam has the habit of talking like that to me. Now in my last place — before I had to leave to look after mother — my madam there used to treat me almost as one of the family and tell me all her troubles.'

'Well, you'll never be treated as one of the family in this house, I can assure you,' said Lily, dryly, 'so if I was you, I wouldn't discuss anything about matrimony when you do Madam's hair thinking that she's interested in the subject.'

'Oh, I would not dream of doing such a thing,' protested Dorise. 'I know my place I hope.'

'I feel sorry for poor Miss Eleanor,' said Cook, assuming the sentimental voice reserved for mention of her. 'First there was the trouble with Miss Elizabeth and now Master Edward. It can't be a very cheerful atmosphere up there.'

'At least Miss Eleanor has her painting and her F.D.W. meetings; she's not dependent on her family,' said Mr Barrett. And she has me too, he thought, and one day they will all know it.

'I wonder if the trouble is anything to do with that girl Master Edward was with. You remember, Mrs Trouson, Mr Carter said he saw them in Oxford Street and the girl looked tarted-up and common.'

'That reminds me, Lily. Lady Farron's butler, Mr Penfold, called here this afternoon. He'd had a letter from Mr Carter and Alice and they asked him to let us know that they are doing fine out there. If we'd like to join him, his brother would employ us like a shot. It's a lovely climate, the Australians are "fair dinkum" — whatever that's supposed to mean — and everybody is equal. He and Alice wouldn't come back to Britain not for all the tea in China.'

'That goes without saying,' said Lily, laughing, 'being as Mr Carter much preferred to drink coffee.'

'For my part,' said Cook, impressively, 'I wouldn't care to be in a place where everybody is equal, if it is true which I take leave to doubt. It stands to reason that some people are better than others; either because they were born that way or they have become so by leading the right kind of life. Don't you agree, Mr Barrett?'

'I agree to the extent that Australians cannot all be equal in brains and position. If they were who would do the dull manual jobs. They must have postmen, dustmen and so on out there, employed by the government. They can't be equal, otherwise they'd be the government.'

'That's just what I mean,' and Cook smiled on the butler, though it certainly was not what she had said.

'When me and my sisters were in the orphanage,' said the kitchenmaid, 'we always had to go to Sunday School and we often sang a hymn, "There's a crown for little children, above the bright blue sky", and one day my sister said, out loud, "Is the crown only for children, no big people?" Teacher was cross and she snapped, "Of course it was not only for children, everybody was equal in heaven and would all get a crown" and our Jeannie said, "Jesus must have a lot of money, then".'

This artless tale occasioned loud mirth from Mr Barrett, Lily, Maud and Flora but disapproving frowns from Mrs Trouson and Dorise. Cook never could, or would become accustomed to a kitchenmaid who 'spoke out of turn', this meaning a kitchenmaid who spoke at all, unless invited to do so.

Before Grace could receive a reprimand, Lily hastily interposed with, 'The conversation has come a long way from Master Edward and whether or no it's to do with that girl. I don't suppose we shall ever find out.'

Retiring to his bedroom the butler thought with glee: I shall find out because Eleanor will tell me, though of course I'll not be able to disclose the information to the staff. And he recited, 'The Master, Madam, Master Edward, Miss Elizabeth,' for the sheer pleasure of knowing that the day would come when these appellations would cease to be said by him — so sure he was of Eleanor's heart and money.

Upstairs in the attics, before Dorise shut her bedroom door, Lily said, 'Why did you have to look so straight-faced when Grace was telling us about her sister? She wasn't mocking religion; it was the sort of thing a child would say; especially a child with no home or parents.'

Dorise, looking rather abashed, answered, 'Mrs Trouson wasn't amused.'

'Oh her! If a Cheshire cat sat and grinned in front of her, she wouldn't be amused. Besides, it wasn't what Grace said that annoyed her, it was the fact that she spoke at all.'

Afterwards, in Maud's room, Lily said that probably she would give in her notice in the near future, she was getting fed-up.

'There's not much fun here, Maud. I know that old Horace and Alice weren't exactly the "life and soul of the party" types, but at least Alice could laugh at a joke. Mr Barrett's all right, but you can't deny that there's not much fun attached to him.'

'Too true, Lil. Mind you, he's all right to work with, not half as fussy as old Horace.'

'You know, Maud, I wouldn't say so in front of Cook, 'cause she's not the type you can be matey with, but when Mrs Stewart and that Edward were having coffee, I did hear odd bits of their conversation while I was hovering on the stairs. I think he's got to start working for his father cause his father's cut up rough about something.'

'Well, that won't kill him, Lil. You and I have been working for years. Not but what I'd pack it in like a shot if I could find a chap that wanted to marry me. How you getting on with that Don?'

'That's just it, Maud, I'm not,' said Lily, gloomily. 'I recokon it's my own fault, I'm always the same. I know that it's fatal to be like it, but a chap's only got to fancy me and immediately I see myself walking up the aisle a vision in white, wedding bells ringing and a ring on my finger. I don't give them time enough to get to really know me before I start talking about the patter of tiny feet. Very soon I can hear the patter of their boots departing rapidly.'

Maud could not refrain from laughing, in which Lily joined, albeit ruefully.

'I say, Lil, would you fancy going out to Australia to work? Old Horace told us there's ever so many more men than girls. Even a "plain Jane" — which we're not, of course — can get hitched.'

'I reckon not, Maud. Course it would really be something to be able to pick and choose. Just imagine going to a dance and finding more men than girls. No more wallflowers sitting round; no more hanging around in the ladies room on the pretext that one's nose needed a rub over with a *papier poudré*. No more salaaming to some weedy youth who thinks he's a budding Fred Astaire. Still, for all that I wouldn't leave this country.'

'I s'pose you're right, Lil,' and Maud gave a sigh. 'But don't some of those Australians look lovely? Remember that book Horace shewed us with pictures of them men on a sheep farm They were all sun-tanned and looked ever so healthy. I could have fancied any of them.'

'Don't believe all you see, Maud. Those pictures are just to get the likes of you and me out there. It stands to reason not all the men are tall and handsome, they weren't when they emigrated. Take old Horace for instance, can you imagine him looking like those pictures in that magazine? Not likely you can't. 'Sides,' added Lil, laughing, 'who wants to be stuck on a farm, with a lot of smelly sheep, miles from anywhere? Your chap wouldn't be much of a Romeo by the time he got back at night. It's not likely they got bathrooms and all out in the back of the country, and he certainly won't sing any "songs of Araby" to you and gently entice you to share his tent.'

Endeavouring to stifle her laughter, Maud said, 'I'll tell you what, Lil, are you seeing your friend Etta this Sunday? You're not? Then I'll take you to a party. My cousin Queenie is getting engaged and as her fiancé works in a pub there's bound to be a few unattached fellows there. When my aunt wrote and invited me, I thought well, if Queenie can snaffle a man there's hopes for me yet. Honestly Lil, she's got hair as straight as a yard-of-pump-water, two currants for eyes and as sure as I'm sitting here, Lil, last summer when we went to Southend for the day and she was floating on her back in the sea, people thought it was a whale and they all rushed out of the water.'

Amid giggles Lily, feeling more cheerful, went off to bed thinking, I bet there's nobody laughing on the floor below.

Chapter 19

How right Lily was in her supposition that there was no laughter above stairs, was further demonstrated in the ensuing weeks by the air of gloom which pervaded the house; so much so that, as Lily remarked, one felt as though a funeral was imminent, the blinds waiting to be lowered and obsequies already determined.

Mr Stewart, never noted for his contribution to the small talk of breakfast and dinner, now in the evening either retired to his study or club. Edward, going sullenly to work and arriving back home even later than his father, complained bitterly to his mother that the nature of his work in the office was such as any ignoramus could do and boring in the extreme. At weekends he departed to see his friend Foxy Reece and confided to his mother that any week now he would be off. Reece was looking for a shop with a flat overhead from where they could sally forth to look for bargains in antiques. As soon as Victor Trentham returned to town, Edward had sought him out to explain that no further help with Norma Parks was necessary. He had no idea, and never would know, that it was Victor Trentham who had sent the anonymous letter to his father. Victor opined it was Cissy Clegg; he considered that such was her spite and hatred towards 'toffs', she would do them an injury even if, in Edward's case, it meant losing out financially. Victor professed sympathy with Edward's predicament, with the fact that he'd now been forced into such an uncongenial occupation. Privately he thought Edward was a ninny. It was all right to have a bit of fun with a girl, she'd only herself to blame if she let a man take advantage of her, but never would he be so idiotic as to give his real name and address. Anyway he, Victor Trentham, had effectively scotched any more of Eleanor's money being borrowed, never to be returned.

Nevertheless, Edward was not quite as simple as he seemed to Victor, for he omitted to disclose his future prospect of joining up with Foxy Reece and making large profits with the minimum of labour.

Fortunately, Mr Stewart's ill-humour was not further exacerbated by the sight of his youngest daughter in the house. Elizabeth had decided to help a widowed schoolfriend run her farm in the Cotswolds. Mrs Stewart, half-wishing for her daughter's company, was yet relieved that Henry would not be subject to a constant reminder of Elizabeth's failed marriage and his inability to make her see the error of her ways. For Mr Stewart had a strong aversion to the idea of a woman leaving her husband, no matter for what reason or however unsatisfactory was the home life. His own marriage coming into that category, Mr Stewart nevertheless would never have sought to change it.

Only Eleanor was unaffected by the discord prevailing for she, ever since that sudden and unexpected embrace in the morning-room, had felt as though life was a dream. At the age of thirty — for she had just celebrated that annniversary — Eleanor had become accustomed to the fact that she never had been pretty and now was even less so; that, as she could never shine at social occasions it was sensible to refuse invitations. Of a modest and retiring disposition, Eleanor exaggerated her plainness, the more so in contrast to her sister's good looks and capacity for lively conversation.

But she had not been unhappy. Although, after her disastrous 'coming-out', her mother's indifference and occasional contempt had been hard to bear, in time she had ceased to notice it, and always there had been her father's affection, and encouragement for her artistic talent.

Now, like a miracle, love had come into her life. She loved, and was loved in return. In vain she told herself that it could come to nothing, that she and dear John could never marry, that all her family traditions were against the very idea of a marriage into the lower class. Besides, how could she hurt her poor father, he would never recover from the blow to his love and pride and certainly would never forgive her? But still she imagined herself and John in a little home of their own and still the memory of that kiss remained to warm her in the privacy of her bedroom.

She and John Barrett had met outside only once since she'd had the temerity to suggest, nay demand, that they should use Christian names whenever they could do so with safety. A week ago, she had used the pretext of a workers' meeting to meet John some few miles from the house. He had insisted on taking her to a quiet little restaurant and paying for the meal. They'd sat at a table that was covered in a red-checked gingham tablecloth, and held hands under the table. John had reproached her for going out with Victor Trentham on two occasions. How delicious it was to be chided by John with his warm and protective manner. She had protested, 'But John, it was only to the Royal Academy to view the exhibition of Parisian artists. Victor, knowing my interest in paintings, offered to take me, and I could not very well refuse his company.'

'But what about the second occasion, Eleanor? I was in the hall when you left with that Victor Trentham and you were smiling up at him and laughing. I felt that you had forgotten about me; I was just a below-stairs butler, not to be thought of in the same breath as a Victor Trentham.'

No such thought had entered John Barrett's head, but he knew, by suggesting to Eleanor that she had hurt his feelings, she would immediately be contrite. As it proved, for Eleanor, tears starting to her eyes, exclaimed, 'Oh John, how could you imagine such a thing? I was laughing because Victor had just made an amusing comment on Cubist art — if one can dignify it by that name.'

'I don't like you mixing with that man, Eleanor. He is a no-good. He keeps the right side of the law but his name has been connected with one or two rather unsavoury affairs. I don't want you falling in love with him.'

'John, I never think of him in that way, he is just an acquaintance. His mother is a friend of my mother, that is all.'

They strolled home in the dark and when, at some distance from the house, John had taken her hand in his, he'd made no attempt to kiss her, although she was longing for him to do so.

But John Barrett knew women — he should do, they had pursued him from early youth — and he knew that a show of restraint was necessary with certain types like Eleanor: shy, nervous and full of emotion. Later that evening lying in bed he thought, I must put pressure on Eleanor, make her agree to marry me, and he smiled complacently, visualising such a change of status. He had complained to Eleanor of the indignities — largely imaginary — that he'd had to suffer; Edward's bare civility and her father's increasing irascibility, finding fault with, 'Barrett, this suit is creased; Barrett, my shoes aren't polished.' He could hardly wait for the day to come when he could tell his employer just what he could do with his suits and shoes. As was only natural, Eleanor had endeavoured to placate him; saying that dear Daddy had much to put up with, Elizabeth and Edward were a great disappointment to him. It was impossible to make her understand how he hated being below-stairs, waiting on them above, standing in the hall to take the guests hats and coats, waiting on them at table. Yes sir-ing and madam-ing. Eleanor had averred it was honest work, a silly statement if ever there was one. Presumably all work was honest unless you were a burglar. Would that count as work, removing people's goods and chattels illegally? And John Barrett thought with pleasure of the last meeting he'd attended of the F.D.W. A huge navvy-type person had stood up in the hall and bellowed that all he wanted was work, work with his bare hands. Not like all those bloody Jacks-in-Offices who lived in luxury and did nothing but work out why a decent working-man couldn't get a job, or those business nobs stuck away in their posh offices who'd give a man the sack if he so much as blew his nose in front of them. John had given Eleanor a quick glance, but of course she never associated dear daddy with such business men. Still, and this surprised him, he liked Eleanor. There was something appealing about her simplicity, her lack of all pretension. Take this affair of her brother's, for instance. Her concern was all for the girl but, in spite of continuous animosity from Edward, she refrained from running down his character; merely said that he was weak-willed and spoilt by his mother. John Barrett mused, Eleanor never mentions her money, I suppose it is all right, she does have it. He'd certainly need to make certain of that before it was too late. What a catastrophe if he married her only to find the ten thousand pounds, far from having increased in the bank, had vanished or never was. Assuredly she would get nothing from her father except maledictions. Ah well, he must get to sleep, ready for another day of 'honest work'. At least there could be no more turmoil above stairs and below would go on in the usual dull manner.

Chapter 20

Contrary to the butler's prediction, things were not destined to go on in the same old way below stairs. For, in the early hours of the morning, Mrs Trouson developed severe internal pains, was rushed to hospital and discovered to be suffering from acute appendicitis. Grace, with the assistance of the lady's-maid who volunteered to help, managed the breakfast for above and below, while Madam, after expressing her sympathy for poor Cook's removal to hospital, sent Eleanor off to the registry office to engage a temporary cook.

'Yes, Miss Stewart,' said the secretary, brightly, 'we have several cooks on our register. Now, let me see,' and she foraged among the correspondence on her desk as though numberless cooks wrote in every day seeking situations that only her agency could provide.

However, it eventually transpired that of the seven cooks on her register, two were still working out their month's notice, three would never take a temporary situation, and one was having a rest. That left only Mrs Annie Dunn whose name was offered, somewhat dubiously, to Eleanor.

'Why not Mrs Dunn?' enquired Eleanor. 'Is she not a good cook?'

'Oh yes, we have had no complaints about her ability to cook, but she is rather old, Miss Stewart.'

'How old?'

'Well, she admits to sixty. But I know she is free now and as it's only temporary would you like me to send her along?'

As a cook was an absolute necessity, Eleanor agreed that her mother would try Mrs Annie Dunn, though when she appeared Mrs Stewart was convinced, such was the ancient and emaciated appearance of this prospective cook, that she too needed hospital treatment.

'I'm as strong as a horse, ma'am,' asserted Annie Dunn. 'I've always been thin and scraggy-like. My old mother — God bless her, taken to his arms she was this day twenty-five years ago — always said, "It ain't a bit of use feeding-up our Annie, a waste of good victuals, cause she never puts on no flesh, she's just a bag of bones." I ain't never changed, ma'am, but I'm as strong as an 'orse.'

Inwardly wincing at this highly coloured description of Mrs Dunn's physical capabilites, when what she needed to know was how well could she cook, Mrs Stewart said, 'The work is not hard here, Mrs Dunn. There is only four in the family and we do not entertain a great deal. You will find Grace, my kitchenmaid, very efficient.'

So, to the subsequent amusement of the staff, Mrs Dunn was installed below stairs as a temporary substitute for Mrs Trouson.

Flora had tided Cook's bedroom and put away all of her knick-knacks, which was just as well as Mrs Dunn seemed to have a motley collection of her own which she distributed around the room.

'Ah, my gal, I never goes nowhere without my bits and pieces,' she told the bemused under-housemaid. This paraphernalia consisted of various photographs — presumably relations — a dressing-table set of bilious green china, several heart-shaped pin cushions and a collection of crest china of which the prize specimen was a dog of incredible ugliness labelled, 'A present from Margate'.

'Everywhere I go I buys myself a bit of crest china,' said Mrs Dunn. 'I reckon I got almost all the seaside towns now. Here, have a look at this two-handled pot, I got it in Southend when I was working in a boarding-house. Course, they calls 'em guest-houses now-a-days — funny kind of guests I say. See what it says on this pot: "Here you will find pot-luck",' and, handing the pot to Flora, Mrs Dunn gave a cackling laugh.

Seeing Flora's bewilderment, she added, 'Cor gal, don't you get the point? Ain't it like the pot you put under the bed, 'cept that it's got two handles?'

Before such vulgarity Flora hastily departed to have a word with the head-housemaid. Lily, although amused at the tale, reckoned that if Mrs Trouson knew what kind of person was occupying her bedroom, she'd want the room fumigated before she used it again.

The kitchenmaid found the temporary cook far more easy-going than Mrs Trouson inasmuch as there were no sharp commands to hurry up, neither did she seem to expect so much waiting on. Also, Mrs Dunn preferred to be addressed as Cook, for, as she explained while they were having supper, 'I never have been legally a Mrs, so I don't want to be called one. Never had much use for men — saving your presence, Mr Barrett and Mr Seymour — 'cause I saw too many of them at home. What with my Dad and four brothers all in the pits it was wash, wash from morning to night. Wore out my poor old Mum it fair did. She passed over twenty-five years ago this day and it was a blessed relief.'

The chauffeur, who owing to his slight disagreement with Mrs Trouson seldom stayed for a meal, said, with mordant humour, 'Who felt the relief, your mother or those she left behind?'

Whereas Mrs Trouson would have taken umbrage at this remark, Mrs Dunn gave a loud laugh and said, 'Oh, Mr Seymour, what a thing to say. Me Ma of course. She had a lovely funeral. My Dad got some money from the Slate Club and we had Ma's death insurance money with the bonuses. The horses had black feathers on the bridles and there were four carriages and ever so many people came to the church. And you should have seen the spread we sat down to; everybody in the village said Ma couldn't have had a better send-off. I was thirty-five then and I was all set to stay and look after me Dad and brothers. The village said Dad was heartbroken but in less than six months he upped and married a young widow only half his age. Gawd knows what she saw in him but she soon had him under her thumb. When I think how my poor Ma slaved over the 'ome and all those men and never said a word, and yet in no time at all this Molly Jenkins — as was — says to my Dad, "You ain't coming the old soldier over me". I heard her say that with my own ears.'

'You never did,' exclaimed Lily, nobly refraining from pointing out that Miss Dunn couldn't have heard it with other ears than her own.

'I did that, gal, and what do you think? You'll never guess what happened next.'

'Don't keep us in suspense, Cook,' murmured the butler.

'Well, that Molly told my Dad she wasn't going to 'ave them sons of his in the home. She'd got enough to do looking after him; they must find lodgings. My Dad let her do it too; ah, she could twist him round her little finger, proper Delilah she was.'

'Perhaps your father was afraid that one of his sons might feel like a Samson to her?' suggested Mr Barrett.

'Eh?' with a look of bewilderment. Then understanding, Cook gave a raucous laugh, 'I never thought of that! Course, I cleared out too; got a job as housekeeper to an old gent and stayed there ten years until he died. I did everything for him, there was only me and the chauffeur.'

'Did he leave you any money, Cook?' enquired the kitchen-maid, feeling free to ask a question.

'Not a blind penny, gal, not a smell of it. I thought I'd have got something but he'd never made a will. The breath was hardly out of the poor old man's body before a pack of relations came down like —'

'Like the Assyrians,' interposed the butler, but Cook, knowing nothing of Byron, went on, '— like they were so eager to pay their last respects, and none of them had come near 'im while he was alive. The chauffeur didn't get nothing either and he'd been with old Mr Hayling ever so long. He had more nerve than me 'cause he told one of the nephews that Mr Hayling had promised him five hundred pounds. It didn't do him no good though 'cause the nephew said, ever so snooty-like, "As my uncle did not leave a will there is no evidence that he intended to leave you anything." And he offered him fifty pounds. Would you believe it — fifty pounds after all those years in Mr Hayling's service.'

'Well, I suppose he got wages ever month,' said Mr Seymour, dryly. 'He wasn't working for nothing.'

'That's true, but still and all I reckon Jack had a right to expect a little nest-egg. Anyway he refused the fifty pounds; Jack said he wouldn't lower himself to accept such a paltry amount.'

'Were you offered the same, Cook?' asked Lily.

'That I was, gal, and I took it too. I says to myself, what's the use of the likes of us being too proud to take the money? Them relations wouldn't have cared, it was just more money in their pockets.'

The staff, much amused, sat around the table listening to Cook's revelations and thought how different she was from Mrs Trouson. For, apart from her frequent references to working for 'the highest in the land' — without ever specifying who they were — Mrs Trouson seldom spoke of her past.

Cook went on, 'The chauffeur, Jack Duncan his name was, suggested why didn't 'im and me get spliced. We could get a job as a married couple or even perhaps as caretakers. He shewed me his Post Office Savings book and he'd got a few hundred in it too. But I says to him straight — course I'd had a few ports at the time — I says, "Thank you Mr Duncan, but in forty-five years I ain't never been in bed with a man and I don't aim to start now." "Ah, Annie", he says, giving me 'and a squeeze, "you don't know what you're missing." "Well," I says to him, "if I'm missing what my Mum got, what sent her to an early grave, an husband an' four great lumps of sons, all I can say is I'll go on missing it." And the nerve of that Jack Duncan, he said, "Well, at our time of life we ain't likely to be having a family." "Our time of life," I says to him, all haughty-like, "you may be knocking sixty, Jack Duncan, but I'm only forty-five. If so be as I felt that way inclined, I could shew a man a thing or two."'

Gratified by the laughter from everybody except the lady's-maid, Cook explained it was then she decided to do temporary work. 'I got myself a room and furnished it with a bed and a few other bits so I have somewhere to stay in between jobs. I like doing temporary work, there's more freedom to do as you like cause the ladies are so thankful to get a cook in an emergency. Last job I had before this one I was there three months; the old lady had a job to keep servants, she was a bit queer in the head like. She wouldn't have a man in the house; parlourmaid instead of a butler and even the gardener was a woman.'

'Didn't she have a chauffeur, then?'

'She didn't have a car, Mr Seymour. Every afternoon, come rain or shine, she'd walk round the square and then back indoors; that was all the outings she had. Madam never came down into the basement, I had to go up to her bedroom for my orders, but at least once a day she'd open the baize door and call down, "Cook, did I hear a man's voice in the kitchen?" I was fit to burst with laughter sometimes 'cause one of the tradesmen would be sitting at the table 'aving a cup of tea as large as life, but I'd go to the bottom of the stairs and say, "Indeed no, Madam, there's only us down here." But she was a sweet old lady for all that. I reckon p'raps she was crossed in love like that what's-'er-name woman in that Dickens book we had to read in school.'

'You mean Miss Havisham in *Great Expectations*,' said the lady's-maid.

'That's it, that's the very book,' exclaimed Cook, admiringly. 'Fancy you knowing the name.'

'I have the book in my room,' said Dorise. 'I'll lend it to you if you would like to borrow it.'

'No, thanks all the same though. I ain't what you would call a reader. I likes me *Reynolds News* and me *Crimson Star* every week and that's enough for me. And I reckon I've talked enough for one night, it's time I went to bed. Come on Grace, I'll give you a hand with the dishes.'

When the rest of the staff had gone upstairs, the butler asked Cook if she would like a glass of port.

'That I would, Mr Barrett, you're a man after me own heart. I always say a drop of port builds you up, like.' Then, noticing a smile on the butler's face, Cook too smiled, 'Yes, I know it looks as though I'd need more than a bottle of port to build me up but I've always been the same, never put on no weight. But what's a handsome man like you doing in domestic service? I'd have thought you'd be a manager of some shop or one of those floor-walkers who walk up and down between the counters, dressed like a gentleman, and speak as though they'd got a plum in their mouth.'

'I could be if I wanted to, Cook, but I have my reasons for working below stairs. It's a kind of an experiment for the time being. I think I'll join you in a glass of port,' and with mutual expressions of goodwill they drank and went to their respective rooms.

Up in the attics the staff were deriving much amusement from their discussion of Miss Dunn.

'Ain't she a caution?' said Lily, laughing. 'There she's already got me at it. I mean, isn't Cook a caution?'

'All those dropped aitches,' said Dorise. 'I wonder if she realises she's doing it?'

'Probably not and probably wouldn't care anyway,' said Flora. 'Besides, what's a few lost aitches. I can see it's going to be much livelier in our servants' hall while Mrs Trouson is away — not but that I'm sorry she's ill.'

'She is not such a good cook as Mrs Trouson,' put in the parlourmaid. 'Mr Stewart complained about the soup. I heard him say, "Edith, has the new cook previously worked in the salt-mines" — that was because the potato soup was too salty — and when Mr Barrett served him with the lamb chops — they were much too brown, I must admit — he turned his chop over on the plate and said, "To whom are we offering a sacrifice tonight?" I didn't dare catch Mr Barrett's eye in case I laughed. All Madam said was, "It is Cook's first night, Henry, you must make allowances."'

'Ah well, Maud, Mr Stewart's never a ray of sunshine at the best of times. But I reckon Cook's knocking on more than sixty, don't you? I bet she's seventy if she's a day, she's that wrinkled. Though I suppose that could be because she's so skinny and bony, not much of an advertisement for her own cooking. But I reckon we laughed more tonight during supper than we have in a month with Mrs Trouson.'

'Yes, for sure we did, Lily, but speaking personally, I thought she was rather vulgar,' said Dorise, primly.

'Oh, you would Dorise,' retorted Lily. 'For fear of being thought vulgar you'd swallow a plum-stone rather than spit it out,' and as Dorise, looking offended, went into her bedroom, Lily shrugged and muttered, 'A bit of vulgarity might make you more human.'

'I was that surprised when Cook helped me with the washing-up,' said Grace. 'Mrs Trouson's never given me a hand, said she'd had her years of being a kitchenmaid bending over a sink full of greasy dishes. Still, I don't blame her. I bet when I get to be a cook — if ever — I won't want to look at a bit of washing-up.'

Flora and Grace going to their room, Lily and Maud

settled down for a few minutes' private chat.

'Did you notice, Lil, that for all his air of gentility, Mr Barrett didn't seem to mind Cook's rather crude conversation?'

'You're right Maud. Probably his gentility — like beauty — is only skin deep. Anyway, it will be nice to have a bit of fun, vulgar or not. Just wait until Cook and old Daniel get going.'

'It's certainly not very lively in the dining-room, Lil. Mr Stewart is that disagreeable lately, it's as much as he can do to say thank you.'

'Perhaps it's his time of life, Maud. You know, like females, only it takes men in a different way.'

'Does it? How do you know? Anyway, he must be well past that time surely, he's a good bit older than Madam. Mustn't it be dreary, Lil, when one gets too old to feel that way inclined. Can't be much fun left in life.'

'I wouldn't worry, Maud, it will be a long time before it happens to us. Besides, in my Mum's last letter she said that my aunt Zenia is getting married again to a retired widower — he will be her fourth husband. Just imagine Maud, four husbands, it's as good as a legal harem.'

'Harems are full of women, Lil.'

'Oh, you know what I mean. 'Sides, why should men be able to have a collection of women; why can't a woman have a male harem? Just think of it, Maud, opening the door and saying, "No, Raschid, not you tonight, I'll have Ali; or perhaps I'll choose Ahab",' and Lily collapsed into giggles.

'Lily Chambers, you are awful, you've got no morals at all. Anyway, Lil,' said Maud, laughing, 'we wouldn't have the stamina even if we had the inclination. But fancy your aunt getting four husbands and we haven't any signs of snaffling one. What's unusual about your aunt?'

'Nothing that I know of Maud, except her name. She's very jolly, talks non-stop, has a double chin and weighs about twelve stone. Obviously it's quantity, not quality, that's needed in the matrimonial stakes. By the way, Maud, you remember that night when you saw our butler and Miss Eleanor leaving the morning-room and you were suspicious that something was going on. Have you noticed anything since?'

'No Lil, but I wasn't making it up. Miss Eleanor really did look a bit ruffled.'

'I told you it was nothing. It's only in romantic novels that one of them marries one of us, and even then it always turns out that the lower-class hero or heroine is really the rightful owner of some castle or mansion.'

'What about your friend, Etta? She's pretty enough to marry anybody she fancies. I thought our butler was really smitten.'

'I think he was, Maud, but Etta's completely taken up with that painter chap; I'm really worried about her because he's just come back from Italy. Next time I see her, I'll try to make her see sense. That man will never marry her; he's not the kind; anyway, it's no use worrying now, I must get some sleep.'

Chapter 21

When Lily next met her friend Etta and began to proffer good advice, she was summarily cut short by Etta announcing that when Lance Melville went back to Italy, she was going with him.

For a moment Lily was too astounded to speak, then she burst out, 'Henrietta Aston, you must be stark raving mad. Leave your own country to go far away with a man you hardly know, a man years older than you? How do you know that he's not already married?' Receiving no reply from Henrietta, she added suspiciously, 'You do mean to get married before you go. You're not going to live in sin?'

'Why must you be so melodramatic, Lil,' said Etta impatiently. 'There's no question of marriage or living in sin. I'm going there as his guest and can stay as long as I like. I can have a room in the same house where he lives; it will be a sort of holiday for me.'

'Henrietta, you don't really believe that you can go to Italy with a man like Lance Melville, a painter who has nude models and probably dozens of girls; that you can live in the same house with him, see him every day and nothing immoral will happen. You know you're in love with him, you can't deny that.'

'Oh Lil, you just don't understand the way other people live. Lance has a housekeeper and a woman who does the cooking; it won't be just him and me shut up in a house. Just imagine, Lil, getting away from domestic service and going where there's warmth and sunshine, where people are light-hearted and friendly, where you sit in the sun and drink wine and watch the world go by.'

'Henrietta Aston, I never heard such guff in my whole life, you talk like a travel guide. I suppose that Lance has been spinning you all those fairy tales. To hear you talk one would think there were no poor people in Italy. I bet the poor work as hard as we do and have little time or money to sit in the sun drinking wine. Besides,' added Lily, dryly, 'who's going to pay for all this jaunting off, and if you don't happen to like it out there how are you going to get back?'

Henrietta, by now thoroughly annoyed with her prosaic friend, said sharply, 'I have money saved of my own and I'll have more before we go in three or four months' time. Anyway, Lil, I don't want to talk about it any more; I thought you'd be pleased for me.'

'Oh Etta, don't be like that. It's just I'm worried — you are so trusting. Let's forget it for now and go to see George Robey; he's always good for a laugh. Oh, I almost forgot to tell you the good news, Etta. On our free afternoon and evening we maids are to be allowed out until eleven o'clock at night.'

'High time too, Lil. I told you long ago that no servants would stay in a place where they have to be in by ten o'clock. That's what I told m'Lady when I applied for the situation. But how did you manage to get the extension?'

'It was our temporary cook. She told Mrs Stewart she'd never been used to coming back by ten o'clock and that an hour later was the accepted rule. So of course, if she could have another hour, we all had to be the same.'

In fact Cook had expressed surprise when she discovered that the servants were expected to be back by ten o'clock. 'That's an old-fashioned idea,' she said, 'and I'm certainly not going to do it.' Where she was last, not only were the staff allowed until eleven o'clock, but if there was something special they wanted to be at — a party or late theatre — they could be out until midnight.

Of course, being a temporary cook, she wasn't afraid to ask for what she wanted. Cook wasn't dependent on a reference from her employer because she had many references and could always account for the gap in between by saying she was resting.

Lily and Maud had thanked Cook profusely for getting them this privilege, it made going to a dance far more of an event. The butler, perhaps feeling some slight on his position, mentioned that before Mrs Trouson came back, he'd intended to speak to Madam about this very matter of free time. That he had not done so up to now was purely because he didn't want to upset Mrs Trouson and cause friction below stairs. Whether this was true — and Lily doubted him — they had to accept his explanation. After all, he was the butler.

Later that night, talking to the parlourmaid about Henrietta's rash plan of leaving Lady Moreham, Lily said, 'You know, Maud, I just don't understand Etta. Fancy leaving a good, well-paid job to go to a country where the Mafia murder people.'

'I think they're in Sicily, Lil.'

'Well, it's the same thing. They're all hot-blooded and fiery and carry daggers. Etta's so sensible and clever in some ways, and yet she can be so soft. She's a splendid cook, earns high wages — could get even more if she wanted to — is well-read and so pretty. She's had chances galore to marry, fellows with good jobs too. And she's going to throw it all up to go off with this no-good painter fellow.'

'What makes you think he's a no-good painter, Lil? If he's going to have an exhibition of his paintings in London, he must be a good artist; otherwise he'd never sell any.'

'I don't mean no-good in that way, Maud. What I mean is, why is he taking an interest in Etta? He must have opportunities to meet dozens of good-looking girls, especially in Italy. Can you see him marrying Etta, for I can't?'

'Come off it, Lil. Your friend knows what she's doing all right. I reckon it's a marvellous opportunity to get away from service, chance how it turns out. I'd go like a shot if he asked me. Anyway Lily, I reckon I'll soon give in my notice, there's not much fun in this place. Miss Eleanor's the only one with a smile and even she seems to be in a dream lately. As for the old man, I'm nervous even to serve him at dinner, he seems that irritable.'

'Perhaps having his son in the business is a source of irritation, Maud. I wonder how high up the ladder of promotion he's reached by now?'

In fact, Edward was still on the bottom rung, but — unbeknown as yet to his father — as this was his last week Edward cared nothing at all for his failure to rise. He was hesitating over the problem of leaving the firm. Should he just fail to be available next Monday when his father enquired where was he? Or should he have the satisfaction of telling his father that from now on he was independent, had a place to live and a congenial occupation? Yes, he'd decide on the latter, it would be worth it just to see the old man's face when he knew he no longer had power over his son. So Edward chose Saturday, after dinner, for his small triumph. And yet, much to his mortification as he stood outside the study door prior to knocking, he felt the old familiar feeling of ineptitude and indecision, and might have gone away if the study door had not been suddenly opened by his father. Surprised to see him there, and even more surprised to know that his son wanted a few words with him, he asked Edward into the study where he told his tale of Guildford, the flat, antiques and Foxy Reece.

For a minute or two Mr Stewart was silent, then he spoke, with an air of resignation, 'A man called Foxy Reece? Tell me, Edward, what kind of a man would be designated Foxy? And why is he called that? It cannot be his real name.'

But Edward didn't know; in fact very few people were aware of how Foxy had acquired this soubriquet. For Foxy's origins were shrouded in mystery and he intended to keep them that way. His parents, never mentioned, but to do Foxy justice, surreptitiously visited once a month, ran a market stall for 'seconds' of china, glass, artificial silk stockings, lace curtains, and other soft goods. It was at this stall that Foxy had served his apprenticeship in selling to a gullible public. At the end of the day, counting up his profit, he would gleefully say to his father, 'I foxed them well and truly today, Dad,' so eventually the family called him Foxy. He had a good reason for keeping his first name a secret from business and club friends, and for this he blamed his mother. Mrs Reece always had, as she put it,'been fond of a bit of romance'. One would have thought that living in a two-up-and-downer, in a back street of Lambeth and working in a street market, would effectively have killed off any romantic inclinations. But when a son arrived — after six girls — poor Mrs Reece got quite carried away with the novelty of this change of sex, and against strong family opposition, insisted on naming the son and heir Vivian. Even now Foxy shuddered when he remembered his schooldays. No boy, in Lambeth or its environs, had ever gone to an elementary school with the name Vivian. As he ascended each year to a higher class and had to call out his name, whistles and catcalls followed and even the teachers, inured to shocks as they were, looked mildly surprised.

However Foxy, graduating from the street markets to more profitable financial dealings — though always just within the law — was now an accepted member of the commercial hotels' 'smoker'. He belonged to two or three clubs, admittedly not in the highest echelon where members sat around like petrified fossils; in his clubs the members drank and joked and told stories that were a bit near the knuckle — but everybody laughed.

Such was Foxy Reece with whom Edward would be associating. Of course he knew Foxy wasn't 'out of the top drawer', but he had his head screwed on all right and, as Mr Stewart asked again, 'Who is this man and why is he called Foxy?' Edward thought, I can tell the old man any kind of yarn, what can he do about it? I'm over age and I'll be leaving this house in a day or two.

'I knew him at University, Father; he's called Foxy because he's mad about hunting,' and seeing in his mind's eye Foxy attired in pink and galloping madly over fences — when Foxy hardly knew one end of a horse from the other — Edward nearly exploded with laughter.

'Well, I hope you know what you are doing, Edward. It seems a precarious sort of business to me, nothing regular about it. Now if you had stuck to my company you could really get somewhere in time.'

Yes, in time, thought Edward, when I'm middle-aged and too old to have any fun with all the money I've made. But feeling it politic to remain silent he walked to the door only to receive a last word of warning, 'No more Norma Parks episodes, you understand.'

Mrs Stewart was waiting anxiously to know the outcome of the study conversation. Henry's moods of late had been so gloomy; she hoped that Edward had not added to her husband's sense of injury.

'Was your father angry or upset because you are leaving the company, Edward?'

'Well, Mother, he didn't exhibit any overwhelming signs of grief. But then there is no reason why he should as my contribution to the company can hardly be noticed.'

'Your father has always hoped you would take his place one day, Edward. You are the only son.'

'Mother, I think you are romancing. Father has never mentioned the idea of my reaching such eminence, rather the reverse in fact. Anyway, that sort of life is not for me, it's too much like being a machine'

'Oh Edward, I wish you were not leaving home; it will be so dull and quiet here. Your father is out all day and Eleanor, well, Eleanor and I have never been close.'

'I was bound to leave sometime, Mother,' said Edward, not unkindly. 'I'm not going miles away, you'll be able to see me from time to time. When I've made enough money to buy a car I'll come up and take you out for a drive.'

Knowing her son well enough to realise that this offer was a remote possibility, Mrs Stewart nevertheless managed a smile. For of her three children, her son was the only one for whom she felt a real affection. As children she'd had little to do with them, apart from an hour or so when Nanny brought them into the drawing-room. As they grew up, Elizabeth had early shown an independent spirit and a determination to have her own way; her good looks and liveliness ensured that almost as soon as she 'came out', she was engaged. How different it had been from her sister's 'coming out'. Plain and awkward, Eleanor had been forced unwillingly to balls and social events and had simply made no effort to make herself agreeable. Mrs Stewart had felt so angry and, what made it worse, Henry had seemed to encourage Eleanor in her isolation; it was almost as though he was against marriage for his favourite. But Edward, prior to leaving for university, had always shown a preference for his mother's company as a refuge from the demands of a martinet father and his continual exhortations to do all the things that Edward hated, and was afraid, to do, such as riding, climbing and swimming in the icy sea. At the end, Edward had come to dread seeing his father and hearing his harsh voice call him a milksop.

And now he was leaving home and she would be left with

just Henry and her daughter. Really more entertaining would have to be done, otherwise life would be so boring. At least there would be less friction once Edward was absent; Henry could talk to Eleanor without interruptions, there would be no more alarms and upsets. Eleanor had her uses in keeping Henry good-tempered.

If only Mrs Stewart could have seen into her daughter's mind, she would not have felt so complacent. Poor Eleanor, in love with John Barrett as only a woman of thirty could love who had never before experienced such emotion. Yet, Eleanor thought, how could they marry? It would kill Father if she was to do such a thing. No, of course it would not kill him, that was an exaggeration, but he would hate her for ever more. Dear Father, always so kind, ever ready to listen, encouraging her talent. If she married John and left home, never would she be able to return, it would be to Father as though she'd never existed ... And poor Eleanor, going down to the basement with a message for Cook and hearing laughter, envied the servants their carefree life. For, kind as she was and concerned for the poor, Eleanor, in common with her class, thought that servants, being ill-educated, and leading constricted lives, were incapable of deep feeling or the finer emotions. Of course this opinion did not include dear John; apart from an accident of birth he was quite a different person from an ordinary servant. If Eleanor had been present at the servants' mealtimes and heard the butler making Cook laugh with some of his ribald stories, she'd have realised that, underneath his 'above-stairs' gentlemanly demeanour, her beloved John was just another servant. As the lady's-maid remarked to Lily, rather plaintively, 'Mr Barrett doesn't seem the same man now that Mrs Trouson is away. He never used to be so free and easy in his conversation.'

Poor Mrs Trouson had not made such a good recovery as was expected from her appendix operation and was now going to a convalescent home for a few weeks. Visiting her in the hospital prior to her departure, Lily and Maud were closely questioned about how the kitchen was functioning in the absence of its rightful mistress. Knowing full well that the last thing Mrs Trouson wanted to hear was that all was going well, they said truthfully that the temporary's cooking did not come up to Mrs Trouson's. Omitting all mention of the much livelier atmosphere Lily, absent-mindedly eating the grapes by Mrs Trouson's bed, said that Miss Eleanor very seldom came into the kitchen now.

'Ah!' said the cook, beaming complacently, 'dear Miss Eleanor came to see me yesterday. She brought me those grapes'—removing them from Lily's reach—'and she went round the ward speaking to several of the patients; such a sweet person.'

'Like a Florence Nightingale in fact.' Mrs Trouson gave Lily a sharp look to see if she meant the remark sarcastically, but Lily, smiling sweetly, added, 'And has Madam been to see you?'

'Well no, but I didn't expect her to with all the problems she's had lately. But Madam sent me a lovely card and wrote that I'm not to come back until I'm really fit.'

When they left the hospital, Maud said, 'Isn't it pathetic, Lil. All she talked about, and wanted to know, was about upstairs and downstairs. Domestic service is her whole life, no wonder her conversation is so restricted. I hope to goodness we never get like that. What has she got out of life?'

'True Maud, but if we don't marry, what else is there for us females? We are definitely the inferior sex. For one thing, there's too many of us. If you think of it, just as it's difficult to get a decent job when there's a surplus of labourers, so is it equally difficult to get a decent man when there's such a surplus of women. Honestly Maud, sometimes I feel I'd marry the devil himself just to get out of service.'

'I don't know, Lil. Conditions are a lot better than they used to be. You ought to hear my old Gran talk about when she was in service. Six pounds a year, one outing a month and practically salaaming to the Master and Madam.'

'Yes, but I still say we are nothing if we don't get a man. No status, a spinster on the shelf, and yet one of us is worth three of the weedy types that have the nerve to think they're doing us a favour if they ask us out. You take that little squirt I met a few weeks ago at the Palais,' and Lily giggled reminiscently. 'Five feet nothing he was and if he'd stood sideways you'd not have seen him. He minced up to the row of wallflowers and selecting me from the bunch he just stood there and never opened his mouth. I suppose he considered that I should rise and curtsey to him. Anyway, having sat on my rear for so long, it ached more than my feet, so I got up to dance with this proper Romeo. God knows what he'd put on his hair — and it was under my chin — it smelt like ashes of violets that had gone off years ago. He never said a word while we danced, not even the usual, "Good floor, good band, do you come here often?" Well, he danced with me two or three times but of course by ten-thirty I had to leave and was I surprised when this pip-squeak offered to see me home. I said, "Whatever for? You don't want to leave the dance yet," and would you believe it, Maud, he had the nerve to say he felt in the mood and he was sure I did too.'

Trying to suppress her laughter in the street, Maud asked, 'What did you tell him, Lil?'

'Tell him? I told him to ask me in fifty years time when no doubt I'd be glad of anything in trousers.'

'Oh Lil you're awful. But wasn't it funny this morning with old Dan and Cook? If Ma Trouson could have heard them she'd have had a fit.'

Perhaps not a 'fit', but Mrs Trouson would certainly have considered it beneath the dignity of a cook to indulge in frivolous conversation with the gardener; especially a gardener that came only two days a week. Daniel Oates, incapacitated by the gardener's complaint, 'a crick in me back', had not seen the temporary cook until today, but the minute she saw him, Cook exclaimed, 'As I live and die, Daniel Oates,' and old Dan, equally surprised, said, 'Miss Dunn, well I never, where did we meet last?'

'Why Dan, you remember, down at The Limes, in Kent, where the old man went off his 'ead.'

And during their midday dinner Cook and Old Dan had talked nineteen to the dozen about the peculiarity of The Limes.

'Must be all of ten years ago,' said Dan, 'I was a full-time gardener then, had me own little cottage in the grounds. You remember, Miss Dunn — sorry Cook — let me see, how long were you there, three months was it?'

'Yes Dan, and you remember how the old gent, Mr Rothsey — and he wasn't no more than sixty — got away from his male nurse, came into the kitchen and chased my kitchenmaid — and she only fifteen — round the kitchen table. I screamed and you came running in from the garden.'

'I remember Cook,' said Dan, grinning hugely. 'And the old gent was wearing only a night-shirt which he kept lifting up; your poor Teresa didn't know where to put her face, she was that upset.'

'You're right Dan, I told her not to worry, I'd seen many such a sight when me Dad and brothers came home from the pit. It might be a man's best friend but I ain't never 'ad no wish to pal up with it.'

Amid laughter from the staff, the lady's-maid, as usual pained to hear anything of a bawdy nature, said, 'Oh Cook, what a thing to say to a young girl.'

'Go on with you, Dorise, she'd hear worse than that before she got through service. 'Sides, Teresa went to confession every week so she 'ad nothing on her conscience.'

'It reminds me of my great-aunt Matilda,' said the butler. 'I never knew her but my father said when she was a child she was taken to the Zoo and saw a kangaroo with a baby in its pouch. And when she was married, such was her ignorance of the facts of life, that when the doctor told her she was expecting a baby, she kept waiting for her pouch to grow.'

There was a chorus of disbelief on hearing this unlikely story, though Mr Oates said, 'Ah, I believe you Mr Barrett. There's a sight of funny things that females think and do. I call to mind when I was about eighteen; I had the pick of the girls then I can tell you.'

Receiving incredulous looks from Lily and Maud, Daniel chuckled, 'Ah gals, you never knew me then. Why, mothers who had pretty daughters used to lock their front door if they saw me in the street. Mind you, I got took down on one occasion. I'd taken a young girl to the music-hall, Cora her name was, pretty as a picture. Anyway, a chap in the seat behind us kept on pushing against the back of Cora's seat; I turned round to tell him off, I thought, lucky he's a small chap — I didn't realise he was sunk down in his seat. When I said, "D'you mind keeping you knees to yourself, mate," he stood up, saying, "D'you want to make something of it, then?" I was fit to pass out 'cos he was over six foot and shoulders on him like Joe Louis. I muttered pardon, pulled hold of Cora and we sat as far away from him as possible. You should have heard the names she called me, the language — and her with that pretty face and all. Course, it was all round the village next day. You can't trust girls, God bless 'em.'

'There was a lady came to the orphanage that used to take some of the older children to the pictures,' said the kitchen-maid. 'Some of the spiteful girls said she only took the pretty ones but it wasn't true because she took me sometimes.'

'Why,Grace,' said Cook, smiling, 'you ain't a bad-looking gal,' at which Grace blushed crimson, never having heard such a compliment from Mrs Trouson; for to Mrs Trouson it would come under the heading of 'putting ideas in a girl's head'.

'Now my cousin Patty,' went on Cook, 'she was well behind the door when they handed out good looks. She 'ad stringy mouse-coloured hair, her nose looked as though it 'ad been hit by a bus and her mouth, well me mum — God bless 'er — used to say, you could post a parcel in it. And yet, as true as I'm sitting 'ere, she got one of the best-looking fellows in our neighbourhood. What he saw in her, 'eavens only knows, 'cause I don't.'

'Perhaps she had a kind nature,' offered the lady's-maid. 'Looks don't last but a kind heart is always there.'

'She didn't have no different nature from me,' exclaimed Cook. 'Why, we went to the same school and sat side by side in class.'

'You often find that good-looking men marry plain girls,' proffered Lily. 'It saves all that wondering what she's getting up to while you're away.'

'Talking about good looks,' said the parlourmaid, 'I heard Mrs Stewart on the telephone inviting Mrs Trentham, her son and niece to dinner on Saturday. You haven't seen the niece, Mr Barrett, she's pretty enough to be a film star.'

'I'm not complaining,' said Cook, whose voice intimated that she was, 'but when I came here Madam said they seldom entertained. I do think it a bit off to 'ave a dinner-party when I ain't been here five minutes so to speak.'

'It's not a real dinner-party, Cook,' said Mr Barrett soothingly, 'more a few friends in. There will be only eight including the family, and I expect Madam will order a simple meal.'

'Oh it's not that, Mr Barrett,' Cook was up in arms at this imputation that she was not exactly a Mrs Beeton. 'There's nothing in the way of fancy dishes I can't do; why I could show you testimonials from the real aristocracy praising my cooking. But I think Madam might have asked me if I minded.'

'Perhaps she will, Cook, maybe she's waiting until the day,' said Dorise.

'Leaving it a bit late, isn't it?' put in Lily, dryly 'For sure, all the guests are already invited. Can you imagine her face, Cook, if she asked you, "Do you mind?" and you said, "Yes I do, unfortunately." '

'I wouldn't dream of saying it, Lily; you might get asked to do the cooking. Though Grace here is not bad at all, I must say.'

Again Grace went red-faced, and thought what a wonderful person was Cook.

Chapter 22

It was not until the day of the dinner-party that Mrs Stewart heard one guest would be missing. Mrs Trentham telephoned to say that Victor had a bad cold and thought it advisable to stay in bed. The truth was far different for the previous evening he had proposed to Eleanor and been rejected.

Over the last few weeks his attentions had been such that she had seen him two or three times a week yet, because she had known him for such a long time, it did not occur to Eleanor that Victor had a specific purpose in mind.

She was not attracted to him as a man, but he did have a genuine knowledge of and love of fine painting, especially water-colours, and as well as giving her expert advice and praise for her talent, Victor had taken her to several art exhibitions. Nevertheless, Eleanor was taken wholly by surprise when he asked her to marry him.

He'd not meant to propose quite so soon but his debts were pressing; with her money — and for sure her father would cough-up another ten thousand for his favourite — he could pay off the most urgent. Victor Trentham considered himself a sharp dealer but it hadn't occured to him that Mr Stewart would extensively enquire into a prospective son-in-law's character and financial position before he parted with his daughter.

Pressing Eleanor for the reason she rejected him, Eleanor, much embarrassed, stammered that she looked on him as a friend, she could never care for him in another way and that in any case she was older than him. Protesting that age did not matter, what was a few years one way or the other, Victor had stressed how well they got on together, how compatible they were, how long they had known each other, that he had always liked and respected her and liking had turned to love.

As level-headed and unassuming as Eleanor was, she found it impossible not to feel flattered to some degree by Victor's apparent desire to marry her; even perhaps she might have accepted him if she had not been so deeply in love with John Barrett that all other men were insignificant in comparison. Eventually, before Victor had left, she had promised to think about him and he would ask her again in a month or so. Poor Eleanor, she was too soft-hearted to be firm, to make Victor realise she could never marry him. It was a strange fact that both John Barrett and Victor Trentham had in the beginning felt indifference towards Eleanor, but as they got to know her, found themselves really liking her company. Still, Victor decided to stay away from the dinner-party; there would have been a certain awkwardness in speaking to Eleanor.

Fortunately for Mrs Stewart, she was able to make up the numbers by inviting an impoverished would-be poet who was thankful for a free meal. Adrian Lomas would have received more hospitality but for his apparently incurable habit of reciting his poems, whether or not he was asked to do so. On the last occasion he had dined with the Stewarts, they had been forced to listen to a long poem, entitled 'The Ballad of Banktown Billy'. By the time the poet had got to the twelfth verse, a less crass person would have realised tht his audience was barely listening, and when at the end of the ballad Billy died, Mr Stewart was heard to mutter, 'Well if he hadn't, I would.'

Apart from Mrs Trentham and her niece, the other two guests were a retired colonel and his rather meek wife. Among many grievances of Colonel Nollis, the chief one was that he had not been made a general in the Great War. In his opinion — and his contemporaries found it expedient to agree, if only to avoid his extreme belligerency — *he* would not have made such a bungling mess of the war as a certain general he could name. The fact that he never did name him was allegedly because 'he wouldn't speak ill of the dead'. Mr Stewart rather liked him; as he intimated to his wife before the guests arrived, 'If you must have people to dine, Edith, I'd sooner talk to old Tim Nollis than that hungry-looking Lomas fellow. It is to be hoped he's left his soulful sonnets at home. At the first sign of him erupting I shall receive an urgent telephone call.'

Mrs Stewart, with some qualms about her temporary cook's culinary skill, had tried to make the meal fairly simple.

Nothing was wrong with the first two courses of clear soup followed by boiled salmon, cucumber and mayonnaise sauce, so Mrs Stewart, her apprehension lulled, was able to take an interest in the conversation. Unfortunately, the cutlets, though not as over-done as those Henry had referred to as 'sacrificial objects', were certainly too brown and the pale and squashy Duchesse potatoes would have been rejected by the holder of that title. Fortunately, Mrs Trentham and the colonel's wife were old friends and sympathised with their hostess and her problems with a temporary cook. Eleanor and Louise — the pretty niece — appeared to be engrossed with the lean and lyrical poet while Henry and the Colonel were talking about Hitler, so Mrs Stewart was able to relax. Perhaps, she thought, Henry will not notice the cutlets and the pudding is Charlotte Russe, I know that is all right. Suddenly, at the end of the table where Colonel Nollis sat, there was a bellow of rage. Oh dear, thought Edith Stewart, has he found a caterpillar in the spinach? I'll never live it down if he has. But no, it was merely the Colonel giving way to his anger over 'this Hitler fellow'.

'Mark my words,' the Colonel barked, 'in two or three years time, maybe less, we'll be at war with Germany. We should have stopped the fellow years ago. Would have done it if the Government wasn't so spineless. What we need in this country is conscription, so as to be ready for the day war comes.'

'Now then, Timothy,' his wife murmured, 'you know what the doctor said, you mustn't get excited, it's bad for your heart.'

'Stuff and nonsense, Rhoda, fellow doesn't know what he's talking about. Nothing wrong with my heart, I'll outlive him and that partner. This country will need a man like me if war comes.'

'I don't believe in fighting,' said the poet. 'I am a man of peace. Surely in these days disagreements can be settled round a table, not by slinging bullets at each other? But if people are so idiotic as to fight, I shall be a conscientious objector.' Adrian Lomas sat back in his chair as though that settled the matter.

For a minute there was silence while the Colonel's complexion became a mottled red and purple. Alarmed, Mrs

Stewart thought he was going to have an apoplectic fit. Then he burst into a furious denunciation of the poet and all cowardly and unpatriotic men like him who would let their country be taken over by a horde of ravening Huns. His wife, obviously not as meek as she appeared to be, said sharply, 'That's enough, Timothy,' and, to Eleanor's amazement, the Colonel mumbled, 'Sorry me dear,' and continued talking to Henry Stewart as though nothing untoward had occurred. Adrian Lomas shrugged his shoulders and continued his exposition of the art of poetry to Eleanor and Louise.

Later, leaving the men in the dining-room while the ladies drank coffee in the drawing-room, Rhoda Nollis apologised for her husband's outburst.

'I'm afraid, Edith, that the news from Germany upsets poor Timothy. He won't admit it of course, but he's really getting old and feels he would be of little use if we ever had another war.'

And then, while Eleanor took Louise upstairs to show her water-colours the three older ladies discussed trivial affairs and Mrs Stewart proudly displayed photographs of her grandson. She explained that dear Elizabeth's health, since she'd had the baby, didn't allow her to live in India with her husband; it was very sad to be separated. Whether or not Mrs Trentham and the Colonel's wife believed this tale, they expressed their sympathy. Probably Rhoda Nollis was sceptical, having had five children and still accompanied her husband wherever his regiment was stationed. The men joined them — the Colonel considerably mellowed by Henry's good port — Mrs Stewart quickly suggested they should play bridge, thus forestalling a possible repetition of the Billy Ballad or another equally as piffling.

Below stairs everything was proceeding amicably. The chauffeur's wife, engaged to help Grace with the washing-up, was getting on famously with Cook. In the normal way, Mrs Stewart wold not have provided extra help for a small party of eight, but thought it best to placate her temporary cook by offering Mrs Seymour, thus leaving Grace more time to help Cook.

On dinner-party nights Mrs Trouson, feeling that all the

staff had worked harder, always provided a good hot supper for them, but tonight, it was just cold beef, tomatoes and pickle. Still, as Lily remarked later on to Maud, 'one has to take the bad with the good'. Cold beef and 'tongue sauce', or casserole and sobriety. Furthermore, after their meal, a bottle of port was put on the table; such an event would never have happened with Mrs Trouson.

'Well how did the meal go upstairs, Mr Barrett?' enquired Cook. 'Did Madam seem satisfied?'

The butler, calling to mind Mrs Stewart's harrassed face thought sardonically, if Mrs Stewart was satisfied, then I'm no judge of what she was thinking. Aloud, he said, 'I'm sure she was, Cook, what was there to complain about?'

'Well, the cutlets were a bit too brown, I thought, but some people like their meat well done.'

The parlourmaid suppressed a smile as she remembered chippy pieces flying off the cutlets as the guests endeavoured to cut them.

The chauffeur, slightly disgruntled at receiving a cold supper instead of the usual hot meal, said, 'People like them eat too much, in my opinion. Half a dozen choices for breakfast, three-course lunch and a five- or six-course dinner, while some people are starving. If you ask me, it's only because they've nothing to do that they eat so much, it passes the time away.'

'That doesn't apply to Mr Stewart,' interposing the butler. 'He is out all day.'

'Yes, maybe so, but he's not doing hard physical work. I drive him to the company building, and fetch him back; wait around if he's going out in the evening and fetch him back again if he does,' said Mr Seymour, looking aggrieved. 'On top of that, I am at the beck and call of Madam during the day. And the nerve some people have. I had orders to take that fat Mrs Trentham and her niece out to Hampstead. Why should I have to work for other people? I nearly gave in my notice, I was that provoked.'

'But she did give you a couple of quid, Bob,' said his wife.

Frowning at her for thus making light of his grievance, and annoyed with the butler for 'putting his spoke in', Mr Seymour said, 'And so she ought; previous few tips come my way from any of the friends and guests.' He added, to embarrass Mr Barrett, knowing full well that the butler did get tipped, 'I expect you find it the same, Mr Barrett. It's not like the old days when the gentry thought nothing of passing over a fiver.'

Mr Barrett was saved from answering by the lady's-maid who cried, 'I quite forgot to mention it. Madam told me this morning that dear old Nanny Smith has passed over.'

'Passed over,' the chauffeur exclaimed, 'what does that mean? Sounds like she was a cloud or a storm. Do you mean she died?'

'She died in the flesh and passed over in the spirit. Nanny Smith was a believer,' said Dorise.

'What makes you so certain she's passed over? I thought that "many were called but few were chosen". Is she one of the lucky few then?'

Before Dorise could think of the right words, Cook said, 'Who is, or was, Nanny Smith?'

'She was Nanny to Miss Elizabeth's husband,' said Lily, 'and she stayed here a few weeks looking after their baby. Nanny told us our fortunes by the cards, she said she had the gift.'

'Did any of it come true then?'

'Well, not yet Cook, but it was for the future so we won't know yet.'

'My friend, Pearl, is a rare one for telling the fortunes,' said Cook, 'but she doesn't use no cards, she's got one of them crystal balls and what she sees in it would take your breath away. She took it up when her Wally died and left 'er a widow with four kids.'

'Pity she didn't take it up a bit earlier,' said the chauffeur dryly, 'then she could have seen she was going to be a widow and given Wally the go-by, married a long-liver and never given a thought to a crystal ball.'

'Go on with you, Mr Seymour,' Cook was not at all put out by the chauffeur's remark. 'I'll bring Pearl to tea on Sunday and if you care to be here I'll get her to look in the crystal. Course, she don't do it for money nowadays, only to oblige, like. But she's a real wonder I can tell you, many a thing she's told me has come true.'

'And how many things has she told you that haven't, Cook?'

'Ah well now, nobody's always right. I remember Pearl and I 'ad our fortunes told on the pier — this was before Pearl got'er gift — and this woman, Madam Rachel she called herself, told me I'd meet a soldier who'd marry me and take me abroad; five bob it cost me and all.

'Oh, I met one all right. Couldn't very well not as a regiment was stationed just outside the town. But did 'e want to marry me and take me abroad? Not on your Nelly, he didn't. First night we went out as a foursome, Pearl had 'er Perce and I 'ad this Joe. That was all right 'cept they didn't so much as buy us a few sweets. On the second night we separated and that Joe took me to the park and we sat on a bench in a dark corner. In no time at all his 'ands started wandering. I wasn't standing for that I can tell you. I gave 'im a kick in the shins and ran. So much for that Madam Rachel.'

After the laughter had subsided, Cook said, 'My dad should have married Pearl instead of that bossy female who turfed out my brothers. She'd have been a sight better for 'im. Course she hadn't got Molly's looks; who could have after 'aving four kids?'

'Perhaps your father wasn't keen on taking on another family,' said Lily.

'I don't know about that Lil. If Pearl was ready to take on my brothers, a few more wouldn't have made no difference to note.'

'Did she ever get married again?' enquired the butler.

'Time she got the chance, Mr Barrett, 'er kids was grown-up and, as Pearl said, it wasn't worth it. She 'ad years of the wash-tub without starting again for some man who wanted an unpaid housekeeper and to be kept warm in bed. Pearl said — she was always a rare one to make you laugh — Pearl said to me, "Annie, an 'ot-water bottle's just as good in bed and you can chuck it out when it's cold." Ah, Pearl was a good mother, all her kids 'ad a good education, none of 'em left school until they was fourteen. Her Pansy — that's the youngest — writes love stories.'

'Does she really, Cook,' said the under-housemaid, open-mouthed with admiration. 'Does she get them printed?'

'That she does, Flora. There was one a month or two ago in *Peg's Paper* called "The Tender Heart", lovely story it was. Funny thing, though she writes these love stories, Pansy never got married and she ain't bad-looking. Never fancied no man she says; 'er and Pearl share a house out Clapham-way.'

The bottle of port being long since emptied, the servants finished their various duties and retired to bed. Just before Cook went to her room, she remarked to the butler, 'This is the first place I've been in where there ain't a cat. I'm used to 'aving one in my room at night. Don't they like cats in this house?'

'I believe that Mr Stewart has an antipathy to all cats,' said Mr Barrett. 'It's the same as some people cannot be in the same room as a canary if it's not in a cage. It's known as a phobia.'

'Is it, Mr Barrett,' said Cook vaguely, not having heard of such a word as 'phobia'. 'Well, it's a pity, 'cause I do like to see a cat around, it makes a place more homely-like.'

In his own room the butler gave a satirical laugh; 'homely-like'. Anything less homely than their servants' hall with its brown-painted walls, brown linoleum and one centre light would be hard to imagine. John Barrett thought, I'll have to leave here soon or I'll go mad. There is nobody below stairs who is intellectual, no stimulating conversation. It is livelier now, but that Dunn woman is a non-stop talker, I believe I prefer Mrs Trouson in spite of her somewhat dour character. The next time that I am alone with Eleanor I must be determined. If she won't leave her home and marry me I'll tell her, then I must go away; it's up to her.

Up in the attics the parlourmaid said, 'The dinner was a bit of a scream; you should have seen the look on Mr Stewart's face when Mr Barrett handed him the cutlets, I had to look away for fear of laughing. And those Duchesse potatoes; what went wrong with them, Grace, you've made them before?'

'It wasn't my fault, Maud. I'd mashed them with some cream and an egg when Cook put sour milk in as well. She said it gave a flavour, but it made the potatoes too soft. I hope Madam won't blame me.'

'I shouldn't worry, Grace. I reckon Mrs Stewart was too nervous about the conversation to think about the food. When that young Mr Lomas said that if there was a war he'd be a conscientious objector I thought old Colonel Nollis was going to have a fit. He went purple in the face with rage and burst forth about ravening Huns; it reminded me of a film that I saw years ago. There was this emperor, Genghis Khan he was called, and every time words came up on the screen, they were about his ravening hordes and the women being ravished — of course they didn't shew that part, you just had to imagine it. All the hordes looked so ferocious it was hard to imagine them even thinking of women, let alone stopping to ravish them.'

'All those handsome and athletic men in pictures,' said Flora, 'why is it that one never sees them in real life, not in the street or shops, or anywhere? It's not just because we're below stairs; I've never seen any of the well-to-do that look like film stars.'

'Wouldn't it be lovely to be carried off by a sheik and live in a tent in the desert,' said Grace, sighing. 'Don't you think so, Flora?'

'That's not for me,' said Lily, firmly, 'I wouldn't care for the sanitary arrangements.'

'Lily Chambers, you have no romance in your soul,' Maud laughed, adding, 'Wait till Sunday, maybe Pearl will look in her crystal ball and discover your fate. But that Cook is the last word, isn't she, always got something to say to make you laugh. When Mrs Trouson comes back I'm sure I'll be too nervous to speak for fear of being too free.'

'Wasn't it funny the other day when Dorise said that perhaps Cook's cousin Patty had a kind nature and that's why the best-looking chap married her. Cook was almost indignant at the idea. You remember, Maud? She said, "Patty ain't got no different nature from me, we went to school together." As though that settled the matter! Anyway, as soon as Mrs Trouson comes back I'm giving in my notice. I might get a job in the country, especially if Etta goes off with that painter. D'you know what I'd like to do, Maud? I'd like to learn to type and get a job in an office. You can earn a lot more money being a typist than being a housemaid.'

'I don't know, Lil, whether you'd be that much better off. Don't forget you'd have to keep yourself and find somewhere to live — unless you went back home.'

'Not likely, Maud. But just think of the freedom you'd have; no more watching the clock for fear of being late. Every weekend and evenings free. Besides, in an office there'd be men around.'

'Lil, what kind of men? You don't imagine the bosses are going to hob-nob with a common-or-garden typist. So that leaves clerks and office-boys, stamp-lickers. My friend Ena married a clerk; he earns a miserable wage and nags all the time about keeping up appearances. I'd as soon marry a dustman and not have to worry about appearances. You know, Lil, it's really funny when I go to my friend's for tea. I knew Ena when we were kids and her parents were worse off than mine. They never even had a tablecloth, it was newspaper on the table; Ena's Mum got the paper from where she went charring. It was a scream to see her Dad nearly dislocating his neck trying to read the paper while he was having a meal. But now, Ena has a proper tablecloth and when I go to tea we have to use silly little doilies — which her husband calls serviettes, though they're not. Her Alf — though you are not allowed to call him Alf, it's Alfred now — is a weedy specimen with a long skinny neck like a giraffe and he won't take his collar off, not even indoors. And as for his voice — well, his old dad used to b — and f — every Saturday night when he got drunk and many a time he got thrown out of pubs. But this Alf — pardon, Alfred — speaks in a mincing tone of voice; I can just imagine him in his office saying, "Yes sir, no sir, very good sir." A man like that's not for me.'

'Too true, Maud. People from our station of life can't ape them above, not without making fools of ourselves. Can you imagine us discussing politics, music and literature? There's me at the dining-table, one of twelve guests. The footman is handing me the vegetables; I say, "No thanks, James, no peas, they will slip off the knife." Then I turn to my neighbour and say, loftily, "What do you think of the Indian question, Mr Rahjit?" — 'cause he's dark so I assume he comes from India.'

'And what does he say, Lil?' said Maud, giggling.

'He says, "Madam, I am unaware that there is an Indian question. But if there is I cannot answer it." Well of course Maud, if I was a real lady, I'd turn to my other neighbour but as it's me, I smile at him and say, you and me too.'

Dissolving into laughter, Lily added, 'You know, Maud, perhaps I really will go back to work in the country. It's easier to save money and the guests seem far more generous with giving tips. When I was an under-housemaid I worked in a lovely old country house, called Hetfield Hall. The entertaining that went on there you'd never believe. As well as the head-housemaid there were three of us unders. One of the regular guests was an elderly bachelor, I suppose he was about sixty. He used to leave his bedroom early in the morning, before breakfast, to walk in the grounds. If I was brushing the stairs, as he went past he'd always lightly pat my rear, walk to the bottom of the stairs then up again, give me another pat and slip a ten-shilling note in my apron pocket. It really was funny 'cause old Miss Bury, our head-housemaid, could never understand why us three competed to do the stairs. Not a word did he ever say but I often felt like telling him that for one pound note he could go a bit further.'

'Lily Chambers, you are awful, you really are,' exclaimed Maud. 'Anyway, it's time we went to sleep so that we can wake bright and cheerful to face this merry household. I wonder how that Edward's getting on?'

Chapter 23

Edward Stewart was, as yet, far from living the life-style he had envisaged from Foxy Reece's enthusiastic account of the profits they would make dealing with 'simple country folk'. On close inspection country folk's simplicity had been greatly exaggerated by Foxy, and on more than one occasion — to Edward's discomforture — he had been told to clear off and had the door firmly shut in his face. Foxy complained bitterly that it was all due to the simple country folk possessing wireless sets. They heard programmes about country houses and the valuable objects to be found in them and then developed inflated ideas about the value of Grandma's revolting vases which no doubt she'd won at a fair. Nevertheless, Foxy had devised a plan for dealing with such impediments to an easy living. By offering a very low price indeed for a desired object, he allowed the owners to bargain until a higher price had been reached. Then, praising them for their cleverness in making him pay more than he intended, Foxy often managed to induce the gullible couple to part with other family heirlooms. For decayed gentlewomen, forced to sell their treasured possessions, Edward alone called on them. His upper-class voice and good clothes were an assurance of probity; one of their own class must be safe to deal with.

But, apart from the work, Edward was finding that continual association with Foxy Reece had disadvantages that he was unaware of when they met only occasionally. Although Edward had his own room in Foxy's flat, they shared the living-room and kitchen, and some of Foxy's mannerisms grated on the more fastidious Edward. His habit of drinking tea or coffee while he had a mouthful of food, his habit of picking his teeth, and his cheerful whistling early in the morning. Edward had sourly protested that Foxy's whistling got on his nerves and Foxy had good-humouredly suggested that if Edward had a bit more joie de vivre — Foxy was proud of that touch, joie de vivre — they might do a bit more business.

But what irritated Edward most of all, was Foxy Reece's girlfriend. He simply could not understand how a chap like Foxy had managed to acquire her. If Nina Scott had been a girl such as that Norma Parks, Edward would have felt a certain pleasure in knowing that Foxy was no more experienced where women were concerned that he, Edward, had been. But Nina was most emphatically not another Norma. Her parents were cultured, intelligent and above all wealthy. It was obvious that Nina herself was well-educated, and very attractive indeed with her beautiful complexion, fair hair and blue eyes. What on earth such a girl saw in a fellow like Foxy was a mystery to Edward. And Foxy was so off-hand with her. Many times Edward had heard him speaking to Nina on the telephone to cancel an appointment, merely saying he was too tired. Sometimes Edward had a wild hope that on these occasions Nina might say, 'What about your friend, Edward, is he free?' but she never did say those words. Once or twice, while Nina was waiting for Foxy to finish dressing, Edward had tried to impress her with a description of his grand home, the dinner parties and the large staff. He hadn't the sense to realise that Nina, who lived in the same style, was not in the least interested in Edward's revelations. She would have liked to hear about Foxy's background but this he was far too astute to disclose.

Edward thought, if I could present such a girl as Nina Scott to my father, he really would be surprised. He'd have to admit that his son wasn't quite the nonentity he'd called him; and of course mother would be delighted.

Mrs Stewart had written to Edward to say that she missed him, hoped he was doing well as she was looking forward to seeing him driving up to the house in his own car. When he'd read this part of the letter aloud, Foxy had facetiously suggested that next Sunday he could drive home in the van, 'be a bit of an eye-opener for your old man'. Poor Edward, although he hated his father, at the same time wanted to impress him. Driving up in a van would most certainly not be the right kind of 'eye-opener'.

Mr Stewart had no idea — and would have vehemently denied it if anybody had suggested it — that his method of raising a son was more than half to blame for Edward's blighted outlook on life. Naturally a timid child, he had been terrified of his father's insistent demands that he must learn to swim, to box and above all to ride. Edward was as terrified of horses as he was of his father. If Mr Stewart had been kind and patient, his son might have eventually 'become a man'. As it was he sought only his mother's company, while his father with contempt used epithets of which soggy and nincompoop were the mildest.

So Edward had become sullen and spiteful, especially so with his sister, Eleanor, because without having to strive, she had her father's approval and affection. Although he would never admit it, not even to himself, Edward would have liked to have that approval.

He and Elizabeth had not so much 'got on' together as tolerated each other, though there were times when he envied her apparent indifference to her mother's complaints of unladylike behaviour and her father's irate demands to know why she had not come home from a party until the early hours of the morning. So he was surprised to receive a letter from Elizabeth, saying:

'Dear Edward, Mother wrote that you are now "in antiques", whatever that may mean, and are no longer living at home. Good for you, it was time that you broke away. If the antiques don't work out, we could do with some help on this farm. My widowed friend is only thirty, you'd like Ellie, she's really go-ahead. Your sister — me I mean — has taken to this country life; I would not live in London again, amazing as it may seem to you. And country society is by no means dull, some of the farmers are really dashing. Don't mention it to the parents, but I'm asking Eric for a divorce. Father no doubt will have an apoplectic fit. By the way, if time and inclination permit, you might call in on Mother. Going by her letter, she seemed rather depressed; of course she and Eleanor were never very close.'

Me work on a farm? thought Edward. Not likely; I'm not cut out for 'back to nature'. I reckon Elizabeth had already met another man and that's why she wouldn't go back to India with Eric. Well, good luck to her, everybody has to look out for number one these days. Of course the old man will have plenty to say, he's such a reactionary.

Edward did travel to London, but not in Foxy's van. His mother was pleased to see him but full of complaints about her life, it was so dull. Henry seldom wanted to go to the theatre or accept dinner invitations, preferring that people came to his house to dine. He complained about the temporary cook, everything was over-cooked and his breakfast kedgeree was worse than Mrs Trouson made. She at least left only the odd bone but now he was chewing the backbone. Thank heaven that in two weeks' time Mrs Trouson would be back. And Elizabeth had invited them down to the farm, but Henry was adamant that he wouldn't go. 'I'm longing to see my grandchild,' Mrs Stewart finished in a plaintive voice.

Mother must have mellowed, thought Edward. Aloud, he said, 'But Mother, you always said that you didn't care for young children. They were noisy, messy and required too much attention.'

Looking embarrassed his mother murmured that she had only one grandchild and besides, now that she had a far less busy life, she had time to spare for her own family.

'Eleanor does not need me,' she complained, 'in fact she hardly seems aware that I exist. Oh, she still does everything I ask her to do, and is never cross; but in a way that I cannot understand she seems remote. I have even tried to show an interest in her paintings but she just smiles and makes no comment.'

'Well Mother, I suppose it's not to be wondered at. You haven't exactly been a doting mother where Eleanor was concerned, so presumably she has learnt to do without you.'

'Edward!' his mother exclaimed, 'I didn't expect that you would be on her side. Why have you changed?'

'I haven't changed, Mother. I'm just pointing out that after years of indifference you cannot alter now. It's too late.'

Mrs Stewart would have thought her daughter was deranged if she could have by some miracle divined why Eleanor was so remote. Deeply in love with John Barrett, she had succeeded in banishing from her mind all thoughts of him as the butler. He was her John, so handsome, kind and gentlemanly who, by some present misfortune, was prevented from mixing socially with his equals. She loved him so and dreamed of a little cottage where they would be happy together. But still she could not see how that halcyon state could ever come about. She would never be brave enough to leave her family, to lose her father's love for ever, never to see him again. She lived for the rare occasions when she and John could meet, just to be together, to hold hands and to kiss. She wondered all the time if John was thinking of her, and how marvellous it was to be loved. She had even given up going to church because John said he did not believe in all the mumbo-jumbo spouted from the pulipt and an intelligent person, as she was, must feel the same. Besides, more crimes had been committed in the cause of so-called faith, than through any other source. Was he not right?

Eleanor had agreed, gone no more to hear the Word, but in the privacy of her bedroom she had her own 'stool of repentance'.

Poor Eleanor was incapable of realising that John's affection was lukewarm — liking maybe but certainly not love. Not that it affected his determination to marry Eleanor. What did love matter anyway? Many women had professed undying love for John, had wanted to marry him and failing, had very soon found consolation in another man's arms.

John Barrett viewed with a certain amount of cynicism Eleanor's oft-repeated assertion that she would be so happy living in a little cottage and doing all the cooking and cleaning for her dear John. Brought up as she had been with every comfort that money could buy, she had no idea at all of how the poor lived. Oh, she spoke at her F.D.W. meetings, but that was a far cry from going into their homes. John Barrett laughed inwardly thinking of Eleanor, who bathed every day, having to put buckets of water on the gas to bath once a week in a zinc bath. Well at least she wouldn't miss the sparkling conversation; he could speak as well, if not better, than many of the so-called high-ups who came to dinner. One heard a lot of old chit-chat about the latest plays, horse-racing and fashions, no great intellect was needed to keep that going. Take that Member of Parliament for instance: he claimed everybody's attention by virtue of being in politics, yet if one analysed his conversation, he said nothing that one couldn't read in the daily papers. And that good-for-nothing Victor Trentham talking about Burlington House as though he was one of the trustees or something. As for that Sir Samuel Beeston, it was common knowledge that he bought his title and as for ancient lineage, until his grandfather made all that money in coal and iron and bought the Malvern estate, the Beestons were absolute nobodies.

Thus John Barrett, the butler, denigrated his employers and their circle; reckoned, and really believed, that he was just as good as them above stairs. In that, he differed from the other servants, who although they often said, 'We are just as good as them,' knew very well that they were not. Morally good yes, but, lacking money and a good education, there was an enormous gulf between below and above. Mrs Trouson considered that it was only right that above-stairs should be on a higher plane. She asserted, 'I would never work for people who were not born into the aristocracy, who are not real ladies and gentlemen.'

The lady's-maid, never averse from introducing a note of piety, had remarked, 'One doesn't have to be of blue blood to be a lady. I have known simple country wives who were ladies in spite of their humble homes. They regularly went to church and visited the destitute to comfort them with kind words.'

The head-housemaid, with mild sarcasm, had answered, 'I should think the destitute would have appreciated more solid comforts. Kind hearts may be more than coronets but they don't enable one to have such a luxurious life.'

'Ah, too right they don't, Lily,' the gardener had interposed. 'You take the couple of old ladies where I go every Monday. I don't do the garden 'cause they haven't got one, it's all paved over, but I cleans their silver and brass. They got what they call entrée dishes and sauce-boats, silver salvers, tea-things and cutlery with fancy handles. What they haven't got is money yet they won't sell a bit of their silver 'cause they got to "keep up appearances". Daft, I call it, why not have a bit of comfort, never mind about letting the family name down.'

'That is only your opinion, Mr Oates,' Mrs Trouson very primly had replied. 'People like that have high ideals and loyalty to their class. I respect them, I'm sure they belong to the real aristocracy, the backbone of this country. Of course, a man like you wouldn't understand that it's not the lack of money that worries such people so much as having to lower their standards.'

Nettled at the cook inferring he knew nothing of good service, Mr Oates had announced that, starting as an under-gardener, he'd worked for establishments ten times the size of this one and as for his two old ladies worrying about their standards, they'd already reached the lowest level. Starting with the staff of twelve all they had now was him once a week; you couldn't get much lower than that. Anyway, judging by what went on upstairs, one couldn't say this house was a model of aristocratic behaviour.

Chapter 24

'Madam was so pleased to see Master Edward this morning,' said Dorise. 'When I went into her boudoir to put away her clothes she looked really happy. It's not my free Sunday, but Madam told me that if I wanted to go to church she would not be needing me this evening. I thought it was so kind of Madam.'

'What about the Master,' enquired the chauffeur, somewhat satirically. 'Was he too "really happy and full of the milk of human kindness", because his son had condescended to call?'

'Probably bubbling over,' said Lily, laughing. 'Are you going to church, Dorise?'

'Indeed I am Lily. It is the Sunday that Father Humphrey preaches; he gets really to the heart of things and when he fixes you with his eyes, it's quite as though he is speaking just to you.'

'I never had any time for all that stuff,' said Mr Seymour. 'Clergymen always seem to me like pale imitations of men; niether fish, fowl or good red herring.'

'Go on with you, Mr Seymour,' exclaimed Cook. 'There must be more to them than that judging by the amount of children some of them have.'

'Our vicar at home had only two children,' said the under-housemaid, 'and one day when he called on Mrs Martin, our neighbour, he got such a welcome he never called again. Poor Mrs Martin's husband had deserted her, and she'd seven kids; holy terrors they were too. She was complaining to the vicar about her hard life and the stupid man said, "Mrs Martin, one day your children will rise up and call you blessed. It says so in the Bible." Mrs Martin was that livid; she said, "Well, until that unlikely day comes vicar, perhaps you'd like to take a couple of the bloody kids off my hands, you've only got two of your own."'

Dorise looked pained but all the others laughed and Cook said, 'You wait until my friend Pearl gets here, she can tell you a few stories about kids. I think that's her now at the door, or else your friend, Etta, Lily.'

Pearl arrived with Pansy, her daughter, followed shortly after by Lily's friend and the chauffeur's wife, keen to have her fortune told in Pearl's crystal ball. Etta, who most definitely had not changed her mind about going to Italy with her painter friend, had no wish to have her fortune told, whether by crystal ball, cards or some other legerdemain. She knew what her fortune was and was not interested in hearing a different version.

Between them, the kitchenmaid and Cook had made a large selection of cakes for the servants' tea. Mrs Stewart, if she had known, would undoubtedly have considered such a spread far too lavish, but as Cook would shortly be leaving, and was in no need of a reference, she considered her loyalty lay below stairs where she was appreciated. Certainly, Grace would be sorry to see her go, Cook was far more easy-going than Mrs Trouson, though as Flora pointed out, Grace was not likely to learn the higher arts of cooking from this Cook. Besides, as Lily said, cheerfully, 'it's well-known that suffering ennobles, so Mrs Trouson might come back with the disposition of an angel.'

'Pansy said she'd like to come with me, I hope that's all right, Annie?' said Pearl.

'The more the merrier,' said Cook airily. 'I'm sure nobody down here objects.' The implication being that it was of no account if above-stairs objected to such an influx of visitors.

To Etta, Cook's friend Pearl looked just like the picture of Tweedledum — or it could have been Tweedledee — that she had seen in a library copy of *Through the Looking Glass*. She was so short and rotund, yet with such slender legs and small feet, it seemed as though with a slight push she would overbalance. Whatever troubles she'd had had not soured her expression, for her round shiny face beamed with good nature.

'Come on Pearl and Pansy, and you Mrs Seymour, tuck in,' said Cook, dispensing hospitality with a free hand, knowing it had cost her nothing.

'The doctor said I've got to watch my weight, Annie, because I get so breathless. He told me if I wasn't careful I'd get fatty degeneration of the heart. I can't understand it, I never ate more than you, Annie, and yet here you are, still as thin as a lath.'

'Well, wait till tomorrow before you start starving yourself, Pearl. Me and Grace ain't made all these cakes for nothing, 'ave we Grace?'

Lily, surveying the well-laden table, thought: if Mrs Trouson could see this, she'd have a fit. One fruit cake a week with scones on Sunday was her limit. I bet when Mrs Stewart gets the grocer's account, there will be an inquest to find out why it's so high. Miss Dunn will be gone by then, so she won't worry.

The under-housemaid, excited by having an author at the tea-table, asked, 'Miss ...'—'Oh, do call me Pansy.'—and Flora stuttered, 'Miss Pansy, have you written another love story?'

'Yes, I have Flora, it's called, *Love Conquers Delphine.*'

'Did she stoop to conquer?' enquired Etta, but as Pansy knew nothing about Goldsmith, Etta's wit was not appreciated.

'I like my Pansy's stories,' said Pearl. 'They always end up happy ever after. I got no time for tales about murders, people hating each other and somebody dying at the end of the book. Who wants to get miserable reading that stuff. Not me, that's for sure.'

'Real life doesn't always end "happy ever after",' said the butler, 'and I reckon it would be very dull if it did. Everybody wants a bit of excitement in life.'

'Ah, you're right there, Mr Barrett. Me and Pansy went down to the country last weekend and laugh, we saw a man being chased by a bull. He got over the fence only just in time, Pansy and me were like to split our sides with laughing, cause *he* split his trousers.'

'Can't you make a story up about that, Pansy?'

'No, Mr Seymour, I write love stories, not comedies,' and Pansy looked slightly annoyed. She added, 'In any case, I write for women's magazines, and they want only sentimental stories about young people in love. I sent them a story about two middle-aged people, a widow and widower who met and fell in love. But the editor sent it back; she said their readers wouldn't be interested, older people were not of the stuff of romance.'

'I reckon no men are romantic be they young or old,' said

Pearl. 'You take my Wally now; he was a good-hearted chap before —'

'Before the Lord took him,' murmured Dorise.

'No, it wasn't the Lord, it was the dust got in his lungs, like. He was good-hearted but as for romance, he'd never hear of it. On our honeymoon night there I was, wearing the pink crêpe-de-chine nightdress I'd made, and what do you think, Wally got into bed wearing his long woollen pants! I was that taken aback, I can tell you. I says to him, "Haven't you got pyjamas?" and he said he wouldn't waste his money on such useless objects, he always slept in his underwear and he didn't look to alter his ways just because he was married. Still and all,' and Pearl smiled reminiscently, 'after a bit of practice like, it was a good night.'

Amid laughter, Cook interposed, 'Now come on, Pearl, what about having our fortunes told in your crystal ball?'

The lady's-maid went upstairs, she was against such an activity on a Sunday; but the chauffeur's wife, Flora and Grace eagerly gathered round. Pearl explained that unlike fortunes told by cards, which could be done in the full light of day, a dim light was needed for pictures to be seen in the crystal. So the curtains were pulled across the windows — as though there was a death, muttered the chauffeur — and Mrs Seymour was the first 'victim'. With much fluttering of hands, pressing of brow and murmurs of, 'it's all dim as yet,' Pearl told the chauffeur's wife that she would receive news from abroad and a young man would be coming to stay at her house. Mrs Seymour, being of a frivolous disposition, was pleased to hear the latter statement, though later on, the reappearance of her brother-in-law, Don, who couldn't get on with his landlady and wanted a room, did much to diminish her pleasure.

Then Flora had her turn, and Pearl, by now aware that Flora liked romantic stories, purported to see in her crystal ball that in the near future Flora would meet a young man, perhaps at a party, and yes, he was dark and handsome. But Flora, although she read romantic tales of young love, was far too sensible and aware of her lot to imagine that a Prince Charming would seek out an under-housemaid; so she just giggled and didn't believe a word of it.

The chauffeur sourly refused to have anything to do with fortune-telling, saying testily, 'It stands to reason that nobody can foretell the future, for if they could, and it was a bad one, they'd alter it, and nobody has been able to do that.'

'You are wrong there, Mr Seymour,' said Pearl earnestly. 'You remember, Annie, when times being so bad, my Wally was going out one night with the lads to do a bit of poaching?'

'That I do Pearl, and two of his mates got caught and sent to clink.'

'Well, I hadn't got my "gift" then, like, but the night before, my neighbour Connie came in — as nice a woman as you could meet and suffered something cruel with the dropsy —'

'A drop too much most days,' murmured Pansy.

'Connie says to me, "Pearl, I'm not long for this world, I read it in the cards last night." Well of course I cheered her up like, we had a drop of stout and I got her to read the cards for Wally. As sure as I'm sitting here, may I never tell a lie, she saw that Wally would very soon be in trouble, perhaps an accident at the pit. But I thought of him going out with his mates and maybe getting shot by a game-keeper, so I persuaded him not to go. And wasn't I right, Annie?'

'That you were, Pearl, and what I say is, some people got a power, people like Connie Young.'

'Yes, but don't you see it was nothing to do with her reading the cards. Your Wally wouldn't have gone poaching because that was his future, a pack of cards couldn't alter it. And,' Mr Seymour added, 'did your friend Connie have an early demise?'

'If you mean, did she die, no. Con lived another ten years and got carried off by flu,' said Cook. 'But that ain't to say she didn't have a power.'

'Perhaps she had will-power,' said Mr Barrett. Pearl and Annie burst into laughter, explaining that Con's husband was named Will, and added Pearl, 'Old Con didn't have much will-power when her Will was around, 'cause she had nine children and none of 'em was twins.'

'Mr Barrett,' said the chauffeur's wife, glancing at him rather amorously — much to her husband's annoyance — 'are we not going to hear your fortune?'

Not even condescending to smile at her, the butler said, grimly, 'I know my future and I don't need a pack of cards or a glass ball to tell me what to do. My future is to get out of domestic service, to get away from being treated as an inferior person, answer bells, fetch and carry, wait on people who are no better than me — if as well-bred. I'm sick to death of hearing; "Barrett, my suits need pressing," "Barrett, you have put out the wrong tie," "Barrett didn't you hear the bell?" You mark my words, I'll be revenged on them before long, revenged on all the slights that have been inflicted on me. There will be no more, Yes sir, No sir, or Very good sir. I'll be free of the lot of them, that's my future.'

An uneasy silence followed this outburst, then the head-housemaid said, quietly, 'I think domestic service is what you make it and there are worse jobs. Besides, it is improving, just look at all of us in this servants' hall. When I started in service, we were allowed to invite a friend to tea only once a month and in some places — not this one I'll admit — the servants have a well-furnished sitting-room and a comfortable bedroom and can choose their own uniform.'

'Yes, and that's about the limit of the concessions made to servants,' said Mr Barrett, cynically. 'A servant still has no freedom, has to wear a cap on her head to denote her servitude — just in case a visitor should make the heinous mistake of thinking she was an above-stairs person. She — or he — is still addressed by the surname, just in case, if you were a Mr or Miss, you might get the idea that you were of some importance instead of less than the dust,' and the butler laughed scornfully.

'Well, I ain't never felt like that, Mr Barrett,' said Cook. 'What I say is, life is what you make it. I remember my Mum, just before she was took, saying to me, "Annie, my girl," she said, "never you mind that you are a bag of bones" — Mum was always a one for straight speaking — "some day 'appiness will come your way and you'll find a man who fancies you." Course, my Mum, God bless 'er, didn't believe me when I told 'er I wouldn't never fancy no man, seen too many of them to wait 'and and foot on at home.'

It was doubtful if this tale had any connection with the butler's diatribe, but it effectively lightened the atmosphere, especially when Pearl said, 'Ah Annie, many's the time my Wally grumbled, "if you were more like Annie Dunn there'd be a bit more room in this bed."'

Her daughter, laughing, said, 'If I had to listen to you two often, I'd never be able to write romantic stories about love-lorn maidens and rags to riches.'

The chauffeur, with mordant humour, said, 'Well, we have a ready-made story for you. Here is our Grace, not a bad-looking girl, brought up in an orphanage and has risen to the heights of being a kitchenmaid. Of course, the glass slipper hasn't arrived yet, but it will, eh Grace?'

Poor Grace, not realising that Mr Seymour was being sarcastic, blushed and giggled, but Pansy looked offended. Lily quickly averted any further comments, by asking, 'Have you sons, Pearl?'

'Yes Lily, I have two, Percy and Patrick. I named them after my wealthy great-uncle, Percy Patrick Dixon; thought it would please the old man and keep us in his mind.'

'Did it please your great-uncle Percy?'

'Well if it did, it made no sort of difference cause he never left us a smell of his money, alive or dead. I reckon him and Scrooge were blood-brothers. He was ninety-six when Old Nick called for him and when his will was read — and there we all were, not daring to look at each other, all hoping for a share — he'd left his house, his treasures and all his money to have a museum called after him. Me and Pansy have never set foot in the place I can tell you. Anyway, we must go, I know you all have work to do. Thank you for a lovely tea, Annie.'

Later that evening, Lily was talking to the parlourmaid in her bedroom. 'We had quite a bit of excitement at tea-time, Maud, with Cook's friend telling fortunes in her crystal ball.'

'Did you have yours told, Lil?'

'I was going to, but that Madge Seymour — you know how she makes eyes at Mr Barrett — simpered at him and said affectedly, "Oh Mr Barrett, are we not to hear your fortune?" Well, Maud, he launched forth into a long rigmarole about being a servant and how in the near future he would be revenged on them above stairs. I wonder what he meant, Maud?'

'Probably nothing, Lil; I expect he was just letting off steam. What were the visitors like?'

'Oh, all right. The daughter, Pansy, got a bit annoyed when she thought Mr Seymour was taking the mickey about her romances. What did you do, did you go to the pictures?'

'Yes, I went to the Roxy to see Buster Keaton. Laugh, Lil, the tears were streaming down my face. Good job I had a laugh because after I came out I went to see my Aunt Nessy, my Mum's sister. Mum kept on at me in her letters to call on Aunt Ness, she was lonely and had no friends. Honestly, Lil, I'm not surprised she's lonely, for a more embittered and sour old spinster I have never met. She was engaged to a young man who got killed just a month before the armistice and either she never had another chance to marry, or didn't want to. All her conversation was about the awful neighbours, rude bus-conductors and people out to do her down. Just imagine Lil, if we never found a husband and got like my aunt Ness.'

'Not all spinsters are like your aunt, Maud. Take my Mum's friend, Miss Paley; weighs twelve stone, fifty if she's a day, never a hope of getting married but she's that lively; goes to old-time dances, likes a drink and a joke. She's always saying that she can't be on the shelf because there isn't one strong enough to support her. And take our Miss Dunn downstairs, you can't say she is sour and disagreeable.'

'I suppose you're right Lil, but I still hope to be a wife to somebody. We shall miss Cook when she leaves and Mrs Trouson returns to her rightful place. It will be the same old routine, dull and monotonous.'

But Maud and Lily would have needed more than Pearl's crystal ball to foresee the great changes shortly to take place in the household.

Chapter 25

Mrs Trouson's return to her basement domain was in the nature of a small triumph. Mrs Stewart had sent down flowers to make the servants' hall look less grim and the staff had also bought flowers to make her bedroom look attractive. Suffering had not changed her disposition, unfortunately for Grace. Not that the cook was a really bad-tempered person, it was just that her occasional sharp and brusque way of speaking gave that impression.

Poor Grace, who could not immediately change from equality to a kind of subservience, came in for a deal of acid criticism which, though probably beneficial to her role as a kitchenmaid, did nothing to make her life easier. Grace confided to the under-housemaid that she'd give in her notice if Mrs Trouson continued her carping ways, and eventually she told the cook that she wished to see Madam. On Mrs Trouson enquiring for what reason, Grace burst into tears and stuttered that she was tired of being continually 'picked on'. Thereupon the cook explained that it was for the kitchenmaid's own good that she, Mrs Trouson, corrected her, for she wanted Grace to 'get on', to learn all the arts of kitchen lore so that she in turn could become a cook. So harmony was restored and everything, at least on the surface, appeared to be as usual.

The butler had, however, made up his mind that he'd had enough — and more than enough — of being a domestic servant. The very next time the opportunity occurred of talking to Miss Eleanor, he'd tell her that he was determined to quit the house and change his occupation.

He'd point out, with apparent verisimilitude, that he simply could not see her every day and yet, because he was a below-stairs person, be unable to even speak to her except in the way of duty.

Such was Mr Barrett's opinion of his own good looks, charm and Eleanor's love, he felt almost sure that he would not leave the Stewarts' as Mr Barrett the butler, but as Mr Barrett, their future son-in-law. Whether or no they would ever come to accept him in that capacity was a matter of indifference to the butler; he would have accomplished what he'd set out to do.

But that calm below stairs and Mr Barrett's plans were shattered by a certainly unforeseen event. Mr Stewart, that rock-like man whose way of life in the home, and rule of life at work, never deviated, suffered a stroke in his office, was taken to a hospital where, for the time being, not even his closest relations were allowed to see him. Mrs Stewart notified her children, Elizabeth and Edward, and a few days later a family conference was held.

Edith Stewart, though sorry for her stricken husband, saw in his absence a splendid opportunity for Edward. 'You are the son, Edward, you have every right to take over your father's affairs.'

'But Mother, I don't know anything about the business. All I ever did there an office boy could have done. How could I possibly take charge?'

'Don't you see, Edward, this is just your chance to prove to your father that you've got brains.'

Elizabeth laughing at this and Edward giving her a sour look, his mother hastily added, 'I didn't mean it in that way, Edward. What I meant was, a business brain. I know you feel you couldn't take over, but old Berry — your father's chief clerk — would be there to initiate you. Think of your father's astonishment when he discovers you were perfectly capable of running his affairs.'

'Suppose poor Daddy doesn't recover,' said Eleanor, weeping.

'Of course he will,' said Mrs Stewart, sharply. 'There is no reason why not. Your father is having every care and attention and he has a strong constitution.'

'Do you think Father would approve of Edward sitting at his desk and going into his affairs?' enquired Elizabeth.

'Well somebody has to do it and Edward, as the son, is the right person. I'm sure he could manage. Will you try, Edward?'

With strong doubts of his ability as a business man, but not averse to getting away from antiques and Foxy Reece, Edward agreed to give it a trial. His mother said she'd accompany him to the building tomorrow as she'd known the chief clerk, Mr Berry, when he first came into the firm. She would explain the circumstances and ask Mr Berry to give Edward all the help he needed.

'I know quite a bit about Daddy's affairs,' put in Eleanor, rather timidly.

'You,' exclaimed Mrs Stewart, in a disparaging voice, 'how could you possibly know anything about your father's business interests?'

'Daddy used to talk to me about the ramifications and complexities of the business world and I understood a great deal of it.'

Before Mrs Stewart could comment on this statement, Edward, to everybody's surprise, said, 'If Eleanor can be of assistance, I'd be grateful to accept her help. I'm certainly going to need advice.'

So unusual was it to hear him speak to Eleanor in a pleasant way that Elizabeth fancied he was being sarcastic. But no, Edward really meant he'd be glad of help.

Elizabeth said that she must return to the farm as her friend couldn't manage on her own, especially with the child left for her to mind.

'I do wish you'd brought my grandson to see me,' complained Mrs Stewart. 'As things are now, I cannot come down to see you.'

'I will next time, Mother. Will you telephone the hospital before I go back?'

The news being that Mr Stewart was 'comfortable', Elizabeth departed, while Mrs Stewart telephoned to cancel her various social engagements.

Below stairs there was much speculation as to what would happen if Mr Stewart died. Mrs Trouson said that it wasn't the first stroke that had a fatal effect; she personally had known an old lady who survived two strokes, only to succumb to the third. The lady's-maid volunteered the information that Mr Stewart might never be able to work again; one of the women in the Mothers' Union had developed locomotor ataxy and was confined to a wheel-chair.

The chauffeur, ever ready to be satirical where Dorise was concerned — because of her church-going — said, 'Perhaps if you offered up a prayer it might get the old man on his feet again?'

'I have already done that,' Dorise told him reproachfully, 'and had prayers offered up in church as well. You might be sceptical about the power of prayer, Mr Seymour, but I have known it to cause wonderful cures. One just has to have faith, that only is needed.'

'You are right there, Dorise,' agreed the cook. 'Why, with my very own eyes didn't I see the mother of a friend of mine open her eyes when everybody thought she had gone. I was sitting by her bed with my friend when the nurse said she'd breathed her last — the mother I mean, not my friend. Then, as sure as I'm sitting here, the rector, a fine old man, came over to the bed to touch her forehead and my friend's mother opened her eyes, smiled at him, and then passed away.'

'Well, I can't see what good those extra few minutes did for her,' remarked Mr Seymour. 'If she'd recovered altogether, that would have been something to talk about.'

'I heard Madam telling Mrs Trentham over the telephone that the doctor said it was overwork, and that Mr Stewart might never make a full recovery,' and the parlourmaid added, 'Madam said something about Edward taking over. Can you imagine it, Mr Barrett?'

But the butler had no opinion to offer. He was busy in his mind wondering how he could turn the event to his own advantage. What a pity that Eleanor was so fond of her father; for surely now was the time to break away from her home. There would never be a better opportunity.

'I think we're all too pessimistic about Mr Stewart's chances of recovery,' said the head-housemaid. 'After all, he has always been a fit man, never been ill since I've been here.'

'Ah, Lily,' said the cook, gloomily. 'That doesn't mean anything because when you've never been ill the body has not built up a resistance to germs.'

'A stroke has nothing to do with germs,' interposed the chauffeur.

Before he could go on, the kitchenmaid said, 'You are right,

Mrs Trouson. When I was at the orphanage there was a family come in because their mother had to go into hospital. Ever such dirty children they were but when we got whooping-cough they didn't and the doctor said it was because they'd swallowed so many germs they was im, im —'

'Immune,' finished Lily.

'That's the word, fancy you knowing what I meant.'

For several weeks following Mr Stewart's stroke it was uncertain whether he would ever be able to speak again; or rather, speak coherently. But came the day when he was able to say a few words quite clearly and the doctors gave assurances that, given time, Mr Stewart would make a fair recovery. He would never be able to work as hard nor walk without the aid of a stick, but, meantime, with the aid of peace, quiet and mild exercises, he slowly improved.

During all this time, he had never once asked, by means of writing on a slate, how the business was going and who was looking after it. But, as yet unbeknown to his wife and family, a profound change had taken place in Mr Stewart's nature. As he lay in bed, unable to communicate, he'd thought about his life and the little pleasure he'd derived from it. Only Eleanor really cared about him. Was it his fault? He had despised his wife for her shallow nature, Elizabeth for her independence and his son because he was weak. Could he have been less strict, shown more love and care? He might have died there and then in his office and nobody but Eleanor would have mourned his death.

There he was mistaken, for many people from his business had shown concern and enquired of the chief clerk, 'Is Mr Stewart getting better?'

Mrs Stewart had also been agreeably surprised by the amount of telephone enquiries. Not only the Trenthams, the Courtlands, old Colonel Nollis and the poet, but several people whose names she'd never heard mentioned. Many were the offers of help and to every one she was able to reply that, with Eleanor's and Edward's help, she was able to cope.

Nobody was more astonished than Edward himself at the facility with which he had managed to grasp the main points of his father's affairs. Neither was he averse to admitting that he had been greatly assisted by Eleanor and the chief clerk, Mr Berry. Without his father's dreaded presence, given authority and opportunity, Edward discovered that he liked the office, the regular hours and the feeling that he was doing something important. Gone was all interest in antiques, though he and Foxy Reece had parted amicably, both realising that they could not have worked together indefinitely.

As below-stairs noted, the atmosphere above stairs was considerably lightened by the absence of Mr Stewart; even to the extent of occasional laughter being heard in the dining-room. As the cook remarked, it was so pleasant to know that dear Miss Eleanor was appreciated at last, and Mrs Trouson recalled yet again the occasion two days ago when Miss Elizabeth had arrived with the child and Miss Eleanor had carried him down to the basement to see the staff. Cook had exclaimed, 'Oh, isn't he sweet,' and was tactful enough to refrain from commenting that the child took after his father. When Eleanor had gone upstairs, Mr Seymour, with his customary asperity, had remarked, 'I suppose by displaying the servants to her nephew, she wants him to realise he belongs to the privileged class.'

Mr Barrett, whose aspirations were to belong to that particular class, replied tartly, 'And why not, or would you prefer him to be a chauffeur?'

Lily hastily averted further acrimony by saying, 'I wonder what will happen when Mr Stewart is well enough to come back here. Will Edward still carry on as he's going now?'

Lily needed to 'keep in' with the chauffeur and his wife because now that his brother Don was living with them again, Don was taking an interest in Lily to the extent of taking her out to the cinema and the Palais. The parlourmaid told Lily that, as this Don had ditched her for a while she should now play 'hard to get'. But Lily, with no boy-friend, protested that she wasn't 'hard to get', and besides, Don wasn't the type to play catch-as-catch-can with. Poor Lily, with her friend Etta constantly talking about the delights of Italy, to which she would shortly be transported, felt that she needed some diversion in her spare time.

'If Mr Stewart is in a wheel-chair he won't be able to work I suppose,' said Maud. 'And—'

'Ah,' the gardener interrupted, 'I knew a man' — you would, thought the cook, you always do know somebody — 'he warn't no more than forty-five to fifty odd, lost the use of his legs in an accident. But did that stop him working? No, by gor, it didn't. Every morning he used to wheel himself right across the town to where he worked and he was as merry as a cricket. He married a young girl that worked in a Woolworths and had twins in no time.'

Mr Barrett gave a derisive laugh, 'Well, as Mr Stewart never showed any signs of being "as merry as a cricket" even when he could walk, and it's not a remote possibility that he'd be interested in a girl from Woolworths, I don't think we shall see him trundling his chair along with a smile on his face. Besides, how do you know that crickets are merry?'

'Stands to reason they are. They wouldn't make all that chirping noise otherwise, would they?'

This very same question of when — or even whether — Mr Stewart would be able to walk again, was being discussed in the drawing-room. Julia Trentham was endeavouring to cheer up Eleanor by describing two cases she'd known of strokes, and both persons were now getting around with the aid of a stick.

'I am not so much worried about that aspect, Julia,' said Edith Stewart, 'but will Henry ever be fit enough to conduct his business again? His doctor has emphasised that it was probably overwork that caused his stroke, and Henry must be protected from having another — with perhaps fatal consequences.'

'How does he seem now, has his speech improved?'

'Yes, he speaks very well, I can easily understand what he's saying. But it seems so strange, Julia, that he never asks any questions about his business. I wondered whether Mr Berry, Henry's chief clerk, had been in touch, but he said no, he was waiting to hear from Mr Stewart. Surely Henry must be worried about what is going on, but when I started to say a few words about his work he just looked at me and smiled. He seems a changed man, Julia. You know that Elizabeth and

Eleanor have been to see him and now he's asked to see Edward. I've told Edward he ought to go but the poor boy is nervous; especially as he's doing so well in the business.'

Mr Stewart was a changed man, and he thanked the fates — whoever they were — that had enabled him to change before it was too late. Oh, he'd not become saintly, he smiled wryly at the thought, but he knew he'd become far more tolerant. And he was determined never again to make his work a full-time occupation. He would delegate authority, let others take the burden. He thought almost wistfully of his son; if only Edward would come into the business. But he must not mention it when Edward came to see him. In another few weeks he'd be able to go home; already he was able to move his leg on the paralysed side.

Great were the preparations made for Mr Stewart's return home. The morning-room on the ground floor had been made his bedroom, his desk and his books installed for easy access, a telephone extension, everything with a view to making him feel less helpless.

The lady's-maid, convinced that her prayers had helped to save Mr Stewart, felt justified in remarking lugubriously, at frequent intervals, 'The poor man will still have a hard furrow to plough.'

Even Mrs Trouson got irritated and said, acidly, 'Not so hard as a poor man would if it had happened to him. I expect Mr Stewart will have a nurse for a while, until he can do for himself. It will seem strange having the Master home all day. One thing I do know, above-stairs has been a lot more human since he was took with that stroke. Madam tells me to sit down when we're working out the menu — of course that may be because I had the appendicitis — and Master Edward always speaks if I happen to see him.'

'Can't say that I've noticed any difference,' said the butler, sardonically. 'We still do the same work every day, answer bells, wait on them hand and foot.'

'Isn't that what you're paid to do?' enquired the chauffeur with false joviality. 'Of course I don't know everything; perhaps there's a special butler's post where he does nothing but wear the uniform. Just put me wise.'

Giving Mr Seymour an angry look, Mr Barrett marched off to his pantry muttering maledictions on people who couldn't keep a civil tongue in their head.

Observing the cook's frown, the chauffeur hurriedly said that he had news of old Horace. He'd met Fred Penfold in the Mariner's Arms and Fred had just received a letter from Australia. Old Horace was doing well out there, still loved the country, but his wife, Alice, wanted to come back to England. Alice had enclosed a note saying that Australia was no place for a woman, they counted for nothing, it was a man's country. Men got together in droves and a refined woman had no chance to have an intellectual conversation.

'The refined woman being Alice, I suppose,' laughed Maud.

'There, didn't I say that no good would come of traipsing off to them foreign parts,' exclaimed Mrs Trouson. 'Of course they're not like us; how could they be, thousands of miles away.'

'Well, most of them came from this country in the beginning,' murmured Robert Seymour.

Ignoring the chauffeur's remark, the cook, quite pleased to know that her adverse opinion of a country where 'below stairs' was non-existent was justified, went on — and really imagined she had said it — 'I remember saying to Madam, what's a refined girl like Alice Beach going to do in that rough country?'

Hardly a girl, thought Lily; well over forty and lucky to get even old Horace. Still, old Trouson is right in a way, Alice was hardly the type to show any pioneer spirit.

'And are they coming back to England, Mr Seymour?'

'Fred Penfold said old Horace wrote that he would never come back here. Over there he was a somebody and if Alice was muggins enough to want England, she'd have to come back on her own.'

'Poor thing,' said cook, sentimentally, 'all those miles away with only her husband for company; no kith and kin to care about her.'

Suppressing mirth Lily thought, well, Alice had nobody over here in the way of relations; old Trouson implies that Alice was the centre of a loving family, when in fact, domestic service was her whole life. I never imagined she'd leave it. I certainly hope to do so at the earliest opportunity, though I must admit it is pleasanter working here now. I wonder if things will change when Mr Stewart comes home.

Chapter 26

Two days after he arrived home, Mr Stewart asked to see his chief clerk and over three hours elapsed before Mr Berry left the house. Mrs Stewart, anxious to know what had occurred, what the chief clerk had disclosed about Edward, fearful that Henry might be in one of his cold rages, went into the morning-room with a certain degree of trepidation. What a relief it was to see that Henry was smiling, looked even happy, called her 'my dear', without that sarcastic intonation to which she had become accustomed.

'Edith, my dear, I have just been hearing such splendid news, though I find it hard to believe. Our son is in the business and old Berry says he is doing well, that he takes after me in his grasp of foreign affairs. Why didn't you tell me?'

'Well, Henry, you never spoke about the office and the doctors warned us not to mention it unless you asked. It was I who asked Edward to give up his antiques and see how he could help in your affairs. Edward was afraid you might be angry.'

'Angry, my dear. Why should I be?' and then recollecting his previous contemptuous attitude towards his son, he fell silent. After a while he said, 'You know, Edith, I have had many hours to think about life. I never really prized it until I almost lost it. I realised that for years I'd been just a money-making machine, become almost inhuman in my dealings with you and the family. But now, strange as it may seem, I don't care if I never see the office again; there are competent people to run it. When my — I mean our — son was born, my one idea was to make him in my image; to take over when I could no longer be "the boss". Instead of showing him love and understanding, I became harsh and tyrannical when he could not conform to my ideas of manliness. No wonder Edward hated me.'

'That is not true, Henry. Edward longed to be loved by you, but he was a timid child and I encouraged him to spend a lot of time with me which did not help. And when Edward found that he could not come up to your standard he simply gave up; became idle and a spendthrift, got into bad company, envied Eleanor because he saw you cared for her. But all that is altered now, he and Eleanor are friends and he freely admits that she has helped him tremendously in coping with your business affairs.'

Henry gave a sad smile as he said, 'What a fool I have been, Edith. I must have a talk with our son, that is if he feels like talking to me.' And half to himself, he murmured, 'Stewart and Son, it's what I used to dream about.' And in his new-found pride in his son, Mr Stewart quite forgot that his daughter had been a considerable help towards Edward's grasp of business affairs. For years Eleanor had listened to her father talking about finance, cartels and contracts, as they sat together in his study and inevitably—although by the nature of her sex unable to enter into that world—she absorbed the information. Now, with Edward having long sessions with his father discussing the firm, poor Eleanor to a certain extent felt shut out from her place in her father's affection. Her mother, with, for her, rare understanding, sensed her daughter's feeling of rejection and tried in many ways to help; but years of indifference to Eleanor could not immediately be overcome.

This state of affairs was accentuated when Elizabeth, on one of her now fairly frequent visits, brought her child. So much had Mr Stewart's nature changed that instead of barely tolerating the infant, he now made a tremendous fuss of him, laughingly pointing out that here was yet another generation to carry on the firm. He never mentioned Elizabeth's absent husband or the impending divorce; as Elizabeth remarked to her sister, 'Father is not the same man that I used to know. Oh, he always made a fuss of you, but Edward and I seldom pleased him. But now it is a pleasure to come home to see our parents.'

Prior to her father's illness, Eleanor had lived her secret dreams of John Barrett and how wonderful it would be if they could always be together. At times, in the privacy of her bedroom, she was almost overwhelmed with the strength of her feelings for John. Accustomed to the indifference of men, in fact not even caring now whether or no a man showed an interest in her, Eleanor had resigned herself to being an 'old maid'. Until circumstances had caused her to meet her father's butler away from the house, she had hardly been aware of his presence, he was just one of the servants. But, from the time he had stood up in the hall to ask a question about slum housing, she had become aware of him as a man.

Gradually John's quiet manner, his deference, his pleasure in her company, had released emotions in Eleanor that had caused her alarm, but also intense delight. The alarm was occasioned by the thought of her father's incredulity and fury if he knew that his daughter was falling in love with a below-stairs person, a butler. That she, with all the advantages of high lineage, tradition and society, could sink so low as to feel a personal interest in a man of the lower class. Her father would think she was mad and should be put away, her mother would probably have hysterics and Edward and Eleanor treat her with cold contempt. Nevertheless, Eleanor, though well aware of the consequences, had no intention of giving up the opportunities of meeting John Barrett; he had become the mainspring of her life.

When her father had collapsed and might have died, added to the ensuing chaos over his business affairs, Eleanor had given up her workers' meetings, therefore the chances of being alone with John Barrett had rarely occurred. But now that her company was not so necessary to her father, she made the excuse of an important meeting an opportunity to be with John on his free evening. And now, here she was sitting on a park bench with him and he was declaring he loved her; it was unbelievable.

They walked along a secluded pathway and sat down on a bench. John put his arm round her shoulders, and with one look at her face, he knew it was the right moment to take his chance. He kissed her, murmurming, 'Eleanor, I love you, I love you.' In fact, though he did not love her, he found it surprisingly pleasant to kiss such a soft and inexperienced woman.

As for Eleanor, in spite of her thirty years, she gazed at John with wonder that such an attractive man should profess love for her and could not refrain from asking, 'Why do you love me, John? You must know dozens of girls far prettier than me.'

It not being polite to agree with this obvious fact and even less politic to say that the prettier were not in the possession of ten thousand pounds, John Barrett murmured that in his eyes she was beautiful and sweet. After a further interlude of kissing and caressing, John, with assumed gravity said, 'But what do you love in me, Eleanor? I am nothing compared to the kind of people you mix with. I'm only the person who waits on table, answers the bell, a factotum. You would never marry a man in my position,' and he laughed bitterly.

'I would, John, indeed I would,' protested Eleanor. 'What do I care for the kind of men I meet in society? Men interested only in pleasure, in making money from the toil and low wages of the workers. I despise them.'

'But your family, my dear, they would never let you marry a man like me, a butler.'

'There is nothing legally they could do about it, John, I'm over twenty-one. Of course, father would be terribly upset and I'd be sorry to cause him grief, but that cannot be helped, John dear.'

John Barrett, assuming a gloomy air, said, 'How can I take you away from the style of living that you are accustomed to, my dearest.' Such blandishments came easily to him, were in fact the small coin of his dealings with women. 'Your father will probably cut off your allowance, and I will have to find another situation — which I will do of course — but it will be a hardship for such as you, it's selfish of me to want you to share my life.'

'John, my dear,' whispered the besotted Eleanor, 'I would share your life if you hadn't a crust. I love you for what you are, money means nothing to me.'

Perhaps not, thought the butler, cynically, but it means a lot to me. Has she, or has she not, got over ten thousand pounds? I need to know for certain before I proceed any further. Aloud he said, tenderly, 'My dear, have I the right to ask you to live in poverty. Could I make you happy?'

Eleanor laughed happily as she answered, 'We would not have to live in poverty, dear John. I have money of my own, left me by an aunt; over ten thousand pounds in all. The family cannot keep me from using it.'

'My dear, I could not live on your money,' exclaimed John, with false indignation. He added, hastily, in case Eleanor had any fanciful ideas of disposing of the money, one never knew what these benevolent types might do, 'Though you could use it for yourself. We could take a little cottage and you could furnish it in any way you like. Buy things to make your life as easy as possible. But I don't want your money; I'll earn a living even if I have to dig ditches.'

He managed to suppress his mirth at the very idea of doing such hard manual work. In any case, why did men, who wished to demonstrate that no work was too menial for them, always state, "I'll dig ditches", as though Britain was one vast swamp that needed to be drained?

Eleanor indignantly exclaimed that he'd do nothing of the sort. She was sure her John had enough talent to accomplish anything he set his mind to. Apparently it did not occur to her that if this was so, John Barrett must have set his talent to becoming a butler.

Risking all, John said, with great emotion, 'Eleanor, will you come away with me? I'll get a special licence, we'll marry and be together always. I cannot go on as we are now, seeing you every day and not able to even speak. I must leave the house, leave you if you haven't the courage to come with me.'

Equally emotional, Eleanor said they could not be parted for ever, she could never lose him. Eventually, after shedding tears at the knowledge of the unhappiness she would cause her parents, interspersed with tender assurances of future happiness from John, plans were made to depart secretly on the following evening. John was too apprehensive that Eleanor's courage would fade away if she had to wait longer.

When Mr Barrett arrived back he thought, this is the last evening that I'll be descending these basement steps and he found it difficult to greet the servants as Barrett the butler; if only he could have casually mentioned that he would soon be Barrett the son-in-law. What incredulous faces they would have at first and as for Mrs Trouson, she would in all probability faint on the spot at the very idea of below-stairs mingling with above.

He found the servants visibly excited because Mrs Stewart had come down to the kitchen — first asking Mrs Trouson if it was convenient — to say that Mr Stewart wanted to give them all a rise in wages. It was such a surprise to Cook that she hadn't known what to say at first, but eventually managed to thank Madam on behalf of all of them.

'Isn't it really something, Mr Barrett, to get higher wages without asking for them,' said the lady's-maid, who seldom used an original sentence if she knew a ready-made one, and added, 'You could have knocked me down with a feather.'

But Mr Barrett, knowing he would not be in service long enough even to receive the wages that were owing to him, could not be bothered to pretend gratitude for such a pleasant event. Pleading a headache, he told Maud to see that all doors and windows were locked, said a curt goodnight and retired to his room.

Poor Eleanor had a real headache and, in spite of swallowing some tablets, was wide-awake and likely to remain so for most of the night. Alternatively filled with remorse at the plan to leave her home in such a secret way, and exaltation that soon she would be married to John, she spent most of the night composing the letter she would leave for her parents. She thought to herself: dear John doesn't really understand how hard it is to elope. It's not as though I'm a schoolgirl, I shall be thirty-one on my next birthday. How can I explain to them that my feelings for John are not an 'old maid's fancy', that I care deeply. I'll never be able to make them understand because to Mother and Father he is not a person to be spoken of in the same breath as a person of our class. How fortunate it is that Father and Edward are now friends, and Elizabeth too; he does not need my companionship as he used to do . . . And so on through the night, Eleanor mused, but was not shaken in her determination to marry her John.

The maids too were awake in their attic bedrooms, thinking of the rise in wages. 'I wonder how much we'll get, Grace? I know what I'm going to buy with mine,' and the under-housemaid giggled.

'What are you going to buy, Flora?'

'I'm going to buy myself pink silk cami-knickers. I've always wanted to ever since I saw those that Miss Elizabeth had—only hers were satin.'

'Ooh Flora, cami-knickers are not decent, specially when you climb up the steps in a bus. What about the conductor looking up?'

'If he's a gentleman Grace, he won't look up.'

'Can a bus-conductor be a gentleman?'

'Course he can, Grace. It's not the uniform and the ticket-punch, it's what's inside.'

'That would be passengers, Flora,' and they laughed so much that Lily knocked on the wall to hush them.

After Dorise had retired to her room, Lily and Maud settled down for their usual chat and to share the box of chocolates that Don had bought Lily.

'You are lucky, Lil, getting chocolates. Last fellow I went to the pictures with was that mean; he bought a quarter of liquorice allsorts and picked out all the striped ones for himself.'

'You do pick them, Maud. Where did you find this one?'

'I didn't find him anywhere, that's just the point. I was introduced to him all right and proper by the woman who runs that little shop where we buy our stockings. She said he was her nephew, Arnie, and he was a stranger in London. As far as I'm concerned he can go on being a stranger if a quarter of liquorice allsorts and one-and-sixpence at the pictures is his idea of a good time. You seem to be getting on all right with your Don.'

'Ah, is he my Don, Maud? On the nights I'm not free, he doesn't stay in, he says his sister-in-law gets on his nerves so he has to go out. But what does he do?'

The friends commiserated with each other over the iniquities of men and the scarcity also.

'Lil, didn't you think there was something peculiar about our butler tonight?'

'In what way, peculiar?'

'Well, he seemed as though he was hardly aware of us and never showed any excitement about the rise. Besides Lil, a butler is not supposed to let the parlourmaid lock up, that is his job. Mr Stewart would be annoyed if he knew. I do believe there is something not right going on. The other day, when we were laying-up for dinner he had such a funny smile on his face. You mark my words, Lil, I can sense that something nasty will happen.'

'Go on with you, Maud. We've had enough predictions from Nanny Smith and Pearl. Don't you start. I reckon something went wrong with his evening and he went to bed in a huff. Everything will be normal tomorrow.'

And so it would be, until late in the evening.

So confident had been John Barrett that Eleanor would consent to leave her home to become his wife, he had, over the last two or three weeks, secretly conveyed some of his clothes to the house of a friend where he intended to stay until they were married. The housemaids were unaware of this, he always kept his wardrobe locked.

Now, as he lay in bed, he ran through his plans: tomorrow morning, Eleanor will book herself a room in a small quiet hotel and, after dinner, pleading letters to write, she will retire to her room and pack a small case. Mr Stewart does not seem to need her so much now that he cares for his son. Perhaps she feels a slight resentment about this. As for me, after coffee has been served in the drawing-room and they are not likely to ring for at least half an hour, I shall tell Maud that I'm just going down the road for ten minutes to say goodbye to a friend. Then I'll slip out with my small leather bag. Soon after, Eleanor will follow me, and that's that.

Of course, John Barrett mused, I had dreams of a far different marriage. I envisaged myself walking up the aisle with a radiant vision in white. Unfortunately — and he smiled wryly — I never met a vision with money. Not for me the 'dinner of herbs where love is', I much prefer the 'stalled ox'. At least, when penury sets in, one can eat it. But Eleanor loved him, would leave her home and marry him; yes him, just the butler in her father's house. What a compensation for all the years of servitude, the bowing and salaaming, the 'Yes sir,' 'Very good, sir.' How much as a child he'd hated his parents' subservience to their employers; his father coming back to the cottage late at night, sometimes still wearing his butler's uniform, his mother being expected to help in the kitchen whenever there was a large party at the Manor. It was even worse when they all stayed with the grandparents. To hear grandfather or grandmother eagerly asking about dear Madam, or dear Miss Mary, was sickening. His whole childhood was steeped in this atmosphere of fawning on 'them'. And now he had his revenge. One of 'them' would be his wife. Everything was against him ever getting 'above stairs', becoming one of 'them', he'd been resigned to that. People like 'them', with wealth, power and position, formed a phalanx, no outsider could penetrate their defences. But now he was revenged; one of the élite was leaving her class, stepping down, becoming a below-stairs person — metaphorically speaking, of course.

With Eleanor's money he would be able to leave domestic service. Not for a life of idleness, oh no, but some occupation where his good looks and attractive voice would be an advantage. Perhaps they could rent a studio where Eleanor could paint her water-colours and he could arrange an exhibition? If that Victor Trentham, who was an expert, praised Eleanor's work, then they must be saleable. Of course, he would never have taken her on without the money, even to be revenged on 'them'. But Eleanor wasn't too bad as regards looks, and she had a soft disposition. But as he drifted off to sleep, John Barrett thought: I have never seen a prettier girl than that friend of Lily's; such lovely eyes and beautiful hair, why on earth is she wasting her time in a basement? Pity I can't have her as well as Eleanor.